We Want for Our Sisters What We Want for Ourselves

POLYGYNY ~ *CO-PARTNERING*

A Relationship, Marriage
and Family Alternative

Patricia Dixon, Ph.D.

Oji Publications

We Want for Our Sisters What We Want for Ourselves
Polygyny~*Copartnering:* A Relationship, Marriage
and Family Alternative

Published by Oji Publications, a division of
Nuvo Development, Inc.
P.O. Box, 372453
Decatur, GA, 30037-2453

ISBN 0-9719004-7-7

To Anna Mae and Genie J. Dixon
I am eternally grateful

A culture of domination is necessarily a culture where lying is an acceptable norm. It in fact is required. White supremacy has always relied on structures of deceit. . .

Within the colonizing process, black people were socialized to believe that survival was possible only if they learned how to deceive.

bell hooks, 1993

Notes:

Co-partnering — the practice of women openly consenting to be in a relationship or marriage with a man simultaneously with one or more other women. Under such an arrangement the women may love, care, and be concerned for each other, and work cooperatively to build their families and communities.

The terms *polygyny* **and** *co-partnering* are used interchangeably throughout the text. In the first part, polygyny is the term primarily used. Toward the latter part, I shift to the term co-partnering. I do this for several reasons. The first is the necessity of naming. It is, I think, the first step in defining and constructing a world. The second is that polygyny has been stigmatized through European American cultural domination. I therefore think it is necessary to move away from the term. The third is to emphasize consent by women. The fourth is to emphasize that the practice is not male-centered or focused around patriarchy or male supremacy. Instead, it is female-centered and focused around women working together for the benefit of each other, their families, and the African world community.

The sculpture from Sierra Leone represents a woman who has just completed initiation into a women's association. It is used here to symbolize passage of women into an association of women who are able to shift to a womanist ethic of care for sisters. It also symbolizes women who are able to make the emotional, psychological, and spiritual shift to co-partnering.

The *Duafe*-wooden comb on the spine is an adinkra symbol of the Akan people of Ghana which symbolizes good things associated with women. Duafe "represents the feminine principles that form womanhood." It is a symbol of good feminine qualities: patience, prudence, fondness, *love, and care* [italics added]. (Willis, pp. 94-95).

CONTENTS

i

FOREWORD

The condition of African American women is deeply embedded in the history of the European enslavement of Africans. This is not the whole story, but it is an intricate part of the process of creating the conditions out of which our women have had to rise and create. Professor Patricia Dixon, a clarion and revolutionary voice, has provided a pioneering work in the interstices of race and gender.

We Want for Our Sisters What We Want for Ourselves is a provocative and brilliant exposition of the crisis confronting the African American woman. It speaks to the manifold difficulties of existing within the framework of a brutal system of enslavement, segregation, and criminalization. What Dr. Dixon has done is to open this crisis to the reader in ways that others have seldom done in order to draw critical attention to the urgency of the social situation.

This book demonstrates that the principles embodied in the founding of the American nation were against the African concept of family, indeed, antagonistic to any idea of family. Dr. Dixon has astutely dealt with the context for the present relationship crisis pointing to the characteristic beliefs, values, and ideas in African culture. She has demonstrated the evolution of both thought and practice in the contemporary setting. Thus, the book is a masterful account of our evolving relational sojourn in this land. But the book is more than a simple recounting of the destruction of our households, the degradation of dignity, the encouragement of instability and creation of dependency. What the book, *We Want for Our Sisters What We Want for Ourselves*, does is to provide a positive and dynamic pathway toward solving the problems that we have found in the American nation.

Professor Dixon suggests that African American women, perhaps even African women of other areas, may need to re-examine the basic philosophical patterns of our culture and find ways to deal with the ever-growing issue of women without men. This is a pro-women book, but it is not anti-male. Professor Dixon demonstrates her unswerving commitment to African women in ways that few feminists have ever done. She seeks to project the idea of relationship as the central canon of progressive and mature families. Denial of relationship is itself anti-woman. The infinite possibilities of human relationships should not be gainsaid, nor should they be open only to a few. If our community is to become whole again it must be on the basis of a freedom that is explored in this new creative paradigm advanced by Professor Patricia Dixon.

Molefi Kete Asante
Temple University
2002

PREFACE

¶If Harriet Tubman, an enslaved African woman, could one day rise up and walk away from the worst human bondage the world has known, and then return nineteen times to free over three hundred others, then surely I, as a free woman, can attempt to free us from attachment to paradigms that keep us in mental, emotional, and spiritual bondage. It is upon this legacy of struggle that I present this work. During Harriet Tubman's time, with some exceptions, it was the general view that slavery was good for African Americans. It was never believing this to be true, or making a shift from such a paradigm, that Tubman was able to free herself. It, however, took deep love for African people, extending herself beyond herself, faith and trust in God, and tremendous sacrifice, for her to return to free her brothers and sisters in slavery.

It is in this tradition that we, people of African descent, must free ourselves from dependency on ideas and ways of being that clearly are not working for us. If we look around us, it is clear that our relationships are plagued with hostility and conflict, our families are in disarray, and our communities are falling apart. Although there are many factors contributing to this, e.g., racial oppression, restructuring of the global economy, confusion over gender roles, etc., there is none, in my opinion, that contribute more to the problems we face than our fixation on Western paradigms and the values that stem from them. Exclusive monogamy is one.

If we look squarely at this, most of us know fully well that the notion of America as a monogamous society is bogus. From the first men who formed this country, to those holding the highest seat in government in contemporary times, we know that a closed form of polygyny has always been practiced. During slavery and after, it was to the disadvantage of women of African descent. In contemporary times, any woman may be subjected to a polygynous type of relationship, whether she is single or married. And because the convergence of capitalism, the sex industry and the inferiorization of women structures in mechanisms for males to engage women for sex or sexual fantasy only (through various forms of pornography, strip bars, etc), there are many who are reduced to objects for sexual exploitation. Strangely, African

Americans are trying to conform to a standard set by those who are not even conforming to it themselves, while our social circumstances clearly indicate that there is a need for other options.

One reason for our troubled relationships, families, and communities is the dishonesty, deceit, and dishonor that occurs when polygyny is practiced in a closed manner. It is crucial however, that we come to understand that we cannot build healthy relationships, families, and communities with lies as an integral part of them. Although there may be individual cases that thrive, when the foundation is built on lies, the whole will eventually fall.

A question that has occurred to me is why African American leaders and intellectuals have not taken a stand in support of polygyny. I think the major reason is that most of our leaders are male. Although many engage in polygynous formations, whether single or married, they have not had the courage to say outright that it is needed and to practice it in a way that is honorable to the women with whom they become involved, or to themselves. There are, in my opinion, several reasons for this. One is lack of information about the practice of polygyny. Because of this, African American male leaders are not in the position to see through the dishonest and negative propaganda perpetuated about it. The second is fear of losing status, position, and financial support by their white benefactors (who also do it), which many eventually lose anyway, once their covert practice of polygyny is found out. The third is fear of wrath from feminists. The issue at hand here is that African American male leaders cannot take a stand in support of polygyny without support of African American female feminists/leaders. The problem with some African American female feminists/leaders is that many are dependent on Western feminist paradigms, and are therefore caught in the web of propaganda on patriarchy that is assumed to be uniform the world over. What also prohibits many African American female feminists/leaders from seeing the need for and supporting an option like polygyny, is that they too, are wedded to Western paradigms of individualism, or "self centeredness," which is crippling our minds, bodies, and spirits, the monogamous, nuclear family, which can be stifling to human growth to say the least, and structures of dissimulation that maim the human personality and subsequently stifle divine potentiality.

  ¦ Whatever the case may be, I believe that the only way that our relationships, families, and communities will be mended is if polygyny is practiced openly. As an alternative marriage and family form, polygyny can eliminate the potential for dishonesty and deceit (which is divisive) as the basis of relationship formation, provide a larger pool of men for women to select from, avoid women being reduced to their sexuality, potentially hold men accountable to all women with whom they enter into sexual relationships with, and provide a mechanism for women and men to work together to build our relationships, families, and communities. As with Harriet Tubman, however, it will require love for African people in general, and love for sisters by sisters in particular, extension of self beyond self, faith and trust in God that we will be all right even if we step outside of the norm, sacrifice, and other principles which I expand on throughout this work.

  Along with Harriet Tubman, the work of other women and men of the past has deeply touched and inspired me. The activism of nineteenth century club women taught me the importance of "lifting as we climb," or, in the words of contemporary writer-poet Maya Angelou, "When you learn, teach." I am deeply grateful to Ida B. Wells, W.E.B. Dubois, Kwame Nkrumah, Fannie Lou Hamer, Malcolm X, and many others whose names I do not have the space to include here, for how their work has inspired me.

  There are contemporary big brothers and sisters whose work not only informs my own, but has empowered and transformed me. I am deeply grateful to Molefi Asante, a warrior-prince, for freeing my mind and spirit from bondage to Western paradigms, for transforming how I see, approach, and experience the world, for introducing me to others, past and present, who have struggled for the liberation of African people, and for literally saving my life. The works of Patricia Hill Collins and bell hooks have shaped how I understand the oppression of African women and have empowered me as a woman. I am grateful to Marimba Ani, whose work helped me to return home (to Africa), and to myself, spiritually. I am thankful for Maulana Karenga, who has taught me the importance of shaping the world in our own image and interests, whose work continues to inform my own, and teaches me, in the tradition of the most ancient of our ancestors, what it means to be human. I am grateful to Wade Nobles and Niara Sudarkasa for teaching me to look to Africa for values upon which to understand and shape our families. I am grateful to Haki Madhubuti, whose work has helped me to understand African American men. Finally, I am indebted to Ben Ammi Ben Israel and Ra Un Nefer Amen, warrior-king-fathers, and their wives or queen-mothers and the women and men of their communities for their courage to step outside of captivity to Western paradigms. Their communities provide practical examples upon which the rest of us can model ourselves, relationships, families, and communities.

ACKNOWLEDGMENTS

I would like to extend special thanks to Trenyaae Jehar Bondojia, who probably knows more about polygyny than anyone in America. The numerous conversations I had with him helped me to understand the seriousness of the subject and helped to shape how I think about it.

I thank my mother, Anna Mae Dixon, and my sisters Lonnell Williams and Regina Dixon for their enduring support and especially Regina, who worked arduously at transcribing the taped interviews. I also thank Darlene Jones who has been very supportive, not only through the writing of this book but also through doctoral studies and tenure, Gary Dubuisson, and David Hill for their financial assistance, Yvette Chapman, who has been like an angel in my life, and Abdul (Winfred Alton) Kennedy for his continuing support.

Others who have supported me along the way include Ruth and Chris Roberson, Barry Grimes-Hardie, Tammy Jenkins, Anita Dixon-Thomas, Antoinette Barksdale, and Samuel Scott-Jones.

There are those whose assistance made this work possible. I thank Ben Ammi Ben Israel of the African Hebrew Israelites for inviting me to come to the community in Israel and supporting me in every way including providing housing. I also thank Naseek (Prince) Rahm Ben Yehuda and Aturah (Crown Sister) Yafah Eshet Adiel who assisted me in making the trip, and Aturah Yafah Kitnah and the many others who really looked out for me and treated me well once I got there. From Ausar Auset society, I thank Tchet Sesh Am Neter for helping me to gain access to members of that community. For assisting me in gaining access to members of the Muslim communities, I thank Nadirah Geder, Opal Muhammad, and Kamilah A. Pickett. I thank all the members of all the communities who allowed me to interview them. Not only did their interviews broaden my understanding of the practice of polygyny, but also helped me in my own spiritual growth. Most importantly, I thank the women for showing me how women can really love and take care each other, even if they are sharing the same husband.

For their contributions, I thank Naseek Gavriel HaGadol and his wives Aturah Rofah Karaliah, Aturah Tekiah, Zeeherah and Yielah; Ahkeazehr Ben Israel and his wives Aturah Rofah Ezreeyah, Sigulah, and Eliezrah; Sar Ahmadiel Ben Yehuda and his wives Rakedah, Aheedalyah, and Ahavatyah; Ahk Bakooryah Ben Israel and his wives, Ahdeevah and Shalaymah and Meneshe Ben Naseek Aharon and his wives Shefrah, Devorah, and Naavah.

Others I thank for their contributions include: Iman Plemon T. El-Amin, Iman Jamil Al-Amin, Antar Ibn-Stanford Smith, Rashid Na'im, Safiyyah Shahid, Khayriyyah H. Faiz, Tasneem Sauda Abdul-haqq, Kayah Bayette, Khadija Yakini, Baherrah Akbar, Abu' Shaka Abdush-Shakur, Terry Harrison, Obediki Kamau, Donald Cook, Timothy Styles, Lance Jeffries, Cleveland Solomon, Robert Alexander, Ronald Pace, Derek Harris, Ronald Stephens, Steve Roberson, Gregory Bethea, Eddie Wright, and the many others whose names I could not include for various reasons.

I am grateful to Georgia State University for the African American Research Grant that provided financial assistance for the research, Dr. Charles Jones, Chairman of the Department of African American Studies for financial assistance for editing, and Dr. Makungu Akinyela for reviewing the manuscript.

Finally, those I would like to acknowledge who did not live to see the publication of this book include Graduate Research Assistant Kim Redd, and a friend who was very supportive, Michael B. Felton. I also thank all those whose names I have forgotten.

INTRODUCTION

After ending a six-year relationship I had been in since my early years in college, I began to evaluate my life. It seemed I had nothing—no mate, children, or work to give my life a sense of meaning or purpose. Although I had sister-friends whom I spent a great deal of time with, I went to a meaningless job and came home to an empty apartment. In search of someone to fill the space, I began dating. It seemed, however, that meeting a man who was willing to make a commitment to a relationship, let alone a monogamous one, was unlikely. I had heard numerous times of the disproportionate ratio of African American females to males in the population in Washington, D.C. But it was not until I began dating outside of campus life that I got an understanding of what this meant. Essentially, the situation is such that the higher number of females to males in the population makes it easy for men to engage in relationships with many women at the same time, without having to be accountable to any of them. This makes it difficult for women who so desire, to form stable, monogamous, committed relationships and marriages. When this became clear to me, I decided it might be better to seek meaning and purpose in something else. I applied to a doctorate program, was accepted, and left Washington, D.C.

While living in Philadelphia, the situation—that is, the number of men available for a committed relationship or marriage, seemed to worsen. I worked on research in which the aim was to evaluate the effectiveness of several drug treatment programs in rehabilitating homeless men who were addicted, primarily to crack-cocaine. Approximately 95 percent of the 700 men in the study were African American. My first introduction to the homeless shelter was startling. My thought was, "This is where the men are."

In the course of the research, I visited several shelters. I found predominantly African American men, primarily in their mid-and late twenties and thirties, and some in their forties and fifties. In some instances, they were wall-to-wall, as if on a military base. I visited drug rehabilitation centers and found predominantly African American men.

1

When I visit prisons and jails, I am absolutely astounded by the number of African American men I see. And as I visit inner cities across America, on any given week-day, I see African American males between the hours of 9-5, when one would typically be in school or working, outside of the opportunity structure, standing on street corners, leading unproductive lives.

It is these observations and experiences that led primarily to my exploration into the practice of polygyny. My thinking was that because racial oppression sets in motion dynamics that deplete African American men from the population and/or marginalizes them in the economic sector, making it impossible for every woman to have an exclusive mate, a practice such as polygyny is needed. Also, because the high ratio of African American females to males makes it easy for males, whether they are married or single, to engage in multiple relationships, something akin to polygyny is already being practiced. However, the closed, dishonest and often dehumanizing manner in which it is practiced is not beneficial for women. I also began to think about how such a practice could be structured to be more beneficial for women.

As I ventured into the life stories of the men at the homeless shelter, it became painfully clear to me that it is oppression in its complex forms that leads many down the path of addiction. It is the way that it weighs on the human spirit that leads many to self-destruct from the inside out. In my very first interview, the brother broke down into tears. The next three years only added to this experience. As a sister, potential wife, and mother, I could not help but to connect what the men were going through in their addiction and their being unavailable as potential husbands and fathers, to my loneliness. I could not help but to connect the pain that they were experiencing to my own.

While I was in graduate school, I experienced some of the most trying times of my life. Not only did I not have my sister-friends, who had been my emotional support, I did not have a consistent mate to support me through the arduous endeavor of pursuing a doctorate degree. *For Colored Girls Who Have Considered Suicide When the Rainbow is Enuf,* the play written by Ntzoke Shange in 1975, was never more real to me than during these years. I'd lie awake many nights reflecting on what I was learning through

2

graduate studies about the connection between African American experiences in slavery and the experiences of the men in the shelter, and the connection between their being in the shelter and not having someone in my life. These experiences, at times, left me feeling lonely, saddened by the circumstances many African American men find themselves in, and hopeless with regard to finding a mate.

Although I have had such experiences at different times throughout my life, I know that I am not alone in this. From what I have observed while living in six metropolitan areas, my research on male-female relationships, and the numerous conversations I have had with African American women I know personally, in my profession, encounter on a day-to-day basis, and who take my courses, I know that many are having similar experiences. Also, based on what I have observed of men throughout my life, and what I have discovered in my research and in conversations with men (which for me is always research), and because there seems to be general acceptance of it by men in U.S. society, I have come to believe that regardless of their marital status, engaging in multiple relationships, is more the rule than the exception for men.

The idea that polygyny is needed and that it is already being practiced began to weigh on me. Questions began to plague me: If engaging in multiple relationships is so common among males, then why is there no structure to support it? And since men could not engage in such relationships without participation from women, how can they be structured in ways that are more beneficial for women?

I began to find answers to these questions while enrolled in the graduate program in the Department of African American studies at Temple University. During this time, I was introduced to the concept of *Afrocentricity*. Although it proposes several things, two fundamental principles stand out to me. One is that it challenges hegemonic Eurocentrism in all its forms. The other is that, as African descendants, African Americans can turn to Africa for social structures more conducive for our social reality. With this understanding, I began to explore African marriage and family systems. What I discovered is that polygyny was widely accepted and practiced throughout Africa. In fact, it was virtually universal.

Far more surprising, however, is that before European world conquest and domination, polygyny was practiced throughout most of the world.

As I continued to search, it became apparent to me that monogamy, as an exclusive marriage practice with closed polygyny, is beneficial for men not women. The benefits accrue even greater to men when there is a surplus of women. Under such circumstances, instead of men competing (which is natural) with other men for women, women are put in the position of having to compete for men (which is unnatural). In other words, it gives men the edge in dating and mating. Because every woman will not be selected as a marriage partner, it allows men the opportunity to engage in sexual relations with those women who are not, without having to be socially, legally, economically, or morally accountable to them. Clearly this is not beneficial for women.

It was my speculation that if polygyny were practiced openly, it would be more advantageous for women. I therefore began to search for models. In my search, I found three African American communities in which polygyny is openly practiced. In two of the communities my speculation proved to be correct. What distinguishes these two communities from the third one, however, is consent by the women.

The purpose of this work, then, is to describe how polygyny is practiced in these three communities. The intent is to show that when polygyny is practiced openly, honestly, and by consent, it can potentially be more advantageous for women. More importantly, the goal of this work is show how, when polygyny is practiced in this manner, it can be more advantageous for the African American world.

Overview

In Part I, I examine monogamy as an exclusive marriage practice, and show how it is another form of Western cultural domination. I show that, while monogamy is imposed upon the world as a universal norm, polygyny has been practiced throughout most of the world. Even among Western peoples in early Mesopotamia and among the Greeks and Romans, polygyny was practiced. However, because it was done so in the form of concubinage and prostitution, it was dehumanizing for women. I also show how the European form of polygyny was carried over into early America with enslaved African American women, and continues in contemporary times in various forms. In this part, I also provide an overview of studies on the practice of polygyny in Africa. Here I describe what African women perceive as the advantages and disadvantages of the African form of polygyny, and how Western cultural chauvinism, Christianity, and industrialization continue to undermine the practice.

Since questions have been raised about whether there is a population imbalance between African American males and females, in Part II, using census and other data, I explore this. I also explore and critique perspectives from African American women on sharing men and emphasize the necessity of making a paradigmatic shift from individualism, or "self", to an "us" orientation. African American women are encouraged to build relationships on truth and around community. In addition, Part II describes African American male perspectives on what motivates them to engage in multiple relationships. This is followed with an examination of Western masculinity and its impact on African American males.

Part III provides the research findings from the women and men in the three African American communities in which polygyny is openly practiced. Here I show how African American women adjusted to the practice of polygyny, their motivations for engaging in it, what they perceive the advantages and disadvantages to be, and their perspectives on the practice. I also describe why men are motivated to engage in such a practice, the challenges and difficulties, strategies they use to maintain balance and fairness, and their perspectives.

In Part IV, I make the shift to co-partnering, explaining how, when there is consent, it can be advantageous for all women. I also outline the moral, legal, cultural, and personal factors that need to be considered. Finally, African American women are urged to use a womanist ethic of care for sisters to move towards co-partnering.

5

This work has three primary limitations. One is the sample sizes. A small number of families was interviewed in the various communities. This is in part because of the small number of individuals who engage in polygyny even in the communities in which it is openly practiced. The samples from the Islamic communities are extremely small, considering that African American Muslims probably engage in polygyny more than any other African American group in America. This research primarily represents only two Islamic communities in one city.

The second limitation is the selection process. The African Hebrew Israelite community provided the members for me to interview. I was introduced to the Ausar Auset and Muslim communities through acquaintances. In the former case, the community may have introduced me to their model families. In the latter two cases, I interviewed those who were interested in being interviewed. There are also other groups such as some Yoruba communities and the House of Israel that practice polygyny openly. I learned of these communities while interviewing members of the three communities and near completion of this work. Through informal conversations, I also learned that there are individuals dispersed throughout the country who are not members of a polygynous community who also practice polygyny by consent. So this study does not include all of the communities or individuals who practice polygyny.

The research on why men engage in multiple relationships and on women's perspectives on sharing men is limited by the selection process. The men who were interviewed came from among acquaintances and their friends and those who responded to questionnaires reflect the responses of members of the African American organizations and newspapers in which the questionnaires were distributed. The research on women is also limited in these regards, and both studies reflect responses from those who take my African American studies courses. The attitudes and perceptions of men and women in these two chapters therefore may not be generalizable to the larger African American population.

The third limitation of this work is that children were not included. Future research might include young adult children to ascertain the emotional and psychological impact of being raised in polygynous families. In spite of its shortcomings, I believe, however, that this work provides a beginning.

Feminist Critique

Finally, I feel compelled to address potential feminist arguments against polygyny. In fact, I feel compelled to critique feminist analysis of patriarchy in general. A fundamental problem with some analyses is that the Greco-Roman and European-American form of patriarchy is assumed to exist all over the world. Anthropologists have noted that the Roman *Patria potestas*, where the father dominated the clan, was an extreme form of patriarchy. Because the Greco-Roman and European-American form of patriarchy is often used as the basis of feminist analysis, the social structures and practices of peoples in other cultures throughout the world are often inadequately examined, and others that may very well have nothing to do with patriarchy are assumed to be derived from it.

For example, there is a great deal of criticism by feminists of male dominance in public arenas throughout the world. The high prevalence of males in public arenas in societies in which the private and pubic are separate, particularly in those that have not been influenced by industrialization or Western systems of domination, however, does not mean that males dominate over females in the manner they do in Western patriarchies. Nor does it mean that the structures males institute privilege them over females. In many societies there are "male" spheres and "female" spheres, and this does not mean that one is superior to the other. Nor does it mean that women do not have influence in those areas that affect their own lives. I wonder also, if it occurs to those who make such analyses that women have not participated in the past or the present in certain public arenas on a large scale in societies throughout the world because they have simply had no interest in doing so?

Whatever the case may be, polygyny might be thought to stem from patriarchy. Potential feminist arguments against polygyny, then, might be, that it is based on male dominance or that it privileges males over females and subjugates females under male control.

I argue, however, that this is not necessarily the case. I do not think the practice of polygyny throughout the world has had as much to do with patriarchy as it had to do with social circumstances, e.g., a sex ratio imbalance and natural tendencies of males to engage in sexual multiplicity. Many societies, understanding how the two phenomena could lead to family and community disorganization, leaving women and children without economic, social, and emotional support (ills plaguing the Western world), may have instituted polygyny to insulate against this. By contrast, it is those societies with exclusive monogamy and closed polygyny, with male supremacy and female inferiority, where women are dichotomized into classifications of "Madonna" or "whore," with the latter left for males to carry out their natural tendencies without accountability — that seem to disadvantage women the most. The fact is, polygyny can exist without patriarchy. And, rather than being male-centered, it can very well be female-centered and work to the advantage of women.

My position, then, is that because of the population imbalance between African American males and females, polygyny is needed. By comparison to the Western form, however, where there are little or no advantages under closed forms, open polygyny can potentially be more advantageous for women. The intent of this work, then, is to show how African American women, through unification and dedication to care for sisters, love, truth, and community, can, and are, making the male propensity to engage in sexual multiplicity work to their advantage. Furthermore, by bringing to the fore the voices of African American women who are practicing polygyny, this work shows how, by consent, women can become agents in empowering themselves, their families, and their communities.

PART I: MONOGAMY AND POLYGYNY

Chapter 1

MONOGAMY ONLY: THE TRAPPINGS OF EUROCENTRISM?

Marriage has assumed various forms throughout human history and experience. The primary forms observed by social scientists include monogamy, polygyny, polyandry, and cenogamy. These four have been further divided into two forms: singular and plural (Lee, 1982). Monogamy, the only singular form of marriage, is the practice of being married to one person at a time. The other three are polygamy or plural forms of marriage. Cenogamy or group marriage, the least common form of plural marriage is that between two or more individuals from each sex. Polyandry is the practice of having more than one husband at a time. Finally, polygyny, the most common form of polygamy, is the practice of having more than one wife at a time. All of these marriage practices have been found in some form or fashion among peoples throughout the world, which means that all have been recognized among those who practiced them.

It was not until European world conquest and domination after the 15th century that the notion of monogamy as the "only" legitimate marriage practice came to dominate the world. A major force driving this was the development of industry and the capitalistic mode of production. Prior to the emergence of capitalism, production or economies were organized around families and extended kinships. Thus, what a family or kinship produced directly benefitted its members. The larger the family or kin group, the more it was able to produce. The more it produced, the greater its status and subsequent position and power. In those societies in which it was practiced, polygyny served this end. More wives and children helped to increase the family and kin size and therefore its productive capacity. Under capitalistic regimes, however, production shifted from the family to industry,

9

eventually taking on global dimensions. With this shift, rather than working directly for the benefit of their own families and kin, members began to work for the benefit of those who controlled industry. In other words, it was members of the *world's families* who now worked to produce wealth for the members of a few families. Africa played a major role in the early stages as it was the free labor of its peoples in the form of slavery which was capitalized on. A consequence of this is that a few families eventually gained control over most of the world's resources, and to maintain control, it has been necessary to dictate the form marriage and family should take. This is done through culture.

Through cultural domination, European-American social structures are projected as superior and those of other peoples as inferior. Exclusive monogamy has not only been a cultural practice for a majority of European peoples, as far back as the Greeks and Romans, but it supported their economic institutions. In the industrial period, the monogamous, nuclear family continued to predominate because the products produced by such families under the capitalistic mode of production would subsequently be purchased by these families, thereby increasing the wealth of European and American nation and corporate-families who owned and controlled industry. As such, monogamy was propagated as a universal norm and a superior marriage form.

This chapter examines how early European and American scholars helped to legitimate the superiority of monogamy and Christian theologians provided moral sanction. This chapter also provides an overview of how monogamy evolved and was practiced in the Greco-Roman world along with what I describe as a peculiar form of polygyny — concubinage and prostitution. In addition, this chapter provides an overview of Greco-Roman marriage customs, and shows how as Christianity evolved over the centuries, these customs came to be integrated with its ideas of marriage, one of which was exclusive monogamy. Finally, this chapter explores whether the way marriage is practiced in the Western world is in reality monogamy.

Origins of Marriage and Family

As already indicated, early social scientists helped to perpetuate the notion of monogamy as a superior marriage form. In their analyses of the evolution of the human family, it was the general view that as humans evolved from lower to higher stages of development, marriage practices evolved from plural or inferior forms to a singular or superior form. A seminal work in which this was done is that by Henry Lewis Morgan.

In *Ancient Society*, Morgan (1963) delineates the social development of human societies into three epochs according to progress made in food production. These stages include: savagery, which he considers to be the lowest stage, barbarism, an intermediate stage, and civilization, the highest stage. The first two stages are further divided into lower, middle, and upper. From these schemata, Morgan describes several types of marriage and family systems, each corresponding to the various stages outlined above. The systems include consanguine, *punaluan*, syndyasmian (pairing family), patriarchal, and monogamian. Of these five systems he focused on three — the consanguine, *punaluan*, and monogamian — which he contends were influential enough to create three distinct systems of consanguinity. The consanguine family, theorized by Morgan to be the first and most ancient form and thought to have existed in the period of savagery, is believed to have been founded on the intermarriage of brothers and sisters and cousins in the form of group marriage. This means that brothers and sisters and cousins married each other and became each other's husbands and wives. Under the consanguine family, essentially, children in each generation belonged to all the sisters and brothers of the next generation, and intermarriage was allowed between brothers and sisters and cousins in the same generation but not across generations, for example, parent and child, or progeny and ancestor. Since group marriage is a plural form of marriage, Morgan's theory suggests that consanguine marriage encompassed both polygyny and polyandry.

Important to note is that Morgan's conception of the consanguine family is derived from how Malayans (thought to still exist in savagery at the time of the study) described their relations

11

with their brothers and sisters and their children. They described the children of their sisters and brothers and cousins as their own and, likewise, the grandchildren of their sisters and brothers and cousins as their own. Other than this, there is no evidence to support the existence of a consanguine family form. Because it was thought by Morgan that whole groups of men and whole groups of women possessed one another mutually and that they married their own brothers and sisters, it was also thought that this early period in human family development represented a period of sexual promiscuity. However, as already indicated, there is no evidence to support the existence of a consanguine family and, therefore, none to support the notion of sexual promiscuity during this period.

The *punaluan* family, a name derived from the study of Hawaiian family organization, according to Morgan, is marked by a period when brothers and sisters were excluded from marriage relations. During this period, marriage could only occur between cousins. The term *punaluan* essentially means that all the sisters of a man's wife and her cousins are his wives. He, however, calls his wife's sisters' husbands *punalua*, which means intimate companion. Likewise, the woman calls her husband's brothers and cousins her husbands and her husband's brothers' wives *punalua*. The *punaluan* family is thought to have existed among all the tribes of human-kind, even those that eventually evolved to become monogamous, including the Greeks, Romans, Germans, Celts, Hebrews, etc. It is also thought that it is the organization of *gentes* (clans) that permanently excluded brothers and sisters in marriage, and that this practice eventually spread across tribes and became universal. Overall, both consanguine and *punaluan* marriage forms, which were plural forms of marriage, is thought by Morgan to represent human progress during the period of savagery.

The pairing family, according to Morgan, emerged during the lower stage of barbarism and is founded on marriage between single pairs, with several pairs usually living in communal households. Marriages in the pairing family were usually arranged by the mothers and, in some cases, the children were strangers prior to marriage. With the pairing family, generally, the parties stayed together as long as they were happy with one another.

When either of the parties ceased being happy, both had the liberty to leave the marriage (Morgan, p. 463).

Morgan observes that even in the *punaluan* family there was a tendency to pairing, "each man having a principal wife among a number of wives and each woman a principal husband among a number of husbands" (p. 466). What helped the *punaluan* family evolve to a pairing family was organization into *gentes* (clans). At first, organization into *gentes* did not immediately disrupt intermarriage. What it did was to narrow its range. Over time, "the structure and principles of the organization tended to create prejudice against the marriage of consanguine as the advantages of marriages between unrelated persons were gradually discovered through the practice of marrying out of the *gens*" (clan) (p. 437). Thus, the progress of society under the *gentes* prepared the way for the pairing family.

As marrying out of *gentes* became the order, it created a scarcity of wives. This led to the acquisition of wives through negotiation and purchase. In addition, men "did not confine themselves to their own, nor even to friendly tribes, but captured them by force from hostile tribes. . ." (p. 467). Thus emerged the practice of obtaining wives by capture and purchase. Because of the effort involved in acquiring wives by capture and purchase, many men were not willing to share them. The effect of this was that a portion of the group not immediately associated for subsistence would be cut off, leading to reductions in the size of the family and the range of the conjugal system. The stabilization of subsistence and improved architecture enhanced protection of life and increased the formation of families consisting of pairs. "The more these advantages were realized, the more stable such a family would become, and the more its individuality would increase" (p. 469). From this type of family would eventually emerge the monogamous family. However, Morgan discusses some of the particulars of the patriarchal family as an intermediate stage in the evolution to monogamy.

Although he describes the patriarchal family as being "founded upon the marriage of one man with several wives; followed in general by the seclusion of the wives," Morgan points out that polygyny is not the "material principle of the patriarchal institution (p. 474). . . .The organization of a number of persons, bond and free, into a family, under paternal power, for the purpose of holding lands and care of flocks and herds, was the essential characteristic of this family"(p. 474). Essentially, the patriarchal family form is that of a patriarch, or a chief, with authority over those held in servitude, employed as servants, and those joined in marriage. Morgan points out that the patriarchal family marks a peculiar epoch in human progress, a time when individuality of the person began to rise above the *gens* in which it had previously been merged (p. 475). He also compares the patriarchal family form with its predecessors: "In the consanguine and *punaluan* families, paternal authority was impossible as well as unknown; under the [pairing family] it began to appear as a feeble influence; but its growth steadily advanced as the family became more and more individualized and became fully established under monogamy which assured the paternity of children" (p. 475).

Important to this discussion is the matriarchal thesis. Essentially, the argument presented by J.J. Bachofen (1967) in *Myth, Religion and Mother Right* is that all societies had at one time been matriarchal. This derived from the mother-child bond, an instinctual love and one that exceeds all others. It was this bond, and thus maternal instinct, which was the driving force behind societies. However, as the father began to experience the same feeling for the off-spring as the mother, it represented a higher spiritual level of love, since it was not motivated by instinct. Thus emerged the patriarchy which is a higher family form. The matriarchal thesis has pretty much been refuted, although there may have been confusion over the way the term was being used by Bachofen and others, for example, maternal instinct being the driving force vs. matriarchy or women dominating over men in the manner that men did women under Greco-Roman patriarchy. Also, with others who have engaged in the debate over the years, it appears there may have also been confusion in usage of the term "matriarchy." It appears to have been used interchangeably with others, such as matrifocal, matrilocal, and matrilinity, which indicate female centeredness and lineage vs. female domination.

Whatever the case may be, Morgan further points out that the patriarchal family has been found among Semitic peoples, primarily the Hebrews, and Europeans— the Romans and Greeks. Among the Romans, the father had the power of life or death over his children and descendants as well as his slaves, servants, and his wife. He, however, notes that the power of the Roman patriarch was an exceptional human experience and "passed beyond the bounds of reason in an excess of domination" (p. 475). Moreover, "its general influence tended powerfully to the establishment of the monogamian family, . . ." which emerged during civilization (p. 475).

Overall, the argument that Morgan makes is that as humans evolved from a lower level of development, which is savagery, to a higher level, which is civilization, so too did their marriage and family practices. It is not so much that there is anything wrong with Morgan's schemata on the development of marriage and family systems. It is the evolutionary paradigm (and the language he uses) which places the practices along a hierarchy, with those in civilization being more evolved, and the underpinnings of sexual promiscuity in plural marriage (which was supposed to be practiced among savages). The Malayans and Hawaiians were thought to still exist in a period of savagery, (as well as others all over the globe, including Africans) and their marriage practices, which may or may not have been plural in form, were thought to be an indication of sexual promiscuity. By contrast, it was thought that the Greeks, Romans and others of Indo-European stock, although in the past had also existed in savagery, continued to evolve. As they became more evolved, more civilized, so too did their marriage practice. That marriage practice is monogamy.

Monogamy With a Peculiar Form of Polygyny

The evolutionary paradigm underlying Morgan's theory of the origins of marriage and family is clearly problematic. There are, however, factors delineated by him, as it pertains to the evolution of monogamy in the Greco-Roman world, that are important to this discussion. As indicated previously, according to Morgan (1963), the monogamic family appears in a definite form in the later period of barbarism. A fundamental distinction between the pairing family

15

from which the monogamian family derived is that there is exclusive cohabitation. A major factor in the development of monogamous family form was property and the need for legitimate heirs to inherit it. Morgan points out "that the growth of property and the desire for its transmission to children was in reality, the moving power which brought in monogamy," especially among the Greeks, one of the earliest peoples to whom it can be traced (p. 485). Although "a knowledge of the paternity of children had begun to be realized under the [pairing family], from which the Grecian form was evidently derived, . . . it had not attained the requisite degree of certainty because of survival of some portion of the ancient *jura conjugialia*" (p. 485). However, there were two factors in the monogamous family under the Grecian form that negatively impacted women. First, the chief object of marriage was the procreation of children. Bearing children was for the most part the only role that women could assume. Second, women lived in seclusion. Morgan asserts:

From the first to the last among the Greeks there was a principle of egotism or studied selfishness at work among the males tending to lessen the appreciation of woman scarcely found among savages [referring to people of color]. It reveals itself in their plan of domestic life, which in the higher ranks secluded the wife to enforce an exclusive cohabitation, without admitting the reciprocal obligation on the part of her husband . . . their education was superficial, intercourse with the opposite sex was denied them, and their inferiority was inculcated as a principle, until it came to be accepted as a fact by the women themselves. The wife was not the companion and the equal of her husband, but stood to him in the relation of a daughter . . . .(p. 482)

He further observes: "It still remains an enigma that a race, with endowments great enough to impress their mental life upon the world, would have remained essentially barbaric in their treatment of the female sex at the height of their civilization" (p. 482).

In *The Origins of the Family: Private Property and the State,* Frederick Engles (1942) elaborates on this, observing that fundamental to the development of monogamy, especially among the Greeks, is supremacy of man over woman. The central ingredient in this was the need to produce heirs to inherit property.

16

/ Thus, as monogamy entered into the Greco-Roman world, it was for women only, not for men. Engles notes that although there were goddesses in the early period in Greek history and women were freer and more respected in the heroic age, we find woman already being humiliated by the domination of the man and by competition from girl slaves under the system of concubinage (p. 126). Citing an example from Homer's *Iliad,* where captive slave girls were taken as booty back to Greece and brought under the same roof as the wife, Engles remarks:

The legitimate wife was expected to put up with all this, but herself to remain strictly chaste and faithful. In the heroic age a Greek woman is indeed more respected than in the period of civilization, but to her husband she is after all nothing but the mother of his legitimate children and heirs, his chief housekeeper and supervisor of his female slaves, whom he can and does take as concubines if he so fancies. It is the existence of slavery side by side with monogamy, the presence of young beautiful slaves belonging unreservedly to the man that stamps monogamy from the very beginning with its specific character of monogamy for the woman only but not for the man. (p. 126)

Engles also describes how in order to ensure that the offspring of their wives were their own, men kept women in seclusion. Women among the Ionians

. . . lived more or less behind locked doors and had no company except other women. The women's apartments formed a separate part of the house on the upper floor or at the back where men, especially strangers, could not easily enter and to which the women retired when men visited the house. They never went out without being accompanied by a female slave; indoors they were kept under regular guard. . . . Molossian dogs [were] kept to frighten away adulterers, and, at any rate in the Asiatic towns, eunuchs were employed to keep watch over the women. (p. 127)

Furthermore, he points out that a woman was nothing more than an "*oikurema* thing . . . for looking after the house, and, apart from her business of bearing children, that she was . . . [the] chief female domestic servant" (p. 127). Thus, the origin of monogamy is not the outcome of individual sex- love as is often thought. Engles states, "It was the first form of the family to be

17

based not on natural but on economic conditions — on the victory of private property over 'primitive,' natural communal property" (p. 128). In fact, according to Engles, as the Greeks themselves made clear, the "sole exclusive aims of monogamous marriage were to make the man supreme in the family and to propagate, as the future heirs to his wealth, children indisputably his own. Otherwise marriage was a burden, a duty which had to be performed whether one liked it or not, to gods, state, and one's ancestors" (p. 128).

Because marriage was based neither on love or affection but on procreation of children, there was a need for other means through which men could fulfill sexual and emotional needs. What emerged was an elaborate system of prostitution. Engles observes that prostitution was crucial in the development of monogamy, especially the Grecian form. In fact, during the most flourishing period of Athens, an extensive system of prostitution came into existence that was favored by the state (p. 128).

In *Prostitution and Society: A Survey,* Fernando Henriques (1962) points out that the state bought prostitutes on behalf of the citizens and established brothels *dicteria* staffed by women *dicteriades* (p. 49). Henriques notes that prostitutes "in a sense were civil servants, and could exercise no freedom of choice over their clients but were at the disposal of all who came. The fees paid, low as they might be, accrued to the state and were used partly for running expenses. The remainder was a profit to the state which might use the monies in a variety of ways from the building of temples to helping the indigent" (p. 49). Brothels were also arranged in accordance with the social hierarchy — the poorest quarters offering the lowest prices and those catering to the rich offering the highest. Brothels could also be privately owned, however, they were taxed by the state.

There were also various levels of prostitution which Bernard Murstein (1974) classifies in *Love Sex and Marriage Through the Ages*. The *pornae*, where women worked for meager wages, were the lowest in the hierarchy: "These women had no social rights, nor could they make any demands on their children for support. To distinguish themselves from others, they were required to wear a special ornate costume and dye their hair with saffron" (p. 55).

Henriques also indicates that the *dicteriades* were among the lowest in the hierarchy in the early stages of prostitution in Athens. According to him, the *dicteriades:*

...were ... deprived of all their rights as citizens and in the streets had to wear special clothing. Many of these disabilities were passed on to their children who could acquire citizenship only by performing an acknowledged act of bravery. Anyone who was responsible for introducing a free-born female citizen to a brothel could be put to death. Despite this law men could sell their sisters or daughters to the state brothels if they had been convicted of fornication – a serious offense. (p. 49)

Auletrides or flute players were next in the hierarchy. They were usually slaves brought to Athens by a speculator. They "were often rented out to feasts to entertain and, after enough had been drunk, to share the beds of the guests" (p. 61). At the top of the hierarchy were the *hetaerae*. The *hetaerae* were distinguished from lower level prostitutes because they were "neither slaves nor lower-class women, as was the case of other prostitutes, but Athenian citizens" (p. 55). This was one of the few occupations open to women. The advantages of being a *hetaerae* exceeded those of being a married woman. Murstein explains:

She was looked upon as sexually exciting, better educated, well groomed, charming, and steeped in all the social graces. She usually lived in her own home and could have multiple lovers or be 'faithful' to one man. Intellectuals as well as lovers gathered in her salon to pass the time agreeably. (p. 55)

Engles notes that men "who would have been ashamed to show any love for their wives, amused themselves by all sorts of love affairs with *hetaerae*" (p. 128). In addition, *hetaerism*, which Engles describes as being a derivative from group marriage,

... is as much a social institution as any other; it continues the old sexual freedom – to the advantage of men .... but in reality this condemnation never falls on the men concerned, but only on the women; they are despised and outcast in order that the unconditional supremacy of men over the female sex may be once more proclaimed as a fundamental law of society. (p. 130)

Furthermore, it was only through prostitution that women were able to develop their intellectual and artistic capabilities and stand above the conventional level of womanhood, which Engles considers the "worst condemnation of the Athenian family" (p. 128).

Concubinage also provided a sexual outlet for men. Concubines, however, were distinguished from prostitutes in that they were slaves owned by prosperous men and were used for both sexual and domestic purposes. They could be sold from one master to another or might even be lent out. The difference between a concubine and a prostitute was that the former was sexual property owned by an individual, whereas the prostitute was hired out temporarily or for a considerable period.

Finally, according to Engles, when monogamous marriage makes its appearance in history in the Greco-Roman world, "it is not the reconciliation of man and woman . . . [rather it] comes on the scene as the subjugation of the one sex by the other . . . a struggle between the sexes unknown throughout the whole previous historic period" (p. 129). It is in monogamous marriage according to Engles, that the first class opposition appears in history — the antagonism between man and woman. In addition, it is the first class oppression — the oppression of the female by the male (p. 129).

The notion that polygyny is inferior and that monogamy, which developed during civilization (essentially among European peoples), is superior, comes through in the work of other scholars. In *The History of Marriage*, a major anthropological work, Edward Westermarck (1922), provides extensive data to show the prevalence of polygyny throughout the world. He also provides possible explanations for its practice, many of which are discussed in the following chapter. In spite of this objective effort, Westermarck ends his discussion with an explanation for why societies, because of factors stemming from the progress made by Western civilization, have a natural tendency towards monogamy. What is revealing in this discussion is how polygyny is regarded in comparison with monogamy. What is also revealing is how people of color are referred to as savages as a manner of speech:

Our examination into the causes of monogamy and polygyny makes it possible for us to explain why progress in civilization to a certain point has proved favorable to polygyny, whilst in its highest form leads to monogamy. The first tendency is, as we have seen largely due to economic and social circumstances — the accumulation and unequal distribution of wealth and increasing social differentiation; but it should also be noticed that considerable surplus of females which among many of the higher savages is caused by their wars is not found at the lowest stages of civilization, where war does not seriously disturb the proportion of the sexes. The retrograde tendency towards monogamy in the highest grades of culture, again may be traced to a variety of causes. No superstitious beliefs keep civilised men apart from their wives during pregnancy and for a long time after child-birth. The desire for offspring has become less intense. A large family, instead of being a help in the struggle for existence, is often considered an insufferable burden. A man's kinsfolk are no longer his only friends, and his wealth and influence do not depend upon the number of wives and children. A wife ceases to be a mere labourer, and manual labour is to a large extent replaced by the work of domesticated animals and the use of implements and machines. The sentiment of love has become more refined, and, in consequences, more enduring. To a cultivated mind youth and beauty are by no means the only attractions of a woman, and besides, civilisation has given female beauty a new lease of life. The feelings of the weaker sex are held in higher regard, and the causes which may make polygyny desired by the women themselves no longer exist. The better education bestowed upon them, and other factors in modern civilisation; enable them to live comfortably without the support of a husband. (pp. 104-105)

Westermarck then asks the question of whether monogamy will be the only recognized form of marriage in the future. The responses he cites from others also provide insight into views on monogamy. For example, according to Westermarck, although one scholar questioned monogamy as a superior marriage form and another speculated that European nations would eventually legalize polygyny, Herbert Spencer, considered the father of Western sociology, had this to say: "The monogamic form of the sexual relation is manifestly the ultimate form; and any changes to be anticipated must be in the direction of completion or extension of it" (p. 105).

Although the general view was that monogamy is a superior marriage form, there are some scholars who challenge this. In *The Mothers*, R. Briffault (1993) points out that the cultural distaste of polygyny by Europeans stems from the Christian-European concept of sex as evil, the notion of exclusivity as a necessity for male-female relations, and misunderstandings of how women are treated under polygyny. As with other scholars, although there are problems with the language Briffault uses, he nevertheless states:

Early Christian moralists who accounted marriage as a necessary evil, favored monogamy as a reduction of that evil to a minimum, but chastity and continence are not valued for their own sakes in uncultured societies. Monogamy accords with the sentiments of exclusive attachment which are assumed in European tradition to be the foundations of the union; but in primitive societies such a desire is not understood. Polygamy is thought to imply disregard for the feelings of women; but in uncultured societies women are the chief upholders of polygamy. (p. 210)

He further points out that among other peoples the "European objection to polygamy is incomprehensible" and "is interpreted as a sign of mental degeneration" (p. 211). In fact, according to Briffault, "Polygyny is widely regarded as a moral virtue; to support as many fellow creatures as possible is not a mark of wealth but a form of philanthropy" (p. 211). He also examines problems with the way polygyny and monogamy are defined and applied to various peoples:

The term 'polygyny' is now employed in preference to 'polygamy' to denote plurality of wives . . . . But many writers do not make use of the distinction consistently, for they do not employ, in opposition to polygyny, the corresponding term "monogyny," but speak of limitation of marriage to one wife as 'monogamy,' thus conveying a misleading impression. The word 'monogamy' not only denotes a practice, but also connotes a moral or legal standard which precludes anyone having a multiplicity of wives. Statements that a given people are 'monogamous' or 'to a large extent monogamous' . . . are liable to suggest that a principle or law enforcing monogamy is recognized among those peoples. But monogamy in this sense is not known outside Christian nations. (p. 212)

He furthermore asserts, "[T]o term a people polygynous or monogynous, polygamous or monogamous, conveys little concerning the actual extent and character of their sex relations. Even in Europe, it has been said, monogyny has never existed. The Romans and Greeks were monogamous in their marriage institutions but scarcely monogynous in their sex relations" (p. 213). Finally, Briffault observes that among most peoples before the advent of Christianity there were no legal prohibitions against polygyny, and there were no words to describe monogamy or polygamy. The first legal prohibitions against it began with the Romans:

Uncultured races vary considerably in the extent to which polygyny is practiced, but no case is known outside Christian nations, of a people among whom it is morally reprobate. Before the Christian era, the terms 'monogamy,' 'bigamy,' 'polygamy' in the sense in which we use them, were unknown. The 'prohibition' of polygyny, which was alleged to be 'natural' and 'to be met with among all nations in a state of refinement,' was actually promulgated for the first time in the world in the code Justinian [among Romans] in the sixth century. (p. 212)

Overall, early anthropologists, employing an evolutionary paradigm, deemed polygyny to be inferior and practiced primarily among peoples lower on the scale of humanity. Plural marriage was thought to have derived from group marriage during a period of sexual promiscuity. Under this paradigm, humans evolved to civilization (those belonging to the European stock), with monogamy being a superior marriage form. Although the practice of monogamy was proclaimed to be superior among the advanced or superior race (Europeans), concubinage and prostitution, a peculiar form of polygyny, were pervasive among these so-called superior peoples. Parallels to this custom can be found in contemporary marriage — the wife and mistress and prostitute — as sexual outlets for males, much to the disadvantage of women. Two other major Greco-Roman ideas also shape Western marriage: that it should be by consent and that it should be indissoluble. In

23

addition, many rituals found in the Greco-Roman wedding ceremony also persist in contemporary practices.

Greco-Roman Marriage

In *Marriage: Human Reality and Saving Mystery*, E. Schillebeeckx (1965) provides a comprehensive overview of Greco-Roman marriage. He identifies three periods in Roman marriage. In the first period, marriage among both Greek and Romans was not based on interpersonal relationships or on procreation but on a "sacral event," based on the "religion of the hearth." The hearth was a sacred fire that symbolized deceased ancestors or the household gods—referred to as *manes, lares,* and *pemates.* Each family essentially had its own household gods with its own rites, prayers, hymns, and sacrifices (p. 234). The father, who functioned like a priest, was responsible for care of the household gods, and this duty was passed on to the son. Because the domestic hearth was never to go out, procreation assured its continued existence, and this accounts for its primacy in later periods.

In marriage, the woman was transferred from the hearth or religion of her father to that of her husband. "This transference or conversion, could only be accomplished by means of a religious consecration and initiation" (p. 234). To carry this out, there were essentially three ceremonies: the *ekdosis* or *tratitio puellae, pompe* or *domum-ductio,* and the *telos.* The *ekdosis* was the religious ceremony and legal act of the father "handing over" from his *manus* or authority his daughter to the authority of the bridegroom. Before doing this, however, the father made an offering to the household gods. In the next stage, the *domum-ductio,* the bride, wearing a veil, garland, and white ceremonial garment, was taken by carriage to the house of the bridegroom while wedding songs were sung. "After a simulated abduction by force, she was carried by the bridegroom over the threshold of his house" (p. 235). It was at this point that she was initiated into the household religion. "She was then led to the household altar, the sacred hearth, where she was sprinkled with lustral water and was permitted to touch the sacred fire, and was received into the community of the water and fire" (p. 235). During the final ceremony, the *telos,* the bride and bridegroom

24

partook of the wedding cake, the *far* or *panis farreus*, a loaf made of flour that was the "very holy pledge of the marriage," and "entered into communion with each other through communion with the household gods" (pp. 235-236). This consummated sacral marriage, a religious and legally valid ceremony, was called the *confarreatio*.

This marriage ceremony, according to Schillebeeckx, appears "despite certain differences in detail, to have been the original basic pattern of the marriage contract in Indo-European society. . . .It was the principle of the household religion which provided the basis for the monogamous and essentially indissoluble character of marriage" (p. 236).

During the second period — the seventh to the fifth centuries B.C. — a revolution took place in Greek and Roman societies, whereby "social institutions were disassociated from their original religious foundations" (p. 238). The *Turannis* came into being — a form of authority based not on religious convictions, the priesthood, or 'sacral' traditions but on the will of the people through legislation. Included in this change was marriage. In this period marriage came to be based on interpersonal relationships and mutual consent by both parties. Although the ruling class considered marriage without the religious rite worthless, over a period time, those by mutual consent gained the same status as the sacral form of marriage by two means. The first was through *coemptio,* whereby the husband got his wife through a fictitious purchase; and the second was through *usus,* whereby the wife lived with her husband for a year after mutual agreement to marry. "This gave the marriage of consent in effect the same standing with regard to the husband's authority, as the ancient rite of *confarreatio,*" but without the ceremony (p. 239).

During the third period in the Roman empire, the practices of *confarreatio, coemptio,* and *usus* disappeared. Fathers of each family arranged marriage, sometimes when children were quite young. Marriage was concluded without any form of law. Mutual consent was all that was necessary, although in traditional circles they were supplemented by ancient religious customs. During this period, a custom, thought to be an adoption from Western contacts with the East called the *arrha,* was integrated into the betrothal. This entailed giving a pledge, often in the form of an engagement ring. "The two concrete elements necessary to make the marriage valid were *consensus* or mutual consent and the *domum-ductio* or leading the wife to her husband's house" (p. 241). The indissolubility of marriage also waned during this period. Roman law stipulated "mutual consent simply created a condition which lasted only as long as the partners persevered in this mutual agreement . . . [and] laid down that every marriage concluded by mutual consent of the partners in the presence of several friends as witnesses was valid" (p. 241). Thus, other "secular and religious practices surrounding it were expressly placed outside the framework of the legal validity of marriage" (p. 241). In spite of this, religious ceremonies were still commonly practiced, although their essential meaning had been forgotten (p. 242). The ceremony usually occurred as follows:

On the eve of the feast the bride was dressed in white, as a Vestal virgin, with a fiery red veil (the *flammeum*) and a garland of flowers. On the morning of the feast the auguries were consulted and, if they were favorable, the partners' consent to marry each other was heard: Did she (he) wish to become a mother (father)? This was followed by the joining of the bride's and the bridegroom's right hands. Next, either at home or in the temple, an animal was sacrificed, while the bride and bridegroom sat on two seats which were bound together and covered by a sheepskin. The priest pronounced a prayer over the couple who passed around the altar. After a symbolic abduction of the bride, the solemn entry into the bridegroom's house took place. On her arrival at the new dwelling, the bride smeared the doorpost with oil and fat and decorated the doors. She was lifted over the threshold and received by her husband 'into the community of fire and water.' (p. 242)

Overall, from these practices one can see parallels to contemporary marriage. In Greco-Roman marriage we find the ideas of marriage by mutual consent (expressed by saying, "I do"), and the notion of marriage being indissoluble (expressed by saying, "until death do us part"). For engagement we find the pledging of the ring. Finally, for the wedding ritual we find the handing over of the bride by the father to the bridegroom, wearing of the veil by the bride, witnesses, partaking of the cake, and the carrying of the bride over the threshold. These customs, along with exclusive monogamy, essentially Greco-Roman in origin, became widespread through Christianity.

The Role of Christianity in the Spread of Greco-Roman Marriage

Schillebeeckx (1962) also provides an overview of how ancient Greco-Roman views and ceremonial practices came to be integrated into Christian marriage. According to him, in the early stages of Christian development, marriage for Christians was very much the same as that for nonChristians, or "pagans."[1] (p. 245). The primary role of the church during this period was pastoral care, wherein which it was to protect baptized Christians from "pagan" influences, particularly sacrifices to "false gods" (gods other than the Hebrew/Christian God). The church "accepted the subjection of her members to Roman legislature, and matrimonial cases were also brought before the civil law courts" (p. 245). The church played a role only in special cases, for example, marriages by orphans and enslaved individuals.

Under Roman law, those who were enslaved were prohibited from contracting a marriage with free persons, and for those who did, their marriages were not recognized as legally valid. Marriages between enslaved persons were also not considered legally valid and were regarded as concubinage. However, to circumvent this practice, popes undermined civil law and permitted such marriages to occur. What evolved from such marriages was the "marriage of conscience," which was concluded with permission from church officials but was kept secret from civil authorities. Because marriage was essentially a civil and family affair, orphans needed someone to assume the role of father or guardian. Since the role of the church was to provide charitable care, church officials would intervene in such cases and would sometimes conduct the entire marriage. Other than such special

---

[1] From the Latin *paganua*, a country dweller, defined as a person who is not Christian, Moslem or Jew — Heathen. As a form of cultural imperialism, a pejorative term used to clump people of different ethnic backgrounds with different spiritual-religious orientations into one group.

cases, the only role that the church played in marriage in the early stages of Christianity was to ensure that Christians refrained from sacrifices to "false gods" and "pagan excesses."

During the fourth century, the role of the church increased. At this stage, bishops and priests provided prayer and blessings known as the marriage service. Schillebeeckx notes: "This priestly blessing probably developed from the practice—highly regarded by families—of a priest, or especially a bishop, going to congratulate the family in which a marriage feast was celebrated. For the most part, the role of church officials was to Christianize pagan practices" (p. 250). The Christian baptism, for example, was the counterpart of the pagan marriage bath. "As the church became more firmly established, and pagan religions had lost a great deal of their prestige, the church became more receptive towards pagan religious practices in connection with marriage. . . .But the liturgy of marriage only formed a framework around the real marriage which was still contracted civilly within the family circle" (p. 251).

Essentially, marriage in the first centuries of Christianity meant marrying a fellow Christian (two baptized Christians) and was to be experienced according to Christian principles that included "sharing the same faith, participation in the Eucharist, practice of Christian charity and praying together at home" (pp. 253-254). It was not until the eleventh century that substantial change took place, and the role of the church increased in significance.

From the fourth to the eleventh centuries, Christianity spread to various parts of Europe. For the most part, marriage was not conducted according to any ecclesiastical form of law but was based on the statutory or unwritten legal practice of the people in each land. Among the Germanic tribes, for example, marriage was regarded as a contract between two tribes or family groups rather than between the individuals getting married. "Under this contract, the bridegroom acquired from the girl's father or guardian the *mundium*, or the power giving him the right and the duty to protect and to represent his bride" (p. 256).

The Germanic betrothal was like a deed of purchase between the bridegroom and the bride's tribe or sponsor. The bridegroom had to give a pledge, or *wadia*, in the form of presents or sureties before he placed himself under the obligation to take the girl as his wife and to give a certain part of his possessions by way of a *wittum*. The Germanic peoples adopted the Roman custom of the engagement ring. However, among the Germanic tribes, the wedding ring became a sign of the marriage contract itself.

The marriage, according to Schillebeeckx, "began with the drawing up of the marriage document in which the *wittum* (dos) and the dowry for the handing over of the authority over the girl was laid down. Then the 'sponsor' gave the girl to the bridegroom with his right hand, and the bridegroom paid him the dowry. This concluded the 'handing over of the bride,' and all her property to the bridegroom" (p. 257).

Over time, mutual consent became an important element among Germanic peoples. However, it was a while before the church succeeded in getting the *consensus*, based on Roman law, accepted among the Germanic tribes. The single most important element of marriage was the handing over of the bride by her father or a guardian. By the eleventh century, the legal proceedings were enacted in three stages: The proposal and betrothal in which the father or guardian played a major role, mutual consent and the wedding feast, which included bringing the bride home, the festive meal, and the solemn entry into the bridal chamber.

Thus, essentially, during the first ten centuries, the church recognized the jurisdictional power of the state over matrimonial affairs and did not demand that the state be subordinate to the laws of the church (p. 272). During the tenth century, however, the king lost power, and matrimonial affairs came under the domain of the church. However, it is important to note that although power came under the jurisdiction of the church, it did not affect the marriage contract. Marriage was conducted according to the people's customs. During the eleventh and twelfth centuries, the church obtained complete jurisdiction in matrimonial affairs and even became responsible for the regulation of the purely civil consequences of marriage, although in some districts secular authorities retained full jurisdictional control up to the thirteenth century (p. 277).

Over time, the ancient ceremonies decreased in significance, and the priest played a more significant role. "It was

29

usually the priest who gave the bride to the bridegroom, though in some places he gave the partners to each other or conducted the ceremony" (p. 277). It is claimed "that the priest took over the function of the father or guardian in the handing over of the bride, whereas others maintain that his part was that of the third, and neutral, party whose function was to ask the two partners for their mutual consent" (p. 277). Schillebeeckx concludes by pointing out that by the time the church obtained jurisdiction in matrimony "practices proper to the secular society had thus become fully integrated into the liturgy of the church. Worldly things, symbols, and legal proceedings, the *arrha*, the ring, the dowry, the . . . veiling, and so on, objects and practices deriving from the popular tradition of the Germanic, Frankish, Celtic, Longobardic and Gothic tribes — had partly, under Greco-Roman and Eastern influence (especially via the Western Goths in Spain), found their way into the liturgy of the church" (279).

It was not until the nineteenth century that marriage came back under the authority of the state. George Joyce (1948) in *Christian Marriage*, states that "one of the most signal results of the French Revolution was the acceptance throughout Europe of a purely secular conception of the State" (p. 263). The concept of the state with authority to regulate every department of man's life manifested itself in the widespread introduction of civil marriage throughout Europe and carried over into its colonies in the New World. Even so, the customs and ideas underlying marriage, including the basic form it should take, much of which was derived from Greco-Roman and others of Indo-European origin, had already been set and sanctioned by the Christian Church for centuries.

The Biblical Case for Monogamy and Against Polygyny

Although monogamy as the only legitimate marriage form is culturally specific to Greek, Roman, and other Euro-descended groups, the Bible has been used by Christian theologians to make the case that monogamy is what God intended, and other forms of marriage, namely polygyny, are contrary to God's will.

In *Polygyny Reconsidered*, in the chapter "Polygamy and the Bible," Eugene Hillman (1986) provides an overview and analysis of how the Bible has been used to affirm monogamy's compatibility and polygyny's incompatibility with Christianity. Scriptures that have generally been used according to him, include those addressing: the Creation (Gen 1:26-28; 2:7-25); prohibition of adultery and divorce (Matt. 5:27-32; Mark 10:2-12; Rom. 7:2-3; 1 Cor. 7:2-16; Eph. 5:22-33); the Covenant between Yahweh and his people (Isa. 50:1; 54:6-7; 62:4-5; Jer. 2:2; Ezek. 16; Hosea); and marrying multiple wives (Deuteronomy 17:16-17). Scriptures have also been used to support a growing appreciation for monogamy (Pro. 5:15-19, 31:10-31; Eccles. 9:9; Tob 8:6-7; Ps. 45:9-11, 128:3). In addition, it has been argued that "while many of the great biblical figures were monogamists, the first recorded plural marriage occurred among the reprobate descendants of Cain" (Gen. 4:19, 23).

Although numerous Scriptures have been used to support monogamy, Hillman argues that there is "no single passage of the Bible that stands alone as a clear proof of God's intention in this matter, although impressive number of texts may be cited as indications of a positive inclination toward monogamy" (p. 143).

Hillman first observes several substantial differences between the historical and cultural contexts that shaped Old Testament ideas of marriage and those that shaped Western ideas. One is that in the Western world, marriage is understood primarily in terms of the conjugal relationship between husband and wife. By contrast, marriage in ancient Israel was seen in the context of the community, the family, and the clan. The husband-wife relationship was subordinate to the family or clan. "Through daughters being married into different families, there was a mutual strengthening of kinship bonds — each family giving its own flesh and blood to other families" (p. 145).

Another difference is that marriage was consummated neither through sexual intercourse nor a mutually fulfilling personal relationship, as in the West, but through fertility — the birth of a child. Thus, fertility was the primary focus of marriage.

Finally, the marriage form itself was different. Hillman notes that the concept of marriage during the period of the Old Testament was congenial to polygyny. Having many wives was "clearly regarded as a normal and licit practice (cf. Exod. 21:10; Lev. 18:18; Deut. 21:15-17), although among the common peoples it was never very widespread. . . .[Thus] nowhere in the Old Testament is this form of marriage called into question" (p. 145).

With regard to Scriptures addressing the Creation, according to Hillman it is generally argued by theologians that the Genesis (1:27; 2:18-25) account of the Creation "depicts marriage as monogamous in the beginning" (p. 143). Here, since God created one wife for Adam, monogamy is what was intended. Also because Jesus quoted verses from Genesis in a discussion about marriage laws, this "is taken as a sign of divine will that marriage should be monogamous" (p. 149). Hillman, however, points out, "The method of interpretation . . . has been altogether too literalistic and focused too exclusively upon selected words. Instead of allowing these words to speak only as parts of a whole story, they have been lifted out of their proper contexts and analyzed with reference to an exclusively monogamous ideal of marriage which is, as we have seen, foreign to the socio-cultural ethos of the Old Testament" (p. 150). This, he argues, would present major problems if such were done throughout the biblical text.

Genesis (2:24), which stipulates that the wife is to be "one flesh" with her husband, has also been used to support God's preference for monogamy. Hillman again notes that this is taken too literally in support of the monogamy only thesis. The "wider meaning . . . found frequently in the Old Testament (cf. Gen. 29:14; 37:27; Lev. 18:6; Judg. 9:2; 2; Sam, 5:1; 19:12-13; Neh. 5:5; Isa. 58:7) suggests kindred—whereby all the members of a single kinship group "have one flesh which is conceived as a collective reality possessed by all" (pp. 152-153). Moreover, he asserts that it is highly unlikely that by using "one flesh" the author of Genesis "intended to exclude or to derogate the customary [polygyny] permitted by Mosaic law, thus departing substantially from the traditional Judaic conception of marriage" (p. 153).

The frequent biblical analogy of Yahweh's love for his people with a husband's love for his wife, where wife is singular, is also emphasized by theologians to support God's preference for monogamy. Hillman, however, explains: "In the descriptions of the covenant relationship between God and his people, the image of the wife, in the singular, might be better understood in terms of 'corporate personality.' This is a familiar Semitic thought category and biblical manner of speaking, in which a singular, the individual, may stand for and signify a plural (the collective): in the way, for example, that Adam stands for all men" (p. 147).

\ The case against polygyny and for monogamy has also been made through arguments for strong biblical prohibitions against divorce and adultery. Hillman however argues that it is wrong to suggest that these problems are associated with polygyny. In fact, by its very nature, polygyny excludes divorce and does not lead to it any more than monogamy. Furthermore, adultery can only be committed between two persons who are not married to each other. He adds, "The various biblical reactions to abuses that occurred under the existing marriage laws of different periods should not be construed as revealing a divine preference for monogamy" (p. 145). Mosaic law gave equal recognition to both types of marriage and usually made no distinction between the two. The only Scriptures that explicitly admonish against multiplying wives are those found in Deuteronomy (17:16-17). However, it cautions against the acquisition of too many wives, and if put into proper context, it is "simply a warning against an abuse — against the king's taking too many wives, *foreign* wives specifically because they would turn his heart toward their foreign gods (cf. 1 Kings 11:1-8)" (p. 145). In addition, this warning was combined with those against acquiring an excess of other things, such as horses, gold, silver, etc. They therefore reprimand over-indulgence or excess and should not be taken as an attack on the institution of polygyny itself (p. 143).

The teachings of Paul according to Hillman, have also been used to support exclusive monogamy. Three factors are used in making the case: that Paul "speaks of the husband-wife relationship in the singular; he uses the Old Testament expression 'one flesh' with reference to conjugal unity, and he depicts the love of Christ for the church in monogamous terms" (p. 164).

With regard to Paul's singular use of the husband-wife relationship, Hillman notes that this is the "normal biblical way of talking about marriage, which in the sociocultural context of the Jewish people could be either monogamous or polygamous" (p.

33

165). In addition, Hillman observes, "Paul's understanding of marriage was developed in a context of pastoral concern for Christians in a Greco-Roman world where monogamy was the socially determined form of marriage, while polygamy was proscribed" (p. 165). Polygyny was tolerated only in Jewish communities by Roman authorities. It was, however, less prevalent among Hellenized Jews with whom Paul had more contact. Thus, as Hillman indicates, "it would seem appropriate that Paul should speak of marriage in monogamous terms. But this does not necessarily amount to teaching against polygamy" (p. 165). Furthermore, because Paul called for each people to adhere to the laws under their own customs, it seems reasonable to expect that this also applied to those who were in polygamist marriages, although it was not the norm among those to whom the church provided pastoral care.

With regard to use of the expression "one flesh," Hillman notes that Paul's usage illustrates the broadness and flexibility of this Old Testament expression. The expression does not apply just to conjugal unity but also to other relations and does not preclude more than one wife (p. 167).

With regard to Christ's love for the church, it has been argued that the church is the bride of Christ and is monogamous, as Jesus can have only one bride. Hillman points out, however, that although "the church is portrayed as the bride of Christ (not brides), Saint Paul in the very same breath describes the church as a plurality of persons: a husband must love his wife, "as Christ does the church, because we are members of his body" (cf. Eph. 5:28-33; 1 Cor. 5:15; 12:27). This again is taken too literally. Hillman asks, "Is it possible that the union between Christ and the church can be symbolized in a simultaneously polygamous marriage? Christ standing for the husband, is one; and the church, as his spouse, is plural. For in actual historical fact, God's beloved people is a plurality of persons" (p. 168).

Overall, Hillman contends that the arguments against polygyny have stood on shaky ground and what is considered to be divinely willed by God is simply Greco-Roman (p. 140). He states, " . . .[T]he method of interpretation is rather suspect. The whole biblical case against the practice [of polygyny] is developed only by inferences, and it hinges on a number of assumptions which can no longer be taken as self-evident"(p. 141). He then asks, "Is it possible that our theologians have merely searched the Scriptures for evidence of a divinely revealed conception of marriage that is really just Greco-Roman: not strictly biblical, certainly, and not even clearly in the mainstream of the Jewish cultural tradition?" (p. 141).

Finally, Hillman asserts:

Surely, it is the Western cultural tradition, far more than the Bible, that has provided Christians with their basic notions about marriage. For it has been just too easy in the past for theologians and churchmen to read into the Bible what they expected to find there. Considering the pre-scientific methods of biblical exegesis used in earlier decades, it is reasonable to suppose . . . that our traditional Christian theology of marriage derives more from [the] history of biblical interpretation than from what the Bible actually says on the subject. (p. 142)

The Theologian Rationale Against Polygyny

In another chapter, "The Reasoning of Theologians," Hillman provides an overview and critique of the rationale employed by theologians in support of monogamy and against polygyny. These arguments, according to him, have been based on natural laws, cultural progress, and sociological conjectures (p. 179).

With regard to natural laws and in line with the opinions of Saint Augustine and Saint Thomas Aquinas, Hillman points out that polygyny has been argued not to be an evil in and of itself since it was permitted by God in earlier times and serves the primary end of marriage, which is to procreate. In fact, more so than with monogamy, there is the potential to fulfill this end in marriage. However, it has been argued that polygyny does not serve the secondary end of marriage, which is "mutual love, and/or remedy for desires, household tranquility and the sacramental significance of marriage as a sign of Christ's union with the church" (p. 81). Here the case is made that wives under polygyny are treated as inferior; that is, they are not treated as equals and are abused or neglected because attention to them by the husband is divided.

Hillman, however, counters this contending that women in monogamous marriages are treated in this manner as well. In fact, "In some cases of monogamy in which the primary end of marriage (procreation) cannot actually be achieved . . . there follows a strong tendency toward adultery, divorce and remarriage" (p. 183). Although polygyny may serve the primary end of marriage more so than monogamy, it should however, not be concluded that polygyny is more in conformity with the nature of marriage and henceforth, natural law; just as it should not be concluded that monogamy is. Hillman further points to flaws in using natural law in this manner and reminds us that it was the major theologians, including St. Thomas Aquinas, who argued that slavery was natural and therefore justified. He notes, "The demise of slavery in the Western world was not due to the perceptiveness of moral theologians with their traditional natural law rationale"; it continued in lands touched by the Christian Church throughout its history, and with regard to the African experience in Africa and North America, although "secular states had already repudiated slavery, many Churchmen — drawing upon the traditional teaching of the majority of Christian moralists — found ways of compromising with it" (pp. 184-185).

With regard to cultural progress, it is generally believed that Western peoples and their customs are superior and more "civilized," and that the extent to which other peoples assimilate their norms is the extent to which they are progressive. This also applies to the institution of marriage. The monogamic union, exclusiveness, or conjugal love between a single man and woman is thought to be superior, and those nations that subscribe to this through their civil codes are thought to be progressive. Hillman, however, argues that the conception of the ideal marriage is determined by a people's values, and social and economic structures. In earlier times in Western societies, procreation was a driving force behind marriage because economic conditions contributed to high mortality rates. In contemporary times, there is greater emphasis on mutual love between husband and wife.

Often, offspring and kinship bonds do not even factor in. By contrast, in other societies, particularly in Africa, kinship bonds and a strong sense of community are valued. Thus, polygyny is in line with their values and social structures surrounding family, kin, and community. He further notes:

In a society that has no place for unmarried women, where marriage alone offers women the security and dignity required for their normal self-realization, and where economic forces prevent men from marrying at an early age, [polygyny] is apt to be both a social necessity and a positive social value. In such a society the right that every woman has to marriage and the society's need for legitimate progeny is actually well served by the system of [polygyny]; hence the system is widely supported and encouraged by women themselves. (p. 189)

Finally, from a sociological standpoint, it is presumed that the practice of polygyny is vanishing in Africa anyway and Westernization is only assisting in the process. Hillman, however, points out that although Westernization is working against the custom, particularly through economic conditions, and the new values of urban elites, polygyny "is diminishing notably in some regions but is increasing in other regions — even in urban areas and in more sophisticated and prosperous segments of the population" (p. 191).

In conclusion, Hillman's analysis shows that the case for monogamy only, and against polygyny is not well founded biblically or through rational arguments made by theologians. Also, the work of early scholars on the development of marriage and family systems revealed their ethnocentric biases. Thus, Western scholarship and religious imperialism converged to create a "hegemonic monogamy" (Dorman, unpublished). As was shown, a fundamental problem with the theoretical propositions of early family theorists was the underpinning of evolution; that societies evolved from a lower form of consanguine marriage to a higher form of monogamic marriage. Although humans and their social institutions may have evolved from one form to another based on utilization of material resources, the notion of one form of marriage practice being inferior or superior to another is clearly problematic. It was this type of thinking — some peoples and their social structures being lower on the scale of humanity – that has and continues to justify white supremacy, cultural annihilation, and genocide of peoples all over the globe. It was this kind of thinking that reduced Africans and their descendants to commodities, to be sold as chattel during the trans-Atlantic slave trade, a calamity from which we are still trying to recover.

Social scientists now recognize different types of societies and social institutions without ranking them in a hierarchy. Although still guided by a materialistic paradigm, sociocultural evolutionists now classify societies based on their natural environment and use of technology (Macionis, 1997, 96-102). With this schemata, various types of societies are recognized – hunting-gathering, horticultural, agrarian, nomadic, and industrial – along with corresponding social, political, and economic institutions.

As it regards religion, it was shown that early Greco-Roman marriage practices greatly influenced Christian ideology of marriage. In its middle years, although its practices were undergirded by Greco-Roman customs, the church essentially accepted the practices of peoples it came in contact with, and conformed its customs to their own. As the church evolved, in later years, it became more imposing, and, as already indicated, played an essential role in various peoples' conformity to Western ideas on marriage. Thus, ideologies and remnants of marriage customs from Greco-Roman and other groups of European descent can be found in current marriage customs not only in the U.S. but in other places throughout the world where the West dominates. In spite of the imposition of monogamy on the world, it has been shown that much of the evidence used by Christian theologians is more a matter of interpretation than substantive evidence. Thus, it can no longer be assumed that the cultural normative of monogamy only is the divine will of God. Furthermore, there is no moral basis to limit marriage to monogamy only.

The Monogamy Myth

Although monogamy is the only marriage practice that is legally and morally sanctioned and socially accepted in the Western world, particularly in the U.S., some argue that even this is not what occurs. Hillman, for example, argues that "plural marriage or polygamy is found throughout the world in a variety of forms that are culturally determined" (p. 10). In most societies where it occurs, there is *simultaneous* polygamy, the practice of having more than one spouse at the same time. "The familiar form among Western peoples," according to Hillman, is "*consecutive* polygamy," whereby a person may have "one spouse after another in a sequence involving divorce and remarriage"[italics added] (p. 10).

Considering the close to 50 percent divorce rate and various relationship, marriage, and family formations that emerge from it, one social scientist suggests that U.S. society is moving in the direction of *onigamy*. This is a situation in which "each will be married to all" (Tiger, 1978). Interestingly, Morgan (1963) proposed that the pairing family (a marriage form where individuals remained together until they were no longer happy) existed during an early stage in marriage and family development, but the ease with which individuals can get divorced in American society, indicates that such a form is still quite prevalent. If one were to apply this classification scheme to the current state of affairs, one might conclude that U.S. society still exists in the stage of barbarism!

These propositions suggest that one can enter into and out of marriage in ways that indicate the prevalence of plural marriage for both men and women in the Western world. However, contrary to common belief, simultaneous polygyny has also been widely accepted and was quite prevalent throughout human history and experience, especially in Africa.

Chapter 2

AFRICAN POLYGYNY

Monogamy is the only legal form of marriage in the U. S. and most industrialized nations. Because of this it is thought by many to have always the been the most socially accepted and morally sanctioned marriage practice throughout the world. Polygyny, however, has also been widely accepted and practiced. George P. Murdock's investigation of the world's cultures provides evidence of this. In his 1949 sample of 250 societies, for which there was sufficient information on 238, he found polygyny in 193, or 81 percent of the societies. In a later more extensive investigation of 862 societies, which he summarized in the *Ethnographic Atlas*, Murdock (1967) found polygyny to be practiced in 724 societies or 84 percent. There were only 138, or 16 percent of societies in which monogamy was the only marriage practice. Of the 22 European societies included in this study, monogamy as the only marriage practice was found in 21.

In Africa, polygyny was virtually universal and is still prevalent. Of the 297 African societies included in Murdock's latest sample, polygyny was permitted in various forms in all but 13 societies or 5 percent. Only two sub-Saharan African societies did not practice polygyny. The other 11 societies in which polygyny was not found were in North Africa. Other areas of the world in which polygyny has been permitted or was culturally endorsed among indigenous peoples before European domination include North America, including Mexico and Canada, South America, Central America, the Caribbean, Near and Middle East, East Asia, Greenland, Australia, Indonesia, Polynesia, the Philippines, and New Zealand. Only in Europe was polygyny rarely found.

Explanations for the Practice of Polygyny

Although polygyny has been prevalent throughout most of the world, it has been regarded as a social aberration by some Western scholars. Because of this, they have felt compelled to provide explanations for its practice.

Higher Sex Drive of Males

One explanation proposed for the practice of polygyny is the difference in sex drive between males and females and the biological predisposition of males for a variety of sex partners. Here it has been argued that polygyny allows males to have more than one female to satisfy this higher sex drive and their penchant for variety. Arguments have been made to the contrary however. Lee (1979, 1982), for example, argues that no biological evidence supports such assumptions. It is not clear that the male sex drive is any higher than the female's, and there may, in fact, be more evidence to the contrary. This explanation for the practice of polygyny also ignores the reality that males may engage in sexual relations outside of marriage. Furthermore, since sex is obtainable outside of marriage, marrying for the purpose of having sex with multiple partners would be a high price to pay.

Postpartum Sexual Taboo

Another explanation proposed for the practice of polygyny is the period of postpartum sexual taboo found in some societies. Because postpartum can last as long as four years, or whenever the mother stops nursing the child, it has been posited that polygyny provides husbands a sexual outlet during this time. In an early study Whiting (1964) found an association, although it appears to be more complex. According to him, the association between polygyny and postpartum sexual abstinence may be related to dietary factors in certain climates. In the rainy tropics where the primary staple crop is low in protein, a high incidence of the disease kwashiokor occurs, a consequence of protein deficiency. Prolonged postpartum, where there is no other effective means of contraception, averts pregnancy and subsequently protects the lactating mother's milk from a loss of protein that would be harmful to the nursing child. Because the postpartum period may be long, husbands may seek another wife. This explains the acceptance of polygyny as a form of marriage.

41

Women's participation in economic activity is another explanation for the practice of polygyny. Polygyny is more prevalent in societies where women contribute substantially to production. This is particularly true for nonindustrial societies in which the family is the primary unit of economic production. Heath (1959), for example, observes a statement from Gillin (1948) that "polygyny is especially congenial to cultural configurations in which each woman is considered an asset on account of her economic worth or productiveness," and in his study found that polygyny generally becomes more frequent as women's contribution to subsistence increases (pp. 79, 77). Osmond (1965) found that polygynous marriage is significantly associated with female contribution in rudimentary agricultural economics (such as hoe agriculture or horticulture) and that "monogamy is associated with minimal and polygyny with maximal female economic contribution" (p. 11).

In a more comprehensive work, *Women's Role in Economic Development,* Boserup (1970) provides an overview of how polygyny is related to women's contribution to subsistence. First, all over the continent of Africa (at the time of the study) tribal rules of land tenure were still in force. Members of a tribe that commanded a certain territory had a native right to take land under cultivation for food production and, in many cases, also for the cultivation of cash crops. Except for preparing the land for growing crops, which was done by older boys and young men, women did all or most of the work of growing food crops. Wives and their sons were therefore needed; the more wives and children, the larger the plot of land that could be cultivated. The more land cultivated, the more the family could produce, and the wealthier it became. This therefore motivated men and their already existing wives to seek additional wives, and thus polygyny emerged.

Goody (1973) finds a relationship between women's contribution to economics and polygyny but contends that this is not an adequate explanation for polygyny. He notes that women contribute substantially to productivity in hunting and gathering societies where the rates of polygyny are much lower. He also found that women's contribution to subsistence in East Africa is greater, but polygyny is more prevalent in West Africa. In light of this finding, Lee (1990) clarifies the ways in which the various types of subsistence systems are related to polygyny. According to him, its practice varies depending on whether women contribute directly to the economy through their own labor or indirectly through reproduction, primarily of sons. Although women contribute more to subsistence in gathering societies, and such "economies rely heavily on the labor of women, gathering is not labor intensive; large groups are no more efficient than small groups, and consume the available resources in a given area more rapidly" (p. 18). Thus, these societies have the least frequency and the most occasional polygyny. In fishing and hunting societies, women contribute least to subsistence. These societies are also more likely to be characterized by occasional rather than frequent polygyny because polygyny increases the supply of male labor through reproduction (p. 18).

Frequent polygyny is most likely to occur in herding and extensive agriculture economies. In extensive agriculture economies women contribute greatly to agriculture, and in herding societies, multiple wives produce many children who are able to tend flocks of animals (pp. 18-19). Overall, multiple wives are valued and sought after because of their contribution to subsistence, through labor or through the reproductive capacities to produce children, primarily sons who can contribute to the household economy.

Imbalanced Sex Ratio

Another explanation for the practice of polygyny is that it is a response to the imbalanced sex ratio between males and females. Males through all stages of the life span and across cultures die disproportionately more than females. Factors contributing to this are higher male infant mortality and premature death, due to occupational hazards and warfare. Embers (1974), in particular, proposes a relationship between polygyny and high male mortality from internal and external warfare and finds an association between the two. Higher mortality among males results in a sex imbalance in favor of females while polygyny provides a means for

43

all women to be married, even if there are more women to men. Grossbard (1980) also posits that women fare better in polygynous marriages in societies where the gender ratio is smaller than or equal to one. By adding to total production in the marriage, women can gain more than if they remain single.

Progeny

Still another explanation for the practice of polygyny, particularly among African peoples, is their social and value structures. In a comprehensive study of traditional African societies, Mbiti (1969) elaborates on this. According to him, big families are highly valued in traditional African societies. The larger the family, the higher its social status. Polygyny is therefore valued because the more wives, the more children and the more children, the larger the family.

Polygyny is also intricately tied to immortality and beliefs related to ancestry. In African societies, a person lives on even after physical death as long as he/she is remembered among his or her descendants. Therefore the more children an individual has the longer he is likely to be remembered, and the longer he is remembered, the longer he lives. Not only is one's life prolonged by remembrance through one's descendant's, but also is the entire family's life. Thus, polygyny ensures the immortality of the individual and the family.

A few scholars who studied the relationship between women's contribution to economics and polygyny were also careful to note polygyny's relationship to people's cosmological orientation. Boserup (1970), for example, points out that in spite of the relationship between economic production and polygyny, "[t]he desire for numerous progeny is no doubt the main incentive" (p. 41). Goody (1973) also asserts that the reasons behind polygyny are "sexual and reproductive rather than economic and productive" (p. 189). However, Goody (1973) takes it a step further when he questions the need to explain polygyny. He asserts that such a need arises from a European centered view of marriage. The way he sees it, rather than polygyny needing an explanation, it is monogamy that may need to be explained. This is because polygyny is more common throughout the world, whereas monogamy as an exclusive marriage practice is less common.

Experiences and Perspectives of African Women

As indicated, studies on polygyny have focused on possible explanations for its practice. There are fewer studies that have explored it from the experiences and perspectives of women. One study in which women were the focus is by Helen Ware (1995). In her study, "Polygyny: Women Views in a Transitional Society, Nigeria," Ware explores why women would participate in a marriage practice such as polygyny and what they perceive the advantages and disadvantages to be. The data for her study were drawn from the Changing African Family Project, Nigerian Segment 1 (CAFNI) of approximately 6,600 Yoruba women from Ibadan, the second largest city in Nigeria (population close to a million persons). Approximately 250 married women were also interviewed using in depth interviews to ascertain their attitudes toward polygyny. Of these women, one in two were in polygynous marriages, and for those over age 40, two in three were. The numbers of those in polygynous marriages vs. those in monogamous marriages, however, varied according to the level of education. For those with no formal education, 56 percent were in polygynous vs. 40 percent who were in monogamous marriages, and for those who had university training only 3 percent were in polygynous marriages vs. 80 percent who were in monogamous marriages.

In her study Ware found that African women perceive several benefits to being in polygyny. According to her, when the question was asked how they would feel if their husbands took another wife, 60 percent of the women said they "would be pleased: to share the housework, husband care and child-minding and to have someone to gossip and 'play' with" (p. 188). When asked what are the good things about being married to a man who has several wives, 22 percent said none. However, 60 percent cited help in the home as the principle advantage.

45

Another benefit of polygyny for African women, according to Ware, is the contribution that two or more women can make to the economic welfare of the family. Generally, the more women, the more help there is in increasing family wealth. Yoruba women are particularly known for their independence and their ability as traders. This may be why the most commonly cited second advantage given to the question of the good things of being married to a man with several wives was that the women "could plan together to advance the welfare of the household as a whole through trade or other economic ventures" (p. 139).

A third most common advantage for having a husband with several wives was "sharing the burden of the husband's sexual demands." (p. 189). Ware notes that the period of postpartum abstinence in Ibadan is 24 months for women in polygynous marriages and 20 months for women in monogamous marriages. Despite the tradition to abstinence, women in monogamous marriages are more likely than those in polygynous ones to give in to the sexual demands made by their husbands, partly because they fear their husbands may turn elsewhere.

Ware also cites companionship as a benefit of polygyny. She points out that wives are preferred to mistresses because they offer companionship. She also indicates "that companionship may be the goal especially for those who are already cut off from their families of origin by migration or their formal education" (p. 191). In another study on the Yoruba, "African and Afro-American Family Structure: A Comparison," Niara Sudarkasa (1989) also found companionship to be important. With regard to the senior wife, she states, "Traditionally, the Yorubas expected the senior wife to be a companion and confidant to her co-wives, as well as her husband. . . .She was often called upon to intercede with her husband on behalf of a co-wife, and wives of the same husband often cooperated in domestic activities and sometimes economic activities" (p. 45).

In Ware's study, polygyny is also seen as a way to bring a woman with whom a husband may become involved under the control of the family and to keep money in the household. Ware points out that polygyny is seen as the lesser of two evils where the other is extramarital affairs. When asked if they would prefer if

46

their husband took another wife or had a series of mistresses, three-fourths chose taking another wife on the grounds that "men spend less money on their wives than on their mistresses" and that the "position of a wife is defined rather than fluid and uncontrollable" (p. 189).

Although the women cited many benefits of being in polygyny, jealousy and rivalry between wives were regarded as the major disadvantages of the practice. In Ware's study, "When asked about the bad things of being a wife of a man who has several wives . . . 85 percent [said] envy, jealousy, hate, chaos, devilishness or murder," all of which the author suggests are related to jealousy (p. 190). However, she points out that their jealousy is not principally sexual; "it is first and foremost a rivalry to secure maximum access to scarce economic resources" (p. 190). Twice as many of the women indicated the risk of their children suffering from sharing a father vs. wives sharing a husband. Sudarkasa (1989), on the other hand, points out that in her findings, "even though there was some rivalry and competition among wives of the same husband, the relationships among wives of the entire compound were characterized by a considerable degree of comraderie and cooperation" (p. 45). She also provides a description of how wives work together.

[O]n many occasions, including naming ceremonies for newborn babies, weddings, and funerals, the wives of each man, together with other wives of the compound, collectively carried out specific roles that were traditionally assigned to them. On these occasions, the wives were collectively responsible for some of the preparation and distribution of food that took place. They might also have specific social or ceremonial roles to play. For example, during a traditional wedding, as the bride and her procession moves through the town, the wives of her father's compound (excluding her own mother and some older women) bring up the rear of the group, singing traditional songs of sorrow at the loss of a daughter from her husband's lineage. (p. 45)

It is important to note that what children may experience from competition for resources among wives depends on the economic status of the father and the mother's status with him. Generally, the senior wife and her children have the greatest

47

advantage with regard to status and economics. However, because of a husband's emotional and/or sexual attachment to a junior wife, she may be able to garner more resources her way. Philip Kilbride (1994) in *Plural Marriage for Our Times: A Reinvented Option?* presents two cases of what children may experience in polygynous marriages. The first is a case of a 40-year old Ugandan woman with a high school education. Her father is a wealthy agricultural officer with four wives and 25 children. Her mother is the senior wife. The story is as follows:

Before taking a second wife, her father provided her mother with her own home and land near to where two of her other children were attending boarding school. When [she] was in the sixth grade, she was sent to live with her father and his second wife and her children so that she could attend school near their residence. . . .Although her stepmother gave her a lot of chores to do, she did not mind. She liked her stepmothers who she described as being good. On school holidays, she went back to her mother who was stricter with her because it was her mother's job to teach [her] all her female duties. . . .Although their family was large, everyone always had enough to eat and plenty of land to farm. The children treated each other well.

Kilbride goes on to explain that all the siblings recognize each other as sisters and brothers and make no distinction among themselves based on who their mother is. Polygyny in this particular family works well. The father shows no favoritism, and co-wives follow the tradition of respect and deference to the senior wife.

The second case is that of a man in his mid-20s. His father's economic status was less favorable, and he had four wives and 31 children. The man's mother was the second wife:

In [his] early childhood, his father had only two wives, both of whom [he] called "mother." It was not until he was 7 years old that he began to question his status. When he was 8 years old, he recollects going to school for a while with the sons of the first wife. It was not a pleasant memory, for his stepbrothers beat him, made him carry their books to and from school, and forced him to get money from his mother to give them for their own lunches. He finally refused to go to that school, which was 10 kilometers away; he was therefore transferred to a school near his home. After fourth grade he . . . was forced to go to another primary school near the home of the fourth wife. While living in her house, which is 15 miles from the home of his mother and the other two wives who all share the same compound, [he] complains that he was forced to do many household chores, including cooking, cleaning, and tending livestock, at times going without food from breakfast until dinner. (p. 113)

Regardless of their status relative to that of their mothers, or how they are treated, Sudarkasa found in her study that there are "explicit rules or codes defining appropriate behavior for all people in the same group" (p. 45). Everyone belongs to the same family and for siblings, for example, "differential and deferential behavior among them is based on seniority, regardless of differences in maternity" (p. 45). "In day-to-day affairs, all children of the same father are expected to behave toward each other as if there were no differences in maternity" (p. 46).

In "Affines and Spouses, Friends and Lovers: The Passing of Polygyny in Botswana," Jacqueline Solway (1990) points out that among the Bakgalagadi women of South Africa the institution provokes "contradictory opinions in women" (p. 48). On the one hand, because of more sociability and less work, women may feel that polygyny enhances the quality of their and their childrens' lives. On the other hand, it may create a situation where co-wives and their children are seen as detracting from economic resources. As with West African women, the major shortcomings of polygyny among Bakgalagadi women are jealousy and rivalry among co-wives. However, a benefit of polygyny is that it can be seen as "an institution which facilitates cooperation between women" (p. 49). Solway observes that "just as there were stories told about the woman who burned down her co-wife's hut, there were ... stories highlighting nurturance between wives, and shared work load and the freedom polygyny allowed women" (p. 49). In fact, a major benefit of polygyny is the autonomy it gives women. Solway notes that polygyny provides women "more freedom of movement and leisure time than does monogamy. With others to share in care of husbands and affines and less pressure on her to bear children, a woman is freer to pursue other activities" (p. 49).

Overall, the studies show the advantages women see to being in polygyny include child care and domestic assistance, assistance in providing husbands' needs, companionship, and more autonomy and freedom. The major disadvantages are jealousy and rivalry, particularly with regard to economic resources for children. There are also other negatives that were not revealed in these studies. These have to do with injustices some African women experience due to unfairness and disregard shown them by their husbands, as revealed in novels by African women.

In *So Long a Letter,* for example, Mariama Bâ (1980) depicts two experiences illustrative of the injustices African women and their children sometimes sustain under polygyny. In one case, a mother brings home a young woman to marry her son, because she is displeased with the woman he has chosen for a wife. Her displeasure stems from the lower socioeconomic status of the wife's family. When he marries the young woman out of obligation to tradition, the first wife leaves the marriage, pursues a career, and self actualizes through her work.

In the second case, the woman is not so fortunate. She is abandoned by her husband, with whom she has had 12 children during their 25 years of marriage, for a young women who is the same age as one of her daughters, and is, in fact, her peer. The woman stays in the marriage although her husband has essentially left her for his new wife. He dies five years later. However, because he abandons his economic obligations to her and their children, within the five-year period she struggles to make ends meet. To add insult to injury, her husband's brother, who told her of the marriage to the second wife, only after it had transpired, proposes that she marry him after the death of his brother. The story provides a heart-wrenching depiction of the trials and tribulations, and hurt and pain experienced by this woman and what other women who have similar experiences go through.

Buchi Emecheta (1979) in *The Joys of Motherhood* also depicts some of the complexities of polygyny and the injustices women sustain under it. However, hers is a more expansive critique of traditional family practices in Africa and the impact that adherence to such practices can have on women. The story depicts how women are socialized to seek identity and self- worth through their husbands and children, and the trauma they go through if they are unable to get married or have children, or if they do, lose their husbands and/or children through death or abandonment.

Although both stories are revealing, and can leave one with a distaste for the practice of polygyny, it is important to note that the kinds of injustices women sustain under polygyny, they also sustain under monogamy. How a man treats his wife has to do with that individual man, whether in polygyny or monogamy. In addition, the extent to which injustices are supported, and women made to feel powerless against them, may have more to do with patriarchy than with the practice of polygyny.

In spite of the negatives these stories reveal about polygyny, it is still widely accepted by women throughout Africa. According to Ware, one reason "for the widespread acceptance of polygyny is the distaste for the alternative, which in this cultural context is most often not faithful monogamy but legal monogamy paralleled by a series of more or less open affairs" (p. 189). Sudarkasa also points out that "according to African values, having a system of co-wives [is] preferable to having a system where women [bear] children outside of marriage, or where women . . . live out their lives as childless spinsters" (p. 46). Ware notes that the differential response of women to the acceptance of polygyny is based on whether they are traditionally oriented, or whether they have received some formal style of Western education. Those who are Christian and who have the most education are least likely to be in polygynous unions. Sudarkasa also notes that "the negative attitudes of some Western educated African women toward polygyny cannot be taken as representative of the traditional attitude toward the institution" (p. 46).

Polygyny at the time of these studies was declining, at least in some areas although it was thought to be increasing in many areas in Africa (Ware, p. 185). In Ware's study, education is given by women as the most common reason they believe that polygyny is declining. Jealousy, according to Solway, is becoming the most common explanation. She asserts, however:

I believe the jealousy and tension inherent in polygyny can be overstated and these qualities offered by the Bakgalagadi as convenient reasons to

51

explain away a complex social shift. Lefufa and Bagadikano implied rivalry and jealousy a century ago, yet these sentiments were not sufficient to effectively limit polygyny then. Why do they seem to do so now? (p. 49)

In spite of what African women believe, several factors contribute to the gradual decline of polygyny. These include Christianity, Western education, demographics, economic changes arising from industrialization, and disparagement. According to Sudarkasa, "No institution has been more maligned by observers of African societies than the institution of polygyny ... [and this] contributes [greatly] to why polygyny is changing in Africa" (p. 46).

The Impact of Westernization

Although polygyny has been a longstanding and highly valued institution in African societies, Christianity, industrialization, and Western cultural imperialism have and continue to undermine it. Christianity, in particular, has had negative consequences for the practice and, in many cases, it is women who have been most affected. Hillman (1976) describes how Christianity has impacted on African family and kinship systems over the past few centuries. According to him, wherever Christian missionaries have encountered polygyny, men who wanted to become Christian were expected to divorce the mothers of their own children. This has been carried out through canonical regulation, generally known as the "privilege of the faith."

Expressed in the *Altitudo,* a papal document published in 1537, and in subsequent regulatory documents, the "privilege of the faith" essentially means that one is "privileged" to do whatever is necessary to become Christian, even if it means dissolving recognized marriages (p. 28). Under Christian law, if a man wanted to become a Christian, he had to divorce all his wives except the first, the only one held to be valid. The other wives were presumed to be concubines. If a husband could not recall exactly which of his wives was the first one, he was allowed to remarry any one of his previous wives, and the others were "sent away." Even when the husband could recall who his first wife was, the new marriage was still held to be valid and the previous one was dissolved. Valid

52

monogamous marriages could also be dissolved for those who wanted to marry as Christians. Because men had permission to marry again under Christian law, many used this as a way to divorce their wives and marry again. As a consequence, many African women lost contracted conjugal rights, social status, and economic security, and, in some instances, even their relationships with their own children (pp. 28-30). Overall, the imposition of the Greco-Roman ideal of marriage through Christianity virtually destroyed many African family and kinship systems.

Macro-structural changes arising from industrialization have also contributed to the demise of polygyny in Africa. Among the Bakgalagadi, although "cattle (also used in the payment of bride wealth) [has been] the dominant economic resource," and "is still the central sign of wealth in Botswana, the expansion of investment opportunities in business, transport, agriculture, and education and growing wage and salaried employment opportunities," are causing polygyny to lose some of its predominance (Solway, p. 44). Except among the very rich who are able to provide for large joint households, such changes have made it increasingly difficult to maintain polygynous families. Contemporary needs of "education, dress, health care, household furnishing, etc., and the need to purchase food as a result of changing tastes and declining local production make running a household and raising children a much more cash intensive venture than it was in the past" (Solway, p. 51). The increasing need for cash intensifies rivalry between co-wives and half-siblings and "women increasingly view polygyny as a threat to their and their children's standard of living" (Solway, p. 51). The effect of this is more hostility among co-wives and increasing aversion to the institution as a whole. Thus, as societies become more industrialized and cash dependent, polygyny becomes more burdensome, which serves as a deterrent to the practice.

Along with structural changes, cultural factors stemming from Westernization are leading to changing expectations and the basis on which marriages are formed, which again have implications for the way polygyny is regarded and practiced. One Western cultural infusion is the idea of romantic love. In traditional African societies, marriage was not based on romantic love but on the socioeconomic and political relations that could be forged by a couple marrying. Thus, when parents arranged a marriage for their son or daughter, as was usually the case, it was not only the characteristics of the potential spouse that were of primary importance but those of his or her parents and wider kinship group. In addition, the bond between the individuals assumed secondary importance to that of the wider group. Important to note also is that marriage in African societies, unlike the discrete event we are familiar with, is usually a lengthy process and is usually not consummated until the bride wealth is paid in its entirety and/or the birth of the first child (Solway notes that she has seen it paid after divorce or even after death. Among the Bakgalagadi, it was usually paid in cattle, usually eight which is why it may have taken so long). This custom, however, is changing. Solway notes that young people are increasingly in favor of "romance and love," as the basis of a relationship and marriage, and "correspondingly anticipate that their married life will sustain much of the affection and rapport that marked their courtship" (p. 50). In addition, expectations with regard to the marital relationship are changing. "Young women think that sharing their spouse with another woman or marrying men much older than themselves will detract from the quality of their marriages" (p. 50). Ware also notes that, for the Yoruba of Ibadan, personal choice plays a much greater role than it had in the past, and companionship is becoming increasingly important for those who are cut off from their families of origin by migration or formal education.

Despite changes caused by Westernization, polygyny as a traditional custom is still a mainstay in African societies in both urban and rural areas. Along with modernization and changing expectations, there have also been calls for "mental decolonization" and the preservation of traditional values. There has been considerable effort to reconcile the Western form of marriage with the traditional African form. Through such efforts three forms of marriage are generally recognized in African societies: those formed under religious, civil, or customary laws.

In the attempt to fuse customary law with civil law, two types of marriage are officially recognized among the francophone countries: "civil marriage, celebrated according to written laws, which include indigenous laws that appear to conform to modern expectations; and customary marriage, celebrated among the family and regulated by the customary laws of both parties" (Pitshandenge, p. 119). Marriage conducted strictly under religious code is excluded from legal protection in these countries. This was done in order to eliminate religion as a requirement for marriage to be valid, which comes from the strategic move to overcome mental dependence on Western ideas, particularly Christianity (Pitshandenge, pp. 121-122).

Francophone African countries also have varying policies on polygyny. Pitshandenge (1994) notes three legal currents among francophone African countries. These include: (1) exclusive monogamy and the concomitant prohibition of bigamy and polygyny as found in Côte d'Ivoire and the Republic of the Congo, formerly Zaire; (2) optional monogamy found in the Congo, Mali, and Togo; and (3) regulated polygyny with respect to the number of wives a husband may have at one time. Under the first current, there is no legal protection for polygynous unions. There are legal grounds for complaints about bigamy and penal sanctions for anyone who is involved in formalizing the celebration or registration of such unions. In this context, polygynous marriages are null in the eyes of the law, and "in legal terms, the man and the woman are strangers, and have no obligation to feed one another, be faithful to one another or assist one another in any way" (p. 123). Under the second current, optional monogamy, the husband is required to make a declaration in the form of a contractual promise "at the time of marriage, [as to] whether he may take another wife in the future" (p. 123). Although husbands are allowed to go back on their promise in some countries, "optional monogamy, however, implies a legal recognition of polygyny" (p.123). Under the third current, regulated polygyny means that polygyny is an acceptable form of marriage, but the number of wives a husband can have at one time is regulated. Countries where this occurs have a strong Muslim influence. Mali and Senegal, for example, allow a maximum of four wives.

Despite such efforts, there is still considerable confusion about marriage in African societies, particularly in urban areas. Some of it has to do with the inclination among Africans toward traditional practices, particularly polygyny. In some areas where polygyny is not recognized as a legal form of marriage, or where it is not socially popular, males still practice polygyny privately or take girlfriends, concubines, or mistresses as "outside wives."

In a study on an elite group in Lagos and Ibadan, Nigeria, Karanja (1994) describes the phenomenon of private polygyny, or "outside wifeship." First, he notes that although there is no general consensus as to what an outside wife is, it is a woman:

1. Who is financially maintained on a regular basis by a man with whom she has regular sexual relations, with the relationship lasting for several years;
2. with children whose paternity is acknowledged by her parents;
3. who is usually not publicly acknowledged as a wife and always maintains a separate residence from her husband;
4. with no formal legal status because her marriage involves no bride-price or marriage rites;
5. with considerably less social and political-jural recognition than an inside wife. (p.198)

The difference between private polygyny and public polygyny is that the latter refers to "two or more marriages contracted publicly by a man under native custom" (p. 199). By contrast, private polygyny or outside marriage is sanctioned by neither traditional or statutory law. A major component of private polygyny is that the "husband" provides the outside wife with resources. This is why only wealthy males can engage in private polygyny. Karanja notes that it would be "a contradiction in Nigeria and elsewhere in West Africa to refer to a woman as an outside wife if she is *not* financially maintained by her 'husband'" (p. 144).

Children are also another major component of outside wifeship. Because of laws protecting children in southern Nigeria, a woman knows that once she claims to have a child by a man, it would be difficult for him not to have some sort of relationship or obligation to the child. Women know that "a man who is reluctant to acknowledge paternity will receive little moral support from friends and family. His family members may, in fact, leave him little choice in the matter: They may claim the child, thereby conferring legitimacy on it" (p. 207). Thus, the motivation for an outside wife to have children is that first it "establishes lasting socioeconomic and politico-jural ties to the father of her children. Second, because a man is not usually barren according to local beliefs, her fertility and hence her womanhood is established beyond doubt. And third, bearing children links the woman to the man's wider kinship network for the duration of her life" (p. 208).

Karanja notes the motivation for both men and women to engage in private polygyny. The reasons that men engage in the practice include "(1) pressures from peers and . . . the traditional sector to acquire the symbols of power, (2) as an alternative to divorce, (3) the lack of negative sanctions against the practice, (4) creating an image of virility, and (5) attempting to produce children" (p. 203). Although there are social pressures to engage in private polygyny, because of the difficulty of maintaining more than one household, few men can afford to do so. Thus for those who can, having an outside wife is a status symbol. Karanja compares it to acquiring a Mercedes-Benz or building an elegant house. There is also pressure for a newly successful man to have an outside wife to show his adherence to traditional values. For some, it shows family members that they have "not abandoned their roots by having only one wife" (p. 203). Men also undergo pressure to avoid divorce, thus taking on a outside wife is a "convenient way of dealing with or escaping from a bad marriage" (p. 203). In addition, there is also little or no stigma attached to the practice. Overall, Karanja points out that "the practice of keeping girlfriends or mistresses [in addition] to legal marriage practice may represent Nigerian (we might substitute 'African') elite men's attempts to embody Western ideals of a modern man (that is, monogamous Christian, educated, and the like) while secretly admiring the African ideology of polygyny" (p. 197).

There are several reasons why a woman may become an outside wife. A primary one is economic. As indicated previously, in primarily agricultural economic systems women contributed greatly to production. However, with industry and wage employment, especially in urban areas, women have become dependent on men for financial resources. In order to avoid poverty, many attach themselves to wealthy men. Not only do less educated and poor women do this but educated and professional

57

women also do so until the "right man," that is, someone who can reasonably provide for them and their children, comes along. Again, economic support is the main ingredient in these arrangements. Karanja notes, "[T]he ability to regularly support and maintain a woman and her children is not only important; it implicitly defines the relationship" (p 201).

Another reason that a woman may opt to be an outside wife is difficulty in finding a suitable single male to marry her. Because marriage and parenthood are ultimate goals for both men and women, women who have difficulty finding a partner for marriage may opt to be an outside wife; as having the status of an outside wife is better than not being one at all. Another motivation for becoming an outside wife is to avoid the complexities that come along with legal marriage. Outside wives are seen by "inside" wives as having the advantage from an economic perspective, a more romantic life, and freedom to engage in other liaisons if need be. An interesting factor to note is that although inside wives, especially those among the educated elite in Lagos, are opposed to private polygyny for various reasons, they prefer it to public polygyny, which they regard as "backward," or "bush" behavior (p. 197).

Besides outside wifeship, it appears males also engage in relations with women without providing them the status of an outside wife. In "Traditional Husbands, Modern Wives?" Van der Vliet (1992) provides an overview of how the Xhosa of South Africa merge the competing marriage structures into what she describes as "traditional" and "modern" to meet personal and social needs. She describes traditional marriages as those characterized by polygyny, patrilocality, transfer of the bride wealth from the husband's kin group to that of the wife, and mutual social and economic interdependence of extended kin groups. She points out that "for the man the 'traditional' script offered patriarchal privileges, freedom from household chores, and far greater social and financial and sexual freedom" (p. 230). Modern "marriage is characterized by jointness, closure, and marital fidelity. Jointness refers to "husband and wife carrying out activities such as decision-making, budgeting and household chores together or interchangeably and spending much of their leisure time together"

(p. 222). Closure is the nuclear family unit of mother, father, and children seen as "a totally discrete unit in a number of domestic activity areas" (p. 221).

Both men and women fluctuate between traditional and modern when the need to negotiate differences and resolve conflict arises. Although this is the case, women aspire more to the modern form of marriage with an emphasis on jointness — that is, men staying home and participating in joint activities and marital fidelity, whereas men focus more on the traditional, in most instances, to justify relations outside of their marriages. Van der Vliet provides several cases of how tradition has been used to justify infidelity. In one case, a man dismissed a charge of infidelity by "saying all married men had girl-friends—'There are lots of girls'" (p. 224). For some, "modern marriage was associated with whites and to reject this option was also to reclaim some of their own manhood, deprecating white men as henpecked and emasculated" (p.230). One had this to say:

With whites, the wife is playing the leading role. The husband cannot make his own decision. The whites are too serious about marriage. They see love as forever. I would find it intolerable myself. They must always be with the wife, kiss her when they leave. Like educated blacks, the whites are very committed to their wives, but too much so. Your men must always be around the house. We will not tolerate losing our freedom like that. (p. 230)

Van der Vliet quotes a statement made by the Transkei's first foreign minister and lecturer in customary law at the University of Transkei, after passage of the 1978 Transkei Marriage Act, legalizing polygyny: "The African is by nature a polygynist." Others made similar assertions: "Well, I think it was meant for a man because our own fathers used to have three or four wives; it comes from our old tradition. You have a string of girl-friends in the place of the many wives your grandfather used to have" (p. 231).

Whereas women, particularly those who are educated and have more economic leverage, see this behavior of men as deplorable, many are resigned to its inevitability. They believe that men are unlikely to stop having girlfriends. Although the author does not expand on this, it appears a girlfriend can range from a relationship that is similar to an outside wife to casual relations where there are no financial or emotional obligations.

In conclusion, these studies have shown, that African women, depending on their education, economic status and adherence to tradition, see advantages and disadvantages to polygyny. The advantages include assistance with childcare, domestic chores, and providing husbands sexual needs, companionship, autonomy, and a mechanism to build wealth. Major disadvantages include jealousy and rivalry, particularly with regard to resources for their children. Novels written by African women depict the injustices women sustain much of which seems to stem from adherence to traditional roles and expectations by both African women and men and patriarchy. In spite of the disadvantages, polygyny, before Western influence, provided a mechanism for all women to have social and economic legitimacy and the potential for emotional and spiritual support in their relations with men. Unfortunately, because of Christianity, industrialization, and cultural imperialism, polygyny in Africa is evolving to be practiced as it is done in the West — men with a wife and "outside" women, mistresses, or lovers. In the Western world in the past and in contemporary times, such a practice is to the disadvantage of women. As far as America is concerned, no women have been more disadvantaged by the Western form of polygyny than women of African descent.

Chapter 3

WESTERN POLYGYNY

Concubinage and Prostitution

As indicated in chapter one, monogamy may have been the only marriage practice recognized by Greeks and Romans, but concubinage and prostitution, which I referred to as a peculiar form of polygyny was also practiced. Gerder Lerner (1986), in the *Creation of Patriarchy*, explains that such practices even preceded the Greeks and Romans in Mesopotamia and date as far back as 1752 B.C. (with the Code of Hammurabi in Babylonia. It has been argued that the laws existed long before Hammurabi and may date as far back as the third millennium B.C. In the forty years of his reign, Hammurabi amended and restated parts of the law already in force).[2]

In fact, Lerner argues that prostitution and concubinage may have originated with female slavery, and that the female was history's first slave. These practices, she argues, emerged from captured women taken as prisoners of war. Lerner explains that generally, in war, it was the men who were killed because of the physical threat they posed. When they were not killed, they were mutilated and, in many accounts, blinded. Accounts of blinding can be found among the Babylonians, Assyrians, Scythians, and Hebrews (as documented in the Old Testament with Samson, Judges 17-21; Zedekiah, II Kings 25-7; and Jabesh, 2 Samuel 11:2). Other forms of mutilation included tattooing the face, amputation of the nose and feet, and castration. For women, terrorism took the form of rape. It was generally women who were put to work in

---

[2] Lerner identifies ". . . three major collections of Mesopotamian law — the Codex Hammurabi (CH)" ("engraved on a diorite stele <u>ca</u>. 1750 B.C. — encompassed a body of law already practiced for hundreds of years"); Middle Assyrian (MAL) ,and Hittite Law (HL) (Hittite laws and Middle Assyrian laws date from the 15th to the 11th century). Lerner notes that in *The Babylonian Laws*, G. R. Driver and John C. Miles "assume the existence of a common Mesopotamian law in the third millennium B.C." (p. 41)

various of forms of servitude, primarily as domestic servants, and their sexuality appropriated in the form of prostitution or concubinage. Lerner explains how concubinage may have originated with enslaved women:

Women were subdued physically by rape; once impregnated, they might become psychologically attached to their masters. From this derived the institution of concubinage, which became the social instrument for integrating captive women into the households of their captors, thus assuring their captors not only their loyal services, but those of their offspring. (p. 87)

She also explains how the concubine served dual functions to "perform sexual services for the master, with the knowledge and consent of the wife, and to become a servant to the wife" (pp. 91-92). Lerner also makes a distinction between a concubine and a wife in polygyny:

This differs greatly from the relations between first and succeeding wives in many polygamous societies, in which the status of second and third wives is co-equal with that of the first wife. Each wife and her children are entitled to certain rights, to a separate dwelling place, to economic and sexual obligations the husband must fulfill in such a way as not to violate the rights of any wife. (p. 92)

Thus, according to Lerner, "the nexus between sexual servitude to the master and economic service to the wife seems to be a distinguishing feature of concubinage under [Indo-European] patriarchy" (p. 92).

Prostitution also existed in early Mesopotamia. Lerner however, points out that it is generally thought to have originated with "temple" or "sacred" prostitution whereby women who were priestesses provided sexual services for gods or goddesses, in the same manner that they provided other services, such as food or music. Essentially, the basis for "sacred" or "temple" prostitution was that fertility was sacred and necessary for survival. Sexual services were therefore provided by women who were generally daughters of kings and rulers to honor the gods/goddesses to ensure the fertility of the land and people. Lerner, however, distinguishes between "cultic sexual services" and "prostitution," which she refers to as "commercial prostitution" and contends it flourished near or within the temple. ⌐Although commercial prostitution may have originated with corruption of temple prostitutes (through donations of food, oil, wine, and precious goods to honor the deities being kept for one's own personal use, and by priests using lower-class temple servants as commercial prostitutes to enrich the temple), Lerner suggests that it is likely that it derived directly from the enslavement of women. She states, "Military conquests led, in the third millennium B.C., to the enslavement and sexual abuse of captive women. As slavery became an established institution, slave-owners rented out their female slaves as prostitutes, and some masters set up commercial brothels staffed by slaves" (p. 133). She further explains how this led to the establishment of harems, and how the sexual use of women in such a manner became symbols of power among wealthy men:

The ready availability of captive women for private sexual use and the need of kings and chiefs, frequently usurpers of authority, to establish legitimacy by displaying their wealth in the form of servants and concubines led to the establishment of harems. These in turn, became symbols of power to be emulated by aristocrats, bureaucrats, and wealthy men. (p. 133)

Not only was slavery a source for commercial prostitution but also "the pauperization of farmers and their increasing dependence on loans in order to survive famine, which led to debt slavery" (p. 133). Lerner points out that children of both sexes were given up for debt pledges or sold for "adoption" (p. 133). This subsequently provided the infrastructure for women to become prostitutes.

Women might end up as prostitutes because their parents had to sell them into slavery or their impoverished husbands might so use them . . . . Women also became self-employed as a last alternative to enslavement . . . .With luck, they might in this profession be upwardly mobile through becoming concubines. By the middle of the second millennium B.C., prostitution was well established as a likely occupation for the daughters of the poor. (pp. 133-134)

The Veil Separating the "Wife" and "Other"

A major factor in the development of concubinage and prostitution was how to distinguish between women who were wives and those who were for used for sexual purposes. Lerner explains:

As sexual regulation of women of the propertied class became more firmly entrenched, the virginity of respectable daughters became a financial asset for the family. Thus, commercial prostitution came to be seen as a social necessity for meeting the sexual needs of men. What remained problematic was how to distinguish clearly and permanently between respectable and non-respectable women. (p. 134)

This, according to her, was resolved through use of the veil. Legal regulation for the veil was found in the Assyrian laws, which Lerner indicates were representative for the region and in the common body of legal concepts that prevailed in the region for nearly two thousand years. She states, "The practice of veiling, on which it [Assyrian law] legislates, has been so ubiquitous and lasted for so many millennia into this century that one can justify the assumption that we are here dealing with the earliest known example of such a regulation, which was practiced in many other societies as well" (p. 34). She reports the reading of the law as follows:

Neither [wives] or [seigniors] nor [widows] nor [Assyrian women] who go out on the street may have their heads uncovered. The daughters of seignior . . . whether it is a shawl or a robe or [mantle], must veil themselves. . . . When they go out on the street alone, they must veil themselves. A concubine who goes out on the street with her mistress must veil herself. A sacred prostitute whom a man married must veil herself on the street, but one whom a man did not marry must have her head uncovered on the street; she must not veil herself. A harlot must not veil herself; her head must be uncovered. (p. 134)

The law, according to Lerner, also specified that a slave girl must not cover herself. Thus, the veil came to be the "symbol and emblem of the married woman"; the veil "elevated her to a distinguishing mark and its wearing is made a privilege" (p. 135). Lerner, however, notes that it is curious that under this law:

Veiling does not seem to distinguish the free from the unfree, nor the upper class from the lower. Harlots and unmarried sacred prostitutes may be free women, yet they are grouped with slaves. A slave concubine may be veiled, if accompanied by her mistress, but even a free-born concubine may not be veiled if she walks out alone. (p. 135)

She further explains the basis of such distinctions:

On closer examination, we can see that the distinction between the women is based on their sexual activities. Domestic women, sexually serving one man and under his protection, are here designated as 'respectable' by being veiled; women not under one man's protection and sexual control are designated as 'public' women, hence unveiled. (p. 135)

If a woman who should not be wearing a veil was seen doing so, it was prescribed that she be punished. Overall, Lerner asserts that the dress code and the punishment for violation of the code were indications that the matter of "classifying women into respectable and not respectable had become an affair of the state" (p. 136).

Finally, Lerner explains how classes among men differed from those among women. Essentially men took their place in the class hierarchy based on their occupations or their father's social status. Their class position could be expressed by the ususal outward signs — clothing, residential location, ornaments or their absence. For women, however, from MAL 40 [Middle Assyrian Laws] and forward, class distinctions were based on their relationship — or absence of such — to a man who protected them, and their sexual activities (p. 139).

The division of women into 'respectable women,' who are protected by their men, and 'disrespectable women,' who are out in the street unprotected by men and free to sell their services, has been the basic class division for women. It marked off the limited privileges of upper-class women against the economic and sexual oppression of lower-class women and divided women one from the other. (p. 139)

It is this division; women's position, sexual (or marital status), to men — wife vs. other, that separates women. Those who are married are accorded status vs. those who become "other." The veil, although over three thousand years old, and now invisible, continues to separate women and, in the words of Lerner, "still impedes alliances among them" (p. 139).

"Jezebel" and "Mammy": The Early American Concubine and Prostitute

If one examines the plight of African American women during slavery in the U.S., one can see parallels with the concubine and prostitute in early Western history. Also, if one contextualizes the various relations that African American women had with white men during and after slavery — sexual, economic, and sometimes emotional, the roles they performed — domestic tasks and childcare, and their relationship with their wives (including their commitment to the progress of the family) — one can also see parallels with the co-wife found in polygyny.

Deborah Gray White (1985) in *Ar'n't I a Woman?: Female Slaves in the Plantation South,* identifies two stereotypes that were perpetuated during slavery in America to justify the exploitation of African American women's sexuality and labor. These are the "Jezebel" and "Mammy." The Jezebel image projected the idea that African American women were sexually promiscuous and "hot constituted"; that their sexual appetites were above what would normally be expected of women — even beyond that of men. Thus, they had to go outside the bounds of their own race to be satisfied. This stereotype resulted in African American women being used to satisfy the sexual fantasies of white males through voyeurism and sadistic cruelties. They were also raped, rented, sold into prostitution, and forced into concubinage.

Dorothy Sterling (1984) in *We Are Your Sisters,* provides numerous accounts from enslaved African American women of the experiences they had with white men. She first notes that the bodies of African American women were privy to white men at a very early age. She speculates that mothers were reluctant to discuss menstruation and matters of sex with their daughters perhaps because they thought "that ignorance would buy a few extra months of childhood for them" (p. 20).

The naked bodies of African American women on the auction block allowed white men to practice voyeurism and fulfill their sexual fantasies. While on the auction block, African American women could be looked at, fondled, and fantasized about. Sterling points out that "at a time when white women were thought immodest if they so much as showed their feet, slave girls, scantily clad at best, were required to strip for inspection by would-be purchasers"(p. 19). An enslaved African American woman describes her own experience.

We was all chained and dey strips all our clothes off and de folks what gwine buy us comes round and feels us all over. Iffen any de niggers don't want to take dere clothes off, de man get a long, black whip and cuts dem up hard. When Marse Jones seed me on de block, he say "Dats' a whale of a woman."(p. 20)

Sterling notes that "some conscientious owners applied the Victorian moral code to the quarters as well as to the big house, but the majority—and their sons, neighbors, overseers—held to a double standard that coupled veneration for white womanhood with disrespect for black" (p. 20).

Rape was also widespread. Sterling notes that "Rape, white on black, was not a crime under slave law. Even today many scholarly histories of slavery do not mention the word" (p. 24). An example of how common it was for some women can be seen in the following account:

Ma mamma said that a nigger'woman couldn't help herself, fo' she had to do what the marster say. Ef he come to de field whar de women workin' and tell gal to come on, she had to go. He would take one down in de woods an' use her all de time he wanted to, den send her on back to work. Times nigger 'omen had chillun for de marster an' his sons and some times it was fo' de ovahseer. (p. 25)

If they resisted, some women underwent sadistic cruelties. One woman described what her mother experienced:

I don't like to talk 'bout dem times, 'cause my mother did suffer misery. You know dar was an overseer who use to tie my mother up in the barn wid a rope aroun' her arms over her head, while she stood on a block. Soon as dey got her tied, dis block was moved an' her feet dangled, you know, couldn't tech de flo'. Dis ole man, now would start beatin her nekked 'til the blood run down her back to her heels. (p. 25)

White, (1985) also describes how the brutalities had sexual overtones.

Without a doubt, some whippings of female slaves were sexually suggestive. The man who whipped Henry Bibb's wife was often heard by Bibb to exclaim that "he had rather paddle a female than eat when he was hungry." The whipping of a thirteen-year-old Georgia slave girl also had sexual overtones. The girl was put on all fours "sometimes her head down and sometimes up" and beaten until froth ran from her mouth. Solomon Northup's master was not above whipping his slave Patsey in such a manner, either. According to Northup's Master Epps was a man possessed with "brute passion. Nothing satisfied him more than having a few drinks and whipping Patsey" (p. 33).

Concubinage was also widespread. Under the practice of concubinage, African American women were purchased for the specific purpose to serve as sexual and sometimes emotional companions for married white men (Frazier, 1934). Gerda Lerner (1992) in *Black Women in White America*, provides an account from a diary of an slaveholder's wife indicating not only the widespread practice of concubinage but also perceptions that some white women had of African American women:

Under slavery, we live surrounded by prostitutes, yet an abandoned woman is sent out of any decent house. Who thinks any worse of a Negro or mulatto woman for being a thing we can't name? God forgive us, but ours is a monstrous system. . . . Like the patriarchs of old, our men live all in one house with their wives and their concubines; and the mulattoes one sees in every family partly resemble the white children. Any lady is ready to tell you who is the father of all the mulatto children in everybody's household but her own. Those, she seems to think, drop from the clouds. (pp. 51-52)

Court cases also reveal how common the practice was. Sterling points out that in "numerous petitions for divorce, the wife charged that her husband had brought his slave to 'his own wife's bed and there carried out his licentious designs': in some instances these were carried out in her presence"(p. 26). The following is an account:

Your petitioner states that shortly after her marriage with her present husband she discovered that he had taken up with one of his female slaves who acted as cook and waited about the house. So regardless was her husband of her feelings, that he would before her eyes and in every room in which your petitioner slept go to bed with the said slave or cause the said slave to come in and go to bed with him. Your petitioner states that without complaint, she submitted in silence to her husband's infidelity, and attempted to reclaim him by caresses and obedience but in vain. (p. 28)

African American women were also rented and sold as prostitutes to single white men. Many such women were the products of rape or concubinage. They were sold through the "fancy trade" or shipped to "fancy girl markets" because of their light skin, for sexual services to their purchasers. Whereas enslaved African Americans or field hands typically sold for $1600, these women, referred to as "fancy" or "yaller" girls, could demand as much as $5,000 and were often bought as luxuries by wealthy bachelors. Sterling points out that although this was the case, a majority however, were sold to become the "mistresses of wealthy planters, gamblers or businessmen" (p. 27). Below are accounts of some of the intricacies of this trade.

Mr. Mordicia had his yaller gals in one quarter to dere selves and dese gals belongs to de Mordicia men, dere friends an' de overseers. When a baby was born in dat quarter dey'd sen' it over to de black quarter at birth.

Some of dese gal babies got grown an' after goin' back to de yaller quarter had chilluns for their own dad or brother. . . .(p. 28)

Lots of white men had culled wives. Ole man Tom Greene what lived near us comes over to ole Marse Berry one day an' wants to buy mamma. He wants mama but he don't want we uns kids, you see? Mama jus' sits roun' jes' as sad an' cried all de time. She was always nice lookin' an' we all knew what de old Marse Greene want. But ole Marse Berry swear he be damn if he sell her. He say if old man Greene take de chillun he kin have mama. Ole man Greene say he don't want de chillun, so ole Marse Berry sell him nuffin. Well, ole Marse Greene, he buys a nigger 'oman name Betsy f'om some whar. He was a bachluh you know an' he need a 'oman. Dat oman had three chillun and I 'clare if ole man Greene didn't think much o'dem chillun o' Betsy's as if dey as by a white 'oman. (Sterling, p.29)

Although women were raped, sold like prostitutes, and forced into concubinage, Sterling notes that some of the relationships developed into those "in which genuine affection and loyalty were felt on both sides" as was often reflected in the wills of white men (p. 29).

I Thomas Wright give and bequeath to Sylvia, a woman of color, formerly my slave but since emancipated and with whom I have had children, the sole and exclusive enjoyment of the house or tenement on my plantation, also all the household furniture therein, also all the monies of which I die possessed. (p. 29)

In contrast with the Jezebel, the Mammy image depicted African American women as asexual beings. The Mammy image served two functions. One was to ward off negative opinions of the North, of Southern white men's sexual exploitation of African American women. The other was to exploit African American women's labor for the benefit of white women, their children, and families. The Mammy image portrayed the African American woman as an obedient, loyal, and faithful servant. She was depicted as companion and confident of the "mistress" of the

70

house; one who loved and cared for her children — so much so that the sentiments she felt for white children exceeded those she felt for her own. She was the one who cooked, cleaned, and essentially ran the big house.

While African American women were expected to perform all these tasks for slaveholders' families, many had little or no semblance of a family life of their own. When they did, being a wife (not in the legal sense, since slave marriages were not recognized), and mother to their own children was almost nil. E. Franklin Frazier (1939), in *The Negro Family in the United States,* provides a vivid description of how the exploitation of their labor in the fields and the house stifled the ability of African American women to be mothers to their own children. While they were suckling white babies, their own would often be left unattended by anyone other than older children for days at a time. Their children suffered from malnutrition and neglect. As a result, infant mortality was extremely high. For African American men, because slaveholders had full control of the sexuality and labor of African American women, and controlled the economics in their households, their relationships with their women were compromised. As is reflected in plantation and bill of sale records, the African American man was rendered almost invisible in slave family life. Consequently, he is rendered almost invisible in much of the literature on enslaved African American family life. One, therefore, can only speculate, that the time and energy African American women could dedicate to relationships with African American men, was as limited as it was with their own children.

Although the Mammy was projected as an asexual being, she was subjected to rape and concubinage, particularly because she was more accessible to white men in the big house. Thus, although both stereotypes were projected as opposites, more often than not, they were one and the same person.

Long after the slave regime was dismantled, with the prevailing image of African American women as Mammy, they still worked as domestic servants at slave wages (and some for no wages when employers would not pay them), largely because this was the only occupation open to a majority of them. By the 1940s, close to 60 percent of African American women worked in domestic service (Collins, 1991). The author of an anonymous letter sent to the *Independent*, an African American newspaper in the early 1900s, provides an account of the labor that African American women performed in the homes of whites:

I not only have to nurse a little white child, now eleven months old, but I have to act as a playmate . . . to their other children in the home, the oldest of whom is only nine years of age. I wash and dress the baby two or three times each day; I give it its meals mainly from a bottle; I have to put it to bed each night; and in addition, I have to get up and attend to its every call between midnight and morning. If the baby falls to sleep during the day, as it has been trained to do every day about eleven o'clock I am not permitted to rest. It's "Mammy, do this" or "Mammy, do that" or "Mammy do the other," from my mistress all the time. (Lerner, p. 228)

In the meantime, as with many African American women, her three children were being neglected. She was able to see them only once in two weeks on Sunday afternoons. In addition, her children also provided domestic services, such as doing laundry and nursing for white families. While working in this capacity, African American women, were also, among other things, companions to the wife of the house.

   In a study, "A Complex Bond: Southern Black Domestic Workers and Their Employers," Susan Tucker (1990) interviewed "100 black and white women: domestic workers, children of domestic workers, employers, and children of employers, all born between 1880 and 1960 in the area that runs from Baton Rouge, Louisiana, to Pensacola, Florida" (p. 2). Tucker first points out that "Until 1968, [she] had never spoken to a black female who was not either a domestic herself or the daughter, niece, or granddaughter of a domestic" (p. 3). She explains that "even less well-off white families could afford domestics, because black women had little other choice of employment. As late as 1945, it required only half as large a family income to employ a servant in the South as it did in other parts of the country; the South was known as the white housewives utopia" (p. 3). She notes that the domestic is "rooted in the Old South and in the person of the ever-giving, nurturing, and loyal 'Mammy.'" In fact, the African American domestic gave whites status within their own communities. Even the poorest whites exceeded their means to have an African American domestic.

Tucker also notes that for white women in the South "employing a black domestic allowed a lifestyle very different from that of her contemporaries in other parts of the country" (p. 6). This, she suggests, might be why these women were perhaps more conservative in their views on feminism. Because their roles as mothers and caregivers were made easier by African American women; many were able to self-actualize in other areas at the expense of African American women.

The primary purpose of Tucker's study was to show how African American women domestics and their employers remember each other. What she reports is quite revealing of the type of relationship they shared. With regard to how white women remember African American women, some saw them as part of the family, others as emotional support, someone with whom their 'secrets' were 'safe.' African American women and white women shared common experiences with men. A recurrent theme for their daughters according to Tucker is that 'She was closer to me than my own mother' (p. 7). She explains why:

[I]n homes that employed full-time help, black women domestics were the more active caregivers. They were the ones who were there in day-to-day emergencies. They were often the ones who told children about menstruations, about sex, about relationships with men because they were often with these children at crucial times in their lives. One black woman told me of a young white woman in labor who refused to go into the delivery room without her. It was the maid who cut the newborn's umbilical cord. This was in the 1950s long before "significant" others were allowed to be present at birthing. (p. 7)

73

White women emphasized the strength of African American women. They were thought to be stronger emotionally and physically, or as one woman stated, "They stay strong until they die" (p. 7). They were described as more "natural" or more "instinctive" mothers. They were also assigned magical qualities, described as healers, therapists, listeners, someone who "sensed things," someone who "could just pick up a rag or something and touch you and it felt better" (pp. 7-8). Tucker is careful to note, however, that by proclaiming the strength of African American women, white women "continued to ignore their own part in the continued exploitation of black women in the work place" (p. 8). Finally, younger white women spoke of how life, with the assistance of African American domestic workers, had been made easier for their mothers, particularly after the birth of a child. From the examples provided by Tucker, many appear to long for what their mothers had:

The thing I always remembered was how close Rachel was to my mother. I mean, I think about it today and almost yearn for that sort of relationship. I can remember Rachel fixing breakfast for Mama and it would be just a poached egg and toast and coffee on a tray, but just the way it looked, I remember. And how she'd take it into Mama's room and sit it on the dressing table. Today, I feel so . . . tired. I have these two children and I'm pregnant, and I'd love someone to bring me breakfast. And Rachel came everyday—well six days a week and did that. I can never remember her going on vacation or anything. She'd go with us on vacation. . . . And she came at seven in the morning and left at 6:30 after she'd fed us and had us all cleaned up. (pp. 6-7)

The image of Jezebel also persisted. After slavery, African American women continued to be sexually exploited by white men; just as during slavery many were still compelled to acquiesce to the sexual overtures of white women's husbands. In some cases, white women preferred their husbands to have African American women as concubines because of their inferior status. They perceived them as less of a threat than white women whom they saw as

74

competitors. Learner reports an anonymous letter submitted in 1912 to the *Independent* entitled, "We are Little More than Slaves," where an African American woman describes how she was dismissed from her job because she refused to let the "madam's" husband kiss her. This woman pointed out that because of the manner in which he began kissing her, as if it were part of the job, he must have been accustomed to this from his servants. When her husband confronted him, he was cursed, slapped, arrested, and subsequently fined $25. Below is a partial account from the letter:

I believe nearly all white men take and expect to take undue liberties with their female servants—not only the fathers, but in many cases the sons also. Those servants who rebel against such familiarity must either leave or expect a mighty hard time, if they stay. By comparison, those who tamely submit to these improper relations live in clover. They always have a little "spending change," wear better clothes, and are able to get off from work at least once a week—sometimes oftener. The moral debasement is not at all times unknown to the white women in these homes. I know of more than one colored woman who was openly importuned by white women to become the mistresses of their white husbands, on the ground that they, the white wives, were afraid that, if their husbands did not associate with colored women, they would certainly do so with outside white women, and the white wives, for reasons which ought to be perfectly obvious, preferred to have their husbands do wrong with colored women in order to keep their husbands *straight!* (p. 156)

In this description, the woman also described how some African American women were kept as concubines:

And again, I know at least fifty places in my small town where white men are positively raising two families—a white family in the "Big House" in front and a colored family in the "Little House" in the backyard. In most cases to be sure, the colored women involved are the cooks or chambermaids or seamstresses, but it cannot be true that their real connection with the white men of the families is unknown to the white women of the families. (pp. 156-157)

Overall, African American women's relations with white men during slavery were very similar to concubines and prostitutes in early Mesopotamia and in Greece and Rome. After slavery, African American women still provided domestic services and were, in some instances, forced to engage in sexual relations with their employers. Thus, unlike a co-wife whose time, energy and resources would be used to support her own family, for African American women, theirs was used to support white families. This peculiar form of polygyny has not only been to the disadvantage of African American women but African American people. These forms of interactions between African American women and white men and women and their families occurred for close to three centuries in a society that proclaims to be monogamous.

Contemporary Forms of Polygyny

Although the above description provides a depiction of polygynous formations in early America, there are other forms, or rather, various ways in which males engage in sexual relations with females in contemporary times. With regard to intimate relationships, there appear to be two primary types of polygynous formations. There are those in which a man has relations with two or more women, neither of whom he is married to, and those in which he has a wife and another woman, and, in some instances, "other" women.

Such arrangements parallel early male-female formations under Indo-European patriarchy, namely, the wife and the *hetaerae*. The wife in Greco-Roman society existed to provide a stable structure, domestic service, legitimate heirs, and childcare. The "other" woman, as the *hetaerae*, provided a variety of needs ranging from intellectual stimulation to sex, to romantic love. However, viewed from a perspective where genuine care, concern, and love feelings are felt for both the wife and "other" woman, one may think of the arrangement in the way that David Maillu does. *In Our Kind of Polygamy* Maillu (1988), argues that although prohibited in

76

its true form, two types of polygyny are widely practiced in the Western World.[3] One is consecutive polygyny whereby a man may divorce one wife and take on another; the other is simultaneous polygyny whereby a man has a wife and another woman simultaneously. In the latter case, the man essentially has two wives; one who is *"legal,"* and the other who is *"illegal,"* [Italics added] or one who is the legitimate wife, and the other who is illegitimate or a *"secret"* wife.

Although the man's economic, sexual, and emotional interaction with the illegal wife may simulate a legal "wife" type of relationship, the illegal wife, according to Maillu, is the one who is most disadvantaged. What occurs under this kind of arrangement is that the illegal wife and the husband agree to a conditional marriage. In this conditional marriage, the illegal or secret wife must adhere to several conditions, either spoken or implicit. One, and probably the most important, is that she has no legal, economic, or social claims to him. Another is that she must defer her objectives, wishes, and aspirations to those of the legal wife, and she must at all times avoid any physical contact with her. Another is that she is not to be seen in public with the husband demonstrating any kind of affection. He is also at liberty to hide her from relatives and his circle of friends. Most of all, "the understood but unsigned contract of the second marriage stipulates that at any time and place the husband shall reserve and enjoy total liberty to walk out on her without any notice and liability whatsoever" (pp. 30-31).

A most important condition of the secondary marriage is that the illegal wife is not to have children. If, by chance, she does, there may be negative consequences for them as well. Most significant is that they may be treated like their mother. Maillu notes that the child is "by state law, an illegal child; hence a second-

---

[3] The word that Maillu actually uses is *polygamy*, the popular use for *polygyny*. Since he uses *polygamy* in the context of *polygyny*, this term is used for the sake of clarity.

class child, who is known in public places and in records as a bastard" (p. 30). Furthermore, children of such unions may:

Grow up as shameful, second-class citizens, usually abused by relatives and the public, misunderstood and treated with a high degree of rejection both by the public and the law. They are inferior, in as far as social life is concerned, to the children of the licensed marriage. The husband in such a marriage is always ready, at any time and any place, to deny the existence of such a marriage and any children from the union. (p. 31)

The illegal wife is also treated with contempt by the public. Maillu notes:

The Mistress is a public disgrace. She is treated by the public with maximum suspicion particularly by the licensed woman; she is discriminated against, abused and misunderstood. In domestic socio-economic politics, she is classified by the licensed woman as a "husband thief," who deserves to be hunted down and eliminated even by extermination from the life of the husband. Her position in society is insecure. The Church sees her not only as a sinner, but an embarrassment although her failure to secure a licensed marriage was not of her own making. She is therefore, a lonely person. (p. 31)

Overall, because of the way the illegal wife and her children are perceived and treated by relatives, friends, and the public, there may be negative consequences for their emotional and psychological health.

Although Maillu discusses disadvantages, there are some advantages the illegal wife has by comparison with the legal one. One, is that she does not have to deal with the domestic complexities of a legal marriage. Another is that the time she spends with the husband is limited; this therefore helps to keep the luster in the relationship, which in turn may enhance their sex life. Because his visits are usually scheduled, she can always look her best. This also helps the relationship. Another is that there is no obligation on her part to meet his sexual, domestic, or emotional needs, and because he has a legal wife, this can be used for leverage in conflicts. In addition, she is free to engage in liaisons, intimate or other, with other men, which may enhance her overall life satisfaction.

All of these factors may be quite the opposite for the legal wife and may put her at a disadvantage by comparison to the illegal wife. One disadvantage is that she may feel inadequate with regard to providing her husband's needs, or feel that she is no longer desirable, which may lead her to feel insecure. In cases where financial provisions are made for the illegal wife, although they may be substantially less than those provided to the legal wife, it still detracts from her household. Most importantly, the legal wife is deceived by her husband and his illegal wife. If the legal wife finds out about the illegal wife, it may lead to conflict in the marriage, and, in worst case, divorce. Where there are children, besides daughters learning to distrust men, and boys learning to emulate the deceptive behavior of their fathers, the conflict in the marriage may have negative consequences for the children's emotional and psychological development. This is particularly the case if the affair leads to divorce.

The second type of polygynous formations are those in which there is with no marriage license. In such situations, a single man may engage in sexual relationships with a woman as a "primary" partner, often described as the "main" woman, and other women as "secondary" partners. In some cases, because none of the partners meet the standards of a wife or primary partner, all of the women may be engaged as secondary partners. Thus, whether a legal or illegal wife, a primary or secondary partner, it is women who are disadvantaged both psychologically and emotionally. This is primarily because of the deceit involved in how these relationships are entered into and maintained. Because there is no mutual consent between the women, the men often spend a great deal of time and energy juggling the women instead of attending to their needs. Thus, the needs of the men may be satisfied, most of which are sexual, whereas those of the women, in most cases, emotional, may not. This leads to distrust, conflicts, and ultimately unstable relationships, families, and communities.

Besides these two primary types of intimate relationships, there are other sexual outlets for males that disadvantage women. Figure 1 compares Greco-Roman and early and contemporary American forms with the traditional African model.

Figure 1

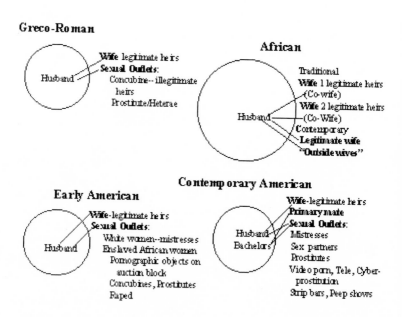

As shown under the Greco-Roman model, the wife's function was to provide legitimate heirs. Other outlets for males included concubines, who also provided domestic support for the legitimate wife, and *hetaerae* or prostitutes. In the early American model is the the wife and enslaved African woman. Enslaved African women provided support for the wife as "Mammy." Some also provided sexual outlets for white males in the form of concubines or through rape. Their bodies on auction blocks also provided pornographic images for white men.

In contemporary America, there is the wife and in cases where the male is not married, a primary mate. Sexual and emotional outlets for married men may include a mistress, while for single males, secondary partners. Other sexual outlets for both married and single men include sex partners, prostitutes, and other mechanisms, such as video pornography, tele- and cyber-prostitution, and peep shows and strip bars. Probably one of the most deplorable sights I have witnessed in contemporary times is the red light district in Amsterdam, of the Netherlands, where various forms of prostitution (except for street) is legal. As one strolls down the streets of the red light district, women (considered business women), like any other object on display for buyers, or like mannequins, scarcely clad (a few were not dressed at all) are displayed in windows. The tour guide explained that when a woman is on display in the window she is available. When the curtain is closed, the woman is with a client. The women work in shifts and are available for men, even before work hours. The women are not just Europeans, but include all nationalities, numerous of whom are of African descent. The only difference between the red-light district in Amsterdam and in cities across the U.S. is that in the U.S. prostitution is not legal and therefore women are not displayed for sale (although they do display themselves illegally under street prostitution). However, peep shows and strip bars, where women do "lap dances," provide an alternative sexual outlet (through voyeurism and sexual fantasy) for males.

Phone sex, another contemporary form of prostitution also provides a sexual outlet for males. Spike Lee's movie, *Girl Six*, provides a depiction and critique of the dynamics of this industry. In addition, if one does a search on the internet for Black women, several sites, called "Black whores" come up. Thus, the cyber age also provides a way for women to sell their bodies, and a sexual outlet for males.

These various ways of engaging women exist along with monogamy and are perfectly acceptable in U.S. society. In the case of the wife and the "other" woman, such interactions leave both women emotionally vulnerable, while the "other woman" is also legally, financially, and socially vulnerable. When they are not married, women are vulnerable in all these respects. The other forms, outgrowths of the pornographic industry, provide sexual outlets for men, but dehumanize women.

In traditional Africa, wives and their children were granted the legitimacy and status accompanying socially sanctioned marriage. Wives were entitled to social, legal, financial, and emotional support from their husbands, and their children were recognized by the family and kinship. The woman was not reduced to an object for sexual use, and there was potential for a socially and emotionally fulfilling relationship. Clearly, this model is more advantageous to women.

All the interactions described here occur and are acceptable in contemporary U.S. society. While this is the case, communities in which polygyny is practiced openly, are castigated. There is no other instance in which this is more evident than in the case of the Mormons.

Chapter 4

THE CASE OF THE MORMONS

In *Polygamous Families in Contemporary Societies*, Irwin Altman and Joseph Ginat (1996) provide an overview of Mormon history in the U.S. According to them, the Latter Day Saints of the Church of Jesus Christ, or Mormonism, began with Joseph Smith. Joseph Smith was born in 1805 into a poor family in Vermont that later moved to upstate New York in Palmyra. He had visions several times throughout his life, the first of which occurred during his teens when God and Jesus Christ were made known to him. He had another at age 18 when the angel Moroni appeared to him. In this second vision, Moroni revealed to him the place of golden leaves, or plates, on which was inscribed the history of a people who had lived in America during ancient times. He was led to transcribe the ancient scripts into what became the Book of the Mormons. In this book one finds an account of who these ancient people were and the role that was destined for Joseph Smith. According to the account, somewhere around 600 BC, led by God, a group of Hebrew Israelites from Jerusalem traveled to North America. The account continues as follows:

[O]ver the course of the next centuries they grew in numbers and built cities and temples but then split into two warring groups. . . .Christ came to the Americas following his crucifixion and instituted a period of peace and tranquility, which eventually gave way to conflict and upheaval and the destruction of one group. The angel Moroni was the last prophet of the defeated group. He hid the record of his people, written on golden plates, until such time as a righteous man appeared in 'the latter days' to restore the gospel and divinity of Christ. (Altman and Ginat, p. 23)

That man was Joseph Smith. In 1829, Smith and a friend were also visited by John the Baptist, after which they engaged in a mutual baptism. In the spring of 1830, at the age of 24, Smith and a few of his followers established the Latter Day Saints of the

Church of Jesus Christ, in Fayette, NY, where they named themselves "latter day" saints to distinguish themselves from "former day" saints of biblical times (Altman and Ginat, p. 23).

Early Struggles

In the early years, between 1831 and 1838, the Mormons established communities in various cities in Ohio (Kirkland) and Missouri (Independence, Liberty, and Far West). Because of conflicts over religious differences and their growing numbers, they became a threat to already existing community members, who were vying for political and economic control. They were eventually forced to leave these cities.

The Mormons first established headquarters for the church in Kirkland, Ohio. However, dissension within the leadership, a bank failure, and increasing debt brought about open rebellion by Mormons who sought to depose Joseph Smith and support a suit by non-Mormon creditors. Combined threats of violence and imprisonment forced Smith and other leaders to flee from Ohio to settle in Missouri.

While in Missouri, their swelling numbers led them to move into counties other than the one designated for them. Also, increasing militancy by a Mormon group of vigilantes called *Danites* (decedents from the tribe of Dan), used the threat of violence to stifle dissension. Their claim to be God's chosen people and the suspicion that they were agitating enslaved Africans and the Native Americans led people in the community to perceive the Mormons as an economic and political threat to non-Mormons (LeSuer, 1987). Conflict ensued leading to a civil war between Mormons and other non-Mormon citizens. The civil war ended in a government-issued order that the Mormons be banished from Missouri or be "exterminated." While awaiting trial in 1839, Smith directed Brigham Young, his eventual successor, to move the Mormons to Illinois, and Smith and others escaped prison and fled there.

84

The Mormons settled in Nauvoo (which means beautiful city), Illinois. While in Illinois, Smith dominated local politics and held all the important offices. He attempted to establish a theocratic government and even considered running for president of the United States. His political aims created a cultural clash between Mormons and non-Mormons who were avid supporters of a democratic government (Hallwas & Lanius, 1995). It was in Illinois that intimidation against dissenters cost Joseph Smith and his brother their lives. Reacting against an anti-Mormon article printed by the *Depositor,* some Mormons destroyed the property of the newspaper owners. Using his political savvy and power, Smith was able to maneuver around attempts to arrest him and bring him to trial. A public uproar ensued in the city of Carthage, in Hancock county. In response to threatened violence, Smith declared martial law in Nauvoo and brought out the Nauvoo region reserves to protect the city. Smith and his brother attempted to flee but returned after they were shamed for abandoning the church in a time of trouble. He and his brother were released from riot charges but were later arrested for treason against the state for unlawfully declaring martial law in Nauvoo. While incarcerated in a local jail in Carthage, Joseph Smith and his brother Hyrum Smith were murdered by a mob (Hallwas & Lanius, 1995).

The Mormons were eventually forced to leave Illinois. Seeking a place where they could have religious and secular control, they began a hard and long journey of more than 1,200 miles to Utah. They arrived in July 1847 and eventually settled in Utah under the leadership of Brigham Young. By 1848, some 2,500 persons had settled in Utah, and the population continued to grow. Of the many hardships they faced in the early years, the most significant was in 1848 when crickets began to destroy their meager crops. "Unable to control the crickets, they fell to their knees and began to pray for divine intervention. Following this, waves of sea gulls came to the great Salt Lake and devoured the crickets. To commemorate this event, the Mormons constructed a monument of a seagull on Temple Square in the Center of Salt Lake City" (Altman & Ginat, 1996).

Overall, the goal of the Mormons was to create an economically independent, church-controlled community, free of the life-styles and practices of the "gentile" world. Through industry, a strong work ethic, and a business entrepreneurship orientation, they "developed factories, farms and dairies, foundries and iron works, machine shops, textile mills and coal mines" (Altman & Ginat, 1996, p. 32). They also built a city. With the guiding principle of a "United Order," their socio-economic structure consisted of collective economics with all things in common, care for the needy, volunteerism, and mutual assistance. By the beginning of the 20th century, Utah had a population of approximately 277,000, of which 65 percent comprised Mormons. They had also expanded into various other areas in Utah, Idaho, Wyoming, New Mexico, Arizona, Nevada, Colorado, California, Canada, and Mexico.

Government Opposition

In spite of their success, the Mormons began to sustain more vigorous assaults from the federal government and their practice of polygyny provided the angle. Marriage under Mormonism is seen as a religious sacrament and is viewed as lasting for "time and eternity," that is, the now and hereafter vs. for "time" here on earth (Altman & Ginat, p.25). Although some of the church leaders, including Joseph Smith himself, had been practicing polygyny secretly in the early 1830s, and more openly by the late 1830s, it was not until 1843, while still in Nauvoo, that Smith made a statement to key leaders declaring a revelation of polygyny on the grounds that Old Testament patriarchs, such as Abraham and Jacob, had several wives. The principle of marriage for "time and eternity," whereby civil marriages were seen to be valid only for the "time," and thus invalid, also gave legitimacy to marriages by the church that included polygyny. In addition, it was established that women needed to be married to righteous men to gain a proper place in the hereafter, and polygyny helped them to achieve this. In 1852, Brigham Young openly declared that polygyny was the doctrine and practice of the Church. After this, it began to be widely practiced (Altman and Ginat, p. 28). During the years 1856 and 1857, the leadership strongly urged Mormon members to engage in polygyny. This resulted in more marriages being contracted than during any other two-year period in Mormon history.

It was the practice of polygyny in addition to what was perceived as rebelliousness to the U.S., including the suspicion that the Mormons were supporting Native Americans against the U.S., along with alleged acts against non-Mormons that contributed greatly to the onslaught by the U. S. government. The Mormons had also established political control on territory that had not yet acquired statehood.

In the late 1850s, President Buchanan ordered troops to invade Utah, after which the Mormons responded with guerrilla attacks (Altman & Ginat, p 33). After negotiations, however, federal troops entered peacefully. Subsequent attacks came through various members of Congress, where the intent was to restrict Mormon independence, including the practice of polygyny. Polygyny, in fact, became a major item on the Republican Party's agenda. The party proposed to eliminate slavery and polygyny, the "twin relics of barbarism" (p. 21). Congress passed a series of legislation that targeted polygyny, including the Morrill Act, passed by Congress in 1862 and signed into law by President Lincoln, the Edmonds Act of 1882, and the Edmonds-Tucker Law of 1887.

The Morrill Act prohibited polygyny in U.S. territories, disincorporated the church, and restricted the church's ownership of property to $50,000. Other intervening legislation also attempted to outlaw the Mormon practice of polygyny. Despite the passage of such legislation, the Mormons maintained their right to practice polygyny under the constitutional right of freedom of religion and appealed the case of George Reynolds, secretary to Brigham Young, all the way to the Supreme Court. The Supreme Court upheld the lower court's decision by concluding that "people could freely 'believe' in certain religious principles, such as plural marriage, but that they were not necessarily free to 'act' upon their beliefs, especially if those beliefs were in conflict with social principles and laws" (Altman & Ginat, p. 39).

The Edmunds Act of 1882 "made plural marriage and cohabitation criminal acts and prohibited those practicing polygyny from serving on jury, holding political office or serving as elected officials" (Altman and Ginat, p. 35). Elections in Utah were placed under the authority of a board of five commissioners appointed by the president to direct elections. Only men who took an oath that they did not practice polygyny or cohabit with more than one woman were permitted to vote. Many men, even church leaders including the president, were forced "underground," into hiding, or into abandoning their families. As a consequence, many families were split up and their living arrangements were disrupted, tearing at the very fibre of the Mormon community. "Within a few years, more than 1,000 men had been convicted and imprisoned for practicing polygyny or cohabitation" (Altman and Ginat, p. 35). To avoid arrest, other families relocated and settled in remote areas of Arizona, Nevada, Wyoming, and Colorado, and in Mexico and Canada.

The final assault came with the Edmunds-Tucker Act of 1887, which was intended to fill the loopholes left in the 1882 Edmunds Act. The Edmunds-Tucker Act allowed the federal government to disfranchise Mormons, required wives to testify against their husbands, and provided a mechanism to confiscate church properties. In 1890, the U.S. Supreme Court upheld the constitutionality of the government's right to seize the financial holdings of the Mormon Church. These actions, in effect, threatened the economic, political, social, and religious base of the church.

However, in 1889, the president of the Mormon Church, John Taylor, who was an advocate of polygyny, died, and to avoid the church's losing its power base, the newly elected president, Wilford Wilson, publically denounced the practice of polygyny. He later issued a manifesto of his intention to submit to the laws of the land and to influence other members of the church to do so also. His intentions were stipulated in the manifesto, however, not all members of the church's leadership signed the document, and they continued to practice polygyny. Although the church publicly denounced polygyny, no penalties were introduced for failing to comply, and there were no structures put in place to address already existing plural marriages. Members were encouraged to find other ways to get around the laws, such as going to Mexico to consummate marriages (Altman & Ginat, p. 37). Because polygyny continued despite its renunciation by church leaders in public statements, new assaults against the Mormons began.

Senator Reed Smoot, a Mormon, had his seat challenged and was forced to pressure President Joseph F. Smith, in the 1904 manifesto, to threaten church officials and members with excommunication if they entered into polygyny. In 1907, the church issued a public document whereby it affirmed separation of church and the state, their loyalty to the United States laws, and polygyny as a violation of church and civil law (Altman & Ginat, p. 38). Church leaders who persisted in the practice were removed from their positions, and some were excommunicated if they continued to openly advocate polygyny (p. 38). Factions developed within the Mormon Church. The conflict shifted from the Mormon Church against the U.S. government to the Mormon Church against Mormon fundamentalists who wanted to continue practicing polygyny (Altman and Ginat, p. 38).

The Fundamentalist Split

Mormon fundamentalists were first led by John Taylor who became a fugitive because of his advocacy of polygyny. They were subsequently led by Lorin Wooley who made a public statement in 1912 about visits of Joseph Smith and Jesus Christ to John Taylor (which he heard while a bodyguard one night outside of John Taylor's room). Smith and Christ told Taylor to hold fast to the principle and practice of polygyny. The fundamentalist were later led by John Y. Barlow, who led the settlement into another area in Salt Lake City (now called the Hildale community) and into a town then called Short Creek (now Colorado City), which was located on the borders of Utah and Arizona.

The new communities continued to practice polygyny and to face opposition from the Mormon Church and the Utah government, where members of the Mormon Church had significant influence. Legislation was passed making it a crime for a person to cohabit with more than one person of the opposite sex (chapter 112, section 103-51-2 of the Utah Penal Code) (Altman and Ginat, p. 44). Other legislation as well as the Utah Constitution were used, and with the cooperation of the Mormon Church, raids were made on Mormon communities. There was a raid in 1935, in Short-Creek, by Utah and Arizona authorities; another occurred in 1944 in various localities (this time involving Arizona authorities and federal agents and Idaho authorities); and yet another, in 1953, on the Short Creek community (by Arizona and Utah authorities). Many members were arrested and convicted of various crimes, such as cohabitation, using males for obscene purposes, and white slavery. As a result, families were split up, children were placed in foster homes, and mothers were forced to give up children for adoption. In spite of this, fundamentalist Mormons held fast to their belief in the practice of polygyny. The communities continued to grow, and estimates for the population range between 30,000 to 50,000 members.

Fundamentalist communities continue to practice polygyny, and until recently, with the case of Tom Green, there has been little concerted action against them by authorities since the late 1950s. It was stated publically "that they [would] not initiate charges against polygamists because no significant harm to the community is being perpetrated, there are too many polygynists to prosecute, and there are more important legal and criminal matters to attend to" (Altman and Ginat, p. 52). The only time legal action is generally taken is when specific issues arise that are linked to polygyny, such as cases of guardianship rights when a parent in a polygynous union dies. This was reflected in an article in the August 1991 issue of the *Salt Lake Tribune*, "Law Looks Other Way if Polygamy is Only Crime." Here the attorney general of Utah during that time, stated, 'Unless it is associated with child abuse, welfare fraud or any other illegal act, polygamy for its own sake has not been a crime susceptible of successful prosecution and uses up an awful lot of resources' (Altman and Ginat, p. 58). In the *Desert News* (September 11-12, 1991), the County Attorney stated, 'If we are going after illegal cohabitation, we'd have to line them up — the older people living together, young couples, even homosexual couples living together — all violate the bigamy/cohabitation law' (Altman and Ginat, p. 58). There have also been proposals that statements about polygamy be revised in the Utah State constitution "on the grounds that the language is archaic, few other states had such a prohibition, and existing laws regarding bigamy would suffice" (Altman and Ginat, p. 58).

The conviction of Tom Green, husband of five wives and 25 children with three on the way (26, 28 and 29 children have also been cited) however may have changed this. It seems the old battle between the state of Utah and the fundamentalist may have been revitalized. It is believed that Green has been singled out because of his appearances on popular television shows, including his 1999 interview with NBC's Dateline (McCarthy/Partoun, 2001). Whatever the reason for being targeted by Juab County prosecutor, David Leavitt, brother of Mike Leavitt, Governor of Utah, Green was convicted on four counts of bigamy.

Although Green was not legally married to either of the five women — as he had annulled the marriage with one woman before marring another one, he was convicted using a combination of common law marriage and bigamy statues. It was determined that he was married by common law because he and his wives held out to the public which is considered bigamy (Fattah, 2000). The jury that convicted Green, also saw him as knowingly trying to "skirt Utah's marriage Law" (Fattah, 2000).

In light of this outcome, it is speculated that this "case has far reaching implications for future criminal prosecution of other polygamous groups" (Fattah, 2000). By contrast, it is also believed that prosecutors would be reluctant to pursue polygamy cases for fear of imprisoning parents and breaking up families.

A group of women, the Women's Religious Liberties Union, organized in 1998 to ". . . protest newspapers and television depictions of all polygamists as incestuous, misogynous and abusive to women and children" (American Civil Liberties Union, 1999). Supported by the American Civil Liberties Union, their major focus is the Utah 1935 Law that made "bigamy into a felony instead of a misdemeanor," and a clause that has made it illegal to cohabit with another person (American Civil Liberties Union, 1999).

Whatever the future holds for the practice of polygyny in the U.S., it seems that what the Mormons sustained in their early years had more to do with challenges the group presented to the local and federal governments and competition for political power in the respective communities in which they settled than with the actual practice of polygyny. Inherent in the practice of polygyny is the threat it can pose to an already established social, economic and political order. From a nation standpoint, as groups grow in polygynous-oriented families and communities, there is always the potential for the development of a tribe or even nation. Scholars who study what they refer to as group marriage in communes, especially when the communes subscribe to a social, economic and political order different from the existing one, tend to use the term in a way that downplays the potential of these communes to evolve into independent tribes or nations. Many of these groups aspire to an order in which church and state are one. The problem with this is that it can be a threat to the most fundamental principle governing the Western world — separation of church and state.

Before European world domination, marriage was considered a sacred institution in most societies throughout the world. However, for most peoples, the sacred was not separate from the secular. In this regard then, marriage, religion, and the state were intertwined. In the West, church and state are separate. Christianity, however, is the religion of the state, which means that it played a significant role in developing the moral basis for marriage. As such, it played a significant role in establishing the moral basis for monogamy only and in proscriptions against polygyny. The practice of polygyny among the Mormons was not a threat because it challenged the religious authority of marriage. It was a threat because it challenged its political base. In the communities in which they settled, the Mormons posed a threat because they were competing for political control. In Utah, they presented the same threat to the entire U.S. government, because until 1896, Utah, although owned by the U.S., had not acquired statehood. Although one cannot ignore that some of the Mormons, through militancy and use of mythical-political ideas in their struggle for power, did provoke hostility against themselves, one also cannot ignore the underlying threat their potential to establish a theocracy on U.S. land posed. In this regard, the Mormons became a threat to U.S. secular democracy. And as is obvious, if one wants to eliminate a potential threat, the most strategic place to start is the family. The practice of polygyny among the Mormons provided local and federal authorities just what they needed.

In spite of what the Mormons have undergone, they have managed to survive. Their experiences over the past few decades demonstrate that polygyny can be practiced without becoming a threat to the social, economic, and political order.

In the case of Tom Green, it is unfortunate that it is more acceptable for a man to go from house to house and engage in sexual relationships with women in secret and without accountability, than it is for him to marry the women and be

93

accountable to them and their children. More importantly, it is unfortunate that most of the world is compelled to adhere to a minority of the world's (white males who create and enforce the laws) ways of engaging women — wife and other women as mistresses, prostitutes, and pornographic sex objects — and that they have convinced women the world over that this is the way. What is needed, it seems, is for groups who practice polygyny to combine their forces. Their efforts united might be what is needed to force the power structure to accept the diversity in the human family, and the relationship and marriage practices that emerge from it. Structural constraints might then be eliminated, and polygyny can indeed become a viable option for those who choose it.

PART II: THE CURRENT SITUATION

Chapter 5

A SHORTAGE OF AFRICAN AMERICAN MEN: MYTH OR REALITY?

There has been a marked decline in marriage rates among African Americans in the past few decades. In 1970, 64 percent of adult African Americans were married (McAdoo, 1997). By 1998, approximately 42 percent were (U.S. Bureau of the Census, 1999). The rate is decreasing so noticeably, it seems that "marriage is becoming a minority lifestyle among many African Americans" (McAdoo, 1997, p. 145).

As shown in Table 1, when combining the proportion in the age group 25-34 who had never been married, approximately 53 percent, with the 6 percent who are divorced, it appears that approximately 59 percent of African American women may be living single.[4] Although this may be because African Americans are delaying marriage, the combined proportions are still relatively high for those in age groups 35-44, which is approximately 47 percent, by comparison with their white counterparts whose combined rates are 33.7 percent and 26.6 percent, respectively, for the two age groups.[5]

The proportion of African American women who may not have a mate consistently present in their lives increases substantially if we add the number who are married without their spouse present, reaching over 67 percent for those in age group 25-

---

[4] These figures many not include those who may be cohabitating; and economic, sexual, and emotional sharing is similar to married couples.

[5] The combined rates are slightly higher for African American males in both age groups, approximately 60% for age group 25-34, and 48% for age group 35-44.

34, and over 60 percent for those in age group 35-44. Absent spouses may include those who are in the armed forces or employed away from home. They may also include those who are institutionalized or away because of separation due to marital discord (U.S. Bureau of the Census, 1992).

Table 1
Marital Status of Women by Age Group, 1998

Age Group	Black Females 25-34	35-44	White Females 25-34	35-44
Marital Status (percent)				
Never Married	53.2	30.0	25.3	9.1
Divorced	6.1	17.4	8.4	15.5
Total	59.3	47.4	33.7	26.6
Married spouse absent	8.2	13.1	3.6	3.7
Total	67.5	60.5	37.3	30.3
Married spouse present	32.2	38.5	62.3	71.6

Source: U.S. Bureau of the Census: Black Population in the U.S., Current Population Survey, Table: 4, March 1998; http://www.census.gov/ population/socdemo/race/black/tabs98/tab04.tx.

The proportion of African American women maintaining families has also increased substantially. In the 1960s, approximately 25 percent of African American families were maintained by women. By 1998, African American families maintained by women with no spouse comprised 47 percent of all families. Some attribute decreasing marriage rates and the number of women maintaining families to cultural trends stemming from the sexual revolution, the increasing number of women in the labor force, and those who depend on social welfare programs. Others, however, attribute these changes to the shortage of African American men. In fact, this is the most frequently used explanation. Although this is the case, there is the question of whether Census counts accurately reflect the African American population in general, and males in particular. Because African American males are more likely to not be counted by the Census, the question that arises is: Is there really is a shortage? Is this myth, or is it reality? If there is a shortage of males, another question that arises is: What is the implication of this for African American male-female relationships, marriages, and families? Furthermore, what is the implication of this reality for polygyny as an alternative relationship, marriage, and family formation?

How the Census Bureau Enumerates the Population

To answer the question of whether there is a shortage of African American males, it is important to understand how the Census Bureau enumerates and reports the population. Essentially, the Census Bureau does a complete count of the population every ten years. These counts are referred to as decennial counts. The Census Bureau also makes estimates of the population on a annual basis. This is done by taking the decennial counts, adding births, net immigration, and net movement of U.S. armed forces to the resident population; and subtracting deaths of residents and civilian citizens of the U.S.

When the Census Bureau enumerates the entire population, it counts all persons living in households and group quarters — persons classified as not living in households (U.S. Bureau of Census, 1992). The two categories of group quarters include institutional and noninstitutional. Noninstitutional or "other persons living in group quarters" include ten or more unrelated persons who share the same living quarters, which include, but are not limited to, rooming houses and homes for the mentally ill, mentally retarded, physically handicapped, drug and alcohol abuse, maternity, and other domiciles that provide communal living quarters, such as college dormitories.

The institutional population category includes those who are *under supervised care or custody*-- inmates in correctional facilities (jails and prisons), persons classified as patients in nursing homes, wards or hospitals for the mentally ill, chronically ill, physically handicapped (includes schools), and mentally retarded (includes schools), drug/alcohol abuse wards in general, military hospitals for patients who have no usual home else where, and juvenile institutions. Reports showing the residential population exclude those in the military overseas. Those showing the civilian noninstitutional population excludes both those in the military in the U.S. and overseas and those in institutions.

In *Using the 1990 Census for Research*, R. E. Barret (1994) reports that the Census goes through several stages to enumerate the population in households. For the 1990 Census, forms were first mailed out. When a housing unit did not send back a Census questionnaire, enumerators were sent out to find someone to fill out the form. If they failed to find someone, they were permitted to obtain *last resort* information, which is information from someone else who lives in the neighborhood. After questionnaires from 95 percent of the housing units were collected, enumerators proceeded to the next stage, which was to obtain *closeout data*. This entailed recording the "kind of structure in which the unit was housed, the number of persons living there (or their names), and whether the unit was occupied" (p. 48). In cases in which a housing unit was occupied but there was no way to find out how many persons lived there, the characteristics were estimated through substitution data from a nearby housing unit. This is called *non data defined* (p. 48).

Barret notes that data were collected from approximately 4.6 million people through the last resort procedure, 1.93 million people through the closeout procedure, and 1.96 million through the non data defined procedure. He also notes factors contributing to difficulty in taking the Census. Some include "poor quality of address lists, poor coordination between the U. S. Postal Service and the Bureau of the Census, unreported new construction, new housing units constructed within existing structures, Census forms left in apartment house lobbies because they lacked apartment numbers and so on" (p. 50).

A factor contributing to difficulty in taking the 1990 Census was non-compliance primarily in low-income neighborhoods in urban areas. Added to this is that enumerators were temporary employees with heavy workloads and little pay. This resulted in high turnover. Also, enumerators felt uncomfortable or unsafe in low-income areas, which may have led to falsification of data. In addition, some persons had never heard of the Census, and others experienced reading and language difficulties in attempting to complete the forms.

Because of problems with taking the Census, there are groups of persons who are "over, under or mis-numerated" (p. 51). To account for this, estimates using two methods are made: the Post-Enumeration Survey (PES) and Demographic Analysis (DA) (Barret, 1994; Hogan & Robinson, unpublished). The 1990 PES involved conducting an independent survey consisting of two subsamples, P and E of about 170,000 housing units in 5,290 blocks, approximately six months after the original enumeration (Barret, p. 51). "The E-sample was a reinvestigation of housing units listed in the original enumeration. It was designed to find persons missing from the household Census questionnaires and to search for erroneous and missing data, including cases where Census (or respondents) falsified data" (p. 51). "The P sample involved interviewing everyone who lived on these blocks at the time of the PES. These data were then compared with the data for these blocks from the original enumeration" (Barret, p. 51). The 1992 PES rates were 4.9 percent for African Americans males and four percent for African American females. With these PES estimates, there were approximately 16,476,225 females and 14,900,868 males, amounting to approximately 1,575,357 more females (July, 1992).

Demographic Analysis (DA) is a method that involves applying a variety of techniques to data from prior Censuses, with measures of demographic data, such as deaths, births, and immigration statistics at the time the Census is taken (Barret, 1994; Hogan and Robinson, unpublished). Demographic Analysis can only be used to estimate the net undercount (that is, the difference between the estimated population and the enumerated population), whereas the PES can be used to estimate the undercount, the erroneously enumerated, and the proportion of questions answered incorrectly (Barret, p. 56).

One advantage of DA estimates is they extend as far back as 1940. As shown in Table 2, the DA undercount rate for the entire population in 1990 was 1.8 percent, whereas for the African American population, the rate was 5.7 percent, compared with the nonAfrican American population which was 1.3 percent. Between

99

1940 and 1990, the undercount rate for African Americans has consistently been approximately 3-4 percent higher than that for nonAfrican Americans. Although both African American males and females are undercounted, the rate for African American males has been close to double that of females throughout this period and was more than double in 1990. These undercount estimates have implications for ascertaining a true index of the number of African American males to females.

Table 2

Demographic Analysis Estimates of Percent Undercount of Resident Population by Race and Age: 1940-1990

Year	1940	1950	1960	1970	1980	1990
Total	5.4	4.1	3.1	2.7	1.2	1.8
Black	8.4	7.5	6.6	6.5	4.5	5.7
Non-Black	5.0	3.8	2.7	2.2	0.8	1.3
Difference (Black/ Non-Black)	3.4	3.6	3.9	4.3	3.7	4.4
Male						
Black	10.50	9.70	8.76	9.10	7.47	8.49
Non-Black	5.18	3.84	2.87	2.71	1.47	1.97
Female						
Black	5.99	5.39	4.42	3.9	1.6	3.01
Non-Black	4.89	3.66	2.44	1.73	0.09	0.63
Difference (Black male/ female)	4.51	4.31	4.34	5.13	5.80	5.48

Source: *Journal of the American Statistical Association*, Estimation of Population Coverage in the 1990 US, Sept. 1993, Appendix, Table 2 & U.S. Bureau of the Census, Unpublished Tabulation.

Although the Census Bureau goes to great measures to counter against, those over, under, or mis-numerated, interestingly, the estimated undercounts still may not be included in actual Census reports. For example, in the 1990 Census, a decision was made to not include undercount estimates. Overall, because of the complexities involved in enumerating the population, and because undercount estimates may not be included in reports, it may be difficult to ascertain the proportion of African American males to females. Despite this, the population demographics of African Americans are still quite revealing.

African American Population Demographics

There are data showing population counts of African Americans back to 1820. Table 3 shows not only the proportion of males to females, but the number who were free vs. those who were enslaved. As can be seen, the majority of enslaved African Americans were males up until the last Census before emancipation in 1860. This means more females than males were free. There were also more males than females in the total population in 1820 and 1830. From 1840 to 1990, however, there have been more females to males.

Table 3

Free and Enslaved African American Population by Sex, 1820-1860

Year	Free		Enslaved		Total	
	Male	Female	Male	Female	Male	Female
1820	112,734	120,790	788,028	750,010	900,762	870,800
1830	153,453	166,146	1,012,823	996,220	1,166,291	1,162,366
1840	186,481	199,822	1,246,517	1,240,938	1,432,968	1,440,760
1850	208,724	225,771	1,602,534	1,601,779	1,811,258	1,827,550
1860	234,119	263,951	1,982,625	1,971,135	2,216,744	2,234,486

Source: U.S. Bureau of the Census, *U.S. Census, 1870, Vol.1*, pp. x/iv-x/ix and pp. 3-8.

Table 4 shows that the ratio of males to females continued to decrease from 1840 to 1990. In the most recent decennial count in 1990, there were approximately 1,645,758 more females than males, creating a sex ratio of 89.5 males to 100 females.

Table 4

African American Population by Sex and Sex Ratio, 1820-1990

Year	Male	Female	Sex Ratio
1820	900,762	870,800	1.03
1830	1,166,276	1,162,366	1.00
1840	1,432,998	1,440,760	.990
1850	1,811,258	1,827,550	.991
1860	2,216,744	2,225,086	.996
1870	2,393,263	2,486,746	.962
1880	3,253,115	3,327,678	.977
1890	3,726,561	3,744,479	.995
1900	4,386,547	4,447,447	.986
1910	4,885,881	4,941,882	.988
1920	5,209,436	5,253,695	.991
1930	5,855,669	6,035,474	.970
1940	6,269,038	6,596,480	.950
1950	7,269,170	7,767,505	.935
1960	9,097,704	9,750,915	.933
1970	10,748,316	11,831,973	.908
1980	12,508,991	13,973,358	.895
1990	14,170,151	15,815,909	.895

Source:.U.S. Bureau of the Census, *Historical Statistics of the U.S. Colonial Times to 1970*, p. 17.

As shown in Table 5, in 1990 there were also more females than males in the fifteen metropolitan areas with the largest proportion of African Americans. The ratio ranged from 79 males for every 100 females in the Cleveland-Akron, Ohio area, to 98 males to 100 females in the San Francisco area. The average number of males to females was 88 to 100 for the fifteen metropolitan areas.

Table 5

Fifteen Metropolitan Areas with Largest Number of African Americans
by Sex, 1990

Metropolitan Area	Males	Females	Ratio
New York-Northern			
New Jersey-Long Island	1,502,182	1,789,637	.84
Washington-Baltimore, DC-MD	488,077	554,133	.88
Chicago-Gary-Kenosha, IL-IN-WI	712,324	2,133	.92
Los Angeles-Riverside-			
Orange County, CA	589,579	636,898	.93
Philadelphia,-Wilmington			
-Atlantic City, PA-NJ-DE-MD	511,190	588,869	.87
Detroit-Ann Arbor-Flint, MI	446,248	527,670	.85
Atlanta, GA	342,974	392,503	.87
Houston-Galveston-Brazonia, TX	316,551	347,676	.91
Miami-Fort Lauderdale, FL	279,391	312,393	.89
Dallas-Fort Worth, TX	261,907	292,375	.90
San-Francisco-Oakland			
- San Jose, CA	264,574	271,203	.98
Cleveland-Akron, OH	200,240	251,941	.79
New Orleans, LA	197,643	233,416	.85
Norfolk-Virginia Beach-			
Newport News, VA	189,681	208,330	.91
Memphis, TN	184,428	214,897	.86

Source: U.S. Bureau of the Census, 1990 US Census Data, Database: C90STF3C1,
Summary Level: Metropolitan Statistical Area; http://venus.census.gov/cdrom
/lookup/940970566.

Although these counts show more African American
females to males, based on what was revealed about the
complexities involved in enumerating the population, one might be
skeptical of the data. However, even with the estimated
undercount, there are still more females to males.

As shown in Table 6, in 1990 there were 14,420,331 African
American males compared with 16,062,950 females, a surplus of
1,642,619 females. The Demographic Analysis estimate showed an
undercount of approximately 1,338,380 males compared with
497,892 females. With these revised net undercount figures, there

were 802,131 more females than males. In the age groups between 25 and 44 undercount rate was substantially higher for African American males compared with females and ranged between approximately 10 and 14 percent for males v.s. 2 to 5 percent for females. This increases the proportion of males to females in these age groups.

Although the proportion of males to females improved with undercount estimates, Hogan and Robinson (unpublished), note some limitations of the DA estimates. One is that assumptions go into the undercount estimation process, some of which can be validated and some of which cannot. The accuracy of these estimates also depends on the quality of the data and the corrections. Research by Hogan and Robinson shows that "net undercount for particular race, sex or age groups based on DA may be subject to considerable uncertainty for measuring exact levels" (p. 5). In addition, demographic estimates for race, sex, and age groups only measure net undercount and tell us nothing about the separate effects of *net coverage error*, which is the difference between those missed and those counted in error, and *content error*, which is the difference between those not placed in the correct category. Despite these limitations, there has been a decline in the undercount rate over the past 50 years (except for the 1990 undercount rate, which was higher than 1980 for all groups). The differential undercount for decennial census from 1940 to 1990 between African American and nonAfrican Americans has ranged relatively consistently, as seen in Table 2, between 3.4 and 4.4 percent.

Although including the undercount shows that there may be more males than reported by the Census, there are other data that show evidence of a sex ratio imbalance between African American males and females. An example of this can be seen for a more recent year in which the most complete data were found – 1996.

104

Table 6

Demographic Analysis Estimates of African American Male and female Undercount by Age: 1990

| Age | Male | | | | Female | | | |
---	Census	Corrected	Revised Net Undercount Amount	Percent	Census	Corrected	Revised Net Undercount Amount	Percent
All Ages	14,420,331	15,758,711	1,338,380	8.49	16,062,950	6,560,842	497,892	3.01
0-4	1,486,287	1,626,259	139,972	8.61	1,453,109	1,582,560	129,451	8.18
5-9	1,371,538	1,485,877	114,339	7.70	1,339,798	1,448,090	18,292	7.48
10-14	1,328,261	1,385,644	57,383	4.14	1,301,212	1,356,088	54,876	4.05
15-19	1,370,304	1,368,147	(2,157)	- 0.16	1,343,940	1,349,463	5,523	0.41
20-24	1,299,074	1,377,297	78,223	5.68	1,355,862	1,390,199	34,773	2.47
25-29	1,322,573	1,514,692	192,119	12.68	1,456,996	1,532,001	75,005	4.90
30-34	1,269,916	1,476,872	206,956	14.01	1,447,773	1,500,057	52,284	3.49
35-39	1,094,253	1,242,390	148,137	11.92	1,265,095	1,293,755	28,660	2.22
40-44	867,892	970,459	102,567	10.57	1,013,737	1,029,126	15,389	1.50

Table 6 (continued)

Age	Male Census	Male Revised Net Undercount Corrected	Amount	Percent	Female Census	Female Revised Net Undercount Corrected	Amount	Percent
45-49	644,853	732,195	87,342	11.93	768,419	787,189	18,770	2.38
50-54	530,296	602,458	72,162	11.98	647,223	657,513	10,290	1.56
55-59	460,001	523,303	63,302	12.10	580,888	580,944	56	0.01
60-64	418,147	466,209	48,062	10.31	553,613	538,143	(15,470)	-2.87
65-69	360,653	368,530	7,877	2.14	499,041	463,239	(35,802)	-7.73
70-74	252,967	263,823	10,856	4.11	385,110	371,163	(13,947)	-3.76
75-79	178,695	176,467	(2,228)	-1.26	304,840	294,902	(9,938)	-3.37
80-84	98,351	103,016	4,665	4.53	189,932	199,667	(9,735)	4.88
85+	66,270	75,073	8,803	11.73	156,362	186,743	(30,381)	16.27

Source: Source: *Journal of the American Statistical Association*, Estimation of Population Coverage in the 1990 US, Sept. 1993, Appendix, Table 2.

First, looking at the Census counts for that year, as shown in Table 7, there were approximately 1.6 million more African American females than males, including those overseas. For the resident population there were approximately 1.7 million more females than males. If the 1990 undercount was added, there were still approximately 870,000 more females to males. If one examines the difference between females and males for the civilian noninstitutional population, plus the armed forces in the U.S., there were approximately 2.3 million more females than males.

Table 7
African American Estimated Population, 1996

Population	Male	Female	Difference
Total Population Including			
Armed forces overseas	15,980,000	17,656,000	1,676,000
Resident Population	15,932,000	17,644,000	1,712,000
plus 1990 net undercount	17,270,380	18,141,892	871,512
Civilian Population	15,736,000	17,594,000	1,858,000
Civilian non-institutional			
population plus Armed			
Forces in the United States	15,042,000	17,429,000	2,387,000
plus 1990 net undercount	16,380,380	17,926,892	1,546,512

Source: U.S. Bureau of the Census, 1997; U.S. Population Estimates by Age, Sex, Race and Hispanic Origin, PPL-57 Rev, Appendices A-D

With the net undercount, there were still approximately 1.5 more million females than males for the noninstitutional resident population. Also, for 1996, as shown in Table 8, the sex ratio of males to females, was 90 to 100. In the 25-34 age group it was 90 to 100 and close to 80 to 100 for those in the 35-44 age group.

Table 8

African American Estimated Resident Population by Sex and Age, 1996

Age	Male	Female	Sex Ratio
Total	15,001,000	16,658,000	0.90
Under 5	1,567,000	1,525,000	1.03
5-14	3,045,000	2,955,000	1.03
15-24	2,739,000	2,735,000	1.00
25-34	2,563,000	2,850,000	0.90
35-44	2,473,000	2,822,000	0.87
45-54	1,238,000	1,857,000	0.67
55-64	936,000	1,217,000	0.77
65-74	671,000	950,000	0.70
85 years & over	81,000	201,000	0.40

Source: U.S. Census Bureau, March, 1997; U.S. Population Estimates by Age, Sex, Race and Hispanic Origin, PPL-57 Rev, Appendix A-D

By looking at data outside of that reported by the Census, one can see evidence of a numerical disparity. First, is the number of males who are institutionalized in correctional facilities. There were an estimated 773,900 African American adults in prison or jail in 1996. For those under the jurisdiction of a federal or state penitentiary, as shown in Table 9, an estimated 528,200 African American males were in prison, compared with only 33,900 females. Viewing this for 100,000 per resident population, the figures are astounding. There were 3,098 African American males imprisoned per 100,000 resident population, compared with 188 females incarcerated. Noteworthy also are the disproportionate number of African American males, 3,098, incarcerated per 100,000 residents, compared with 370 incarcerated white males. These figures also reflect the number of males and females under federal and state jurisdiction for a sentence of a year or more.

Table 9

Number of Prisoners per 100,000 Residents Under State or Federal Jurisdiction, 1996

| | African American | | White | |
	Male	Female	Male	Female
Sentenced Prisoners	528,200	33,900	510,900	33,800
Per 100,0000 resident population	3,098	188	370	23

Source: Bureau of Justice Statistics, Correctional Populations in the United States, 1996, pp. 4, 5.

As can be seen in Table 10, the number of males to females is substantially high. For the age group 25-34, a combined 15,059 males to 1,012 females were under jurisdiction; for those in the age group 35-44, a combined 11,425 males to 844 females were under state or federal jurisdiction.

Table 10

Number of Sentenced Prisoners Under State or Federal Jurisdiction for Over a Year by Age, Sex and Race, 1996

| | African American | | White | |
Age	Male	Female	Male	Female
Total	3,098	188	370	23
18-19	2,615	74	263	17
20-24	6,740	203	762	35
25-29	8,319	415	829	54
30-34	7,052	597	862	73
35-39	6,601	518	759	61
40-44	4,824	326	606	38
45-54	2,768	161	380	20
55 or older	505	18	96	3

Source: Bureau of Justice Statistics, Correctional Populations in the United States, 1996, p. 5.

Although the numbers were substantially smaller in previous years, as indicated in Table 11, a ratio imbalance of African American males to females incarcerated have remained constant from the period of 1980 to 1996. Thus, it appears that if all of the males who were imprisoned in the year 1996 were released in the next year, considering the ratio over this period of time, close to that number would still be incarcerated, thereby decreasing the number of males available to females overall.

Table 11

Number of African American Prisoners Under State or Federal Jurisdiction, by Sex 1980-1995

Year	Male	Female	Ratio
1980	140,600	6,300	22.32
1981	156,100	7,200	21.68
1982	174,900	8,200	21.33
1983	185,900	8,500	21.87
1984	194,600	9,400	20.70
1985	210,500	10,200	20.64
1986	232,000	11,800	19.66
1987	249,700	12,600	19.82
1988	274,300	14,200	19.32
1989	313,700	18,300	17.14
1990	340,300	19,700	17.27
1991	366,500	22,000	16.66
1992	393,700	23,600	16.68
1993	434,900	27,300	15.93
1994	474,800	30,200	15.72
1995	509,800	31,900	15.98
1996	528,200	33,900	15.58

Source: Bureau of Justice Statistics, Correctional Populations in the United States, 1993, p. 8; 1996, p. 4

Another factor indicating the lower ratio of males to females is the death rate. As shown in Table 12, the death rate per 100,000 residents was higher for all causes for African American males for the nation's leading causes of death in 1996. Though not indicated in the table, because they were not a leading cause of death for the entire population, African American males died disproportionately more from causes due to homicide and legal intervention, which was the 5th cause of death, and conditions originating in the perinatal period, which was the 10th cause of death for them. Diseases related to HIV infection was 65 per 100,000, more than triple that of all other groups, and was the 4th cause of death for African American males.

Table 12

Rates for Ten Leading Causes of Death by Race and Sex, 1996

| Cause | African American | | White | |
	Male	Female	Male	Female
All Causes	939.9	753.5	918.1	896.2
Diseases of the heart	234.8	229.0	293.3	294.2
Malignant neoplasms	207.3	157.9	225.8	201.8
Cerebrovascular diseases	50.1	59.7	49.1	76.3
Chronic obstructive pulmonary diseases	24.7	17.0	46.1	43.0
Accidents & adverse effects	24.3	22.8	41.9	16.1
Pneumonia and influenza	26.2	21.6	30.5	36.9
Diabetes mellitus	26.0	37.9	21.1	23.9
Human immunodeficiency virus infection	65.0	20.8	13.6	**
Suicide	**	**	20.9	**
Chronic liver diseases	**	**	12.6	**

Source: Center for Disease Control and Prevention, National Center for Health Statistics; *National Vital Statistics Report*, Volume 47, Number 9; Deaths: Final Data for 1996, pp. 30-33.
** Died from a disease other than one of the ten leading causes of death.

As indicated in Table 13, 16,855 more African American males died than females in 1996. The number of deaths for African American males in age group 15-24 was more than triple that of females. For those of marriageable age, 25-44, approximately 24,894 African American males died compared with 13,334 females. The number of deaths for African American males was more than females for every age group except the over 65, where approximately 14,233 more African American females died. Because the life expectancy for males is approximately 66 years compared with that of females, which is approximately 74 years, a disproportionate number of males die earlier. This may account for the disproportionate number of females who die in the later years.

Table 13
African American Deaths for all Causes by Sex and Age, 1996

Age	Male	Female	Difference
Total	149,472	132,617	16,855
1-4	869	754	115
5-14	1,160	764	396
15-24	6,422	1,830	4,592
25-44	24,894	13,334	11,560
45-64	40,835	27,395	13,440
65 years and over	70,374	84,607	-14,233

Source: Source: Center for Disease Control and Prevention, National Center for Health Statistics; *National Vital Statistics Report.*,Volume 47, Number 9; Deaths: Final Data for 1996, pp. 34-36.

The disproportionate number of African American males who die annually has also been consistent. As shown in Table 14, the number of deaths of African American males has ranged from between approximately 22,000 to 27,000 annually from 1980 to 1995.

Another indication of the number of African American males unavailable for African American females is interracial marriage. In 1996, interracial marriages only accounted for an estimated 2 percent of all marriages. Of all interracial marriages, an estimated 30 percent included an African American spouse. As shown in Table 15, of the 337,000 African American/ white marriages in 1996, 220,000 comprised African American male/white female, compared with 117,000 African American female/white male. Although the number of African American females marrying interracially is increasing, it is still small by comparison with males.

Table 14

Number of Deaths and Ratio of African Americans Males to Females by Sex, 1980-1996

Year	Males	Females	Difference
1995	154,175	132,226	21,949
1994	153,019	129,360	23,659
1993	153,502	128,649	24,853
1992	146,630	122,589	24,041
1991	147,331	122,194	25.137
1990	145,359	120,139	25,220
1989	146,393	121,249	25,144
1988	144,228	119,791	24,437
1987	139,551	115,263	24,288
1986	137,214	113,112	24,102
1985	133,610	110,597	23,013
1984	129,147	106,737	22,410
1983	127,911	105,213	22,698
1982	125,610	100,903	24,707
1981	127,296	101,264	26,032
1980	130,138	102,997	27,141

Source: Center for Disease Control and Prevention, National Center for Health Statistics; *National Vital Statistics Report.*,Volume 47, Number 9; Deaths: Final Data for 1996, p. 16.

Table 15 also shows the gap has been relatively consistent from 1960 to the present, although fluctuating in the years between. The low number of interracial marriages indicates that most individuals marry within their own race. The number of African American females who marry other races, especially by comparison to males, may indicate that a majority prefer a man in their own race.

Table 15
Interracial Married Couples with an African American Spouse

	Total	Husband/ White Wife	Wife/ White Husband	Husband or Wife/ Other Racial
Year				
1996	337,000	220,000	117,000	39,000
1990	213,000	159,000	54,000	75,000
1980	121,000	94,000	27,000	47,000
1970	65,000	41,000	24,000	12,000
1960	51,000	25,000	26,000	7,000

Source: U.S. Bureau of the Census, Current Population Reports, Series P20-514, March 1998 (Update), Table: MS-3, Interracial Married Couples: 1960 to Present http://www.census.gov/population/socdemo/ms-la/tabms-3.txt.

Another factor decreasing the number of African American males available to females is homosexuality. Because the Census Bureau does not include a question on sexual orientation, it is difficult to gauge the number of African American males who have a preference for and are choosing other males only for mates. In the past, to escape the stigma of being labeled homosexual, many had relationships with women, married, and maintained families. Some opted to not act on their orientation to the same sex, and others had "closet" relationships and maintained double lives through bisexuality. In contemporary times, American society has become more open to gay and lesbian relationships, and it appears more are choosing to live a gay lifestyle. Interestingly, when males form relationships with other males, it results in two or more (depending on how many) being depleted from the number available to females.

Females may also opt for a gay lifestyle. If they do to the same degree as African American males, this might have some implication for the number competing for the available males. What is important to note, however, is that the shortage of males

114

may be a motivating factor for females to seek same-sex relationships. Overall, the unavailability of males because of homosexuality combined with all the other factors makes the competition for females who are strictly heterosexual (meaning they are not oriented to the same sex, nor do they wish to have intimate relationships with members of the same sex) even more competitive.

Employment also impacts on the marriageability or desirability of males. As indicated in Table 16, although the employment participation rate of African American males was higher than females in 1996, there were more females overall in the labor force, approximately 706,000. Thus, there were more females who were employed, approximately 6.8 million compared to 6.2 million males. Also, although the unemployment rate for females was higher than it was for males, again, there were still more females in the labor force than males.

Table 16
Employment by Race and Sex for Those over 20 Years of Age, 1996

| | African American | | White American | |
	Males	Females	Males	Females
Civilian labor force	16,838	17,544	58,623	48,686
Participation rate	(72%)	(63.3%)	(77.4%)	(59.9%)
Employed	6,235	6,851	56,356	46,614
Employment-population ratio	(65.7)	(57.5)	(74.4)	(57.3)
Unemployed	598	693	2,267	2,072
Unemployment rate	(8.8%)	(9.2%)	(3.9%)	(4.3%)

[1]In Millions
Source: Labor Force Statistics from the *Current Population Survey*, December, 1996
http://stats.bls.gov/news.release/empsit.t02.htm[1997].

Thus, for that year, in addition to a surplus of approximately 2.3 million (1.5 if the undercount were added) females in the residential, noninstitutional population, approximately 598,000 African American males over age 20 were unemployed. This does not include the numerous males who are not even looking for work. Note that the estimates given for those employed may not be a true indication of those *gainfully* employed, considering that those who are involuntarily stuck in part-time jobs and who experience sporadic unemployment due to short-term work are also counted. Thus, if males are employed, but not gainfully so, it may detract from the their desirability and consequent marriageability. By contrast, a female's under- or unemployment status may not detract from her desirability in the same way it does a male, because a primary role prescribed for a man in American society is still that of breadwinner, while for a woman it is still acceptable to be a homemaker.

Another factor is the disproportionate number of males who are drug and/or alcohol dependent. The data that would help to determine the proportion of males to females who experience such problems is limited. Through observation alone, it appears that problems of this nature are disproportionately experienced by males.

Impact of the Male Shortage on Relationships and Families

In summary, for the year 1996, with the DA undercount added back to the population, there were still approximately 1.5 million more females than males among the civilian noninstitutional population and those in the military in the United States. If one is still doubtful of these figures, the fact that the undercount has been relatively consistent over the past decades might be taken into consideration. But regardless of whether counts from the Census Bureau are close to accurate, what cannot be ignored is the number of African American males in proportion to females that are depleted from the population through incarceration. Again, for 1996, there were approximately 528,200 males incarcerated compared with 33,900 females, which means that there were approximately 470,990 more males than females unavailable for marriage, or if already married, could not play a significant role in the lives of their mates.

These numbers still do not include those who are in jail, which if added to these figures makes the proportion of men who are potentially unavailable higher. For example, the number of adult African American males held in state or federal prisons and local jails was 711,600 compared with 55,300 females in 1996. The implications for employability of those who have been in the criminal justice system and on parole or probation are relevant to their marriageability. These figures, added to the proportion of males relative to females who die prematurely, also decrease the number of males who are available. As indicated previously, for 1996, approximately 149,472 males died, which was 16,855 more than the number of females who died. This annual difference has been consistent from 1980 to 1996. The disproportionate numbers of those who are incarcerated, those who die prematurely, and those who marry interracially, added to those who live a gay lifestyle are evidence of a numerical shortage, regardless of Census Bureau data. The numerical shortage combined with those who may be undesirable because they are either unable to maintain stable and reliable employment, are emotionally unstable, and/or addicted to drugs and alcohol, further decrease the number of marriageable males available to females. Thus, with regard to the question of whether there is a shortage of males, I think the data indicate that there is.

With regard to the question of the impact of the shortage on African American male-female relationship, these demographics result in a surplus of African American females, and create a situation where they must compete for a limited number of males. African American women, as women have done historically, gravitate to economically and emotionally stable men. Because the number of African American men who fit this profile is limited, the situation may lead women into polygynous formations with men of three kind: (1) unmarried, marriageable men who because of the numerical disproportion of males to females *will not commit* to an exclusive relationship with one woman; (2) married men who because of their married status *cannot commit* to an exclusive

117

relationship with "another" woman; and (3) unmarriageable men who may have extraordinary physical or personality attributes but because of their precarious economic status feel *less than adequate to commit* to an exclusive relationship with one woman.

This low ratio of males to females has implications not only for African American male-female relationships, but also for marriages and families. In an early study, "Polygamy: A Futuristic Family Arrangement for African Americans," Joseph Scott (1976) projected that because of the sex imbalance, female-maintained households would be one of two dominant family patterns, the other one being two-parent families (p. 14). This, he argued would impact on two-parent families, particularly in urban communities, because single women outnumber males so greatly, they "would feel little hesitation about trying to attract the husbands of other women and establishing social-sexual and even conjugal-type relationships with them" (p. 14). Two-parent families would be further impacted when women "rather than accept the option of being (childless) simply for the lack of a legal mate, has children" (p. 14).

In his study, Scott interviewed women who had been in relationships with men who were already married or in relationships for the past five years. An important finding is that the women reported that "finding available men 'free and clear' was infrequent" (p. 17). Considering the current ratio between African American males and females, one can only suspect that this is still the case. Scott further projected:

The one-parent family ever increasing the way it is will, I believe, create greater pressure for polygamous type relationships. . . . What today are called broken homes may in fact be polygamous-type families wherein the men are part-time members of the household, but nevertheless emotionally, financially and sexually integrated with them in an organic way. (p. 19)

Finally, Scott asserts with regard to the impact of one-parent families on two-parent families, "The question for the future is not whether they will have to co-exist, but rather how they can co-exist in peace" (p. 17). Considering this, the question one might then ask is not whether polygynous relationship and family formations are an alternative. They already are. The question is how can we construct these relationship and family formations in ways that are beneficial to women, children, men, families, communities, and the African American world as a whole.

Chapter 6

ILLEGANY: WHY MEN ENGAGE IN MULTIPLE RELATIONSHIPS

In his book *Black Men: Obsolete, Single, Dangerous?* Haki Madhubuti (1990) describes "illegany," which he also refers to as the "ball game" in the following manner:

The male is on home plate and has women on first, second and third. . . The male in this arrangement is busy running bases trying to service and control as many women as he can, and responsibility to the "real" needs of these women and their children is not even a part of the equation. (p. 97)

In many instances under this arrangement, the women will have some knowledge of each other but never discuss it "due to deep patriarchal holds most men have on their mates" (p. 97). Some of the most prevalent elements of illegany according to Madhubuti are:

- It is underground, which means that knowledge of affairs is restricted to a few of the male's friends, while the women may undergo a great deal of pressure from other women (some of who are involved in similar situations) for participating in such an arrangement;
- women generally support themselves and sometimes contribute to the male's support, while males contribute little if any to their financial support;
- males have irregular visiting schedules, but usually show up at least once a week and sometimes unexpectedly to keep the women off guard;
- time the male spends with the female is basically sexual;
- these relationships are short-term unless children are involved and in instances in which they are involved, they are considered illegitimate;
- there are few, if any, social pressures on males to become more responsible. (p. 97-98)

120

This arrangement, in which men, single, married, separated and divorced participate, Madhubuti contends, ". . . is becoming the dominant Black male/female social arrangement in the country"(p.97).

Considering the economic status of a large segment of the African American male population and the social milieu shaping the attitudes and approach of some to relationships with women, the description of illegany provided by Madhubuti may indeed describe the form that many African American relationships take, if they last long enough to be called that. Also, considering the decreasing marriage rates among African Americans, Madhubuti's assertion that these types of relationships are becoming the dominant male-female arrangement is more than likely an accurate assessment of the situation.

In light of what Madhubuti has described here, I was interested in finding out what motivates males to engage in multiple relationships. I therefore interviewed 40 men from different parts of the country, but now residing primarily in Atlanta and Washington, D.C., from among friends, acquaintances, and referrals. Included in this chapter also, are responses from another 61 African American males to a survey that was conducted through African American newspapers, organizations, and in African American studies courses. Overall, there were a total of 101 participants.

Ranging in age from 19 to 59 with a mean of 31 years, 92 percent of the participants had attended college. Approximately 51 percent had no degree, but about 75 percent of them were currently enrolled in college. Six percent had an associate degree, 29 percent had bachelor degrees, and 15 percent had a masters or professional degree. All of the participants were either employed, 70 percent, or in school only, 15 percent, and approximately 14 percent were self-employed. Approximately 21 percent were married, 58 percent were single, 4 percent were separated, 12 percent were divorced, and 1 percent was widowed.

The men who were interviewed were asked why they think men engage in multiple relationships, whether the men they know do so, and whether they do it themselves. The questionnaire used in the survey asked the participants to respond to the first question only. With regard to the question of why men engage in multiple relationships simultaneously, there were several responses. The most common were it's natural, peer pressure, variety, ego, and sex. Although these were the most common reasons, sex was an overarching response. For example, when most discussed variety, it seemed to indicate sexual variety. With respect to ego, the motive appeared to stem from the need for sexual conquest. Some of the men also indicated that a primary partner was not providing their sexual needs.

A few participants indicated that they believe African American men engage in multiple relationships because of psychological problems related to: identity and distrust; hurt feelings in a past relationship; avoidance of loneliness; or compensation for inadequacy in providing for a family. Others believe it happens because of excess women to men in the population. There were a few who see it as a spiritual need — the male's need for completion.

When asked whether their friends engage in multiple relationships, all the interviewees said they do or have done so. As for themselves, most indicated that they have done so in the past but do not do so currently. I speculate that some still do and believe the question was answered in this way because I am female.

It's Natural

~"*When God created man he placed in him the desire*
. . . and gave him an appetite. To go against it
is to go against nature."~

As already indicated, several of the participants believe it to be natural for men to engage in multiple relationships. It is believed to be "biblical" and inherited from African forefathers. One interviewee, for example, explained, "It's in our blood to have multiple wives. A lot of it is genetics, and it's passed down like other things are passed down from Solomon, David, Abraham." It was also described as part of the "collective consciousness"of African American men, something that is "culturally or ethnically encoded" and "justified by nature [because] there are more women

122

than there are men." In addition, engaging in relationships with multiple women was described as being "instinctual," "being a man," and as a drive that is in all men. One stated, for example, "Even [for] those who don't mess around, it's there. They just don't pursue it." Finally, according to some of the participants, "It's harder for most men not to have more than one woman," because "when God created man he placed in him the desire . . . and gave him an appetite. To go against it is to go against nature."

Peer Pressure

~"If you say you don't do it, some ask',
'Why not, what's wrong?'" ~

Peer pressure is another reason participants gave for what motivates men to engage in multiple relationships. Although monogamy is the only relationship that is given legal, moral, and social sanction in U.S. society, a major contradiction is that engaging in multiple relationships is acceptable for men, among men. Those who are able to win the affection of several women are held in high esteem by other men. A 40-year old self-employed legal specialist explained, "Peers are judged by popularity. Popularity is judged by how many women you can be with. . . .The more women you have, the more popular you become to your peers." Because popularity among peers is also tied to leadership, the man with the most women, according to this participant, becomes the "leader of the pack." Having several women is expected among peers according to a 41-year old entrepreneur: "When guys get together and talk 'smack,' if you say you don't do it, some ask, 'Why not, what's wrong?'" How one responds to peer pressure, however, may depend on where one is in the life cycle. This participant explained:

I didn't know any better. I was younger, just following the crowd. I was going along with peers. Men think it's okay. I think it is a macho thing. They think that's what a man should do. . . .As you get older, you get more control. Age makes a difference. One, because you are more independent, you can take the pressure of your peers as you mature . . . .

After thirty-five, you don't have to go along with the program; . . . you can shake it. It is a fight. I used to fight all the time. E and them, they used to be mad at me.

When one interviewee was asked whether men still think like this when married, he explained that the peers they "hang around with" after they are married are the same ones they hung around with prior to that. Generally, their values or perspectives do not change, and men are still under pressure from their peers to engage in relations with multiple women.

Making the transition from engaging in multiple relationships while single to being monogamous when married factors into the struggle for some men to remain faithful after they are married. One interviewee explained:

Fathers don't tell their sons to be loving or caring or stay celibate until you're married. Men are taught to be players. But later you are taught that you are supposed to be truthful to one woman. How are men supposed to suddenly turn that way? These are conflicting messages from society that confuse men. You grow up feeding your ego on these type of challenges. Once you get married, it's like someone pulls a rug from under you.

Ego

Ego is another factor interviewees identified as to why men engage in multiple relationships. The phrases used to describe ego involvement included: "a power thing," "the challenge of conquest," "the hunger to feed your ego," and "a powerful drug." When a 52-year old construction claims consultant was asked why he thinks men engage in multiple relationships, he cited variety and ego. "Ego. Because you can do it. It is the same thing if you are going out to a night club and men hit on you. Men take it further—they take her to bed." It is the "ultimate stroke of ego,"

. . . even more of an ego booster, if the woman allows him to sleep with her when he already has a wife or someone else . . . .Most women don't deal with men if they have someone, not if he tells her right up front. If you can tell someone from the very beginning, "I have someone," that is

124

major in terms of stroking the ego, if she is willing to accept a small amount of your time to be with you.

Variety

~*"It's like having pizza one day, lasagna the next day, and crab cake the next day."*~

Variety was also given as a reason that men engage in multiple relations. A 31-year old college professor explained it like this:

You know, it's like having pizza one day, lasagna the next day, and crab cake the next day. You know you're having a variety of different experiences. You may be with a light-skinned sister one day . . . a dark-skinned sister the next day, a brown-skin sister the next day; just a variety of different women, different personalities, different levels of intelligence, different aspirations, different goals, it's just different.

Variety seems to go hand-in-hand with the perception that no one woman can satisfy a man's various needs. "One woman cannot satisfy me"; "No one woman can give me what I need"; "At times there is something one can give you that the other can't or won't"; were a few of their comments. One man said, "A man has needs, and he looks for a woman to satisfy each and every one of them. You need one to show off to your friends, one to satisfy the intellect, one to be a freak that will do anything you want— fulfill your sexual needs and fantasies. Then you want one to be your nice little woman to come home to." Others affirmed this attitude: "If one won't provide you what you need at the time, you will look for some who will." When a 36-year old, self-employed mortgage banker was asked why men engage in multiple relationships, he replied, "They ain't happy at home. The wife is a nag. She makes all these demands. It helps to forget about the woman until you go home." The need for variety is also a factor, as according to him, "Variety makes for the spice of life." He also drew a parallel with forefathers from Africa and observed that white men try to prohibit multiple wives as a way to control: "Back in the day, in Africa, you could have as many wives as you could afford. White men designed it to keep us in check. That's why I have ten children. And I take care of my business."

Women's beauty contributes to the desire for variety. A 44-year old lawyer put it succinctly, "You see, some women are just stunning. You want to be with them." A 37-year old college professor explained, "I just have big eyes. Black women are so beautiful. I have a weakness for [them]. I'm trying to work on my stuff. It's not like I'm being disrespectful. It's just like so many of them . . . You just like people for different reasons."

For men entering into middle-age, it is, according to one 40-year old interviewee, about the "quest for the ultimate woman." He explained that when a man is younger, it is about sex. When he gets older, it's about finding a woman who is possessed with what he described as the "five basics": "beauty, shelter, education, employment, and transportation." The problem is that once he gets the ultimate woman (which most are unable to get, although some come close to it), he then get's caught. This means that he "must turn in his license" and do what is necessary so that another man does not take her, and he gets his heart broken. In addition, when men go through several women during their formative years, they acquire certain skills or have "class A" experience to assure themselves that once they get the ultimate woman or something close to her, they are able "to keep her," and ensure that no man will have the power to pull her away.

Sex

~"It will take a breathtaking experience for a
woman to totally captivate a man."~

Sex was the most common reason participants gave for why men engage in multiple relationships. Some were straight and to the point about this. It was said to be "just for that orgasm," "to bust that nut . . . when she [the wife] is on the cycle — something better to do"; "because we like a variety of pussy, the key word is fucking." It is also not just sex but sexual variety. One interviewee explained, "It keeps your sex drive alive. There are but so many positions with one woman. It keeps it more interesting at home

126

because you have an outside interest." He compared the experience to driving cars: "If you enjoy driving the same car, it becomes boring. If you drive the same car, you know the car, whereas, if you are driving different ones, it keeps it interesting. If I have two, I appreciate both a little more."

A 38-year old self-employed government contractor compared sexual variety to candy: "It's like being in a candy store — she's tall, she has pretty feet, but in the same instance he may see someone just the opposite and lust for [her]." In addition, according to this interviewee, there is the excitement of different responses from women during sexual intercourse. He explained: "Making love to the woman the very first time is an experience that is unbelievable, because a man does not know if she is going to moan, scream, sigh, hold him tight, or simply just whisper in his ear." There is also the desire to please women sexually because of the sense of control it gives. This interviewee continued: "It's really knowing you have this human being and are going to give her all this pleasure. A man knows when he makes her feel this that he is in control." He then asked, "Can you imagine making love to 10, 15, or 20 different women and getting that fantasy of the excitement when you penetrate her?" However, according to him, "after the man has reached his climax, his love, his fascination, the splendor of being between her legs, all leave after he comes."

The availability of women, stemming from the demographic disparity between African American men and women, makes it easy for men to satisfy their need for sexual variety. A 39-year old deputy observed, "It's there and not only is it available and different, it's exciting. Every woman offers a new challenge, new feeling, a new chemistry." When asked about his friends, he claimed that all men do it, "Every last one, married and single, priest and monks." With regard to commitment, he said, "Men won't commit because there is too much to pick from. . . . There are women coming around because they need men . . . There are so many needy women. We find pleasure in being with them physically." Furthermore, he contended, "Black women want us. White women want us. Women want us, period. It will take a breathtaking experience for a woman to totally captivate a man. The saying — a dime a dozen — that is what it is now."

The Need to Feel Loved and Needed

~ *"Most men would not be looking for M[s] Goodbar if he's getting satisfaction in the bedroom."* ~

For some men not having their sexual needs met by a primary mate is a major factor in why they seek sexual relations with other women. One man put it succinctly, "Most men would not be like looking for M[s] Goodbar if he's getting satisfaction in the bedroom." However, behaviors stemming from early childhood experiences may also factor in. A 32-years old male indicated that his parents did not know how to show love when he was a child, so he sought it outside the family. He explained: "My mother and father were orphans, and they were kids trying to have a family. They wanted to give love, but they were not old enough to know how to give love. So we sought love somewhere else." Now, as in his early years, when he does not receive sex from his wife, he seeks it elsewhere. He continued: "My wife is cold, and she doesn't like sex. When we first started dating, we used to fuck like rabbits. We fucked everyday. After she had our daughter, she went cold. She's just not interested in sex. I become intimately involved with women outside of my marriage because I have a lot of love to give and share. So I share it with other women." The problem, however, is "that women fall so deeply in love that they can't handle it. This creates problems in trying to juggle them." He explained, "One girl tried to commit suicide on me twice."

A 41-year old self-employed business consultant said, "Some men are just a 'ho'; they gotta have more than one woman cuz they are whorish." It is also because "they don't get enough attention at home. . . .They go to other women because they are not being served; whether it is breakfast in the morning or dinner." He emphasized the significance of small things to make a man feel satisfied at home and made a distinction between the willingness of professional and nonprofessional women to provide these things. He states, a man "needs a woman on the side to do the little things. Professional women don't do the little things. The women who are not professional do more. The more money they make and the higher their status, the less they give a shit." Although he

128

prefers a monogamous relationship, when I asked if he would go outside of his primary relationship, he admitted: "Maybe, to keep from being lonely at times. To get attention, to relax, to feel comfortable. Sometimes you can't feel comfortable at home." He discussed the importance of finding a comfort zone, particularly because of the tremendous stress African American men are under. If the primary mate will not provide it, most men will find someone who will:

Black men experience stress whether it is working a 9-5 or being an entrepreneur. There's pressure, pressure dating, pressure affording to take a woman to lunch. It ain't nothing but pressure. Sometimes he needs to go somewhere so he can be pampered. No matter how clever he is, no matter how successful, no matter how strong he is, he needs to go somewhere where he can be weak; somewhere he can let his guard down and not be threatened. . . .The more successful he is, the more he needs it. The rest of the world doesn't see it, but he has to find a nest where that can take place. He has to. So what he tries to do is to position himself so he can let his guard down. . . .He needs this to be available whether it is the one he is with or the one he has to get.

A 42-year old marketing director indicated that married men often have extramarital affairs because their sexual needs are not being met. He observed, however, that it may be because many men do not share household and child care responsibilities. Thus, rather than relieving their wives, they seek to have their needs met with other women.

The ones that I know that have extramarital affairs, usually it happens after they have kids. A lot of men don't play the father role; they only provide. The other needs are being met by women—cooking, cleaning, taking care of the children. By the evening, the man's's rested, and he wants to have sex. So he'll go out to have someone on the side to meet his needs.

Seeking a woman outside marriage is related to the ways men have been socialized to support women and to the need for control. This interviewee continued:

The wife may want some of the burdens to be shared. This is what she needs. He may not want to give this kind of help. He wants to help out in the traditional way. In the marriage, she may not want to have sex because of resentment from not having shared responsibilities. It may create a communications barrier. . . .Most of the time, when men go after someone that's not their mate, they are less attractive [and] have less going for them. He [then has] more control to use the money to help out, taking her around, taking her out, doing financial things to make up for not being there on holidays. If the person is struggling, this is the controlling aspect of it. The person is going to spend time with you, have sex with you. You are able to help someone out that is not in the position to be self-sufficient. The gap is pretty big. They're struggling on their own. If they are doing something that's marginal, they'll say I can get better.

A wife may accept it, according to him, "If she doesn't have high self-esteem, or she values the family and don't want to leave and break up the family, she'll stay, knowing. If he's discreet, she'll be able to accept it more; if he's discreet enough to not do it with someone she knows." Unfortunately, according to this interviewee, many men usually get into affairs with someone the wife knows, a girlfriend, or someone at the office." He also described an affair he had himself.

In eleven years I had one affair. It was a sexual need. It was just to the point where my wife and I weren't having sex, right after the child. I had heard that after childbirth, a woman's sex desire diminishes. It lasted for fifteen months. It complicated things. My wife knew about it. She sensed it; I denied it.

When I asked why the affair ended, he explained: "I would see my home, my wife, and son. After a while the sex got better." With regard to his mistress, he claimed, "I loved them both. I was able to meet both their needs sexually and financially, but I was not emotionally involved. I realized I had a real good family, home, job; why was I going outside the home? I just ended up breaking it off."

Several men discussed the constant struggle involved in remaining committed to their marriage. One explained:

In my current marriage, I miss the freedom. You can't engage in an outside relationship without it potentially having a devastating effect on your life. It's male instinct. You have to control it. There are women attracted to me. If they catch you at a weak moment, but it's a constant battle in terms of not allowing yourself to become attracted, or allowing someone attracted to you to allow it to go anywhere. There is nothing wrong with having female friends, but you may be putting yourself in the position for it to happen. Don't allow yourself to be put in the position where it can potentially have problems. That is why a lot of married men don't go out by themselves. Sometimes it just happens.

A 51-year old self-employed medical broker summed it up: "Seventy percent of men mess around. The other thirty percent are spending most of their time trying to figure out how not to mess around. It's almost like a joke when a guy says, 'I'm one-on-one with my wife.' Most that are one-on-one are miserable."

Temptation from Women

~"*Men aren't the only ones being doggy*"~

Some married men have extramarital affairs because women pursue them although they know that they are married. A 36-year old maintenance supervisor claimed, "A lot of women will push a man to the limit. If a woman presents it, I'm a man, I'm taking it. If you want me to fuck you, I will, even though I'm married. When I was single, I had less women coming to me. Now that I am married, I get more 'play.'" Another interviewee said:

Women always say that men are fucked up. But who do we mess around with? When I was married, women hit on me all the time. Black women have utterly no respect for each other. Women always say that men are dogs, but who do we mess around with? Dogs come in two genders. Men aren't the only ones being doggy. We have to have someone to be doggish with. Usually when a man is married, he lets the outside woman know. And she's willing to go along with it.

Another man described an incident where a woman tried to "hit" on him, even while his wife was present. He explained, "I was at a function. There was a familiar face. She kept looking at me. Then she gave me her card when my wife was not looking." He further discussed how the numerical disparities between African American women and men contribute to this. "In areas like D.C. and Atlanta, where you have a lot of women, where the ratio of women to men is higher, women are only going to be lonely for so long. No one enjoys being lonely. So they stoop to or settle for someone who has someone." When asked if he had ever been unfaithful, he described an experience:

I got weak for a moment. She wanted a relationship, but my conscience would not allow me. She had just moved in town. She didn't know many people. We were out, and it just happened. We met at Mr. C's. She invited me over. It didn't happen that night. It could of happened. We were rubbing up against each other. And I went back over there a couple of days later and "it" was ready. I left "it" in the oven when I left, and "it" was still hot when I got back.

This man also had another affair which he said doesn't count; it was just sex. Neither person was looking for anything after. He now struggles to remain faithful. It is, however, difficult when women tempt him:

I try not to mess around anymore, but there is always the possibility that you may see one that you might want. But you try not to put yourself in the position or in places where it can possibly happen. Case in point is this person that lives down the street that did everything but spread her legs to let me know I can "hit it" if I want to. On the other hand, she and I are friends. She admires me for being loyal and not being a dog and "hitting it." On the other hand, she wonders [whether] I'm not attracted to her sexually. She wants to find out. She makes up reasons for me to stop by. She brought me Hennessy; a bottle of wine. She has certain types of clothes on. So I take myself out of that situation. She had on one of those body suits. It was talking. She had that gaze in her eyes. I knew I had to get up and get out, but it's hard. Especially in a town like D. C. There are a lot of women that need somebody. If you are half way decent, are responsible, they are attracted, even if not for looks, [then] how you carry yourself.

A college professor, 38 years of age, also described an experience he had:

132

I think there is a certain attractiveness — women are attracted to men who are in relationships. For some reason, this appeals to them. I remember I was just minding my own business. There were problems in my marriage, but I was not actually looking to get into a relationship. And this woman comes by my office. She didn't really want anything, but she came by, wrote her phone number down, and told me to call her. . . .She said she wanted to talk about her research project, so we set up a date for dinner. The research she wanted was on me. I told her I was married. She said she had no problem, that's the way she preferred her relationships.

This same man described the background of women with whom he has had experiences explaining why, even though they have a lot going for them, they may be drawn to him, despite the fact that he is married.

Another one did that about six months after that. She said she wanted to be my friend, but it was a "booty call" for her. These are very nice women; good paying jobs, educated, carry themselves with respect; not everybody can talk to them. This happened in an institution of higher learning. A Black male with a Ph.D., the perception of status, physical features, all play themselves out.

In addition, he, as others, spoke of how men are drawn into relationships with women outside of their marriages: "Even when a Black man is not seeking, there is the temptation — a woman may present herself in a certain way and they fall prey to the temptation."

Psychological and Emotional Factors

~"*trying to find themselves in somebody else . . .*
moving around, hitting and missing."~

A few interviewees believe that men who enter into and out of relationships with women are suffering from deep psychological problems related to identity and distrust. Some interviewees asserted that a son's relationship with his father plays a significant role in his adult identity. One interviewee, for example, pointed out that when a man enters into and out of relationships with women, besides not "getting satisfaction, sexual or mental, he's trying to compensate for his shortcomings," and if he was raised without his father, "he had no guidance." He further explained, "Guys who don't know their fathers have a big question mark over their head all the time. This leads them to go to extremes in relationships." When I asked what if their fathers engaged in multiple relationships, his response was, "They are acting out because of what they saw their fathers do":

If your daddy don't know what he's doing, they have a strong tendency to do the same. If the father was confused, so is he. If they have a strong bloodline, if it's more stable, they have balance and more confidence in self. Those who be trying to date everybody are trying to find themselves in somebody else. They are moving around, hitting and missing.

Distrust is also a factor. One male who is divorced said, "I'm very distrusting of relationships. I'm leaning toward multiple relationships with people who live in different places (cities). . . .I don't feel like I should put all my eggs in one basket. I tried that. To me it wasn't a good investment. There was too much ownership, too much control, too many expectations." Some men have extramarital relationships because they "don't trust women. So if one drops you, you'll have another one." Although a 27-year old truck driver admitted that distrust was a factor in it for him, he also confessed, "We are just fuck-ups. We don't know why we fuck up so bad; it just seems to happen. Most of us couldn't tell you why." He described the difficulty he has remaining committed to a monogamous relationship, no matter how satisfying it may be. His inability to do so cost him a woman he cared for.

The long-term relationships which I was involved in were very fulfilling for me. I was usually the one that fucked up. When I have a woman that is everything I could want in a woman, I become very distrustful. I start to wonder if I will be enough for her twenty years from now. In my last relationship, I had a woman that was everything I wanted. . . .She had beauty, she was warm, she would do anything for me, and I would do anything for her. I was really into this lady. I fucked up by calling her another lady's name while making love to her. She dropped me like a hot potato. No questions asked; she never spoke to me again.

Others engage in multiple relationships, in the words of one participant, "to avoid a broken heart," or to assuage hurt they experienced in a previous relationship. One respondent recalled, "I was going with this girl for approximately 7 ½ years. We broke up . . . .I was hurt. I started free wheeling." Another man confessed that although he "still loves" her, his ex-girlfriend won't talk to him. Thus, to fill the void, he just says, "Fuck it right now, and [I am] living the playboy lifestyle," but deep down, "I hate screwing a lot of different women."

Loneliness is another factor. One male explained that because he cannot provide for a wife adequately, he engages in multiple relationships. He doesn't "want to be alone"; he doesn't "want to sit around and not have a relationship of some sort with a female."

In Search of Completion

There are those who believe that men engage in multiple relationships because they are in search of completion. One man explained that completion for males is more difficult to achieve than it is for females. The way he sees it, the woman is both self and other because of her ability to bear children. Because she can produce both male and female children, she has a connection to both the male and female child in a way that the male can never have. It is more difficult for the male and female (masculine and feminine) to exist in men; even if this is the consequence of socialization, it is still innately harder for the male to connect because he does not have the ability to produce the male or female child. "If he had the ability to carry the male and female, he would have a natural connection to his female self or the female principle." "The male is on a constant quest to seek the other because . . . his self is not the other." The problem is that a culture with monogamy only, which is thought by some males to be unnatural, prohibits males in this quest. Because they are under domination, many are off their spiritual center and act out in ways that may not be beneficial to women or themselves.

The search for completion was revealed in the responses of other spiritually-focused interviewees. One interviewee spoke of needing another wife because of his need for another family that would ultimately "complete" him. A man in his early fifties, whose wife is past her reproductive years and whose children are about to leave home for college, discussed how this "saddens" him and how he "mourns" their leaving. He therefore longs for another wife to begin a new family. It was also pointed out by interviewees that they need another wife for spiritual growth.

It's Needed

There are some interviewees who believe that given the scarcity of African American men, polygynous types of relationships are needed in the African American community. The numerical disparity between African American men and women contributes to men engaging in multiple relationships, which is the reason some men believe that "sharing is an option that should be explored." One interviewee said, "Whether they [women] want to accept it or not, they are sharing." He also discussed how polygyny might help with regard to family and nation building, asserting: "In America we are constrained to working one way — the Western way. To have a strong nation requires a strong family. If there are Black women who do not have a man and are willing to share, it should be done." Another interviewee expressed similar thoughts:

I think the Black community in terms of numbers need polygamy. Cheikh Anta Diop said that Black women created polygamy. In Africa, if a woman lost her husband, her sister might ask her husband to take her. The woman would have a choice as to who would come into the family. As time went on, husbands started to just bring in additional wives. After the intrusion of the Arabs and Europeans, Black men started taking on the characteristics of Europeans and Arabs. In European and Arab cultures, women are disrespected. This is how Black women lost control in such matters.

This interviewee thinks that although "polygyny would solve some of the problems facing the African American community, Black men and women aren't ready for it, because we are not honest enough with each other and women are too selfish. Only Black women can make it happen."

Finally, interviewees were asked whether they would consider polygyny if it were done openly, became a legitimate marriage option, and women consented to it. A few said they would, and believe they have the capacity to do so. What is most interesting, however, is that although most of the men had engaged in multiple relationships at some time or another, and/or may still be doing so, a majority indicated that they would not do it openly. The most common reason is their religion; they are Christian, and it conflicts with their beliefs.

Overall, the most common reason participants gave for what motivates males to engage in multiple relationships is the desire for sex. It appears that the desire stems from natural urges, which some males find difficult to suppress, particularly when women are tempting and willing to engage them. This also applies to those whose sexual and emotional needs are not being met by a primary mate. Peer pressure, ego, and variety appear to also be motivated by sex. Participants also believe that males engage in multiple relationships because of issues with identity, trust, loneliness, and feelings of inadequacy. The search for completion seems to indicate spiritual needs for those who are focused in this way.

Whatever the case may be, a majority of the responses indicate why illeganous formations are so prevalent in African American communities. Although many of the responses, specifically those focused around sex, may indicate that the desire to engage in sexual multiplicity may stem from natural urges, they also speak to values. And it is clear that these values stem from Western ideas of masculinity. Some of the responses also show the general lack of understanding by some men, particularly those which evolve around peer pressure, variety and ego, of the purpose of the male-female relationship, which is for the parties to provide sexual, material, emotional and spiritual support to one another and to create a stable environment to raise psychologically and emotionally healthy children.

These findings are not encouraging for women. And they definitely do not help women to see co-partnering as an option. However, what is clearly obvious is that it is the preponderance of women that makes it easy for men to engage women in the manner that they do. The fact is, men could not engage in multiple relationships simultaneously without participation from women. What is needed, then, is a way for men and women to engage each other in ways that are healthy for everyone involved. For this to happen, it is critical to examine the value structure males use to engage females. This means examining Western constructions of masculinity.

Understanding the role that these ideas play in their own intrapersonal growth and development and how they shape their approach to interpersonal relationships with females is critical for males. More importantly, redefining manhood is necessary to help African American males make the shift from illegany to co-partnering.

Chapter 7

WHO HAS TURNED US OUT?: WESTERN MASCULINITY AND ITS IMPACT ON THE AFRICAN AMERICAN MALE QUEST FOR MANHOOD

> We became sort of like the European's woman in the slave experience. We became punks, "punktified." Then, when we coopted our women in the slave trade, we became doubly "punktified." And when we married our women and gave them a European name, we became triply "punktified."

> Kamau Ajanaku, 43

In an interview, Nasheed Fakhrid Deen (1998), explained that one of the signs of manhood in prison is to make another man submit to one's will. The objective is to "turn a man out," the way a man does a woman. The individual may make the victim go to the bathroom and sit on the toilet like a woman, take care of his clothes, and perform other functions a woman would typically perform for a man. In the twisted way the term is attached to women, the objective, according to Deen, is to "literally, make him a bitch." In a discussion with prison inmates, he raises a critical question:

When we speak another man's language, adopt another man's culture, adopt another man's religion, when we dress the way another man tells us, when we eat the way he tells us; when another man tells us what kind of woman we want—the blue-eyed blond—when he tells us how to treat our women, to disrespect our women, who's dictating that reality? Who has turned us out? Whose bitches are we? We are another man's bitch because we don't have the courage to seek out and find, to reach back to our ancestors and define reality for ourselves.

Both the statement by Kamau and the question raised by Deen speak to the low value placed on the feminine — that is, women and men who are effeminate. However, in the spirit of one of our greatest warriors and ancestors, Malcolm X, both are critiques of the wholesale co-optation of African American men into the cultural value system underlying the American social structure, particularly as it pertains to masculinity or manhood. One way that manhood is demonstrated in African American male culture is sexual prowess. This adaptation from the slave experience is manifested through conquest and domination of women or, in street lingo, "turning them out." Although many have incorporated this cultural peculiarity into their *modus operandi* in their relations with women, most still have a superficial understanding of Western masculinity or its origins.

Origins of Conquest and Domination in Western Masculinity

\In general, the male gender role in U.S. society is defined as provider and protector. Although the primary roles of a man in most societies have been that of provider and protector, a distinguishing feature in the European American model is patriarchy. This means that, as provider, the man dominates his household, including his woman. This feature of patriarchy is derived from the Roman *Patria potestas* whereby the patriarch or father dominated the clan. Because economic exclusion makes it difficult for many African American males to be providers, they are unable to carry out this most basic dimension of the male gender role. Domination of women through sexual conquest then emerges as a cultural adaptation to this. In other words, since he cannot dominate her through economic prowess, he attempts to do so through sexual prowess. This carries over into multiple women — that is, the more women a man is able to conquer in this manner, the closer he comes to attaining manhood. This explains why ego, conquest, and power emerge as significant variables in why men engage in multiple sexual relationships simultaneously.

Since conquest and domination are characteristics of masculinity in the West, an important task is to examine their origins. One might begin with Cheikh Anta Diop's two-cradle theory as a point of departure. In this theory, Diop (1974) posits that there are two regions on earth in which the human family evolved — the Southern and Northern cradles. Because of different climatic conditions, distinct personality and cultural traits predominate among the peoples who evolved in these two cradles. In *African Origins of Civilization: Myth or Reality?*, Diop (1974) asserts, "The history of humanity will remain confused as long as we fail to distinguish between the two early cradles in which nature fashioned the instincts, temperament, habits, and ethical concepts of the two subdivisions before they met each other after a long separation dating back to prehistoric times" (p. 111). With regard to the Southern cradle, Diop contends:

The first of those cradles . . . is the valley of the Nile, from the Great Lakes to the Delta. The abundance of vital resources, its sedentary, agricultural character, the specific conditions of the valley, will engender in man, that is, in the [African], a gentle idealistic, peaceful nature, endowed with a spirit of justice and gaiety. (p. 112)

By contrast, for those who evolved in the Northern cradle:

. . . the ferocity of nature in the Eurasian steppes, the bareness of those regions, the overall circumstances of material conditions were to create instincts necessary for survival in such an environment. Here nature left no illusion of kindliness; it was implacable and permitted no negligence; man must obtain his bread by the sweat of his brow. Above all, in the course of a long, painful existence, he must learn to rely on himself alone, on his own possibilities. He could not indulge in the luxury of a beneficent God who would shower down abundant means of gaining a livelihood; instead he would conjure up deities maleficent and cruel, jealous and spiteful: Zeus, Yahweh, among others. (p. 112)

He further notes:

All the peoples of this area whether white or yellow were instinctively to love conquest, because of a desire to escape from those hostile surroundings. The milieu chased them away; they had to leave it or succumb, try to conquer a place in the sun in a more clement nature. Invasions would not cease, once an initial contact with the Black world to the south had taught them the existence of a land where the living was easy, riches abundant, technique flourishing. (p. 133)

It follows then that a major personality trait that emerged from these climatic conditions is one that thrives on conquest, and what follows, domination and/or destruction

There are also distinctive cultural traits. In *Cultural Unity of Black Africa*, Diop (1990) provides extensive evidence of the types of cultural traits that evolved in these two cradles. One area which he elaborates on is familial structures. Here he describes how the nuclear family may have emerged to become superior in European cultural practices and the power a man had over his household, including his wife:

In Europe, among the Aryans, the nomadic style of life makes each clan, that is of each family, an absolute entity, an autonomous cell, independent in all its purposes, self-sufficient from an economic or other point of view. In addition, the head of the family does not have to account to anybody; there is no authority higher than his own, no religion above his, no morality outside domestic morality. This situation, born during the nomadic life, perpetuated itself for a long time after sedentarisation;. . . Individual right among Aryans was anterior to the foundation of cities. . . . .This is the reason why for a long time, the state had no power to interfere in the private life of families. [T]hat is to say, that in Rome and Greece during whole centuries a man could kill his son, his wife or his slaves, or sell them, without committing a crime against the state which was then the city. Public authority stopped at the door of a man's house. (p. 144)

Thus, contrary to what some social scientists suggest, the nuclear family may not just be a development from the industrial period but a cultural retention.

Other cultural traits, according to Diop (1990), that characterize the Southern region include the territorial state, social collectivism (because of the agrarian mode of existence, people had to work collectively), material solidarity, xenophillia, matrilinity, emancipation of women in domestic life, circumcision and excision (done to neutralize the masculine or feminine depending on whether one is a male or female; since both, when born, are considered androgynous, which is symbolic of the creator containing both masculine and feminine principles), monotheism (a beneficent creator who showers in abundance), etc. These qualities reflected in the moral domain "[show] an ideal of peace, of justice, of goodness and an optimism which eliminates all notion of guilt or original sin" (p. 195).

In the Northern cradle we find patriarchy, city-states (until contact was made with the Southern cradle, after which it was transformed into a territorial state and an empire), where a man is either a patriot or an outlaw. Other characteristics include xenophobia, individualism, "moral and material solitude, a disgust for existence . . . which is none other than the expression of the tragedy of a way of life going back to the Aryan's ancestors" (p. 195). This outlook is accompanied by ideas of "war, violence, crime and conquests, inherited from nomadic life, with, as a consequence, a feeling of guilt and of original sin, which causes pessimistic religious or metaphysical systems to be built" (p. 195). Thus, two essential components in Western masculine construction are conquest and domination.

To expand on Diop's discussion further, I propose that societies in which survival was tenuous and where continuous warring occurred among various tribes over scarce resources, over-development of the masculine emerged, or at least certain dimensions of it. Over-development of masculine qualities emerged because environmental conditions dictated that feminine qualities be repressed for survival. Men could not be in touch with the feminine in themselves because it could lead to the demise of the family and, ultimately, the tribe. Among some Germanic tribes, a man could go to the highest place after death only if he died in battle. This may be why feminine deities were eventually repressed and masculine ones reigned supreme when contact was made with peoples in the Southern cradle. The various tribes were continually at war, so there was always the threat of women being captured and taken as "booty." Thus, as it pertains to women, over-development of masculine qualities manifested in two primary ways: The outward projection of repression of the feminine within men themselves onto women, and the consequent repression of women through overt social forms: dress, isolation from men, and keeping women under the domain of their fathers until they came under the domain of their husbands. These cultural patterns emerged to protect women and men's property—women themselves—from sexual violation by other males of their own as well as other tribes. Repression of women also ensured that the children who would inherit their property, would be their own. Thus, we have the emergence of extreme forms of patriarchy, as found among the Greeks and Romans and others of earlier Indo-European stock.

Homer and Virgil, Jesus, the Black Knight, and the Bourgeois: Early European Conceptions of Masculinity

Other scholars have traced the historical development of masculinity and the male gender role in the Western world. A. J. Doyle (1983), for example, identifies four models or concepts of masculinity that males were expected to imitate in various epochs of European history. These include (a) the epic male, (b) the spiritual male, (c) the chivalric male, and (d) the renaissance male. The epic male, according to Doyle, is the ideal male depicted in ancient Greek and Rome. He comes to us through the sagas of Homer and Virgil. In these sagas, we find: "a world inhabited by soldiers, adventurers, warriors, kings, and gods. Men were the 'doers,' the conquerors, and rulers of a threatening barbaric world" (p. 25). The epic male was a fighter and leader whose major virtues were prowess and skill in battle. He possessed strength, courage, and loyalty. His role can be summed up as a "warrior-ruler" (p. 25).

The spiritual male was expected to follow the example of Jesus Christ who stressed nonviolence and service to others. Although the "life and teachings of Jesus Christ provided the basic tenets of Christianity, . . . it was early church fathers who largely influenced the male role ideal," which "did not take complete form as we have come to know it until several centuries after Christ's death" (pp. 26-27). Doyle notes:

Patriarchy found itself a highly favorable niche in the Christian church. The male portrayed as the image of God the Father, was seen as the

144

ultimate authority in all matters, both spiritual and secular. Women are to subjugate themselves to all males' rulings, their priest's, father's, husband's. (p.27)

Furthermore, "not only did Christianity portray men as women's ultimate authority, men were also expected to disdain the female" (p. 27). Men, especially those called to be clergy, were to renounce the flesh, including all sexuality. And because of woman's "insatiable sexual nature," she was regarded as the link between sexuality and sin and the "embodiment of evil" (p. 27).

The chivalric male role emerges in the 12th century in Western Europe under the new social order of feudalism. As authority spread from the church to include the cultured aristocracy and military class, it gave rise to the "soldier or knightly class" (p. 28). During this period, it was this new ideal "for the male role which transformed the asexual spiritual male into a sensual chivalric or knightly male" (p. 28). The chivalric male emphasized "physical strength, prowess in combat, loyalty to the king or . . . lord, and devotion to the lady" (p. 28).

This period witnessed the ideal of romantic love between a knight and his lady, to whom he was devoted, but with whom his relationship was consummated with disastrous effects. In relation to woman, the knight was "champion of women and protector of the weak" (p. 30). Despite the arrival of courtly love and man's devotion to woman, a new perspective on womanhood emerged that reflected an ambivalent vision of woman's nature. Women were either "pedestaled virgins" (a secularized Virgin Mary) or "lusty temptresses and prostitutes" (p. 28).

The renaissance male model appeared in the 16th century when there was a growing middle class and the Roman church was losing much of its authority. "The knight riding his horse in quest for glory and his lady's approval changed into a man searching for knowledge" (p. 29). Thus, the rational and intellectual man became the model. By the 18th century, the rise of a strong and powerful middle class in England gave rise to the bourgeois male ideal whose values were shaped by money, status, and prestige. For the bourgeois male, money was the ultimate symbol of power. During this period, women continued to be subjugated to men (p. 30).

Doyle indicates that although the male role may have changed over time in European history, a persistent feature of all the models is patriarchy, the supremacy of the father, his dominance in male-female relations. These four archetypes have provided the basic models for males in U. S. society.

Agrarian Patriarchy to the Iron Man: The White American Male Search for Manhood

Pleck & Pleck (1980) identify four historical periods in the construction of masculinity in American society. These include the period of agrarian patriarchy (1630-1820), the commercial age (1820-1860), the strenuous life (1861-1919), and the companionate provider (1920-1965). The agrarian patriarchy is a period of male superiority in the home, in politics, and in religion. Marriage and family were important primarily for children, for labor, and for care in old age. Primogeniture was firmly established, and men as husbands held supreme authority over their wives and as fathers over their sons. It was also a period when white slaveholders claimed sexual rights over enslaved African women.

The commercial era marks a period of separate but equal spheres for the sexes: men in business and public affairs, women in the home and church. During this period, men were expected to be good providers. The era was also characterized by sexual purity for both men and women. Pure women were elevated to pedestal status, whereas those who were not were outcasts. Important to note is that during this time, while white women were put on pedestals, enslaved African women were raped and taken as concubines, and their sexuality appropriated by white males. It was also during this period, that "males were viewed as the more passionate sex and the goal of the good woman was to help him control his passions for his own sake and for the good of society" (Pleck & Pleck, pp. 14-15).

The strenuous period occurs between the Civil War and World War I. There were still separate spheres for the sexes during this time, but women were beginning to seek equality and were entering the work force. With the threat of the "new woman," erosion of patriarchy, and industrialization, which displaced men as owners of their own labor to the "depersonalized regimentation and routine drudgery of factory work," white men began to experience a "flagging sense of masculinity" (Doyle, p. 39). "At the time of the Civil War, 90 percent of men in the United States were independent farmers or self-employed businessmen or artisans. By 1870, that number had dropped to two of three, and by 1910, less than one-third of U.S. men were economically autonomous" (Kimmel and Kaufman, 1995, p. 33). This resulted in the search for autonomy, male bonding, and "roughing" it in nature experiences men had during the Civil War. A body-building craze, all male organizations, such as the Boy Scouts (to help boys become men), organized sports, fraternal orders, and the establishment of separate meeting places for men, such as saloons, were the outcome of the need for these types of experiences.

The period of the companionate provider is marked by erosion of Victorianism and emergence of a different cultural ethos. There was a rise in cabarets and speakeasies, and other places where the sexes mixed to drink, dance, and be entertained (Pleck and Pleck, 1980, p. 29). It was during this period that men began spending more time with the opposite sex instead of their male friends, and the values of sexual continence and control were replaced with sex as recreation. "With technology and specialization, men no longer validated their manliness in purely physical activities but turned to providing for their families as evidence of their manhood. The role of breadwinner or good provider became the primary element in the definition of masculinity" (Doyle, 1983). With widespread unemployment during the Great Depression, however, men experienced a shaky sense of manhood once again. After World War II, old attributes of manhood were revitalized, and during the 1950s and 1960s, men reasserted their manhood as breadwinners and dominance over women. The feminist movement in the 1960s however, began to challenge male dominance, leaving many, once again, with a shaky sense of masculine identity (Doyle, 1983; Pleck & Pleck, 1980).

In response to this, three primary men's movements emerged. These include the men's liberation movement, or pro-feminists, the men's rights movement, and the mythopoetic men's movement of the early 1990s.

147

Profeminists, men who are sympathetic to the feminist cause, believe that the male role is oppressive for women as well as men. In the initial phase of the movement, during the 1970s, profeminist men began meeting on college campuses and in conferences where they encouraged consciousness raising (C-R) among men. They continue to meet in two primary conferences — Men and Masculinity (M & M) and the National Organization for Changing Men (NOCM) — and both continue to encourage change and personal growth in men.

The men's rights movement maintains that the traditional male role is unhealthy for men and may even be lethal. However, M. S. Kimmel (1995) explains that men's rights advocates "maintain that feminism, instead of helping men or providing a model for male liberation, has actually made things worse" (p. 10). This is because feminism created new options for women, but men have not been given the same range of choices. Thus, it is thought that ". . . a new sexism has come into existence, with men as the victims" (p. 10). In addition, they believe that "feminism has created guilt in men for their own socialization, which is not their fault" (p. 10). The goal of the men's rights movement is to "bring about an understanding of the new sexism and to create laws that protect men against current injustices, especially in the areas of divorce, child custody and domestic violence prosecution" (p.10).

The mythopoetic men's movement emerged with Robert Bly's publication of *Iron Man* in 1990 (Clatterbaugh, 1990; Kimmel, 1995). Scholars' views on this movement vary. Clatterbaugh (1990), for example, sees the movement as a psycho-spiritual perspective on masculinity, whereby men are encouraged to get in touch with their spirituality through traditional stories, myths, and rituals. He explains that men are encouraged "to descend into themselves and come to understand themselves . . . to heal their psychic and spiritual wounds to achieve a better life" (p. 85). What distinguishes the mythopoetic movement from the other two, according to Clatterbaugh, is that the other movements *encourage* personal change and growth as important parts of their agenda, whereas personal change and growth assume *urgency* in the mythopoetic movement.

Although Kimmel (1995) and Kimmel & Kaufman (1995) acknowledge the value of the mythopoetic men's movement in helping men connect with their inner feelings (including their own pain) and with other men, they criticize the movement for its apolitical stance, particularly with regard to the feminist movement, and assert that the mythopoetic movement is:

A retreat to [a] highly selective anthropological world of rituals that reproduce men's cultural power over women and that are now used to facilitate a deeper nostalgic retreat to the lost world of innocent boyhood. It is thus a retreat from women, from adult men's responsibility to embrace women's equality and struggle against those obstacles that continue to lie in the path of gender equality. (p. 41)

Whatever the case may be, the mythopoetic movement apparently has a large following of predominantly middle-class white males, and they hold retreats and workshops across the country to help men deal with the crisis in masculine identity.

From this overview, it is apparent that masculinity in the U.S. has had an unstable history. This is due in part to challenges to patriarchy by women that began with the abolitionist movement. White women worked in the abolitionist movement and then went on to start a movement of their own for women's rights. Free African American women also worked for women rights, the most noted being Sojourner Truth and others like Anna Julia Cooper, author of *A Voice from the South* (1852) that advocated education for women.

Regardless of its unstable history, common elements comprise masculinity in contemporary times. Doyle (1983) identifies five elements. These include: (a) antifemininity, (b) success, (c) aggression, (d) sexuality, and (e) self-reliance. Brannon (1976) identifies four dimensions of masculinity: (a) "No Sissy Stuff" (rejection of feminine aspects of the self); "The Big Wheel" (status and power); (c) "Give 'Em Hell" (aggression and toughness); and (d) "The Sturdy Oak" (emotional strength and invulnerability). "No Sissy Stuff" was the most notable among them. Overall, from these and other studies outlined by Thompson and Pleck (1987), masculinity appears to encompass independence, competition, aggression, power, status and achievement, anti-femininity, and sexuality.

Obstacles to the African American Male Quest for Manhood

As already indicated, proponents of men's liberation have noted limitations of the male roles of provider and protector. Regardless of their limitations, however, it apparent that white males, as a group, still function largely as providers. It is they who dominate industry and the major financial and other institutions in the U.S. and global economy. It is also white males as a group, through the industrial military complex of the U.S., who are the major protectors of the global social, economic and political order.

Because they are still primarily providers and protectors, many may be able to connect with their own power through identification with white male power as a group. The situation is different for a majority of African American males. Although most may not be aware of the politics of masculine construction in U.S. society, African American males know intuitively that their roles as providers and protectors in the U.S. and global social, political and economic order as a group, are almost nil. Madhubuti, (1990) is clear on this:

As part of the political body, Black men do not have much, if any, power to speak of; as a cultural unit Black men do not make important life-giving or life-saving decisions on a local, national or international level. Black men are not able on a national or mass level to protect Black women, educate Black children, employ Black youth, clothe Black families, or house Black communities. Our input into a national Black domestic policy is laughable; our involvement in "Black" foreign policy is minor. Our relationship to Black women is quickly approaching the point of disaster. Black economic-political clout on the world level is minuscule, and our understanding of the forces that regulate our lives is embarrassing—especially since we are supposed to be the "most educated" and the most "creative and talented" community of Black men in the world. (pp. 67-68)

He further states:

150

[M]ost of the Euro-American systems and subsystems are structured to systematically keep *conscious* Black men out. However, if Black men wish to become imitation White men, there exists within the political industrial-military complex significant token positions . . . which are in fact used to legitimize the system and to cloud its true relationship to Black people, a relationship of slave/master. In fact the "slave" position is the major rank that Black men, regardless of title and income, are allowed to occupy. (pp. 67-68)

In "Black Men in America: The Quest for Manhood," Cazenave (1981) also notes, that even minimally "today being a man in American society still means achieving, accomplishing, having a good job, and providing adequately for oneself and one's family" (p. 177). Here, again a majority of white males are still able to actualize these most fundamental components of manhood by the mere fact of their maleness and white skin privilege. This puts them in the position, at least on an individual level, to satisfy their quest for masculine attainment or manhood.

For African American males, obstacles to carry out components of the male gender role began with their experiences in slavery. Their role as provider was undermined by the slaveholder, who distributed material goods to the family and, in most cases, through the woman. Any attempt by African American men to protect their wives and children could result in mutilation or even death. Even after emancipation, their ability to carry out gender roles was stifled by apartheid and various other efforts to starve them and their families and terrorize them into subordination. Since World War II, the unemployment rate for African American males has remained consistently double that of white males, which has kept them, according to Pleck & Pleck, (1980) in a sort of "permanent depression." At present, though more African American males than in the past may be able to be good providers, a large segment of the population is denied the means to carry out this basic role.

In *Black Masculinity*, Robert Staples (1982) compares the position of African American men with white men, particularly as it relates to the men's movement. He points out that most of the literature in the pro-feminist men's movement "has focused on the privileges of masculinity in gaining access to the values and goals of the culture" (p. 7). However, "in the case of black men, their subordination as a racial minority has more than canceled out their advantages as males in the larger society" (p. 7).

Unlike white males, they have few privileges in this society except vis-a-vis black women, and even that advantage is being eroded by black women who have a competitive edge over some black males for certain jobs. Indeed, in comparison to white males, black men find themselves on the negative side of social statistics in the areas of health, employment, education, income, etc. (p. 7)

By contrast to the goals of the white male movement, those of African American males are basic. According to Staples:

It is patently clear that the central concerns of black men are not about relinquishing male privilege or forging new concepts of androgyny or sex role egalitarianism. They must first and foremost deal with the issue of survival. It is not that they have abused privileges accruing to men, but that they have never been given the opportunity to realize even the minimal prerequisites of manhood—life sustaining employment and the ability to support a family. To a large extent, these problems are confined to a certain segment of the black population, but they constitute a very large proportion of all black men. We should realize that the more these legitimate aspirations to manhood are retarded, the greater the tendency will be to assert them in other areas. (p. 13)

Given this reality, Cazenave (1981) asks, "What happens to Black men who accept society's notions of what it takes *to be a man* but are denied the resources to '*earn*' their masculinity through traditional channels? An awareness of this precarious predicament," he asserts, "is the key to understanding the unique psychological and social drudgery which distinguishes black men from other sex/race groups in America" (p. 178). He and others have proposed adaptive strategies that African American men have and continue to use to avert obstacles in their quest for manhood. Applying Robert K. Merton's theory of anomie, Cazenave explains:

[S]ocially deviant or unacceptable behavior results for certain groups in American society because, while the majority share the basic *goals* of society, all do not share the means of achieving these goals. Consequently . . . the very structure of society (especially differential access to the opportunity structure) actually encourages certain individuals to function deviantly to obtain cultural goals (i.e., the material and social prestige rewards of society). (p. 178)

Cazenave outlines Merton's five modes of adaptation that may be used by African American males. These include conformity, innovation, ritualism, retreatism, and rebellion. Using an example from L. Taylor's *Deviance and Society* (1971), he also explains how these adaptations work:

The machine is rigged and only some players are consistently rewarded. The deprived ones then either resort to using foreign coins or magnets to increase their chances of winning (innovation) or play mindlessly (ritualism), give up the game (retreatism) or propose a new game altogether (rebellion). (p. 178)

Adaptive Strategies in the African American Male Quest for Manhood

Other scholars have examined more specifically "alternative modes of masculine attainment" used by African American males (Cazenave, 1981, p. 189). In an early study, Hannerz (1969) identifies what he refers to as a ghetto-specific masculine alternative. These include "sexual exploits, toughness and the ability to command respect, personal appearance with an emphasis on male clothing fashions, liquor consumption, and verbal ability" (p. 79). Glasgow (1980) in a later study found two types of adaptative strategies for young males in Watts. Stemming from various types of *hustling* strategies for survival, these include the *player* who is "highly articulate," "bright," "ambitious," and a clever manipulator who is possessed with an "astute grasp of ghetto psychology"; and the *activists* who obtains money "through acts of vandalism, robbery and theft" (p. 91). According to Glasgow, socialization is toward the development of a distinctive style, "highly ritualized roles," "individual innovation as manifested through personalized styling," such as walk, manner of speech, choices of "threads" and "hairdo," "maintaining cool," the ability to rap and "to be a clever and effective manipulator of person and environment" (pp. 96-97).

In an even earlier study, Grier and Cobbs (1968) describe psychological adaptations. Some of their analyses, however, seem to be plagued with American stereotypes of African American males that were derived from the slave experience. They identify four adaptions — the "postal clerk syndrome," the "bad nigger," "the sexually prodigious" and the "playing-it-cool" male. The description of the "postal-clerk syndrome," and the "passive, nonassertive and nonaggressive," male seems to parallel the happy, docile Sambo. The "bad nigger," although described as coming out of Black folklore, is also found in the stereotype of the African American male as the Black brute.

Other more recent studies also identify adaptations. Oliver (1989) found two adaptions, which he attributes to an inferiorization process of African Americans: "player of women" and "tough guy." The tough guy stems from "norms that define manhood in terms of fearlessness, emotional control, and a willingness to use violence to resolve interpersonal conflict" (p. 261). The player of women image is "based on a set of norms that define manhood in terms of overt promiscuity, dominance, and emotional and sexual exploitation of women" (p. 261). In *Cool Pose: The Dilemmas of Black Manhood in America,* Majors and Billson (1992) examines the "playing-it-cool style" Grier and Cobbs describe and the "cool player" described by Glasgow. They explain that although "cool" is believed to have originated in Africa and represents inner spirituality and inner strength, it was transformed during the slave experience into something different. "Black masking," "Black acting," "shucking," "Black humor," and "inversions" were used as survival strategies and coping mechanisms (pp. 55-66).

In contemporary times, according to Majors and Billson (1992), "cool pose is the presentation of self many African American males use to establish their male identity" (p. 4). "It is [a] ritualized form of masculinity which entails behaviors, scripts, physical posturing, impression management and carefully crafted performances that deliver [a] single critical message: pride, strength, and control" (p. 4). As a survival strategy, it is "one way that disenfranchised African American males struggle to survive in the face of diminished rights and blemished self-esteem"(p. 5). Essentially, it is a cover for a "low sense of inner control, lack of inner strength, absence of stability, damaged pride, shattered confidence, and fragile social competence that comes with living on the edge of society" (pp. 7-8). The positive side of cool is that it shows a form of social competence, pride, search for meaning, and protection. The negative aspect, however, includes distorted and damaged relationships with other African American males and females.

Although most of the aforementioned studies focus on males in the lower socioeconomic stratum, Majors and Billson (1992) note that cool behavior is also found among middle-class African American males and that it "has influenced mainstream culture through entertainment, sports, clothing, and the media" (p. 9).

The White Man's Burden

Although Grier and Cobbs discuss the prevalence of "prodigious Black men" in African American folk lore, they failed however to discuss its origins in white male mythology. The African American males' sexuality is inextricably linked with the sexual politics of the African man's penis which began with European males during the period of slavery.

Winthrop Jordan (1974), in *The White Man's Burden*, indicates that, when Europeans encountered African males, they were surprised by what they described as their "large members" (p. 82). The African man's large member became a subject of interest in European circles and "by the final quarter of the eighteenth century the idea that the [African] man's penis was larger than the white man's had become something of a commonplace in European scientific circles" (p. 82). It was also addressed in letters and journals, as can be seen in the following account by an "officer in the First Pennsylvania regiment about [African] boys waiting on Virginia dinner tables" (p. 82):

I am surprized that this does not hurt the feelings of this fair Sex to see these young boys of about fourteen and fifteen years old to Attend them. these whole nakedness expos'd and I can Assure you It would Surprize a person to see these d_____ black boys how well they are hung. (p. 83)

Europeans conjured up notions of Africans as being oversexed and sexually promiscuous because of their large genitals and practice of polygyny. During the slave experience, Africans were perceived as fecund, and both males and females were used as breeders; the males were specifically used as stallions. Because African Americans were likened to animals, males were neutered in the same way as animals. Jordan (1974) points out that "castration was dignified by specific legislative sanction as lawful punishment in Antigua, the Carolinas, Bermuda, Virginia, Pennsylvania, and New Jersey" and provides examples of the offences for which it was applied:

It was sometimes prescribed for such offences as striking a white person or running away: employed in this way, castration was not a irrational method of slave control, closely akin to the Jamaica law which authorized severing one foot of a runaway. Yet castration was not simply another of the many brands of hideous cruelty which graced the colonial criminal codes; it was reserved for Negroes and occasionally Indians. In some colonies, laws authorizing castration were worded so as to apply to all blacks whether free or slave. As a legal punishment castration was a peculiarly American experiment, for there was no basis for it in English law. (p. 81)

With the idea of superior male genitals imprinted on their psyches, white American males saw African American males as a threat after slavery ended. The idea that they were brutes and rapists, and if let loose, would sexually assault white women was propagated. No longer needed for breeding purposes, African males were castrated through mob violence to assuage the fears of white males.

An important component of masculine construction is sexuality. As a tool of terrorization in war, it expresses itself in the rape of women and castration of men. Men may also be castrated to deter them from reproducing with the victors own women. This raises the issue of reproduction as another dimension of sexual politics.

A great deal of focus has been placed on population growth among peoples of color, or those on the so-called lower scale of humanity in Western history. Such a focus gave major impetus to the eugenics movement which began in the late 1800s and to more recent birth and population control projects. What may underlie the need for population control by white males is an instinctual competition for reproduction. Anthropologists and naturalist alike have argued that there is competition among males in all species to impregnate as many females as possible. In the *Origin of the Species* (1859), Charles Darwin argued that those species favored by nature survive and reproduce themselves. This is why some species in the evolutionary process sustain themselves over time versus those that do not. Darwin also argued that the male of species with superior natural and constructed weapons are at an advantage in the competition of sexual selection for reproduction. However, Darwin did not make a distinction between human beings based on race.

Herbert Spenser applied Darwin's natural selection theory to construct a "survival of the fittest" social ideology. He argued that those who are more fit are superior and therefore survive. Those who are less fit do not. It was this ideology which was used to justify white supremacy and subsequent domination and destruction of peoples globally. Interestingly, in the competition for reproduction, the fertility rate of peoples of color is higher than it is for whites. Thus, although their weapons may be superior, white males are still not favored in sexual selection by mere numbers, although the material quality of life for their offspring may be.

Trenyaae Bondojia (1999) asserts that reproductive competition is the crux of the matter in the white male's distaste for the practice of polygyny. He argues that because the fertility rate of peoples of color is higher than it is for whites, legitimate structures to support an already higher fertility rate gives them advantage in the competition for reproduction. Thus, it was necessary to construct legal, moral and social structures to prohibit polygyny, while simultaneously, constructing the same to promote monogamy only. This, Bondojia calls *"legalistic Darwinism."*

Frances Cress Welsing (1991) in the *Isis Papers* also addresses the issue of reproduction. In the "Cress Theory of Color Confrontation, and Racism" she theorizes that what underlies white supremacy and the systems devised to bolster it, is *numerical inadequacy* — there are fewer people of non-color than there are people of color and *genetic inferiority* — which is the "the genetic inability to produce skin pigments of melanin which is responsible for skin color" (p. 4). Also, "color absence acts always as a genetic recessive to the dominant genetic factor of color-production" and [c]olor always 'annihilates' (phenotypically-and genetically speaking) the non-color, white" (p. 4). Because of whites' inability to produce color and the envy that results from this, they have developed psychological defense mechanisms, one of which is *reaction* formation, which is defined by Welsing as "a response that converts (at the psychological level) something desired and envied but wholly unattainable into something discredited or despised" (p. 5). In other words, because white is not favored in reproduction, and because they desire to have color but are unable to attain it other than by suntanning or using tanning chemicals and equipment, they attribute negative qualities to the color of people of African descent "who have the greatest color potential, and therefore are the most envied and feared in [the] genetic color competition" (p. 5). Thus, it is this which underlies not only white supremacy, but why African American male genitals were targeted during and after the slave regime.

The Black Man's Burden

Whatever, the case may be, overemphasis on the African American male's genitals, has shifted from being the "White man's burden" to the "Black man's burden." Robert Staples, (1982) put it succinctly when he states, "Denied equal access to the prosaic symbols of manhood, they manifest their masculinity in the most extreme form of sexual domination. When they have been unable to achieve status in the workplace, they have exercised the privilege of their manliness and attempted to achieve it in the bedroom" (p. 85). More tragic, however, is when unevolved (domination and control in relations with other males and females) white male conceptions of manhood are used by African American men to objectify and exploit African American women in the same manner that white men did during slavery.

The experience of slavery for African American women was just as horrendous, if not more so, than it was for African American men. They experienced similar barbarities. Not only was their labor exploited in the same manner as males but they were also subjected to sadistic cruelties based on gender. Dorothy Sterling in *We Are Your Sisters* (1984) and Angela Davis in *Women, Race and Class* (1983) and various other works provide explicit accounts of the barbarities African American women suffered during slavery. In the same manner that African American men were used as stallions, African American women too were exploited for reproductive purposes. Whites created the Jezebel stereotype to justify the wholesale rape of African American women and circulated stories that African women had copulated with orangutans because of their lusty sexual appetites. Ultimately, it was the sexual organs of both African American women and men which became the means through which the slave regime perpetuated a permanent labor force. An unfortunate outcome of this is an adaptation in which the penis for some African American men becomes a measure of their manhood. Africa American women also use their sexuality to auction themselves off to men. Most unfortunate is that in carrying on in such a manner, both not only demonstrate the level to which they have coopted a cultural value system that leads them to dehumanize each other, but also demonstrate the acuity with which they can reenact adaptations from the slave experience. This has serious implications for children who are brought into the world through such associations, and has further consequences for families, communities, and nation building.

Towards a Definition of African American Manhood

Because of limitations of the construction of masculinity for African American males, some have begun to look to other sources. In *Dismantling Black Manhood*, Daniel Black (1997) examines how manhood was acquired in traditional West African societies.

According to him, manhood in traditional West African societies was acquired in four stages. These include boyhood rites, demonstration of physical prowess, husbandhood, and fatherhood.

In the first stage, boyhood rites "were highly-symbolic, ritualized ceremonies" to introduce boys to male behavior, social roles, and male-centered camaraderie from immediately after birth through puberty (p. 12). In most communities, boys experienced at least three different types of rites of passage: one immediately after birth, another between the ages of 4-7, and the third between the ages 9-13. Each stage prescribed specific feats to bring the boy closer to manhood. Rituals following birth included singing, the laying on of hands, and speaking to the child, all of which were intended to impress male sensibilities on the spirit of the child. The rites between ages 4-7 included systematic flogging in some societies, circumcision, and various other activities focused on discipline and respect for authority. The focus between ages 9-13 was also discipline but included development of emotional stability, perseverance, strength, and, most importantly, becoming educated in the history and lore of one's people (pp. 14-18).

Between the ages of 13-18, great value was placed on physical prowess. A boy could demonstrate this through outstanding wrestling, warrior training, hunting, and, to a lesser degree, swimming. Wrestling, one way to demonstrate virility, not only confirmed a male's physical strength, mastery of certain skills and mental strategies, but also "established internal rank order, male leadership roles, friendship bonds and social solidarity" (pp. 19-28). Because solidarity was a major goal, the goal of wrestling was not to seek the total destruction of another. It was part of initiation into a fraternal order. Thus, it was important that males treated each other fairly to be embraced by members of the brotherhood. Warrior training, another avenue for males to demonstrate physical strength, taught boys the tactics of warfare to enable them to protect their families and communities from invasion. Critical in the training of a warrior was that the male understood his position in relation to his people. Black states:

[B]oys did not compete so much against as with one another as they attempted to convince others that they were fit to be embraced as men. In fact, it appears as though a boy became a man only after he understood that he was, in fact, his brother's keeper. To abuse a comrade in the demonstration of one's physical abilities was never sanctioned, for the ultimate purpose of physical strength was the protection — not destruction — of one's people. (p. 4)

Although some West African societies never experienced war or the threat of war, young males who demonstrated the greatest potential as warriors became leaders among their people. In many West African societies, "the idea king was the great warrior, larger than life" (p. 26). Overall, physical prowess was not only important to gain respect and admiration but was also important to convince the community that one was ready for the next stages of manhood — being a husband and father. However, a man could not enter into these stages until the community was satisfied that he could indeed protect and provide for a family.

Black points out that "all young males were expected to marry, and to date, no source reports of any man have chosen to abandon this societal expectation" (p. 28). He further notes, "For a young man, the marriage to his first wife marked a major step forward in his social and economic status within the village, comparable in importance only to his [earlier] initiations into manhood" (p. 29). But marriage entailed considerable responsibility. A man had to prove his economic resourcefulness and moral character and had to make gifts or work for years to prove he would be a good provider and would treat his potential wife well. With regard to fatherhood, a major goal in West African societies was to perpetuate the family name and strengthen the family lineage (p. 32). Marrying multiple wives was therefore motivated by producing children who would extend the family lineage. Being a father also meant more than just siring children. Black points out that men were expected to engage in the socialization of their children by disciplining them, teaching them life survival skills, and most importantly, steeping them in the history of their people.

One, therefore, did not become a man by simply attaining age 18 or 21, the age at which most youth are recognized as adults in U.S. society. Entering into manhood was a highly complex

161

process that took place over the course of a male's life. One did not become a man through his ability to have relations with multiple women, but by his ability to care for these women as wives. One did not become a father by the mere siring of children but by the ability to provide for them, protect them, and engage in their development. Under current social circumstances, there is generally no systematic way to guide males through the stages of manhood, leaving many without a clear definition of what it is. This makes them extremely vulnerable to distorted European or "ghettoized" interpretations and leads many males to engage in compulsive masculinity behaviors with devastating consequences for their families and communities. Madhubuti outlines the steps that U.S. society sets in motion to marginalize African American males and disrupt African American families.

First, U.S. society acculturates African American males into the values underlying this social structure. This, according to him, produces African American men who work not in the best interest of their people but in the best interest of their teachers. Ultimately, this is because "*no serious definition of Black manhood is ever contemplated*" [his emphasis] (p. 73). The second step is to exclude African American men from the economic sector "making it impossible for them to take care of themselves and their families" (p.73). What follows is a life of crime. The third step is to incarcerate those who have been forced into crime. Imprisonment, according to him, "breeds hard non-political Black men who for the most part will return and prey on their own communities" (p. 73). The fourth step is to supply them with options such as drugs, alcohol, and unrestricted sex. The fifth step is to drive them "crazy so that they turn against themselves and the Black community" (p. 74). The recourses then are mental hospitals, suicide, and Black-on-Black destruction. The sixth step is to feminize them; "men of other cultures do not fear the 'women-like' men of any race" (p. 74). Also, "Homosexuality and bisexuality [become] the norm rather than the exception" (p. 74). The seventh step is to teach "Black men to believe in force(s) greater than their own people, their own culture, their own destiny" (p. 74). Finally, the eighth step is to kill them — not just mentally but physically — and do it in a way that strikes fear into the hearts of other Black men.

This not only happens to African American males in the lower socioeconomic strata but those on all socioeconomic levels. The impact is such that the majority of African American males become social and political eunuchs, unable or unwilling to participate in the struggle for their own people.

To combat this negative pattern, Madhubuti (1990) provides an expanded definition of manhood for African American males that, in part, includes the following:

your people first. a quiet strength. the positioning of oneself so that observation comes before reaction, where study is preferred to night life, where emotion is not seen as weakness. love for self, family, children, and extensions of self are beyond the verbal. making your life accessible to children in meaningful ways. able to recognize the war we are in and doing anything to take care of family so long as it doesn't harm or negatively affect other black people . . . to seek and be that which is just, good and correct. properly positioning oneself in the context of our people. a listener. as student. a historian seeking hidden truths . . . direction giver. husband. sensitive to Black women's needs and aspirations . . . not afraid to take the lead. creative father. organized and organizer. a brother to brothers. a brother to sisters. understanding. patient. a winner. maintainer of the i can, i must, i will attitude toward Black struggle and life. a builder of the necessary. always and always in a process of growth and without a doubt believes that our values and traditions are not negotiable. (pp. 16-17)

Overall, a most critical task is not only to define manhood as Madhubuti has done but also to ensure that mechanisms are put into place to bring males through the process. Because of the crisis facing African American males, rites of passage programs are being initiated throughout the country. There is, however, a need for them to be initiated on a broader scale. African American men might collectively declare a state of emergency for males. Community and religious leaders, fraternal orders, and other organizations might pool their resources and initiate a nation-wide rites of passage program for African American males. Only then will we be able to tackle the massive problems plaguing our communities.

Shedding the Burden: Moving Beyond Sex

If one recalls from the previous chapter, the desire for sex was the most common reason interviewees gave for why males engage in relationships with multiple women simultaneously. What seems like a never ending need for sex, however, may be attributed to several factors under the current social system. In an article, "The Black Male/Female Connection," Maulana Karenga (1989) examines three dominant values underlying the American social structure that have destructive effects on African American heterosexual relationships. These include capitalism, racism, and sexism. Capitalism, according to Karenga, turns "relationships and parts of relationships into commodities and utilitarian arrangements" (p. 48). Racism "engenders self-hate, self-doubt and pathological fixation on the white paradigm," and "sexism imposes unequal, oppressive and exploitive relationships based on gender or sex" (p. 48). Sexism also "encourages artificial personal power over women as a substitute for real social power over one's destiny and daily life" (p. 48). Karenga contends that these structural values transform African American male-female relationships into what he calls, "connections. . . a short-term or tentative association which is utilitarian and alienated and is designed primarily for the mutual misuse of each other's body" (p. 48). He describes four connections that plague African American male-female relationships. These include the cash connection, the flesh connection, the force connection, and the dependency connection.

According to Karenga, "The cash connection grows out of the commodity character of society, which means that money and material become the basis upon which relationships are formed" (p. 48). The flesh connection "grows out of the pornographic character of society and is defined as an association based purely or predominantly on the pursuit of sex"(p. 48). This is most critical to this discussion because sex was given as the primary reason that males engage in multiple-relationships.

Karenga defines five basic ways pornography expresses itself as a definite social thought. "First it is an expression of species alienation. It reflects man alienated from and oblivious of his species half confused by the contradictory emotions toward thoughts of her as 'whore and high priestess,' mother in public and sex machine in bed" (p. 48a). Second, it "is objectification of the species half, turning a natural partner into an object of use and disuse. It is this objectification which leads men to say while pursuing a woman, I'm going to get 'that' and to reduce women to parts of their bodies" (p. 48a). Third, pornography "is fragmentation of the body, hacking the body into usable pieces [and] rejecting the wholeness of the human personality....No one in a flesh connection wants a whole body, just holes in the body" (p. 48a). Fourth, "it is brutalization, most viciously expressed in the sadomasochistic vulgarities society at its most violent and alienated level has produced" (p. 48a). Finally, it is a "sexual commodity form. Its practical expression is in the selling of the body or its image" (p. 48a).

The force connection arises out of the violent and oppressive character of society, with conquest being a central theme, and men using their greater physical strength to subdue women. The dependency connection emerges when a woman after "being transformed into a commodity" and "reduced to parts of her body, becomes dependent" (p. 49b).

Because of how the pornographic industry distorts the female image, many men are led to see women as nothing more than objects to fulfill whatever their needs are for the moment. It is the pornographic character of society which keeps some males in constant search of, in the words of one interviewee, "the ultimate freak in bed." Naomi Wolfe (1991) in *The Beauty Myth* makes a critical observation about pornography when she asserts, "The consumer culture is best supported by markets made up of . . . men who want objects . . . ever-changing [and] disposable....The fleeting chimera of the airbrushed centerfold, always receding before [them] keeps [them] destabilized in pursuit, unable to focus on the . . . woman — known, marked, lined, [and] familiar. . ." (pp. 144-145). She further points out that "consumer pornography has a built-in obsolescence to ensure that as few men as possible will form a bond with one woman for years or for a lifetime" (p. 144).

There may also be other factors as to why sex is highly sought after by African American males. Audrey Chapman (1995), in *Getting Enough Loving*, points out that besides a "shaky sense of masculinity," stemming from few or no other outlets for power, and fulfilling the "stud" stereotype, some African American men "use sex to anesthetize the pain and hurts that come from living in this society" (p. 140). It may be a way for men to heal emotional wounds, particularly the wound that social scientists, using the Freudian oedipal complex theory, argue the male undergoes in individuation or separation from his first love, his mother. The idea is that after separating from the mother, the boy bonds with the father, which helps him to forge a male identity. With the absence of so many fathers, however, this is a wound Chapman asserts, many African American men may never be able to recover from.

Sex may also be used, according to Chapman, to satisfy deep emotional hunger, and a daily compulsion for it may be "a sign that an individual is looking for the holding and coddling he or she lacked as a child" (p. 146). This may be particularly true for African American men who were reared in households where their mothers were overburdened by single parent responsibilities. In addition, sex for some men, "is the only way they know how to allow themselves some tenderness" (p. 140). Chapman states, "So many men long to express their feelings, but feel ashamed of them at the same time. Through sex they can access their tender side, but they feel angry about having to be dependent on women in order to feel it"(p. 147). This may stem from the struggle some undergo from ambivalence with how to balance the masculine and feminine sides of their personalities, which may in part stem from an incomplete separation from the mother. It may also stem from the anti-feminine component in masculine construction in U.S. culture.

A man's physiological make-up may have implication for the sex drive in men. Biologists indicate that a healthy, potent male produces several hundred million sperm on a daily basis. The pornographic character of U.S. society may interact with the natural biological make-up of males to contribute to the ceaseless desire for sex. The proliferation of sexualized visual images of women and parts of their bodies may lead men to experience a continuous generalized build up.

The ceaseless desire for sex may also be an indication of the spiritual emptiness gripping not only men, but the entire Western world. Because many are spiritually empty, and know of no other

166

means to satisfy this most basic human need, sex becomes the primary vehicle. For men, their bodies, or sex, becomes a way to connect with their souls.

The demographic disparity between African American males and females indicates that an option such as polygyny may need to be explored. Studies have shown polygyny to be most prevalent in societies with a sex imbalance in favor of women (Embers, 1974). Although polygyny may be needed, current illeganous practice is not conducive to the emotional and psychological health of women, or men themselves. In such interactions, women are often made to feel estranged by men who, may be experiencing estrangement from themselves because of definitions of self based on power or, in the case of many African American men, powerlessness. Although polygyny has been widely accepted among peoples throughout the world, only about 25 percent of men in the world's cultures have been in the position to practice it. A majority of African American men are not emotionally, financially, or spiritually equipped to assume such a responsibility.

In a society dominated by men, one would expect African American men to play a significant role (as with Ausar Auset Society, African Hebrew Israelites, and others dispersed throughout various communities), in structuring marriage and family systems. However, because "outside" males are most threatening under any system of domination, and are therefore the direct target of physical, mental, and spiritual annihilation, they may not be able to assume this role on a wide scale.

Despite this, it is important that African American men become more politically and socially astute. They must understand what they do to women when they use them to satisfy their need for power by objectifying or reducing them to their bodies. They must realize that by reducing women to their bodies or body parts, they are in essence reducing themselves to their bodies, or body parts. They must see that God created man and woman with a body and a soul; as full human beings. African American men must understand the necessity of rising above sex. This indeed is a true step towards manhood.

It is also crucial that African American men understand how negative and irresponsible behavior impacts on the development of children. Women who are emotionally and psychologically stressed from unhealthy interactions with men cannot nurture psychologically and emotionally healthy children. If men would spend more time and energy helping women raise children, they would have less time to focus on sex. With more time focused on their children, especially their sons, there would be fewer "wounded" males from lack of relationships with their fathers.

The state of affairs of some African American youth has serious implications for the future of African American people. I think few recognized the irony of the tragedy, that the progeny of one of the greatest warriors in the history of the African global struggle, Malcolm X, set his widowed grandmother, Betty Shabazz on fire, and caused her death. The behavior of many of our youth is a clear indication of the state of relationships between African American men and women.

African American men must therefore be clear on how their behavior contributes to the demise of families and communities. They must know that when the most fundamental human relationship, that between man and woman is in trouble, that people are in trouble. Much of the trouble we are in stems from the widespread ignorance gripping African America, especially among those who are supposed to be educated. As Haki Madhubuti (1990) indicates, it is critical that African American men broaden their understanding of the social, political, and economic factors shaping African life, globally. Most critical, is that there be a clear understanding of what is necessary for co-partnering to become a viable option, and, what we, African American women, need and want.

What African American Women Want

•   We want warriors — men who have a clear understanding of the role they must play in the development of African people — true soldiers for our people.

168

- We want builders — men who are courageous; men who are not afraid to take a stand to define and construct our own social reality; men who understand the necessity of foregoing tribal differences around Western derived religious "scripts," "Greek" orientation, pseudoclass position, or ideological stance; men who understand that everybody can't be a king, but everybody has a significant role to play; men who understand the necessity of solidarity to move us forward.

- We want men who understand the necessity of building political, education, economic, spiritual-religious, and familial institutions that will meet the needs of our people; liberators, rather than indoctrinators; men who can withstand the heat, when what they are building is too revolutionary, even for our own people.

- We want hunters — men who "by any means necessary" will do what must be done to provide the material necessities for our families; so long as what they do is not destructive to members of anyone else's family.

- We want men to be our husbands — to be our companions; men who will talk to us, who will not dominate us; who understand that their "being" does not mean our being less; men who will not reduce, objectify, or use us as sex objects, just because the social circumstances make it easy for them to do so; men who understand what is meant by commitment, and who know how to make one, and stand by it; men who are committed to us, our children, our families, our communities.

- We want fathers for our children; men who know that being a father means more than siring or being financial, men who are actively involved in the spiritual, social, psychological, and emotional development of our children.

- We want men who understand the necessity of self development — mental, spiritual, physical, and emotional — and for those who are financially sound, to know that who you are is not be based on your financial status, but the kind of human being you are.

- We want men — who are seekers of knowledge; true seekers of truth.

- Most of all, we want men of God; regardless of the path they choose, men who seek alignment with God, righteous men, true God-like men. And as we develop these characteristics in ourselves, as we strive to be righteous, true God-like women, with open hearts and open minds, we want you to honor and respect us. With this, you and me, side-by-side, can put our relationships, families, and communities back together.

Chapter 8

SHARING MEN?: PERSPECTIVES FROM AFRICAN AMERICAN WOMEN

> ꜜ*Lonely is a place I used to be*
> *But I'm closing that door*
> *I won't live there anymore*
> *Yes I am alone, Yes I'm on my own*
> *But for the first time in my life*
> *I'm gonna carry on, Yes I'm gonna ache,*
> *But I will not break.*
> *Some things I can choose, and baby*
> *I refuse to be lonely*

i refuse to be lonely [CD, 1995]

"I Refuse to Be Lonely," the title and theme song of the CD that came out after the suicide of Phyllis Hyman, left many with the feeling that it was loneliness that led her to end her own life. Born in Pittsburgh and raised in Philadelphia, Phyllis Hyman began her professional career in 1971 with a group called *New Direction*. After moving to New York and winning over club audiences, she became a featured vocalist on the album "You are My Starship," which was produced by Norman Corners. Her solo career took off in 1977 when she signed with Buddah and then with Arista in 1979. She received critical acclaim for her music, and many of her songs hit the Billboard R&B Chart Top 20.

Although Hyman was known to suffer from bipolar disorder, according to her friend/manager, "at the root of everything was her most basic need: love – to both give and receive love" (Garcia, 1997). This need seemed to plague her and was thematic in many of the songs she sang. Although the songs may have been written by others, the depth with which sang them gave many the feeling that she was singing about her own experiences. In one CD, she sings over and over, "I can't stand this living here alone." The lyrics to "i refuse to be lonely," seem to indicate that she had risen above her struggle to live without love. She apparently had not. Rather than live alone, on June 30, 1995, she opted for death.

Eleven years prior to Hyman's death, journalist Lenita McClain also ended her own life. In an essay "To Be Black, Gifted and Alone," Bebe Moore Campbell outlines McClain's astounding achievements. By the time she was 32, she was the first African American to become a member of the editorial board of the *Chicago Tribune* newspaper in its 137-year history, a position that earned her $50,000 a year; she had won the Peter Lisagor Award from the Headline Club, the 1983 Kizzy Award for outstanding Black women role models, top honors from the Chicago Association of Black Journalists for commentary and had been selected by *Glamor* magazine as one of the ten most outstanding working women in America. In spite of these achievements, on memorial day 1984, McClain took an overdose of amitriptyline and ended her own life. Her words, "I have made it, but where," sums it up for many African American women.

Like Hyman and McClain, African American women are realizing significant achievements. They are corporate executive officers, college professors, administrators, bankers, physicians, psychiatrists, editors of major publications, architects, builders and developers, and serve in national government bodies, including Congress (Reid-Merritt, 1996). Despite such gains, many undergo psychological and emotional distress. This is because with all they achieve, they find they are without someone to share it with; they are alone. This becomes the focal point in the lives of many, causing them to suffer deeply. The suicide deaths of both McClain and Hyman are extreme cases of where loneliness and its associated psychological problems can lead to. Most women would not opt to end their own lives, but the psychological pain some experience from lack of a mate can sometimes be too much to contend with.

Considering the various the factors making it difficult for African American women to find suitable mates, several studies have explored the possibility of sharing men as an alternative. One work is that by Audrey Chapman. In her controversial book *Mansharing: Dilemma or Choice?* Chapman (1986) indicates that the sex imbalance between males and females in American society makes it virtually impossible for every female to have an exclusive mate. However, in U.S. society, most women choose not to deal with this reality openly and honestly and prefer to treat it as if it does not exist. She also indicates that sharing men has been in existence throughout human history and continues today. Another factor affecting male-female relationships, is the impact the rapidly changing post-industrial world is having on the willingness of individuals to commit to relationships. According to Chapman, we live in an era of "declining commitments" not just to people but also to traditions. In a consumer-driven, "throw-away" society, for fear of getting too close, people avoid making commitments to relationships and expect them to be of short duration. "The 'me' decade where self-gratification is exalted above nurturing and caring for others" and the shifting roles for men and women also contribute to declining commitments (p. 34). In addition, although the women's movement of the 1960s has given women relative parity with men, it has failed to define what this means for them socially, particularly in their relationships with men.

Some women, at a loss with how to deal with such changes, are opting to share themselves with many men, in a manner similar to the way men do with women. Although Chapman supports this and makes suggestions for doing so in a manner that is healthy, it is those women who are open only to a monogamous and exclusive relationship with one man who face a serious dilemma. She challenges these women to consider sharing as a means of empowerment and encourages them to make a conscientious choice to do so rather than allow it to become a dilemma in their lives.

Although sharing could provide an option for meaningful and fulfilling relationships, most women do not see it as such. This is evident in the responses from African American women to a survey on African American male-female relationships. In the late eighties, I initiated research through African American newspapers (in ten urban areas containing the largest proportion of African Americans) and various organizations to ascertain the perceptions and attitudes African American males and females have of each other based on their experiences in relationships. The most common response from African American females was their disappointment with the unwillingness of African American males

173

to commit to and/or remain so to monogamous relationships and marriages. Taking this finding into consideration, the questionnaire was revised to include an open-ended question on women's attitudes toward sharing men. I asked the question, "What is your opinion on mansharing?" Although I expected most to be opposed to the idea, I was specifically interested in their reasons. I thought such information might assist me in demystifying and debunking myths about various marriage practices.

Sixty-three African American females responded to the mansharing question (There were a total of 509 male and female participants in this on-going study at the time of this writing). They were from all over the U.S., with a majority being from the Northeast and the Southeast. Their ages ranged from 19 to 67, with a mean of 32. Approximately 56 percent were single, and 22 percent were separated or divorced. Approximately 18 percent were married, and five percent were cohabiting with someone. About 60 percent had some college education, with most still seeking bachelor degrees; 20 percent had at least a bachelor degree, and 14 percent had graduated from high school.

A second questionnaire was designed specifically to ascertain the attitudes of females on sharing men and was administered to undergraduates in several courses on African American male-female relationships and in a course on African American women at a non-traditional university in Atlanta. The questions included: What is your overall opinion of sharing a man, and would you consider openly sharing a man with another woman? There were 155 respondents. A majority were from the Southeast, primarily the Atlanta metropolitan area. Approximately 75.5 percent were single, and 13.5 percent were married. The number separated or divorced was approximately 5 percent, and 6 percent were living with someone. Their ages ranged between 19-51, with a mean age of approximately 27. All of these women were enrolled in college as undergraduates. Approximately 13 percent had already received an associate degree, 13 percent a bachelor degree, and 3 percent a master degree. Overall, 218 women responded to both questionnaires.

It's Wrong

Although there were many responses to the questions, the findings, as expected, indicate that a majority of women are opposed to sharing a man. The respondents gave various reasons for their opposition to it. One is that it conflicts with their moral beliefs. As I discussed in the first chapter, monogamy is perceived as a superior marriage form and is therefore the only one given moral sanction in the Western world. It is also projected as a universal norm in those parts of the world dominated by Europeans. While this is the case, studies show that polygyny has been a morally sanctioned marriage practice by over 80 percent of the world's peoples. Because monogamy is perpetuated in this manner, it is not surprising that women would be opposed to the idea of sharing. Most respondents who gave this as the reason for their being opposed to sharing a man did so from the perspective of what they think God intended. In several responses, the Adam and Eve story emerged. An example of this is the expression by one respondent, "God made man and woman to share with each other. He did not include a third person as a part of that union." Most others who were opposed for this reason see sharing a man, in the expression of one respondent, as "wrong! wrong! wrong!"

I'm Too Selfish; He's Mine

Another reason that respondents gave for not wanting to share a man is that they see themselves as too "selfish." An underlying reason for this is fear that such a relationship would detract from the time they could spend with, and attention they would get from the man. Some indicated that they like a lot of attention from a man. Therefore, if the man is spending time with another woman, they may not get the attention they need. It was expressed that not getting the attention one needs may lead one to feel they are being "neglected." It was also thought that time shared should be mutual. That is, if a woman is giving a man all her time, she "deserves" the same in return.

Another factor is that some see the man as someone who belongs to them. This idea was expressed by one respondent who said, "My man is just plain *mine*."

The Need to Feel Special

The need to feel special to a man was also a common response. The idea here is that if a man is in a relationship with another woman, it can lead one to feel less special to him. "To be upheld as the only one in a man's life," is for some, important. Apprehension was also expressed about how being in a sharing arrangement would impact on one's position with the man. There was concern about being second to another woman. Most who responded in this manner claimed that they would never allow themselves to be in such a position with a man, as was indicated by the expression of one respondent: "I will not be second best to any woman, unless it's his mother."

It Can be Physically and Emotionally Unhealthy

Another concern had to do with how sharing a man would impact upon one's emotional health; there is fear that such a relationship might lead to emotional instability. Some respondents expressed that it might be difficult for them to see a man they are in a relationship with or married to with another woman. It is also thought that if a man is in a relationship with another woman it might undermine the commitment between the two individuals. One respondent summed it up:

I really don't believe that you can be in a relationship sharing a man and really let yourself fall in love. I'm not saying that these relationships don't or won't work; I just think that mentally it's not healthy. Most relationships are really intimate, and the couple becomes really close; you begin to think that you can depend on that person for anything. But when you're sharing a man, it's very possible that he won't be around when you really need him.

There were a few women who admitted that they had been in or were currently in sharing relationships (clandestinely). What helps them to deal with it, however, is that there is no commitment between them and the person they are sharing with another woman. One respondent, for example, expressed that sharing a man "is a sad fact in our society today." She, however, is currently sharing a man and justifies doing so because there is no commitment. She admitted, "I know it is occurring in the situation I am in right now. I am tolerant of it because we are not in a committed relationship, but I dislike it." Furthermore, she indicated that she would not "do it by choice if the man considers [them] to be in a real (committed) relationship."

Sharing a man is also thought to be physically unhealthy for women. Respondents expressed concern with the potential for the spread of sexually transmitted diseases and fear of contracting one themselves.

It's Shortchanging Oneself

It is also thought that one who would participate in a sharing relationship might be shortchanging oneself. To opt to share a man, one may be cutting oneself short because "there could be someone they are missing out on; someone who is willing to commit to them only."

There were a few respondents who expressed that they would never have to even consider sharing because of their ability to please a man. One woman, for example, claimed, "It wouldn't be fair to her (the other woman). After he deals with me, he would not find her a challenge or even of interest."

I'd Rather Not Know

Many of the respondents believe that they may have already shared a man in the past and that they might share a man at some time in the future. Interestingly, almost all indicated that if this occurred, they would rather not know about it. The most common response was that they could not "knowingly" share a man. Although some do not think it possible for most men to have a monogamous relationship, they feel they should be "smart enough not to let their infidelity interfere with their primary relationship." Also, many feel that "what they don't know won't hurt them."

I'd Rather Be Alone

Finally, for those who are opposed to it, sharing a man is perceived as "another form of infidelity," a demonstration of a "lack of self-respect," "as a last ditch effort to have a man," an "act of desperation," and is generally thought to be "degrading" oneself. Many were also straight and to the point in their expressions of opposition to it: "It's disgusting"; "I hate it"; "It stinks"; It's "foul"; "Its nasty,"; "That is a no-no"; "No thanks"; "Hell no"; "I share food and clothes, but definitely not a man." Furthermore, rather than share a man, most proclaim that one is simply "not worth having" and that they would just "rather be alone."

It's An Option Worth Considering

Although most of the respondents were opposed to the idea of sharing, there were a few who think it might be worth considering, especially in light of the African American male shortage. There were several responses in this category: (1) Those who are in agreement with it but do not see it for themselves; (2) those who are in agreement with it, may have been involved in such a relationship, but because of bad experiences are now opposed to it; (3) those who see it as acceptable as long as the parties are dating and are not in a committed relationship; and (4) those who see sharing as acceptable for themselves. Most of these respondents agreed with sharing as long as all parties agreed to it. They indicated that they believe "it can work between consenting adults"; that it "could actually be a good thing" and that there is nothing wrong with it "if you can handle it." However, as one respondent pointed out, "The key word is *handling*, in which all parties are aware."

For those in the first category, although they see sharing a man as a possibility, similar to women who are opposed to it, many expressed the "hope" that they would never have to "knowingly" share a man. Respondents in the second category believe sharing is "necessary in some situations and a legitimate solution to the male shortage." However, because of negative experiences with it, they see drawbacks such as "jealousy," "hurt feelings," and "betrayal." Respondents in the third category see sharing as acceptable if one is only dating and not in a committed relationship. One respondent, for example, explained:

If I were just dating a guy that I was fond of but I wasn't looking for a relationship, knowing that he was seeing someone else would not bother me. On the other hand, when it comes to love I don't think I could share a man with anyone else. I believe that a love relationship is something so special that another person in the picture takes from it.

The women in the fourth category are open to sharing for themselves. Again, these women believe it is a "good idea if the women are informed," or "if all parties agree." However, they believe "it takes a strong individual to do this," and, as one put it, requires a man who is "especially strong willed, loving, kind, compassionate and gentle." It is also thought that it would take "very mature people with realistic expectations of each other" and that "openly sharing a man by a woman causes less stress in her life and gives her more control and less helplessness in considering her options." Although open to the idea of sharing, some of the women expressed concern about how it would be handled by African American men. It is thought to be necessary, but "the problem is that brothers raised with the European culture do not look at multiple relationships with the responsibility that comes along with [it]." One respondent, for example, explained, "If I am secure with myself . . . and the other female is secure with herself, and the brother is taking care of both of us (I don't mean 'well he bought her this, so I want it also'), then I would be glad to share my man." She also expressed how since sharing men does occur it would be better for African American women.

It has become a way of life for a lot of women. We as women like to think that we shouldn't share a man and maintain the attitude that if a man has a woman, it's best as a well-kept secret. Their notion is "what I don't know won't hurt." But I personally feel that it's important for me to be in a relationship where honesty supersedes all else. I would feel better knowing if I were sharing a man, because this gives me the chance to make a conscious decision as to whether I want to be in this relationship, and it empowers me in the sense that I'm not put in a vulnerable position.

She also adds, "I'm not intimidated by another woman, and I am realistic when it comes to the scarcity of 'good' Black men." Overall, it is believed that "sharing a man . . . could work" and that "in America, especially among African Americans, there's a need for it." Unfortunately, "African American men or women are not ready for it."

Finally, a few women described their experiences in sharing relationships. One described the difficulty she experiences because the woman with whom she is now sharing a man will not allow him to be open about it. She feels that if she were to do so, the relationship would be better for both of them. She explained:

I know very few Black men who are monogamous, and I have grown not to expect "fidelity" from a man. My man has another woman. I understand and accept it. I can handle sharing. I don't find it threatening. In some ways polygamy appeals to me, but most women don't know how to handle a polygamous situation. I dislike the lying and the double-dealing. If you're gonna have two or three or whatever, be up front and choose women that can handle the situation. Understand it so that there isn't all the confusion and frustration and game-playing. For example, I know who the other woman is in my case (I jokingly refer to her as my co-wife.). I know her name, what she looks like, a lot about her. My man has opened up to me to such a degree that he doesn't try to hide anything about her; he knows he can come to me to talk about that relationship without my feeling jealous or hurt. Yet, although he has tried to tell her about me (and she knows that there is someone else in the picture, it's all obvious), she refuses to acknowledge that she is sharing. She feigns ignorance. I don't understand why she refuses to deal up front with this, but then everyone is different. Ideally, I would like to be her friend so that the lying and machinations would cease. I feel, and this will sound crazy, that if she could accept the relationship, we would both have him more than either one of us has him now. Because then he could be himself, and the tension would be eased. He could devote the time he spends trying to placate both of us and pacify each of us without fear of reprisal. . . . Sharing doesn't bother me. I could very well live in the same house with him and his woman and be perfectly content and happy. I love him just that much.

Another respondent described a situation in which she shared a man with a woman to whom she became a good friend. The relationship that these two women had with the man ended in the year they met. They, however, sustained a long lasting friendship:

I met her through him. He told me they were not seeing each other at the time. She and I became friends. We started spending a lot of time together. I thought she was one of the sweetest persons I had ever met. We became closer to each other than we were to him. He would come to my house one night; then he would go to her house. We would get on the phone and talk about it. He thought we did not know what he was doing. We'd talk about it and laugh. We found that we had more in common with each other than either of us had with him. Both of us ended the relationship with him when we discovered he was seeing another woman. We still have a wonderful friendship, which has lasted over 15 years. She is like a sister.

It's About WE, US, and I (WEUSI)

Although a majority of the respondents were opposed to the idea of sharing a man, the social circumstances of African Americans indicate that it may need to be given serious consideration. The disproportionate number of males lost through incarceration and death is a true indication of the war we are in. Madhubuti (1990) has noted that in war, it is men who are the direct targets, especially the warrior class — those between the ages of 13 and 30. It is therefore not a coincidence that the leading cause of death among African American males between the ages of 25 and 34 is homicide and that one in four between the ages of 20-29 are in the criminal justice system. (These figures are substantially higher, reaching over 50 percent, in some urban areas. The Sentencing Project, 1991). It is not a coincidence that there are not enough men for every African American woman to have an exclusive mate.

To take the idea of sharing seriously, however, requires a conversion in our way of thinking. African Americans are imprisoned by European-American hegemony, which imposes its cultural practices as universal norms. It is necessary, however, to

181

deconstruct Eurocentrism in all its forms. A most critical value underlying Eurocentered social systems is individualism. Individualism is undergirded by the idea of self at the center, self-centeredness or selfishness. Self-centeredness underlies all Western social systems and institutions, including marriage.

The conversion can begin for African Americans by drawing on African traditions and values. Sharing was virtually universally practiced in the African world. One reason for this was the primacy of the group over the individual. Mbiti (1970) explains:

Only in terms of other people does the individual become conscious of his own being, his own duties, his privileges and responsibilities towards himself and other people. When he suffers, he does not suffer alone but with his kinsmen, his neighbors and his relatives whether dead or living. Whatever happens to the individual happens to the whole group, and whatever happens to the whole group happens to the individual. The individual can only say: "I am, because we are; and since we are, therefore I am." (p. 109)

Thus, it was the group that was the center, not the individual. This left no room for selfishness. It was important that all members were supported, and if one member suffered, so too did the group. It is drawing from traditions of the "old" — African centered traditions and values (which were ultimately human centered — see Linda James Myers, *Optimal Theory*) that Afrocentric theorists argue is necessary for the survival of African peoples. In *Afrocentricity*, Molefi Asante (1989) asserts:

Afrocentricity is the centerpiece of human regeneration. To the degree that it is incorporated into the lives of the millions of Africans on the continent and in the Diaspora, it will become revolutionary. (p. 1)

Using African traditions as a beginning, Wade Nobles (1978) explains that the new values we are forging is shaped cosmologically, by interdependence, ontologically, by oneness of being, and axiologically, by harmony. From this, our values are then shifted to those where "I am because we are" is the operative. Ideologies underlying the U.S. social structure are also shifted. Survival of the fittest is shifted to survival of the group;

individualism is shifted to collective responsibility; and competition is shifted to cooperativeness. Asante (1980) asserts, "A reorganization of our frames of reference is in such a way that WE becomes the center of all that radiates from US. This becomes a source of regeneration in our values and beliefs"(p. 45).

Robert Williams (1981), in *The Collective Black Mind: An Afrocentric-Theory of Black Personality*, further asserts, "Afrocentricity means a reorganization of our thinking about political, educational, economical, psychological, social and spiritual systems. Afrocentricity means that African (Black) concerns must be properly placed at the center of our being and existence" (p. 87). This, according to Kobi Kambon means a psychological conversion to an African Self-Consciousness (ASC). And because spirituality, that is, all phenomena being connected through spirit in the African world, "represents a dynamic synthesizing energy" that allows the self to "extend/ merge into the totality of communal phenomenal experience," there is also conversion to extension of the self, or African Self-Extension Orientation (ASEO) (p. 49). Such a conversion, where one is not separated from one's own center (ASC) or one's extended self, "others" (ASEO), then one's world view, and way of being is shifted according to Robert Williams to a:

"WE-US-I" or "WEUSI" v.s. an "I" orientation.

Ultimately, it is this conversion, consciousness of "self" and extension of "self" to others, or a WEUSI orientation, which is necessary for African American women to construct relationships based on "selflessness" vs. "selfishness." Only with a WEUSI orientation will African Americans be able to construct relationships that are liberating for the group.

The women who were surveyed gave various reasons for their opposition to sharing a man. Some indicated they would not consider sharing a man because it goes against their moral beliefs. A question that emerges, then, is sharing not moral? I do not think one can find in the religious or moral precepts of people anywhere in the world, that sharing is immoral. Some of the women admitted that they are too "selfish" to share. A paradigmatic shift to the

183

"WEUSI" orientation is necessary to move beyond this. Other women said that they would not share a man "knowingly." Unfortunately, this is more acceptable in Western culture than saying one would rather share a man knowing one is doing so. What this says is that we live in a society where lies are valued over truth, a society where persons would rather live with lies in the dark than with the truth in the light. And what does this say about concern for sisters who are kept in the dark?

Some women felt that sharing a man would make them feel they have no self-respect or that it is degrading. Most women fail to realize, however, that they are made to feel this way because of the disrespectful and degrading manner in which women and men engage each other in the Western world. Some relationships between men and women are based on honor and respect (husband and wife), and others (husband and mistress, lover, prostitute, etc.) are based on dishonor and disrespect (of the men to the women and the women to each other). However, relationships between men and women continue in this fashion because women participate in them and do not collectively challenge the ideas and structures that make them reality. Other concerns with time and attention, the impact of sharing on the commitment between individuals, and how it would affect one's emotional and physical health can be managed, if there were structures with guidelines to teach men and women how to conduct themselves in such relationships.

There is a need to break the stranglehold of Western cultural domination on the African American psyche. It is a hold that tells us that one's own happiness is the ultimate good, even if it means that many others will suffer. A question any African American woman can ask herself is: How can I be happy when my sister is not happy? How can any one woman be happy when a multitude of her sisters are not happy? This is not to suggest that women cannot have happy, fulfilling lives without men (some even opt to do so), but it is my belief that there is a part of a woman's being (if she is heterosexual) that is fulfilled only through an intimate relationship with a man. Thus, it is natural to feel incomplete if one does not have one.

The male-female relationship is the basis of family, and it is the basis of the nation. In all nations among all peoples throughout the world, marriage and family are highly valued. Such institutions are valued because of what they provide its members — emotional support and a stable environment to raise children. Although this is so, many African American women have been deceived into believing that there is something wrong with the desire to have a man in their lives. A popular saying among many is: "I don't need a man." Such a saying may be perpetuated to help women understand that they can be whole human beings without a man. It may also help to deter women from entering into relationships that may be unhealthy just for the sake of having one. In addition, it may help women cope with the idea that they may very well not have a man. However, for those who are in the young adult stage of the life cycle, not having a relationship with a man can potentially become a crisis. This is natural in that a love relationship is most critical at this stage in life, especially since they are in their reproductive years.

For those who are entering into middle-life, having a relationship with a man may become decreasingly important for various reasons — including having had more years to make the adjustment, having evolved past their reproductive years, and the increasing importance of generative activities and self-actualization. The problem is that for some women, regardless of where they are in the life cycle, it has become more popular to say "I don't need a man" than to admit that they desire the love, support, and security of one. And while they are saying this, they secretly long for one, while others are engaging in destructive and/or clandestine relationships behind closed doors.

It is important to note that in contemporary U.S. culture a great deal of value is placed on being single. This stems from the shift in U.S. culture from familism to individualism and the value of materialism. In the past, the nuclear family was highly valued. This is because the nuclear, monogamous family helped to fuel the economy of the European American modern, industrial period. Now it is unhappy singles, cohabitants, and married couples who are plagued with spiritual emptiness and confusion stemming from illusions created by a commercialism that is used to sell endless

185

products, that fuel the market-driven economy of the European American postmodern, super-industrial, information age.

Another factor is that many African American women have been lured into the notion that one cannot have both a family and self-actualizing life work. It is not that one cannot have both, but it is trying to do so under the nuclear family model (and for many African American women as single mothers). When families evolved around extended kin and fictive networks, there were other support mechanisms to help couples handle the demands of family life and actualize in their personal lives. This is compounded by inequality in the division of labor whereby women are expected to assume childcare and household responsibilities. The notion of African American women not needing the love and support of a mate also helps to free U.S. society of its responsibility for the dynamics that deplete African American males from the population and marginalizes them in the opportunity structure, thereby decreasing their desirability. Because of the economic and social status of African American men, many women find themselves trying to take it all on, while their natural, God-given mates, who under normal circumstances are naturally, physiologically and emotionally equipped to assume stress, are in prison cells, homeless shelters, on park benches, or are emotionally and spiritually ill and out of it, and/or addicted to drugs and alcohol. But this is not the only reason that some African American women are taking it all on by themselves.

Many have coopted European-American norms (or mythologies) of monogamy (where one thinks they will have an exclusive mate) and prince-charming (where one's husband is expected to rescue one and assume the role of breadwinner, rather than husband and wife working cooperatively). Thus, if they can't have it this way, they would rather "go it alone." Unfortunately, it is easier for the majority of African American women to say, "I'd rather be alone" than it is to challenge the structures that leave them by themselves. And while they are trying to hold it up alone, many are crumbling under the weight of it all.

Some women undergo loneliness, anxiety, stress, and depression to the extent that if they have not attempted suicide, they may have, in the words of Ntzoke Shange, "considered" it.

Meanwhile, others are slowly self-destructing through drug and alcohol abuse, excessive eating and/or dieting, and entering into and out of emotionally unhealthy relationships.

Although a primary relationship with a man may be important for emotional well-being, developing relationships in community is equally, if not more, important. Relationships in the extended family and community are necessary for emotional and social support. When one has other significant relationships, the need for an exclusive relationship with a man, becomes less critical, and one of many. Community, then, may be critical to make the shift to sharing.

Towards Community

bell hooks' (1993) work, *Sisters of the Yam, Black Women and Self-Recovery*, is critical reading for African American women. It explores many dimensions that we must address in our lives to begin to heal; to get on the road of recovery. In contemplating whether to write a chapter on male-female relationships, hooks instead wrote one that deals with the necessity of community, entitled "Sweet Communion." In this chapter she first tells of a conversation she had with a friend:

Girlfriend, I'm struggling with whether or not to write a chapter on relationships. I can't think of anything new to say. I don't wanna repeat all that stuff about black women and loneliness, and not having a man, cause every black woman don't want a man, and do you have any thoughts on the subject? Her contribution: "This man thing is not where it is at. . . .And when are they gonna see that caring and being a friend is what's happening?" We talk and talk, agreeing that the real deal is learning to live and love in community. (p. 150)

hooks goes on to state that although she herself would like to have a committed relationship, she "no longer believes that to be all that's necessary, and that [she] really want[s] to build community" (p. 150-151). She explains that while growing up in the rural South, she knew professional African Americans, most of whom were school teachers, who had chosen this profession over being married (married women at one time in U.S. history could not be teachers) who led fulfilling lives. Although they were lonely at times, and had not given birth to children, "in profound ways they were not alone" (p.151). This is because, by "living in community they had found ways to cope with the gaps in their lives" (p.151). She continues:

It did not matter if they did not have children, for there was always some needy child in their midst on whom they could shower love and care. They had their women's group, usually church related. And they had their romantic relationships, no doubt clandestine, but, of course, always known as everything in a small community is known. (p. 151)

In addition, hooks encourages African American women, as we have always done, to build "communities of resistance" (p. 159). These "should be places where people can return to themselves more easily, where the conditions are such that they can heal themselves and recover their wholeness" (p. 159).

Had McClain, Hyman, and numerous women who have committed suicide been connected to community in this manner, their fates may have turned out different. Building relationships around community may be necessary for survival.

Towards Truth

hooks also emphasizes the necessity of living life based on truth. In her chapter "Seeking After Truth," she states, "Healing takes place within us as we speak the truth of our lives." She asserts that "a culture of domination is necessarily a culture where lying is an acceptable social norm. . . .Within the colonizing process, black people were socialized to believe that survival was possible only if they learned how to deceive" (p. 20). She then goes on to discuss the origins of deception in the slave experience:

[Enslaved African Americans] often told "lies" to white oppressors to keep from being brutally punished or murdered. They learned that the art of hiding behind a false appearance could be useful when dealing with the white master and mistress. Skillful lying could protect one's safety, could help one to gain greater access to greater resources, or make resistance possible. (p. 20)

And although "Black folks expressed anger and rage that they were forced by oppressive social circumstances to commit the sin of 'lying,' they did what was necessary for survival" (p. 20-21). She further explains:

[Enslaved African Americans] expressed righteous indignation that oppressive white people created a dehumanizing social structure where truth-telling could be valued but not practiced and where black people were judged inferior because of their "inability" to be truthful. Caught in a double-bind, on the one hand believing in the importance of honesty, but on the other hand knowing that it was not prudent to always speak truthfully to one's oppressors, [enslaved African Americans] judiciously withheld information and lied when necessary. (p. 21)

Being untruthful continued even after the slave experience:

The realties of daily life in white-supremacist America conveyed to black people in the long years after slavery had ended that it was still not in their interest to forsake this practice of dissimulation. Continued racial oppression, especially when it took the form of lynching and outright murder of black people, made it clear to all black folks that one had to be careful about speaking the truth to whites. (p. 21)

This way of living continues today. According to hooks, "Encouraged to wear the mask to ensure survival in relation to the white world, black folks found themselves using strategies of dissimulation and withholding truth in interpersonal relationships within black communities" (p.22). Furthermore, the "negative impact of these strategies was that truth-telling, honest and open communication, was less and less seen as necessary to the building of positive love relationships" (p. 23).

Even though we continue to use strategies of dissimulation, hooks indicates "[m]any of the survival strategies that were once useful to black people, like dissimulation, are no longer appropriate to the lives we are living and therefore do us grave harm" (p. 23). Finally, she points out, "It hurts to pretend. It hurts to live with lies" (p. 29). Thus, saying that one is willing to participate in relationships with men who are in relationships with other women, but not "knowingly," as many of the respondents indicated hurts not only those directly involved, but those peripherally so. Moreover, it hurts us all.

It is also important that women learn to develop different types of relationships with men. Chapman (1986) suggests that women stop seeing every man as a potential husband or, in other words, stop "husband hunting." It is necessary to begin to see and develop relationships with men in the variety of ways in which they can enhance our lives. Not being confined to a monogamous relationship allows women space for different kinds of relationships with other men so that they can continue to grow and develop.

Most importantly, women must understand the value of developing and maintaining relationships with other women. This is necessary for community. It is also critical for even considering a sharing relationship. Traditionally, in Africa and throughout the diaspora, African women shared sisterhood through their work, mothering, "othermothering," and activism in church and community (Collins, 1991; 2000). What is interesting, however, particularly where European-American culture dominates and puts women in competition for men, when it comes to a man, sisterhood falls apart. Women must unlearn their distrust of the feminine, and they must unlearn distrust of each other.

In my African American male-female relationships and women courses, young women speak of the reluctance they have with developing relationships with other women. They speak of women being catty and difficult to trust. I explain to them, however, that women are held to a different standard than men, particularly in the Western world, and women do it themselves. European patriarchy has taught men not to trust the feminine in themselves, and it has taught women not to trust it in themselves and in other women. This starts from the most powerful myth among us — the Adam and Eve story. Eve is responsible for the downfall of humankind and therefore cannot be trusted. Women therefore are not to be trusted by men, other women, or even themselves. We must not underestimate the power of myth and the role it plays in structuring social relations and institutions and our views of self and relations with others.

It is unfortunate that hooks decided to not write a chapter on male-female relationships because this is probably one of the most critical problem areas facing African American women. In *Body and Soul*, Villarosa (1994) indicates that the "the National Black Women's Health project reports that over 50 percent of Black women live in emotional distress"(p. 369). She also notes that Dr. Denese O. Shervington estimates that 80 percent of Black women are deeply troubled (p. 369). The general depression that many suffer is compounded by problems in intimate relationships (p. 369). Shervington, according to Villarosa states:

In addition to dealing with racism, lots of Black women experience rejection in their relationships that takes a heavy toll on them. . . .As a response to the rejection, the women will often engage in self-destructive behavior such as substance abuse or unsafe sex. They develop a hopelessness and very fatalistic attitude toward life because they don't feel good about themselves or believe they have anything to live for. (p. 369)

In her chapter "Healing Darkness," hooks, using an excerpt from Toni Cade Bambara's book *Salteaters*, two Black women, an elder and ancestor, are in the process of trying to heal Velma, a young woman who has attempted suicide. One asks the other, "What is wrong, Old Wife? What is happening to the daughters of the yam? Seem like they just don't know how to draw upon the powers of the deep like before" (p. 13). hooks goes on to discuss how she had been raised by African American women who taught her the powers of healing, how to "draw upon the powers of the deep," and how she "grieved for this new generation who seemed so modern, so sophisticated, and so lost" (p. 13). It is crucial that African American women unlearn the ways of those who have been our oppressors, those who have caused and continue to cause us pain. It is critical that African Americans turn to old traditions, old values, those of our fore-fathers and mothers, our ancestors; to begin to heal.

It is also important to develop a healthy relationship with self. Sharing a man requires a woman to be secure within herself. Although one may desire a man to enhance one's life, he should not be the basis of one's self value or worth. Moreover, it is with a secure relationship with self that a woman can be at ease in a relationship with a man who is in a relationship with another woman. Most important, as hooks points out, is the necessity of cultivating a spiritual life or "walking in the spirit." This is absolutely critical.

Sharing, if structured in a way that is beneficial to women, can provide an alternative to living without a mate at all. Clearly, a critical factor is that men make the shift from patriarchal ideologies that define manhood in ways that lead them to engage women in less than an optimal manner. However, for sharing to become a reality that can be healthy for everyone involved, it is going to take women to do it. Women can become a formidable force if they unify. Only through unity can women construct structures that hold men accountable, structures that teach both men and women new values upon which to form relationships and to conduct themselves. Dedication to truth may indeed be the most critical factor to help us move forward. Here again, hooks is instructive:

Collective unmasking is an important act of resistance. If it remains a mark of our oppression that as black people we cannot be dedicated to truth in our lives, without putting ourselves at risk, then it is a mark of our resistance, our commitment to liberation, when we claim the right to speak the truth of our reality anyway. (p. 29)

Furthermore, according to hooks, "it must be remembered that to be open and honest in a culture of domination, a culture that relies on lying, is a courageous gesture" (p. 29). "To choose wellness, we must be dedicated to truth" (p. 29).

There are African American women who have already made a move in this direction. The structures they have helped to build, along with men in the African Hebrew Israelite, Ausar Auset, and some Muslim communities, provide models for all women. This is the focus of the chapters to follow. The models these communities provide can be a model for relationship, family, and community building for African Americans across the board. To forge ahead, however, it is crucial that African American women divorce themselves from the lies and deceit upon which the

192

monogamy "only" myth is constructed and perpetuated. A myth that keeps many of us divided, unfulfilled, unhappy, and alone.

PART III: AFRICAN AMERICAN WOMEN AND MEN IN POLYGYNY

Chapter 9

DIVINE MARRIAGE: AFRICAN HEBREW ISRAELITE WOMEN IN POLYGYNY

The African Hebrew Israelites are a community of African Americans who are currently living in Israel under the leadership of Ben Ammi Ben-Israel. After Ben Ammi had a vision in 1967, he led an exodus of 400 African Americans out of the U.S. They settled in the interior of Liberia to purge themselves of the malignities they had acquired under cultural domination in American society or, in their own words, "while in captivity." In 1969, some of them made the journey to Israel. They have been living there for more than 30 years and currently reside in three towns: Dimona, Arad, and Mitzpe Ramon. They also have extensions throughout the U.S., in the Caribbean, and in West Africa.

The African Hebrew Israelites say they are the descendants of the biblical children of Israel, a descendant of Abraham. They believe that as a result of their disobedience to the laws and commandments of God, the children of Israel have been held captive by various nations. Since many had migrated to West Africa, some were brought to the U.S. through the transatlantic slave trade. The African Hebrew Israelites are guided by the laws of Yahweh that were passed down through Moses to the descendants of the twelve sons of Israel, one of whom was Judah, the ancestor of the Jews. Thus, their practices with some variations are the same as those practiced under Judaism. In fact, it was pointed out that most members of the African Hebrew Israelites are descendants of the tribe of Judah although a few are from other tribes (Ammi, 1999). The African Hebrew Israelites, however, distinguish between Judaism, which is religion, and righteousness. Religion requires that one be obedient to the traditions;

righteousness requires one be obedient to God. Consequently, the African Hebrew Israelites do not practice religion but "a way of life" based on the will and instruction of God (Ammi, 1999).

As under Judaism, some of the laws the African Hebrew Israelites observe include the Sabbath (the day of rest that begins on Friday at sunset and continues until nightfall on Saturday), and the holy days that include but are not limited to Passover (delivery from slavery in Egypt); Shavuout (the spring harvest and God's gift of the Torah), Memorial Blowing of the Trumpets; Yom Kippur (the day of atonement), and Succoth (feast of booths commemorating life in the wilderness). A basic practice of Judaism is compliance with the dietary laws given them by Moses to eat only animals with cloven hoofs that chew the cud and only seafood with scales or fins. The diet of the African Hebrew Israelites differs in that they are vegans. This means they eat no food that contains animal products. In addition to their strict diet, the community is self-contained and has an economic system based on a principle of all things in common. The overall goal of the African Hebrew Israelites is to build a new world or kingdom based on the laws of God.

Divine Marriage

Marriage in the African Hebrew Israelites community is practiced under what is referred to as divine marriage, which simply means a marriage that is pleasing unto God. Divine marriage consists of three stages. The first stage is divine pursuit, which means that a man may pursue a woman, or a woman a man. During this stage, the two individuals spend time getting to know each other. Apart from holding hands, physical intimacy is not allowed. If both individuals develop a mutual strong feeling, they enter into *michodeshet* (similar to engagement), a period of sanctification that lasts a minimum of 70 days. Physical intimacy is also not allowed at this stage. Once the couple enters into *michodeshet*, an announcement is made and the individuals are removed from the community of single "brothers and sisters." This means that no one can pursue either of them, nor they anyone. During *michodeshet* the couple must meet with a priest at least ten times.

The man and woman may attend some of the meetings together and they may attend some of them alone.

\ There are several objectives in meeting with a priest. The first is for the individuals to learn the primacy of the presence of the creator in the development of the relationship. The priest ensures that the individuals understand the larger moral obligation not only to each other, but to the community. Because the sessions are based on open and frank discussions, both individuals can discuss issues or concerns, and the priest inquires into personal matters, including sex and fertility issues. Spiritual compatibility is emphasized over physical and emotional compatibility to ensure that the couple understand that once vows are made, the relationship is eternal. After these meetings, the priest determines if the individuals are ready. The period of *michodeshet* ends when the couple either gets married or ends the engagement.

A unique feature of divine marriage is that a man may marry more than one wife. Such a practice was acceptable among the ancient Hebrew Israelites. However, centuries of contact with various Christian European nations (Romans banned polygyny in A. D. 285 and again in A. D. 393) effected a gradual movement away from polygyny among the Jews. The African Hebrew Israelites, however, continue to follow the custom of polygyny in the manner of the ancient children of Israel and is generally given no static from the Israeli government, though there is no official recognition of it either. Although marriage and divorce are handled by the religious authorities of the various communities in Israel, in some matters the state supersedes laws of the religious communities. Muslims, for example, are allowed to have up to four wives. However, only one wife's name appears on the state registry (Ammi, 1999).

With regard to their perspective on polygyny the women are guided by the principle, "We want for our sisters what we want for ourselves." As one crown sister (the highest level in the political hierarchy that a woman may hold) put it, "What we want is happiness, and this is what we want for our sisters." Although a man may take on more than one wife, he cannot consider doing so until after a year of marriage to his already existing wife. In the year with his new wife, he does all he can to strengthen her. When

196

he becomes interested in marrying another woman, or when a woman becomes interested in marrying him, the potential wife may spend time getting to know his family, including his already existing wives and children. The already existing wives may also sit with the man and the prospective wife in sessions with the priest. Overall, the African Hebrew Israelites believe that one of the greatest blessing of divine marriage is that it allows the family to be guided by men of God, and provides images of strong men and emotional, physical, and spiritual security for women.

The Women

The population of the African Hebrew Israelite community in Israel consists of approximately 1600 members, with 25 percent of the families being polygynous. I conducted two- to four-hour interviews with women in six families during my two-week visit to the community in Israel. Women in three of the families were interviewed separately, and those in the remaining three families were interviewed together. A total of 16 women were interviewed formally. Their ages ranged from 26 to 59, with a mean age of 42 and a median age of 43. One family had four wives, two had three wives, and four had two. The women were by profession a nurse, midwife, nutritionist, teacher, and a dancer; two were business owners, and the rest were homemakers. I also had informal discussions with women throughout the community.

"Just Pray for the Right Mind": Making the Adjustment

I was first interested in finding out the women's initial attitudes toward men having multiple wives and how they were able to adjust to it. The responses varied according to the stage the women entered the community. For women who were there in the early years, there was a great deal of resistance in the beginning. What contributed to this was the way their husbands introduced new wives. In some instances, first wives learned of the second wife after the relationship was already underway, and in one instance, after the husband and new wife had already married. Thus, the first wives had not agreed to a second wife and had no input into the selection of the person with whom they would be sharing their husbands and children. An example of this is a woman who made the journey to Liberia before her husband. She explained, "I was looking forward to spending some time together 'cuz we were always busy with the community. When he came, he had a wife coming too, two weeks behind him." Similarly, another woman explained "He had already found somebody and made up his mind. So he said, 'I have somebody and I want you to, you know, try and develop a relationship with her and get to know her, because I'm bringing her into the family.'"

In some instances, the second wives were deceived about the status of the first wife. When one woman, for example, asked her potential husband whether he was married, he told her, "I'm married to God." She described how she discovered that men could take on multiple wives:

We went over to M, . . . and when we went in, . . . he introduced me to the brother and he introduced me to the sisters, but nobody said, "This is his wife, and this is his wife." So we sat there that evening; we talked. Myself and the sisters, we talked. And in my mind, I was saying, "That's his wife? No, that's his wife." I couldn't figure it out, and I didn't ask them. So when we were going back to the temple to get my car, I asked him, "Which one of those sisters is his wife?" He said, "Both of em." At that point, I didn't say nothing else because I couldn't believe it. Two women in the same house? I couldn't even conceive that, and he didn't say nothing, and I didn't say anything. It tripped me out, but I didn't bring it up no more.

She described how she eventually found out that the man she was with was still with his wife.

I found out before I left, but by this time we [were] married already. . . .By chance, one day we were looking at some pictures that had come in from the land, and they were saying, "Ooh girl, Ooh girl. Look at so-&-so, Here's so-&-so." [I asked], "Oh who's that?" [They said], "Oh that's so-&-so." I asked, "Are they married?" and somebody replied, "Yeah, they married to whoever, so-&-so." Then I said, "Who is this? Somebody said, "That's K." Then I said, "Who's she married to?" Then they looked at me. So anyway, I said, "Well who's she? Who's her husband?" Then they stopped. Then they turned around and looked at me like. "You mean you don't know?" That was before I got there. So then I realized that I was involved in something that I really wasn't prepared for, because I had no previous knowledge.

Although she was confused about the whole matter and even admitted that she "didn't want to be bothered with no man and his wife, cause [one] knew how those situations were, and [she] didn't want to be involved in that," she decided to go ahead with it because she thought his already existing wife would understand because she had "been in the truth for four years and knew about [her]." She, however, continued to question, asking herself, "How am I supposed to treat her," and she still "couldn't even imagine being married to a man that had a wife." Unfortunately, she did not know that the first wife did not know about her either, nor had she accepted the idea of her husband having another wife.

Another woman explained that in the early stages, although some wives knew that divine marriage included polygyny, many did not think it would happen to them and were in denial about it. When asked if she knew the community practiced polygyny, she explained, "They had mentioned that brothers can have more than one wife. It was new then. This was something that had never been done before. Sisters would say for years that they didn't know anything about it. Then it began to come around the family." When asked if the first wife knew whether her husband was pursuing her, she responded, "Well, in actuality, she knew, but she was not accepting of it and did not realize the seriousness of it. . . . I began meeting the family and everything, but by the time we went to meet his wife, she was like, 'I don't know anything about this.'"

Although the women initially resisted the idea of a man having multiple wives, and even organized against it, it appears that as divine marriage became more structured and the men persisted in bringing in new wives, the women began to see value in it and came to accept it. Emphasis on the vision of the kingdom and spiritual development were key. One woman saw it as a part of the kingdom. She pointed out, "I was in pursuit of the kingdom. One day it just came to me that, hey! I'm talking about following this, and I believe in this, and I believe in that, but I'm separating things and leaving things out, the parts that I don't want. If I'm accepting it, I've got to accept the truth as the whole. You can't separate anything from it. So, at that point I realized that I had to accept everything and just prayed for the right mind to do whatever I had to do." Another woman also described how prayer helped her.

We had been married for 18 years before the second wife came into the family. . . .And it was something new to me. I had to learn about it, and I had to pray because in that society we were accustomed to the man having one wife. Of course, now we all know that men had more than one woman, but we were not accustomed to living with each other. So I had to get an adjustment in my mind as to, you know, could I accept it? Could I get an understanding with it? Because like I said, I was also just coming into the kingdom, learning about the kingdom, learning about the guidelines and how to really share and how to be sisters with someone.

As with others, a most crucial factor for this woman was that in spite of her husband taking on a new wife, it was important to feel that he still loved her:

I had to talk and really get an understanding with my Lord [how women refer to their husbands], because he was learning too and basically what I told him was I just wanted him to be truthful. That was the most important thing, and I wanted him to give us both consideration and have balance and judgment in his decisions. . . .So after talking to him, he said, "I love you for your attributes and I love S . . . for her attributes, but me loving her does not end my love for you. You have been with me 18 years already and we already have children." We had two children at that time, and I was pregnant with the third child. And he said, "I love you." So with that understanding I prayed.

What also helped some women adjust to polygyny was that they knew it was common in African American communities in the U.S. They knew that men had other women. What they were not used to, however, was its being done openly. As the women above indicated, they were not used to the idea of having to live with the "other" women. Those who came into the community later in its development seemed to be more open to polygyny for this very reason. When one woman who entered the kingdom approximately

13 years after the exodus from America was asked her impression of polygyny when she first came to Israel, her response was, "I didn't have a problem with it because most men in the world had another girlfriend." Another woman also indicated, "I can't think of any time in my relationship with my fiancee from the world that he didn't have another woman. . . . I feel that the way they talked about it coming into the community was a little more honest."

There are also those who were raised in the community in Israel. This means that not only are they socialized to multiple wifeship, but they have also been raised in such households. One young woman, however, had spent eight years in America. When asked how her friends in the U.S. reacted when she would tell them about the lifestyle, her response was, "People just think it is unheard of, yet they can have girlfriends and be going with women and married, sleeping around. They just don't bring it to the house, but they do it. It isn't called divine marriage but they do the same thing."

"How Do I Treat Her?": Relationships Between the Wives

Besides how they eventually accepted polygyny, I was interested in knowing how wives eventually came to accept one another and what their relationships are like. Initially, having a second wife imposed on them caused a lot of hurt and pain for first wives. This resulted in a great deal of resentment, which strained relations between them and their husbands and their new wives. Because of the love they hold for the kingdom and their husbands, however, they eventually accepted their new wives and even developed friendships. The women now participate in choosing wives for their husbands, express a great deal of love and respect for them, and refer to each other as "sister-wives."

An example of how second wives were received by first wives in the early stages of the kingdom is that of one family in which it "took 16 years to get to work together, live together and have some harmony." Although the first wife does not feel that she and her sister-wife had a friendship all those years, she did note that "it's kind of hard not to love somebody that you live with, the love for the children, helping one another, doing for one another,

201

and just being there." When the second wife was asked how she initially felt about the first one, she responded:

First of all, I still felt that I had been done wrong, because I would have preferred, I would have felt better, had I come in knowing. I felt that I had been cheated, but then what I did, I said, "O.K., leave that alone. . . . Ain't no sense in you going on, dealing with that. Now, where do we go from here. How do I treat her?" I had to keep asking myself, "How do I treat her?" The only thing that kept coming to my mind was, "Treat her the way that you would want to be treated." So, I started trying to do that, but in the beginning, she was hurt too, because she's here one day, and then here is somebody telling her about that's her husband, I mean, that ain't no easy pill to swallow. So, you have to look at both sides of it. You can't just look at one side like that, because it's not easy.

Interestingly, it was the first wife, who was initially against the second wife, who years later encouraged a third wife to become a part of the family. She explained, "I had chosen her cuz at one point she was fixin' to get involved with another family. I told her she was getting ready to make a mistake — that wasn't her family." The third wife agreed: "I could very well have gone in the wrong direction. . . .She saw me sitting out one evening talking to someone else. . . . She grabbed me. She said, 'This is our family here.' She pulled me away, and it put something in my mind." From that point on, she kept "pressing" it on her mind until she finally made the decision to join the family.

A second wife explained that when she married her husband, his first wife took it "pretty hard." However, they "understood that was the way it was going to be." A key was that she and the first wife talked. She explained further, "We talked about everything and shared our thoughts together and our being that close helped the brother to better understand how to deal with the two of us." In this particular instance, the relationship between the wives outlasted the relationship with their husband. Their husband eventually left the kingdom. Remaining together, they were put back into the sisterhood, which meant that they could pursue again or be pursued. In fact, they were "so close" it was suggested by members of the community that they should "have married the same brother again." They both married three years later, however, to different men.

In some instances, the women are already good friends. This makes it relatively easy for them to sustain a good relationship after they marry the same man. In other instances, as above, the woman may pick out a sister-wife. For example, when one woman who already has a new sister-wife was asked whether she thinks her husband will eventually take on a third wife, her response was, "Oh most definitely. I have already picked her out. I love her dearly." In other instances, women encourage their husbands to take on a new wife out of love and concern for a "sister." With regard to a third sister-wife, one woman explained, "She needed to get married; she had been single for a while, and she was the type of sister that was so giving that she deserved a good family." Her sister-wife expressed similar thoughts: "I always wanted him to marry her. I had been trying to get her to marry him for years. . . cuz she's a good sister." And still in other instances when a man begins pursuing a woman, she will introduce herself to already existing wives and spend time getting to know the family. When one wife was asked how she felt about her husband pursuing a second wife after a year into the marriage, she responded, "It was all right. I didn't have a problem with that. [She] came and let me know that she was interested in him." With this woman, as with others, initially, the concern had to do with difference in age. Her potential sister-wife was twenty years younger than she. She, however, eventually resolved: "It really has more to do with personality. I actually have a younger spirit. I'm fun, whereas she sits back and have the children. . . .I told her, 'You are the old one.'"

Another wife also described how she dealt with an incoming wife who was twenty years younger than herself:

My main concern too was the age, because I have a son, 32, and she's 32, and when she first started coming around, and our Lord was talking to her, I mentioned this to her. I said, "Well, do you realize that we have a son that's your age?. . . . I'm somewhat concerned about your age, are you going to be able to make the adjustment?" And also I mentioned, naturally, at that age group, you want to still be partying, I know I did. Going to the various parties that they have here and with our Lord being older, I told her, "he might not want to go to all of the parties. . . . I know he's going now, because when they're pursuing, they gotta show they still got it, but when he gets married, he probably will wanna stay home and relax. You might still wanna go partying, how you gonna feel about that?" She said that she could make the adjustment. She was O.K. with it. She didn't see anybody else, and she knew that he was an older brother, that she loved him and felt that she could adjust. After she said that, and after I discussed it with him, I said, "It's gonna be an adjustment for you," and they still had their minds set, and I moved on.

When this woman's sister-wife was asked about her feelings with regard to the husband bringing in a younger wife, she said,

They say, it's a man's world, and it's like that all over the world. Because he might not be marrying anyone younger, that doesn't mean that he's not out there. . . . So, it's just real, it's brought home. You know who the person is, you know her attributes, you know her hygiene, and you know her personality. So it makes it better. It doesn't have to be in the dark.

I was also interested in how the wives adjust to each other's different ways of doing things. I was particularly interested in how already existing wives adjust to the new wife. Understanding that "everybody has their own personality and spirit"; "everybody does things different"; being open minded and open to change, and "striving toward oneness," were thematic. When one woman was asked how she felt coming into a situation in which the routine was already established, she explained, "R . . . had established an order. She had a way she kept the children, folded the clothes, and did the ironing. She had to adjust and say it may not be my way, but it is still getting done. We try not to criticize because it is not the way to do it. We are different people; you may put something different in your cornbread that I don't, but if it's good, say hallelujah!"

The women were asked what they find most difficult about being in a polygynous marriage. Someone else being attentive to their husband is one. One woman explained:

I guess I was just so used to it being just us, the sharing. All of a sudden you look up and it's not just you any more. When you have been with him for 10 years, you get comfortable and relaxed. It's like, "Okay baby, I'll do your hair when I get to it." Now all of a sudden it is someone running to do it. I think to make a personal and spiritual space for another person in

204

the family is really a growth process. It is an adjustment, but it is now more easy.

I asked this woman how having a new wife affects her space psychologically. She pointed out the importance of the relationship with the husband and said, "I feel that I have my own space. I'm secure in myself, in my personality, in my relationship with my Lord, and I'm not concerned about anybody taking my space, cause I feel that my space will always be there."

Another adjustment is assuming responsibility for children when one has none. This may be particularly difficult for those who have a career, business, or likes to travel. A woman who is the third and newest wife, although she loves the sense of family that her sister-wives provide, stated, "I have 15 children and I have to answer to things. I think that was the hardest adjustment because I like freedom." When one woman married, she had no children but her sister-wife had six. She, as others, however, loves the children and treats them as her own. She said, "I never separated; it wasn't like I didn't have any children. When I got married, I had six children. That meant when I went to the store, I bought enough for six children." In fact, some women spend so much time with the children of their sister-wives that others in the community have difficulty distinguishing whether or not they are their biological children.

I was also interested in how the women adjust to assuming responsibility for new children after their own have already reached the age of maturity. One woman has three children who have already reached adulthood, and her sister-wife has four, the oldest being seven. When she was asked how she feels about raising children all over again, she pointed out that some women are so attached to the children of their sister-wives that even the children get confused about which mother is the biological parent. In her case, her sister-wife's child thinks she is her brother's biological mother and tells people in the community that her natural mother just has "a spiritual connection with him." The boy also thinks she is his biological mother.

The women were also asked how conflicts are resolved and differences handled. They seem to have simple solutions. One pointed out, "We come together on our love for him." Another woman said, "If there is a problem, you go ahead and air it out. We all have the freedom to say how we feel." With regard to differences, this woman continued, "If there is something she is adamant about, I will give in, and if I am adamant about something, she will give in, whether it concerns the children or the house."

The Benefits of Having Sister-Wives

Research on polygyny among African women shows that women find several benefits to being in polygynous marriages. These include assistance with child care, husband care and domestic tasks, companionship, increased wealth, and bringing women with whom the husbands may have extramarital affairs into the family (Solway, 1990; Ware, 1979). I was therefore interested in finding out what women in the African Hebrew Israelite community see as benefits in having sister-wives. With few a variations, the benefits are similar to those among African women. The African Hebrew Israelite women cited the sense of family that comes from having sister-wives and their children (particularly if one does not have children of her own). They also like having a helpmate for child care and household responsibilities. In addition, they like having someone to help provide the physical and emotional needs of their husband. However, before expanding on this, let me first discuss the responsibilities of the women in the kingdom.

As indicated previously, the African Hebrew Israelites live in a self-contained community. They own a soybean factory that manufactures a variety of soybean products that are distributed throughout Israel. They also have a sewing center, a cafeteria, which serves over 600 children two hot meals six days per week, a school, and the House of Life, a natural childbirthing center. Although the sewing factory manufactures most of the clothing worn by members of the community, some wives make most of the clothes for their families. For example, I met a woman with 8 or 9 children. She, her husband, and the children had on matching outfits. The women are also responsible for cooking and making basic foods from scratch, such as mayonnaise, ketchup, and salad dressing. Besides cooking, sewing, and other domestic duties, women are responsible for child care. In addition, they must provide emotional, physical, and domestic support to their husbands.

Some women also work outside the home, within the community and outside it. Within the community they are nutritionists and healers and are responsible for childbirth and other health-related matters. They work in the sewing factory, operate the center where the children eat, and are largely the teachers. Regardless of her work, within or outside the community, domestic and extracurricular activities, each sister is required to commit a minimum of six hours a week to the community. Overall, I am compelled to say that these women work! Having sister-wives helps them to meet the many demands.

Domestic Tasks and Child Care

A benefit of having sister-wives is that if one woman works outside the home, there is someone to focus on domestic tasks. Another benefit is that if one wife needs to work, or go away on a vacation or extended trip, there is a sister-wife to care for her children. Women find comfort in knowing that when they leave home their children will be taken care of. For example, one woman explained that because they see their sister-wives' daily interaction with their children, when they are not around, they can feel comfort in knowing their children will "still be loved; they're still going to get a hug; they're still going to get a kiss; they're still going to be all right." She exclaimed, "I just love it. I love it!" Overall, it is important to know that there is someone they can depend on and trust to care for their children as if they are their own.

Two reasons why having sister-wive(s) is also helpful is how the menstrual cycle and afterbirth are handled in divine marriage. With regard to the menstrual cycle, which the community refers to as the period of "inactivity," women are allotted seven days to refrain from cooking. The Kefar (community) even has a house for women, if they so choose, to go to during this time. Although this may seem an antiquated practice, women who go through extreme mood swings and illness during this period

207

may see the benefit of it. With regard to postpartum, women abstain from sexual activities with their husbands for 80 days. During such times, sister-wives help with the newborn, assume responsibility for other children and household duties, and provide the needs of the husband.

Husband Care

Women find security in knowing that someone is there for their husbands, especially when they are away on an extended trip. In fact, some of the women claimed that not only is this a benefit, but an essential need. In one instance, when a sister-wife left Israel for a two-year assignment, the other wife had relied on her so much, that she "prayed for her to come back." With regard to providing her husband's needs, she declared, "I don't think I could do it alone. As a matter fact, I know I can't. I feel that a man needs more than one wife. . . .I prayed every night that she would come back. When you have a man that demands a lot and loves attention, and you have children and different responsibilities, I need my sister-wife to share the load."

Similarly, a second wife went to spend six months with her husband who was away. This was something she looked forward to because as a second wife she never had the opportunity to be alone with him. The demands, however, were more than she anticipated. She explained, "That meant that I was the only one to cook for him, the only one to clean for him. I was the only one in the bedroom. I was the only one, you know, everything was just me and him. It showed me, and it helped me to really appreciate R. . . I was so glad to get back home."

Having sister-wives also provides more opportunity to pursue other interests. This same woman continued, "When it's just you, you have to constantly think of him and constantly think of the children, constantly think of his needs, but with R, I can say, "Okay, I need to travel, tomorrow she'll watch the baby. Then, if next week she wants to travel, then I'll do it. So it allows you the freedom and flexibility to do things." When two wives whose husband is pursuing a third wife was asked how they feel about having to divide their time with a third wife, one explained, "You know, after a certain stage, you kind of want your time and space. There are things that you want to do; you want to read, you might want to sew or what not, it gives you a little time and space." The other one agreed with her, saying, "I'll go in my room and get my book out in a minute. After I put my little one to bed, I'm at peace, read my book, and go to sleep."

Companionship

Companionship is another benefit of polygyny. The women see it as "great, having a friend that you can talk and laugh with," and "a blessing that you don't have to leave home to get this." This is especially the case for those who have husbands who spend substantial amounts of time away from the kingdom. A first wife who initially had difficulty accepting the second wife described the role she has played as a companion:

Well, for one thing, you have a sister you can feel close to right in the same house with you. You have a helpmate that you know you can count on when you need things, or when something is needed for the Lord, that you're not able to be there to take care of. And you have a friend to discuss things with. Quite often, . . . when our Lord wasn't there, we had to go to various functions together. . . .So for many years we have been the companion for each other when he wasn't here.

The women also discussed the benefits of each other's skills, talents and strengths. For example, one woman explained, "You know, people may look at it like a job interview, but it's like what can she bring, what can we give her, what can we do for each other." Another woman stated, "After you get everyone's attributes together, everything is covered." She went on to describe those of her sister-wives and herself: "Like she's the doctor, Crown-sister, wife, mother, and I'm the secretary, bio-nutritionist, wife and mother. The new sister that's coming in the family, she's a seamstress. . . .I don't sew for brothers, so she does, so she'll be the seamstress for our Lord. Once everybody pulls all the attributes together, everything should work out smoothly."

Another wife explained that they both cook and sew, but that the other one does most of the sewing for the family. A few also talked about the personality attributes of their sister-wives. One woman described herself as the balancer and sees herself as more serious. Her sister-wife is funny, and she feels it is good to have the "laughing and the joy."

Finally, there is security in knowing that all woman can potentially get married if they so desire and that they and their children can be a part of a family. No woman has to be without a husband, and their children can have fathers. When asked the single most important benefit, one woman replied, "Security. In Babylon [America], for so long I was both the mother and father for the children; protector and provider, and that's a lot of work. He makes me feel secure, and the children feel secure, and I don't have to worry about anything." She further noted, "Once you get to be forty in America and [you are] a Black woman with children, you are finished, and I didn't have any hope. It is a great sense of security from him and each sister-wife. It is just great."

"Anticipation of the Reunion": Time Arrangements

An important aspect of polygyny is how time is divided between wives. The arrangements are left to the individual families, but there are primarily two ways it is done. The most common method is for the wives to plan the conjugal visit around their menstrual cycles. Generally, when it is a wife's turn to be with the husband, she spends the night with him in his room. When there are two wives, each generally spends time in their husband's room for two weeks at a time. When there are three wives, each spends about 10 days; with four wives, each spends about seven days on a monthly basis.

The other and the least common way is that the husband decides. Overall, a major benefit of the time away from the husband is that it helps to keep the luster in the relationship. As one crown sister put it, "There is always anticipation of the reunion."

"In the Room": Jealousy

In studies on African women, jealousy and rivalry between wives were perceived as the greatest disadvantages of polygyny. Based on research, I was interested in finding out whether the women experience feelings of jealousy, and if they do, how they deal with it. Most admitted to feeling jealous. These feelings usually emerge when their husband is "in the room" with a sister-wife. One woman explained, "I had been his first wife for 18 years. So when he was spending time in the room, at first there were funny feelings about that." What helped her deal with it is knowing he would eventually spend time with her. She explained, "So I had to get my mind situated; that there wasn't anything to feel funny about because he was gonna spend time with me."

Prayer is the way that most women deal with jealousy. When I asked one woman what makes her feel jealous, she responded, "When I want to be with him, and I can't. That's when I have to pray because some of those thoughts I am really shocked to know I am having." Consideration for one's sister-wife also helps. She explained, "I'm like, you have a lot of nerve; she wants to be with him too. She wants to be happy and laugh and joke and experience all of that too. So why should you just feel that it is just you who should get all of that? So during those times I have to really go and pray and get myself together. Sometimes it is easy, and sometimes it isn't."

When I asked another woman whether she ever feels jealous, she responded, "No. I am very secure. Sometimes I just want to be with him all the time, not taking anything away from her. . . . I just want to be with him. I don't like it that I have to leave the room, but I do it with a smile because I am sure she feels the same way."

One woman explained the importance of not being selfish: "In divine marriage, you cannot be selfish in no kind of way. . . . If when he comes home, I want all his time, then that is selfish. He has to divide his time [among] the three of us and fifteen children. He has no room for that."

Although for most of the women, jealous feelings emerge when a sister-wife is in the room, there are those who have evolved to see the benefit of being out of the room. One woman declared, "Initially, when you first get married, you be concentrating on what's happening in the room, but after a while, you concentrate on what's going to happen when you get out. This is your quiet time when you don't have to deal with him calling you. The one who is with him is the one who "attends to him.""

One thing that helps to mitigate feelings of jealousy is when husbands are openly affectionate. One woman explained, "He is free with his wives and I like that. I don't want a man that is going to be sneaking, and ducking and dodging, and only being intimate behind closed doors."

When another woman was asked whether it bothers her when her husband is affectionate with her sister-wives, she indicated that being considerate of their feelings helps: "Sometimes, but not often, because I want them to get the same pleasure and joy that I'm getting when he is doing those things for me. It wouldn't be right if I didn't."

One woman summed up how to deal with feelings of jealousy: "The most important thing is to know that you are human and know how to control and not let that take over and you start acting out."

Other Factors

There were two issues I became interested in ascertaining the women's perspectives on while staying in the community. One is what appears to be a double standard: men being allowed to enter into relations with other women and marry them, but women being prohibited from doing the same. The other issue was the rigid gender roles prescribed for men and women, whereby women are responsible for the domestic arena, no matter what other obligations they might have.

With regard to the double standard, I found that the women generally feel such deep love for their husbands and hold them in such high regard that they have no interest in relations with other men. One woman said that her husband "fulfills" her and that it has taken her "all of [her] life to find that one brother." Another woman had this to say:

212

When I compare all this to the fact that A . . . is a man of God; he is truly, sincerely, and earnestly trying to live a righteous life. He is a good father and a good husband; [a] God head, he has a big heart, [is] a good provider. Then I ask myself, why would any women want anyone else, let alone be attracted to anyone else? Compared to what the world has to offer, the brothers in the kingdom are precious jewels to be valued!

] Concerning gender-roles, again, the women explained that because of how deeply they love their husbands and the great respect they have for them, they do not mind providing domestic support for them. They also pointed out that although women are responsible for domestic work, some families in actuality have egalitarian arrangements whereby the men contribute just as much as women to household tasks and child care.

I was also interested in what the wives perceive to be negative about polygyny. Besides limited space being an issue for the community in general, most could find nothing. The strained relations in the beginning and jealousy were seen to be positives in the growth process. In fact, they could find nothing but positives. One woman explained:

There is nothing that I don't really like about it because, like I say, I know how it is in the American society, and I've seen it with my own eyes. I was thirty-nine when I came here, so I had lived there for [almost] 40 years of my life. . . .There were things that I could see going on there with my uncles and what not having extra-marital relationships and things of this sort. So I knew what was going on there, so I felt that it was more positive to know the person, to develop a relationship with her, and to just bring her into the family and try to make a harmonious relationship of it. So I was willing to try.

Overall, the women expressed the feeling that "it is not done enough" and that polygyny is "great for the children . . . great for the [men] . . . and great for the sisters."

Finally, I asked the women what they would say to African American women in the U.S. The comfort they feel in knowing where their mate is and who he is with is one thing:

I like to know where my man is. At least I feel more comfortable and secure with a sister-wife. Knowing how clean she is, and if she is this way or that way. Knowing your husband is off to North Carolina and you are in another state, and not knowing who he is sleeping with, I don't think I can deal with that. I would have to know that he is with someone clean and picky like myself. I feel secure knowing the background of the woman. . . . If I was in the world, I would not know who he is with. This just feels more secure to me.

Because sharing men is so prevalent and also needed, it is perceived that women may not have a choice. One said, "Growing up, I never had a man that was dedicated to one sister. If they want to be happy, it is the only way, or they will wind up miserable." She also explained the advantage of being married in the manner it is done in the African Hebrew Israelite community rather than the clandestine way it is done in the U.S.: "Here, at least, if you are married to him, you are spending all of the holy days (Hebrew holidays) with him. Over there, if you are with a married man, you are not spending any holidays with him. He is going to spend them with his family, and you are going to be sitting there by yourself — alone. She contends, "They (African American women) are going to have to give in."

An important factor is that the women do not experience loneliness as they do in the U.S. This has to do not only with polygyny being a part of divine marriage, but the communal arrangement of the African Hebrew Israelite community. One woman had this to say:

I would tell any other Black woman, righteous single mother, who has walked in my shoes . . . to come on home, because they don't have to walk alone anymore. You don't have to be alone anymore. I have never been alone since I have been in the kingdom, but I used to be lonely all the time. That is something that we don't have to worry about here. You are never alone.

Chapter 10

AUSAR AUSET SOCIETY
WOMEN IN POLYGYNY

The Ausar Auset Society, founded in 1973 by Ra Un Nefer Amen, provides an alternative way of life for Africans in America and throughout the diaspora. Because they believe that many of the social problems plaguing African diaspora communities stem from cultural and spiritual crisis, the objective of Ausar Auset society is to provide an alternative lifestyle based on traditional African culture.

Headquartered in New York City, Ausar Auset has established fifty chapters throughout North America, the United Kingdom, West Africa, and the Caribbean. Its organizational hierarchy includes: Chief Priest, Ra Un Nefer Amen, Shekhem Ur Shekhem (king of kings); paramount kings who are heads of major chapters in various cities; queen-mothers who head major chapters and other locations; shekhems (chiefs) who also head other locations; techetu (spokespersons); and a priesthood that comprises kerihev (chief priests and priestesses) and serts (elder priests and priestesses).

Major chapters are located in New York, Philadelphia, Chicago, Washington, D.C., Atlanta, and Milwaukee. Each community is independently owned and operated and has its own social center, school, restaurant, and grocery store. The community centers offer adult classes on Kemetic (Egyptian) cosmology and philosophy, rituals, the reading of oracles (Medu-Neter), meditation, and health and nutrition. There are also shekhems and priests to provide counseling and guidance for Ausar Auset society members as well as to individuals in the larger community. The purpose of the schools is to provide African-centered education to children. The grocery stores provide food to members to support their vegan diet (no animal products) and the community at large.

Based primarily on Kemetic, Dravidian, and Canaanite traditions, the basic principle of Ausar Auset is that human beings share the divine qualities of God. According to Ra Un Nefer Amen (1992), there are essentially seven major divisions of spirit in human beings. Four comprise the lower parts of the spirit, and three, the higher parts. The four lower parts of the spirit include: Khab, Khabit, Sahu, and Ab. Khab, the seventh, or lowest division, is the physical body. Khabit (the shadow and animal spirit), the sixth division, is "the seat of sensory perceptions, sensations (pain, pleasure, irritability) and emotions. It is the animating principle which allows man's psychical (emotions, desires, attractions, repulsions) and physical movements," and "its functions are coordinated with the reptilian and mammalian brains in man" (p. 23). The fifth division, Sahu, "houses man's lower intellectual faculties (memory, imitation, syllogistical logic, and the imagination)" (p. 23). It is "limited to the perception of external aspects of events and is dominated by earth-born experiences" (p. 23). Ab, the fourth dimension, is focused on the internal and houses the higher mental functions (the will, circumspection, analysis, and synthesis).

The three higher parts of the human being include Shekhem, Khu, and Ba. Shekhem, the third division, allows humans to influence physical events through spiritual power. The second division, Khu, "enables man to suppress the thinking process in order to intuit the correct solution to all problems" (p. 23). Ba, the first division of the spirit enables humans to experience oneness with "all entities making up the world as parts of oneself" (p. 23).

Although there is focus on developing all aspects of the human being, a major aim in Ausar Auset society is to help individuals develop the three higher parts of the spirit. This is done through mediation and rituals. Amen (1992) notes that in African societies learning was focused on a "graduated awakening and development (initiation) of the higher divisions of the spirit" (p. 27). This is in contrast with Western education which focuses on the Sahu part of the spirit (lower intellect) (p. 27). He contends that "to solely feed information to someone expecting upliftment in the character is analogous to feeding someone, and expecting physical well being without exercise or physical activity" (p. 27). In addition,

Amen (1992) points out that "while nature will evolve[humans] up to the lower third of the spirit, the rest is up to his/[her] own effort through spiritual cultivation (culture)" (p. 27).

Marriage

The purpose of marriage in Ausar Auset is to provide individuals with primary relationships within a family. The philosophy on marriage is that a mate is one who helps one in his/her spiritual development and ultimately his/her incarnate objective, destiny, or reason for "being." Essentially, a mate helps one on his/her spiritual journey. The Ausar Auset perspective on love is that it should be based on "selflessness behavior to another" and giving "not seeking in return" (p. 28). When one focuses on love in Ab, the higher intellectual part of the spirit, then one may be able to achieve this. However, if there is focus on love in the lower intellect Sahu, then it becomes understood and is experienced in "animalist" terms. This is why, particularly in the West, love is often equated with sex.

A major component of Ausar Auset society is the use of oracles. An oracle is a tool that allows one to communicate with God. Essentially a form of divination, oracles are used to guide every aspect of one's life including marriage. For pre-marriage, oracles are consulted to determine whether one should pursue a potential mate, the feasibility of marriage for a couple, and to indicate to a couple things they need to work on for a successful marriage. Once married, oracles are consulted to help family members make general decisions, to assist in conflict resolution, and to give the family overall direction.

There are two primary ways in which the courting process is initiated and individuals eventually marry in Ausar Auset society. One way is through a shekhem, and the other way is through an individual (either a man or woman) approaching a potential wife. If a man is already married, he and his already existing wife or wives may approach the woman. Whichever method is used, the oracles are consulted.

Paying careful attention to gender roles in some traditional African societies, Ausar Auset places special importance on

217

equality for women. In some countries in East and West Africa, particularly in Khamit (Egypt) and Ghana, women participated in all areas of social, economic, and political life, including holding the highest seat in government. With this as a guide, women participate in all levels of the socio-spiritual-political hierarchy as queen-mothers and shekhems. They play a significant role in the realm of spiritual matters, because Ausar Auset society recognizes that women have special powers to intuit spiritual knowledge.

Although there is emphasis on gender equality, Ausar Auset society also recognizes that there are differences between men and women. Amen (1992) teaches that although power was shared and was equal in many African societies, the roles of men and women were not identical. African societies were keen on role playing based on physiological and psychic differences. According to him, the male body generates greater heat and adrenaline, has less body fat, and is stronger (as in weight lifting) than the female body (p. 41). Thus, nature "gave men greater heat generating capacity because it intended that the male should carry out the tasks that taxed the psychic and physical heat output of the body and spirit" (p. 41). "Excess heat creating and sustaining activities such as fighting, soldiering," and various sports, such as long-distance running, "cause women to lose too much body fat, the ovaries to shrink, ovulation to be suspended, etc." (p. 41). The effect of this can be "sterility, reduced fertility and can seriously lower the quality of offspring produced if impregnation occurs at the time the woman is engaged in such activities" (pp. 41-42). In addition, engaging in heat generating tasks interferes with women's psychic abilities as mediums and their overall general ability to intuit (intuition). Thus, in Africa, "so as not to jeopardize the quantity and health of children . . . and women's ability to contact the spirit world to seek guidance and perform psychic healing for the people, women performed the 'cool' tasks, while men did the 'hot' ones" (p. 42).

An aspect of marriage in Ausar Auset society is that men are allowed to marry more than one wife. Because there are more women than men within the community itself, the society instituted polygyny to enable all women the potential to marry and have the benefits of a family life. In this regard, polygyny is thought to be especially beneficial for women.

The Women

Women from five families were interviewed, three of whom live in two northeastern cities and two in a southeastern city. Two families had two wives, two had three wives, and one had four. There were a total of 14 wives. Their ages ranged from 28 to 51, with the mean being 42. The number of years married ranged from three to 25, with the mean number being 12. The mean number of years of education was approximately 16. All of the women had some college education; eight had degrees; one had an associate degree, four had bachelor degrees; and three had master degrees. All were employed; with three being self-employed. Eleven worked full-time, and three worked part-time. Among them there is a librarian assistant, director of special education, director of a private school, registered nurse, and a bio-feedback therapist. Their professions also include sales agents, managers, teachers, secretaries, and clerks. The number of years they have been with Ausar Auset society ranged from six to 25 years, with the mean number being approximately 18 years.

"If the Women [Are] . . . into Each Other as Much as They [Are] into the Man": Entry into Polygyny

As indicated previously, there are primarily two ways women in Ausar Auset society enter into polygynous marriages. One way is that a husband and/or wife may ask a shekhem about a particular woman, and he/she approaches the potential wife. The other is that a husband and/or wife may approach the potential wife themselves. In Ausar Auset society, individuals may not come together based on conventional norms of romantic love. There are a variety of reasons that individuals might come together and eventually marry; the most significant being an individual's attributes, how the marriage might help an individual in his/her spiritual growth and development, and what the oracles indicate. Thus, many of the second and subsequent wives did not enter into

219

marriage based on romantic love feelings for their husbands. What was important, however, was that there was some affinity for already existing wives. In cases where both the husband and wife approached the potential wife, it was the wife who took the lead. For example, a second wife had been to visit the family she would eventually marry into. She explained that about two months later, "They called me on the phone and asked me. I just said yes, and we proceeded from there." When asked if there was at least an attraction to the husband, she responded, "I did have an attraction for my husband, but I also had a very strong attraction to his wife in the sense of her as a friend."

In one case in which a shekhem approached a wife about joining a family, he asked her how she felt about polygyny. She told him, "I thought that polygamy was something that could work if the women were really into each other as much as they were into the man. . . .The women had to really be basically in love with each other as much as the man." In fact, in this instance, feelings for the already existing wife took priority over feelings for the potential husband. This woman explained how, in the beginning, she was not even attracted to the husband, wasn't "thrilled" with him, but that she "really liked the sister because she had worked with her." She continued, ". . . one time when I had come out of the hospital . . . she came to visit me with her daughter. I thought she was a really nice sister; I really did like her. Plus I always thought she was just beautiful." The readings were positive, and she was encouraged to join the family because it was thought it would be "good for [her] spiritual growth." The relationship with the husband began to develop while she was sick. As he nurtured her during this period, she became more attracted to him.

When a first wife was asked who actually invited the second wife, she responded, "I did. I invited her. I knew he was interested, but I was inviting her. . . .I was not inviting anyone in unless I felt it was someone that we could really work with." Some women indicated that they felt better when the wife approached them. In this situation, the second wife reported, "It was really weird because when they asked I remember asking her, 'Well are you asking me or is he asking?'. . . She said, 'I'm asking'. . . .That was really important for me to know who was asking." In one

220

situation, a second wife was already living close by, which made it easy for her to join the family. She explained, "We lived in the same apartment building down the hall from each other. So we were already really used to cooking together, eating together, and sometimes we would shop together and watch each other's kids. So we were interacting in a friendship situation. . . ." Though she was originally, "down on polygamy, didn't want anything to do with it . . .thought any woman who'd do that was stupid," when the first wife asked her to join the family, she accepted. With regard to the husband, "First there was a hate thing, then there was a friendship thing, and then there was an attraction."

The women believe there are two significant factors for first wives to consider when entering into polygyny. One is to transcend "conventional conditioning" and the other is to be "secure" within herself. A first wife put it this way, "It takes a lot to accept polygamy and live in it. And I talk to other wives, the first wife will say, 'Yeah, I even accepted it, but when all of a sudden you are under one roof, then like conditioning or other thoughts come into play. You have to put them in their place and decide to deal.'" Also, "being the first wife you really have to be okay with yourself in order to do polygyny. Because when you have a sister coming in who's spending the first four or five weeks [with your husband], . . . you have to be okay with yourself and your mate enough to say, 'Okay sweetie, go ahead, I know that's our wife, I know you're gonna be out there kissing and hugging her, go ahead.'"

"To Help a Sister in Need": Motivating Factors

Most of the women had originally been opposed to polygyny prior to entering into a polygynous marriage. Although they were committed to the society and its goals, they still did not regard polygyny as something for themselves. They, however, eventually entered into polygyny. There were several reasons for doing so.

One was wanting to provide a family for another sister. One wife stated, "I do realize that there are a lot of women who need to have family relationships." Another woman said she did it because "I think it's the right thing." She went on to explain how, because of her circumstances, a man hired her at 14 years of age even though she was too young. From that experience she learned, "Whenever you're in a situation to help someone, you help. That's what we're here for, to help one another, to be with one another, to share one another.... And if there's something that I have to share with someone else, then why shouldn't I?" The women talked about how, after they accepted polygyny, they even began looking for a sister-wife. This same woman explained, "I opened myself up to it, I guess on some level, I was kind of looking for it everywhere ....Once I saw someone it was like, 'Oh yeah, I wonder how she would fit.'"

A third wife was motivated because she was impressed by how the society practiced polygyny. Originally, when a friend of hers got into a polygynous marriage, she "thought she was out of her ever-loving mind," and that it was something she "would never, ever entertain doing." However, after joining Ausar Auset, the idea that "sisters would bring another sister into their family so she would have the opportunity to be a part of a family, to have children, to be in a nurturing environment and have her children raised in an environment where there were many other mothers to help her raise the children, she "thought theoretically could work." She, however, "had to watch ... to see how the sisters treated each other, how the brothers treated the sisters, and how the family worked as a unit." She explained, "From what I saw, I was quite impressed. I saw sisters grow closer. I saw brothers stepping up to the plate and embracing children that weren't necessarily their biological children, and I saw children really benefitting from being part of a large family like this, where they had many mothers. I also liked the idea of children who may not have had fathers present in their lives, now having [one] who's there to help them to grow."

Although she also saw some down sides, "the potential that polygamy had to offer in terms of family coming together," still outweighed them. She began thinking about the families of different "sister-friends," saying, "Hmm, I wonder if I could be part of their family." A friend of hers indicated that she thought she would do well in a particular family and approached them. Thus, when she was asked to join the family, she felt she was ready.

Another motivating factor is to deter husbands from having extra-marital affairs. Two women's current husbands had affairs in the past, and others had previous husbands who had also done so. They were originally opposed to polygyny for this very reason. For example, a first wife pointed out that she had to "transcend" her feelings about the affair her husband had to get to the point where she could accept a new wife coming into the family. The issue for her was infidelity. She had to ask herself, "Is polygamy an excuse for infidelity?" Other questions also emerged, such as, "his readiness," how he would deal with more than one wife, whether he would be fair, and what other kind of changes [she] was going to have to go through because of "his immaturity." These questions were particularly important because they were "pioneers." Another woman, whose husband had an affair, decided: "Either I'm going to . . . just cut my losses and start all over again, or I'm going to accept the fact that this is something that happens; this is something men do. And if men do this, then I may as well just open myself up to it and do it right." This woman describes another situation in which a friend "knows her husband cheats, but uses it as a weapon to get material things from him." She, however, is determined that "this is not the type of relationship" she wants. "Either you're going to be up front with me and we are going to deal with this, everything out on the table, or I can just . . . go." When asked if she accepted a new wife because she thought her husband might have another affair, she pointed out that he could do that in polygyny. Honesty is most important to her while an ultimate motivation is "to help a sister in need."

Besides these reasons, participants see advantages to being in polygyny. For a second wife, it was the opportunity to have a sister. Initially she saw "polygamy as a man's thing, just [a] brother having a whole bunch of women, . . . just getting his thing off, [and] was turned off by it." She thought "it was just another way men were getting over on women," and so "never really considered getting into it." However, when she was asked to come into a family, she saw it as a chance "to have the sister she never had." Another reason for entering into polygyny is that choices are limited outside of Ausar Auset society. A second wife pointed out that when she left the society for a while it was difficult to find someone:

While I was out there, I could have gotten anything I wanted to. I still didn't like being around smokers, I don't like people who drink....I don't like to go to bars, and I had gone out with people who did these things, thinking it's okay, it not that bad. After a while, I really didn't want to be [with them]; I didn't want to be in this kind of environment. So that limits me. Also, I'm a vegetarian and even when I left the society, I couldn't go back to eating meat. I just couldn't. . . .You got Black males, and you got ones who are eligible . . . [But] who's going to tolerate a vegetarian who's not going to go ahead and fix them a slab of meat?

She explained further, "And then being in society, you want somebody who can at least appreciate what you are doing or understand what you are doing." Other reasons include more time for oneself to do other things and someone to help meet family obligations. One wife, for example, said, "I looked at polygamy because it was like, 'Yes, I am married, yes, I know I have responsibilities, but there are other things that I want to do in my life also, and I looked at polygamy as a opportunity for me to do those other things." A third wife was adamant about not wanting to be the only wife:

When I used to think about marriage, it was like, "Oh God, the brother is going to be with me in my room all 24-7." It's like . . . you're responsible for another person and not that I really mind that cause I'm very giving in that sense, but because I'm that way I know that it would eventually burn me out. So when I thought about polygamy I was like, "Wow, the best of both worlds!" . . . That time when he's with the other wives, I can have my freedom. Just the fact of having my room to myself and being able to do things — if I want to read or sew or whatever. Because when my husband is with me, I feel as though I have to accommodate him. Not that you really have to because other wives probably don't do that. You know like, "Oh, you're here; I'm still going to do my thing." But I feel . . . that's rude if he's there, trying to spend time with me, and I'm here, trying to do something else.

Because her husband has a position with a lot of responsibilities, she thinks it's good that [her family has] three wives. She continued, "I welcome more to share the responsibilities....I think if I were his only wife it would just overwhelm me. Even if we weren't in the society, the things that I . . . love about him is based

224

around polygamy." Besides, she declares, "I just don't see us together by ourselves. I think he would drive me up the wall."

Finally, one woman stated, "I never felt that a man is going to define my being, so I don't feel threatened by the presence of another woman around somebody who[m] I have a relationship with. . . .I don't remember having a drive . . . to have someone all to myself." She also welcomes sisterhood. ". . . I [feel] very comfortable having other sisters to talk with. . . .You can share with other sisters like you can't share with a man."

"Oh God, What Have I Done?": Personal Issues, Insecurities, and Adjustments

There were several personal issues or adjustments the wives experienced before and after their marriage. For second and subsequent wives, one concern was that already existing wives might feel they are trying to take their husbands. In fact, it seems that when Ausar Auset society was first formed, this was an issue for the society in general. One woman pointed out that when she came into the society years ago, "I . . . thought this is so nice, all the sisters getting together. I've always felt that women had a lot of power, and I thought that we just were disunited; that we could get together and use that power. Unfortunately, . . . we had a little rap session, and the sisters were talking about how one of the reasons they didn't want or invite the new sisters that came to the community into their homes was because they found that a lot of the sisters wanted their husbands."

There were also problems with developing friendships because of this. This interviewee said that sisters in monogamous relationships were afraid of befriending other sisters because they might want to come into their families. She also discussed how a relationship with a woman whom she "really liked," someone with whom she "had a lot of fun," and used to "do her hair," went bad because her husband was attracted to her. Although she thought the woman's husband was "very nice," she had no interest in him and was disturbed when she found out that he had been telling his wife of his attraction to her and had gotten a reading. She continued, "I really didn't appreciate that because I felt like our

225

friendship was jeopardized ... now she didn't want anything to do with me because she thought I wanted her husband."

This same woman was eventually asked by another wife to join her family. She pointed out, "I've always felt that women's problems were men because women would always compete with each other for a man's attention. I've always felt that wasn't necessary. So when I came into the family, I didn't want my sister-wife to feel that I was coming in to take her husband. I wanted her to feel like okay. . . .I really wanted my wife to feel comfortable, I looked at her as my wife."

Another wife discussed the shock she underwent when she realized that she was with "somebody else's husband." According to her, she would "wake up and say, 'Oh God, what have I done?'" Some participants also had problems getting comfortable with their status as a wife in the eyes of members of the Ausar Auset community. Because they are not married in the legal sense, some stated that in the beginning they did not feel like a wife, and it still bothers them from time to time. One woman explained: although "I knew I was in polygamy, in my mind, I thought I was with somebody else's husband." When asked if she felt like a mistress, her response was, "No. I didn't feel like a wife though. I didn't feel like this is my husband."

Some of the women are also confused about how to present themselves to the broader society. One woman said, "I'm not comfortable saying things like 'my husband' because someone in the office might know that I'm signing all my forms [as] single." When asked why she does not just say she's married, she pointed out that "technically he's married to somebody else, and I don't know where or when it would become an issue." Similarly, others who are not first wives may like to present themselves to the public as married, but still have to sign forms and various legal documents as single. Participants also indicated that they feel isolated from the outside world. One woman, for example, described the feeling as being "off on an island." There is also concern about how women in polygyny are perceived by the outside world. One woman stated, "There are other kinds of freaky, crazy things that are more accepted," but, in polygyny, "it is like you're dumb, the women are dumb and stupid, and the man is getting all the . . . favors"; or, in polygyny, "it's men who are doing it to women." One wife had concerns with how society perceives her as a mother with children. This was expressed in the following dialogue:

Interviewer: How do you present yourself to the public? Do you present yourself as a married woman or a single woman?
Interviewee: Well, it depends. Most of the time I'm married. But if it's something legal, I can't put that I'm married because legally I'm not married.
Interviewer: How do you feel about that?
Interviewee: I don't have any problems with it.
Interviewer: You don't feel insecure about it in the eyes of society, being a wife?
Interviewee: Well, in the eyes of society I'm married.
Interviewer: I mean in the broader society.
Interviewee: Well, if it's something legal, they don't really know me anyway. It's just submitting a form or whatever; I'm talking about legal documents. I would have a problem with it if I had to say I was single and have a child. I would feel a little insecure because a lot of people look at me and think I'm really young. So for them to think I'm young with children and not married, I don't like that.

Other areas of concern evolve around making the transition from being single to being married. These include giving up personal space, making decisions independently as a single person vs. interdependently as a married person, and adjusting to different personalities. With regard to personal space, one woman said, "I cried [about] giving up my own personal space." Although she admits that, she doesn't think it was "solely [about] giving [up] her space; [she] just had no idea what to expect. . . .[And] that was kind of scary." Giving up one's independence and adjusting to their new family's way of functioning was also difficult. When one woman was asked what was her most difficult adjustment, her response was:

The independence. I was a single mother for seven years, and I was used to doing things the way I was used to doing, . . . I wouldn't say that I didn't agree, but they were different [from] the way I would have done [them]. I didn't feel like I had input on the way things were done because

227

things were already in place. . . .I just felt like I didn't have any say so. Even the things that I didn't agree with, even if I made a statement about it, it was like, "Well no, this is the way it's done," and so that was difficult for me. And some things are still difficult, but I'm working through them, and I'm learning that just because I'm used to doing it a certain way, changes can be made, and there are different ways of doing things. Now, when you're dealing with more people, there are more dynamics. You can't do it the way you're used to doing it, it doesn't work.

Coming into a situation with long-term established relationships was equally difficult. This woman continued:

It is only recently that I began to feel more comfortable with certain things. It was very tense in the beginning, very tense, because I came into a relationship where 20 years, 18 years, 16, 15 years they had a lot of ties. They had a lot of established relationships. So when I came in, I had to adjust to that. I felt insecure about some things. I was uncomfortable with other things. I made mistakes. I did things because I was uncomfortable.

Feeling like an outsider is another adjustment. When one wife was asked the most difficult adjustment for her, her response was, "Learning to get over feeling like an outsider, like people are ganging up on me without giving me a chance because I was the new person." Also difficult for some is the decision-making process. One woman explained, "I used the oracles, but I didn't have to go through three other people before a decision could be made. There are family meetings to make some decisions, and it takes time. Sometimes, I don't have the patience. I wanna just [say], 'This is not a big deal, let's just do this, or let's not do this.' . . . It seems like it's a big issue all the time to come to a decision. . . .I get real anxious." She, however, admits that the process is beneficial.

As far as adjusting to different personalities, it was particularly difficult for those who have spent a large part of their lives alone or with far fewer people. As one woman pointed out, the adjustment was "getting used to being around people all the time, getting used to personalities." Finally, it is quite an adjustment to have more than one person tell you about yourself. One wife explained, "In monogamy, one person can tell you about your stuff, if it's raggedly, but you can say it is not valid. But when you have two or three people telling you about your stuff, you kind of have to listen. . . .That's difficult."

"Women Need to Put Themselves in Each Other's Shoes": Jealousy

The relationships between wives ranged from what seems like sisterly love, where they appear to have deep affections for one another, to estrangement, where a wife had just recently come into the family; to distant relationships, where some wives have more in common with other ones; to those that are conflicted.

It seems a major factor contributing to good or bad relations is how the husband treats one wife by comparison to the others. One woman said that although she wasn't aware of it, a sister blamed her for some of the "injustice the brother was doing. So as a result she became cold towards me, and it was a certain level of rejection, and I felt crushed." The dialogue continued as follows:

Interviewer: What is the relationship like now?
Interviewee: Now, it is just tolerating.
Interviewer: Is it hard living together?
Interviewee: Yes, I think so.
Interviewer: Do you ever want to get out?
Interviewee: Yes, I've considered it.
Interviewer: Because of the relationship with the sister more so than with the brother?
Interviewee: Both, I would say both, but there is a big part of me that is really committed to what I'm doing.
Interviewer: Do you think that it's beyond being repaired?
Interviewee: No, I don't, and that's what I'm working on, my part. I can only do it based on what God has told me. . . .I can only work on my part.
Interviewer: Are the others working on their part?
Interviewee: Yes, I guess so.

She further explained how significant the role of the husband is in the relationships between the wives:

How is that brother functioning in the relationship, that's really a key part. We say we don't want the man to come between the women, but how is

229

that brother functioning in that relationship. If that brother is taking sides and showing favoritism, I don't care how sisterly you are, that is going to create a problem in the relationship.

Although this interviewee and one of her sister-wives have problems, she did admit that she appreciates the times that she has been there when she was really in need. "There is [a] certain history that I have, that even though we might have problems on the surface I do have a certain love for her. . . . Even though we might not have a girlfriend type relationship, I have a certain amount of respect for her and what she's doing. That may not always come across to her, but I do have that."

With regard to a husband's potential to be unfair, one wife noted the importance of a schedule. "You can't control wants and desires with a schedule, but you know the schedule is in place, so it's a matter of waiting until your day comes around."

It was pointed out that there are various kinds of jealousy. Not only may there be jealousy of another wife's interaction with the husband but also of the interaction between other wives. A wife may also be jealous of another wife in general. There may also be jealousy connected with the children. Some children have different extended relatives, which means that they may get the opportunity to do things outside the home or they may have access to more or have more things bestowed upon them. With regard to jealousy between wives, there are sometimes cliques. This occurs, according to one interviewee, when a wife "gravitates" toward another wife with whom she has more in common or with whom she feels most comfortable. A husband may also gravitate toward the wife with whom he feels most comfortable. One wife explained that even though she had gone to the oracles for some things that she thought were not right, and they had corrected her, "It still sometimes can be difficult when [I] see him dealing with the one he is comfortable with." There have also been situations that have made all the wives feel "left out." The women however explained that it is important that individuals commit to balancing this.

Jealousy may arise for other reasons. One wife pointed out that she was dealing with the issues of feeling like a wife. Her thoughts were: "His first wife is his wife." However, after she was put on bed rest and both her husband and his first wife took care of her, it became apparent to her that it was a "family affair." In this instance, instead of the second wife conflicting with the first wife, she did so with the husband. In her words, she was always "butting heads" with him. The first wife, however, was supportive of her and helped her learn how to deal with him. The first wife, in this instance, said that initially the second wife and her husband "being in the room with the door closed all the time bothered" her. But then she thought, "Oh, just grow up." This didn't always work, because she knew he was "very attracted to her," and this made her feel insecure. She continued, "My husband, the one I had been with all this time, is now spending all this time with her because she is able to go out [she was pregnant at the time], she's shorter than I am, people from the neighborhood think that they are married and I'm the nut who just hangs around with nothing better to do. All these thoughts go through your mind."

A second wife said that for her, "insecurity" arises when a new wife comes into the family. Even after being with her husband for 17 years she still deals with it. She thinks, "I'm not good enough or he's gonna like her better than me, or there's something I'm lacking, that's why he wants somebody else." She, however, has gotten to a point where she feels, "There's nothing wrong with me, and it's not something I did wrong, or that I'm lacking something."

According to one participant, one way to avoid jealousy is not to discuss one's personal relationship with the husband with another wife. When asked why not, her response was that, depending on the individual's personality, it might "breed jealousy. If you are going to tell them something personal about what you and the husband did, then they might be like, 'Oh well, we didn't do that. . . .' Not thinking about, 'Well okay, that's what you two like to do.'" She further pointed out how each wife's relationship with the husband is different, and that the kind of things they do or share together might be different for each wife. She explained, "I wouldn't have a problem . . . if he was to take one out to the movies every week if that's what she likes because I'm not a movie person. So I always tell him if that is what one wife likes, or if you see something that you think that wife would like, buy it. Don't feel like if I buy for one, I've got to buy for the other."

Although each relationship is different, some wives still get jealous when their husband does something for one that he does not do for the other. When asked if she gets jealous, this interviewee said, "No, it was not so much jealousy, but [giving] my husband too much time because I didn't want the others to feel jealous. It still is a big thing with me now." Thus, in attempting to be fair, if he would ask her to go out, she'd ask, "Well, did you take your other wives out?" When asked if she thinks the wives are jealous of her, her response was, "Yes, that's why I tend not to go out or downplay it." According to this interviewee, things come up, such as, "He took you out and didn't take me out for my birthday." She also admits that it might not be jealousy as much as it might be "they (the already existing wives) were not really ready for another wife." Whatever the case may be, she explained, "You never know what's going on in another relationship or the reasons that something didn't happen. . . . I don't even try to think about it. If he takes me out every two weeks to the movies and they are having problems in their relationship and that's what he needs to do to correct it, I'm not going to try to analyze it. As long as my needs are being met, I'm fine. And if theirs are not being met," they should blame themselves for it, "not someone else."

Nevertheless, the wives stressed the importance of the man being fair. One explained, "I think the man has to be in the middle; he can't cater to one wife or the other. He really has to be in the middle, regardless of his position. He really has to get in touch with that female side of himself and really put himself in his wives' shoes and really see how his behavior is affecting his wives." It is also important that wives do the same. This interviewee continued, "I think that the way polygamy should be practiced is that if you see a brother that's being unfair then it's up to the women to say, 'Wait a minute, that's my sister. You're not going to treat her like that and you can't come snuggling up to me, and you're not being right to her.'" In addition, the importance of wives caring about and looking out for each other was also stressed. This woman continued, "I think the women need to do that as well, put themselves in each other's shoes and say, 'okay, it might be something simple like, 'Honey, so and so kind of looks down. I don't know what she's going through right now. Why don't you go talk and spend some time with her, even if it's your night. . . .Baby, go ahead and spend some time with that sister.'"

Others indicated that they have no problem with jealousy. One wife said that jealousy is a concept she never accepted for herself because she has always felt that "there is no need to be jealous of anything that anyone else has because she has the ability to get it for herself." She said she has never felt jealous of her sister-wife, and she has never "sensed" it from her. In one situation in which the wives seemed to be close, one stressed the importance of making sure that they keep good relations, which is done by being open and trusting and being able to talk to one another. She said, "We got enough walls in the house. I wanted no new walls." Overall, it was pointed out that the relationship between the wives is the most important one. This interviewee added, "It's important for the women to form a good bond in their relationships." Finally, it was made clear that when jealousy arises, it is important to "want for your sister what you want for you . . . to remember that you have to want for her . . . what you want for yourself."

"It's A Nesting Thing": Areas of Conflict

Two major areas of conflict revolve around household cleaning and children. With regard to cleaning, there may be extremes, such as one wife wanting an extremely clean and organized environment, while another may be indifferent. Timing is also important with regards to cleaning. One may desire the house to be cleaned daily, while another may have the attitude to get to it when you get to it. Whatever the case, this seemed to be a major area of conflict. One woman explained:

I like things a certain way and my environment will tend to dictate my happiness. . . .It's just that I have a certain way of functioning. I mean you could come to my home anytime and it was clean; I didn't have bugs. So when you come into a situation where someone is not as clean as you, they leave stuff here and there; some people can function in clutter, I have a problem with it. That's one of the big problems, just different people's way of functioning.

She, however, concluded, "It doesn't have to be a big problem. It's just how big a problem you make it." Another wife pointed out that what could help alleviate problems with housekeeping styles is each wife having her own space:

My ideal situation would be we all have our own little apartment, like a triplex. I think that would be good, not to be separate from everybody but back in the day in Africa each wife had their own little hut. . . . It's like in nature when a mother bird makes her little nest. It's a nesting thing. You want to have your own little area.

With regard to children, issues generally revolve around parenting styles and goals for them. The issue for one wife was wanting the biological parent to relinquish some of the control and give her more responsibility for the children. In some instances, a child may become more attached to the non-biological parent, particularly when the natural parent is ill or works. This may be because the non-biological parent may play a greater role in the child's life. One woman explained that when her son was 14 months, "it was like [she] was in the back seat" to her sister-wife. She asked, "What is wrong with this boy? He is totally confused." When asked how she felt about that, she responded, "It bothered me a little, but I felt so comfortable being out and knowing he was there, I knew she would take care of him." Another concern for wives as it regard to their children has to do with their having to adjust to different personalities and parenting styles.

There are also other issues that might emerge from the women living together. One wife, for example, had an issue with a sister-wife's wearing her clothes. She explained: "I don't really like to loan [sic] out my clothes and stuff because like when I get it back, I always pick up the psychic energy of the other person. That was before I was in polygamy. I said, 'Well, this is my sister,' and I had a lot of clothes. So I said, 'Okay, I'll let my sister borrow my clothes,' I mean that's my sister." She was, however, perturbed by how the sister would treat her clothes:

You expect people to take care of your stuff the way you do, but when you get it back and it's stained or torn, you're like, "Wait a minute, that's not my stuff!" I just said, "Okay, she's not going to borrow my stuff." Where I was a very vocal person: "I know that's not my dress on the floor." Well, of course, it raised tension because some people you can say anything to them, and it's not a big thing, but some people you can't.

Finally, it was pointed out that problems plaguing polygynous marriages are not much different from those in monogamous marriages. One woman explained, "We have no more deeper problems than other people have. . . .We've got kid problems, we've got health problems, we've got attitudinal issues, just like regular people who are not in our society. . . .Sometimes you get dysfunctional people with their dysfunctional behaviors in the marriage. That has nothing to do with polygamy."

Another woman also noted, "You take any problem and multiply it by four, it looks major. You could have the same problem in monogamy but it's only two people." In addition, she noted that when marriages are dissolved, they are done so for the same reasons monogamous ones are. The husband and that particular wife gave up on trying to make it work.

"What Does God Want?": Conflict Resolution

As already indicated, one way that members of Ausar Auset society resolve conflicts is through the use of the oracles. One woman for example, stated: "It's not about what you want, what he wants, or what she wants, but what does God want?" Thus, the oracles can be consulted to find out the right thing to do in any given situation. Although the oracles can be used to resolve conflicts, it was pointed out that sometimes individuals fail to adhere to the readings. Some also fail to "transcend their emotions." Individuals can also seek counseling to help resolve problems. It was pointed out, however, that many fail to get counseling when it is needed.

The interviewees noted the importance of having family meetings, which all families seem to have. A couple of families also have "wifely" meetings, which are between the wives only. Communicating, not letting issues "fester," and not avoiding issues, is important. One wife said that her way of dealing was to "just not deal with it." It is her view that although one may take such an attitude, it still "bothers" them. Then, "when something comes up, they blow up because [there's] so much build up." She stresses the importance of seeking counseling and continuing to do so. She further noted that one may take an issue to counsel when the person is really trying to change. Fortunately, this is usually revealed through the readings. What is also revealed is when the person is not changing for the better. In addition, it was pointed out that its not the big things, it's the small things that have to be "taken care of right away."

Although open and honest communication is generally seen as a way to resolve conflicts, one participant stressed how disadvantageous it can be when it is not with the right person. She indicated, that one "might be communicating and talking about problems with someone else instead of trying to resolve the issue. It might be discussed but it's not really helping." Another factor is how one communicates. An interviewee discussed how her communication style would lead to problems between her sister-wife and herself. "I know that's one pep-peed (something a person is particular about) that really bothered my sister. . . .She wouldn't say things sharply; I mean she would say things nice that are just as deadly, but the fact that I would use a very sharp tone would create problems. She pointed out, however, "In our society, you're supposed to be under certain guidelines. You don't just come out of your mouth and say something. I mean if someone does something incorrect, [you] could use a gentle approach. I could have said, 'Oh sister, I would really appreciate if when I give you something, you would take care of it.' But I didn't say that, I was like, 'I know that's not my dress!! I know that's not my stuff!!!' So it puts the person on the defense and creates problems."

Reactions from Families of Origin

A critical factor in an individual's level of comfort with polygyny is how members of their family of origin responds to it. This is particularly important because family members can influence whether one's marriage is successful. There were a range of responses from participants' family members. Some have family members who were opposed to their marrying into polygyny; others were liberal about it; and others act as if it has not happened.

236

With regard to the participant's fathers, most of them were opposed to their being in polygyny. One woman reported that her father "freaked out." She, however, explained to him that she thought it was necessary for women who do not have husbands, and that instead of "wearing war paint" to attract a man and "just running around," doing it the way it is done in Africa is a better way. His response however, was, "Baby, that's not your problem. Let the other women do that, you don't have to do that."

Another participant reported that her father, "didn't take it too well. He has not accepted it, and said he will never accept it, and he doesn't want to talk about it."

Another participant's father told her not to bring it around him and that he didn't "want to have anything to do with it at all." One woman's father told her to let other women "find their own husbands."

Although a majority of fathers were opposed to their marrying into polygyny, there is one interviewee who said that because she has a son and "had been struggling by [herself] to raise him," her father "thought it was good idea." He was glad for her to have some support.

Some of the participants' mothers were opposed to polygyny. One wife's mother thought she has "always been too giving, too sharing" and that she needed to "put some limits" on it.

Another wife's mother called her husband a "pimp" and said, "he had a lot of wives on welfare, and he was just collecting the paychecks, and that [she] was being brainwashed." She threatened to call the cops. In the case of this woman, no one but her sister came to the wedding. One participant's mother "boo-hooed," "cried," because she never "thought her daughter would do anything like this."

Although mothers reacted to polygyny in various negative ways, there is only one case in which the mother interfered. In this instance, the mother expressed her concerns about her daughter, "dragging the children" into it. According to this participant, her mother said, "If you want to be involved in that 'cult' and do what they're telling you to do, then that's your choice. But you're not going to do that to the children." The day after she and her husband got married, her mother filed a custody suit. She also called her husband's job to try to get him fired.

Some mothers make an attempt to accept it. One woman reported that "it's hard" for her mother, but "she tries to be open ....When Christmas comes around, she tries to make sure she gets gifts for her co-wife's children." Although most mothers went through changes about it in the beginning, many have generally come to accept it. One wife's mother supported it from the beginning, but thinks she "picked the wrong family."

The participants reported that their family members thought the men were "getting over on them." One woman said that when she gets negative feed-back she generally responds by saying: "He's responsible for taking care of an entire family. It's not one wife, but two or four. . . .When you are held responsible for this, you're not skipping out when things get rough. You are held responsible for taking care of the family whenever difficulties [arise]." When she says such things, it "just starts them to thinking."

As far as their siblings are concerned, there have been similar reactions. One interviewee reported a sibling who "freaked out" and told her, "You cannot come to my house, don't bring that man to my house, none of you come to my house, that's the most ungodly thing I have ever heard of." This however was the most extreme case among the siblings. Most accept the marriage. Some only "tolerate" it; others take the attitude, "It's your life," and still others are liberal and regard it as something to be expected from the "strange"one in the family. Finally, there are those family members who will not talk about it because they don't acknowledge that the individual is married in polygyny, and still others reported that they had not told their family members so they do not know about the marriage.

Economic Matters

A major shortcoming of being in polygyny according to participants is insufficient money. According to interviewees, this is probably the greatest disadvantage of polygyny and is accompanied by lack of autonomy in making decisions about how money is spent. The interviewees pointed out that when one is single, the person can basically spend money the way she desires. When they marry, they have to defer to the family. In most families, it appears that money is pooled for expenses, and each person has his/her personal money.

The participants pointed out the importance of dealing with finances prior to getting married. This, however, may make one feel uneasy, as one wife indicated; she wanted to discuss finances but didn't do so because she felt it was a "sensitive" issue.

It was indicated that if finances are not dealt with prior to marriage, it can lead to problems "down the road." A couple of wives said that their financial status has declined as a result of marrying into polygyny. One woman complained, "Economically, it's been real hard, a real hard thing, because, just for me, I felt like I did not achieve economic goals I set out for myself. I had my own hair salon and was paying my bills, traveled a little bit, and when I didn't want to work, I didn't have to. Then I come into the family, and all my money was family money." She further explained how later she began to see value in the way things were done. "I didn't see my sister-wife; she was working and in school at the time; she wasn't getting paid, so I was like, wait a minute. That was from a very immature perspective, because later I really saw value in what she was doing. She was teaching in school. But I guess I didn't see it because I didn't have children. After I had children, I really saw it."

Another woman said, "It's a change because, before I got married, I was very financially independent. I had money, market accounts, CD accounts. I had money. I was frugal that way. By the time I was 21, I [had] saved about $5,000. I paid my way to school—cash. I had credit cards; I didn't owe anybody anything. I had money." She explained that now that she is married, "I don't have the personal money, my credit cards are to the limit, and I don't have anything materialistic to show for it. But spiritually, I have a lot to show for it. We got our own business, and we have a place where people can come for classes free of charge. So we have to look at the whole picture, not the personal gain."

How the families generate income varies. In one situation, one wife stays home and takes care of the children. The other wife works part-time, and the husband is sometimes employed in two full-time positions. In another situation, two wives run a family-owned restaurant; another wife is a principal in the school, and the husband is employed. In another situation, the three wives work outside the home, while the husband runs a business.

Legal Matters

Legal considerations include marital status, property, insurance, and taxes. A major issue for families is health insurance. If the husband is the only one with outside employment, only the first wife can be put on his health insurance policy. This is particularly difficult, as in the case of one family, where the second wife desires to have children. Another problem is that only the husband and first wife can file taxes together.

With regard to marital status, as indicated previously, this is a concern for wives who are not the first wife. Some wives struggle psychologically with whether they are really a wife, especially because, in the legal sense, they are not recognized as wives. This is compounded by having to sign legal documents as being single. Although some wives may present themselves to the public as being married, most are uncomfortable with revealing their status as a wife in a polygynous marriage. Many, in fact, believe their jobs may be put into jeopardy if they reveal such a status. Others, to avoid any future problems that may arise, do not even present themselves to the public as being married. In addition, the first wife is the only one recognized as the legal wife, and is therefore the only one with the status of being married and the only one with rights to property.

Some wives indicated that they also feel like outsiders with regard to legal matters. One family, for example, was applying for a loan. Because only the husband and first wife's names were on the application, the second wife felt like she was outside the process and became concerned about her stake in the property. She explained, "I never thought about it until last night because we never really discussed it. I think the thought came back again of whether or not I'm a wife. . . .Before it was from a feeling view; I don't feel like a wife; I'm not a wife; what am I doing? I used to say that to myself a lot. But when we were going over the loan, it was more from a legal view. I felt uninvolved because everything is in their name."

When one wife was asked how she feels about not being protected under the law, she said, "Well, I guess that's something that I had to come to terms with before I accepted him. We can't depend on, or I can't rely on the government of the United States. I can't go crying to them if something happened." She explained that contracts can be put in place to handle property. However, she pointed out, "We (Ausar Auset society) decided that the law of the United States is not the supreme law. . . .When you come into a situation like this, you know you're going against what the law states, and you're not going to be protected." She added: "I really feel that if we're really going to exist as a people we have got to stop totally relying on these governments for helping us out because all they do is keep splitting us apart. That is one reason I'm in this society. . . I don't have to run to the white man for this, that and the other if I get in trouble. . . .He's not my great white father." In this instance the woman is relying on the integrity of the parties involved, and she expects them to stick to their commitments.

Regardless of their perspectives, feelings, or how legal matters are being handled by families, Ausar Auset society has devised ways to handle them. A contract is an instrument that can be used when property is involved. Wills can be used for inheritance. If there is a lease involved, it is suggested that all names be put on it. With regard to real property, families can form tenants in common or corporations. It can be problematic when real property is already owned by a husband and his first wife. Since the husband and already existing wife are already invested, they have to determine at what point and by what means to allow subsequent wives to be invested. One family was incorporated, and another had tenants in common. Other families had not dealt with legalities but reported that they would be putting these matters in place at some time in the future.

Benefits

The benefits of being in polygyny for Ausar Auset society women are similar to those for African and African Hebrew Israelite women. A major benefit is assistance with child care. One woman had this to say: "I was a single parent before I came in. I stay out late a lot and usually my daughter was with me, but when I came into the family, I have a family now to leave her with. I don't have to take her with me. She's at home, she can go to bed, [and] she can eat. So that's a real advantage for me." Several of the women also reported that it helps in their spiritual growth and development. I asked what the advantages are for a first wife, and one said, "The opportunity to grow spirituality." She explained that interaction with other wives helps in this. "It benefits to share a household, running a household where you don't have to figure out everything by yourself. You have someone to bounce things off of." Another one said, "It really pulls out the best in me." The opportunity to form "sisterhood and comradery" with people who are different from oneself is also an advantage. There is also the opportunity for children to grow and learn how to live with other people in a community. It was pointed out that it will help them when they get older to come together and get along with other people.

Another benefit to women is someone to assist with the husband's sexual needs, especially if one has children. One woman said, "I have three children, and they are all pulling at you all the time, all day. At night it's someone else pulling on you." Autonomy is another advantage. This woman continued, "The sharing of the husband is one thing I like about polygamy. I don't see myself in a monogamous relationship with him because I enjoy having my time and not having to worry about him. Like if I have a week by myself, I don't have to say, 'Well, who is going to cook for him? Who is going to clean?' If he wants the sexual thing, you know his needs are being met elsewhere. So I have my freedom and I'm not worried about it."

Finally, a benefit is being part of a family and the joy of children. One woman who was single without children prior to entering into polygyny explained, "When the children . . . come in the room, and it's like 4 o'clock, 5 o'clock in the morning, I feel like,

242

you know, you don't feel like getting up. But they come in with these little smiles looking so cute, and your first reaction is like 'Oh God.' But then you look and you see this little face and all these little smiles and you kind of smile too." In addition, she expressed, "I like the fact that I'm not always coming home to an empty apartment or an empty space."

What is Necessary for Polygyny to Work

Overall, the interviewees pointed out several factors they believe necessary for polygyny to work. First and foremost, is that it must be practiced in a community. There needs to be some larger spiritual-religious and social or community support structure. It was also suggested that there be pre- and post-marital counseling. Although the oracles are used to help determine if individuals should marry, there needs to be formal counseling to teach members what to expect and how to be. Members think that legal matters, finances, and issues related to children should be discussed prior to marriage. Another important consideration is space. Some of the participants think it would be better if each woman has her own space. This might mitigate conflicts around children and house cleaning, as well as feelings of jealousy. Another thing that is important is that all the wives agree with each other and the husband on bringing a new wife into the family. This helps to eliminate resentment and problems that can arise if already existing wives do not agree to it. Finally, of all the factors necessary for polygyny to work, it is that wives have good relationships with one another. This, it was indicated, is critical.

Chapter 11

AFRICAN AMERICAN MUSLIM WOMEN IN POLYGYNY

Al-Islam

Al-Islam, which means total submission to the will of Allah, emerged through the revelations and experiences of the Prophet Muhammad ibn 'Abdullah. The Prophet Muhammad was born in Arabia (570-632 AD) and raised in Mecca, a commercial center, prior to becoming a sacred city to the Arabs. He, himself an Arab, came from a respected merchant family of modest means of the Quaraysh tribe. At age 25, Muhammad went to work for a wealthy widow, Kadijah, whom he later married. They bore a daughter, whom they named Fatima. Prior to age 40, Muhammad's life was not much different from other merchants. However, at that age, he began spending more and more time in the mountains meditating. Around the year A.D. 611, he began having extraordinary experiences, where the archangel Gabriel would appear and recite to him. These revelations would become the holy Scriptures of the *Qur'an* (Koran), the major text upon which the Islamic faith is based (Ellsworth, 1982).

There are five core practices of the faith, referred to as the five pillars of Islam. The first is the *shahada*, which is acknowledgment of God or Allah and his messenger, the Prophet Muhammad. The second is *salat*, worship or prayer, which is done five times a day. The third is *sawm* or fasting. Here Muslims are expected to refrain from food, drink, and other activities from sunrise to sunset during the holy month of *Ramadan* (a period of 28 days in the Muslim calendar) and to spend these hours in prayer and frequenting the *masjid* (mosque). The fourth is *zakat*, or almsgiving, which is the giving of a small amount of one's wealth to the needy. A person's surplus wealth is taxed at a rate of 2.5 percent. The fifth is the *hajj*, the pilgrimage to Mecca, Muhammad's birthplace. In addition to these obligations, Muslims are prohibited from eating pork or ingesting alcohol, must refrain from fornication and adultery, and are expected to be modest in their dress. They are also expected to study the *Qur'an*, and the Arabic language. Estimates range from 600 to 900 million persons all over the world who are of the Muslim faith (Ellswood, 1982; McCloud, 1995; Toropov and Buckles, 1997).

African American Islam

In *African American Islam*, Aminah Beverly McCloud (1995) divides African American Islamic communities into two eras; those which emerged between 1900 and 1960 and those which developed after 1960. She makes the division based on the focus of African American Muslim communities during these two periods. Prior to the 1960s, according to McCloud, the focus for African American Muslim communities was nation-building or, as expressed in Arabic, *'asabiya*. Thus, "African American Islam during this period can be viewed as the history of a people's attempt to create *'asabiya* in a hostile environment" (McCloud, p. 4). After the 1960s, many African American Muslim communities placed priority on *ummah*, connecting with and/or participating with Muslim communities throughout the world.

Although the African American Muslim population grew considerably during the twentieth century, scholars believe that African American Muslims have been in America since the period of enslavement. Many West African populations had converted to Islam before the transatlantic slave trade. Thus, it was during this period that Islam among African Americans became implanted in America. As with other African cultural traits, Islam was retained and passed down intergenerationally but on a very limited basis. Organized Islam began in the early 1900s with the Moorish Science Temple, grew to a high point in the early 1960s under the Nation of Islam, and has now become a major religion among African Americans.

Moorish Science Temple

Although various organized African American Muslim communities began to emerge in the early 1900s, the Moorish

Science Temple appears to be the first. The Moorish Science Temple was founded by Noble Drew Ali when he established the Canaanite Temple in Newark, New Jersey in 1913. The teachings of Noble Drew Ali spread to other Northern cities — Pittsburgh, Philadelphia, and Harlem, in New York City; Midwestern cities — Detroit, Chicago, and Cleveland; as well as various Southern cities — Pine Bluff, Arkansas, Richmond and Petersburg, Virginia, and Baltimore, MD (Karenga, 1993; McCloud, 1995). In response to the social and political climate of racial segregation or apartheid, race riots, and brutalities including lynchings, nationalism was central to the philosophical-political core of the Moorish Science Temple and was reflected in its flag. The Moorish Science Temple taught that African Americans' salvation lay in casting off the epithets of Negro, Black, colored or Ethiopian and in embracing their national origins as Asiatic, or more specifically, Moors (Lincoln, 1961).

Because literacy was low among African Americans during this period, the priorities of the organization included "attaining literacy and becoming informed about subjects such as African history, world geography, and mathematics" (McCloud, p. 13). To this end, "the Moorish Science Temple published a substantial amount of literature in the African American community" (McCloud, p. 13). Noble Drew Ali published a *Holy Koran*, (as distinguished from the Islamic *Holy Qur'an*) also called the *Circle Seven* of the Moorish Science Temple to help members gain a knowledge base. When the English translation of the traditional *Holy Qur'an* became available in the U.S., it was read by the membership of the Moorish Science Temple along with other sources of information, such as the *Moorish Guide National*, the *Moorish Science Monitor*, and the *Moorish Review*, which were published out of the Richmond, Virginia Temple (McCloud, p. 17).

Besides encouraging African Americans to return to the religion of their ancestors, the Moors of Morocco, the Moorish Science Temple taught members to work hard and strive for economic independence. The Moorish Manufacturing Company produced various products, such as heating oil, a bath compound, and a tonic (McCloud, p. 17). The community was also "very active in feeding the poor, providing drug and alcohol rehabilitation, and creating wholesome, disciplined community life" (McCloud, p. 17). Membership eventually reached an estimated twenty to thirty thousand.

Noble Drew Ali was murdered in 1920 (due to a brutal beating), and the organization split into smaller groups at the Unity Convention in 1929 (McCloud, p. 18). Two primary factions were those led by C. Kirkman Bey (Ali's former secretary), and John Givens-El (Ali's former Chauffeur) (McCloud, p. 18).

Nation of Islam

The Nation of Islam, according to Eric Lincoln (1974), "is the most powerful and in terms of numbers by far the most attractive alternative religious community that has ever been available to Blacks in the country" (p. 155). Beginning with Master Wali Fard Muhammad, its founder, to the Honorable Elijah Muhammad who brought the organization to its apex, to Minister Louis Farrakhan, the current leader, the Nation of Islam has been one of the premier organizations imparting ideas of racial and economic empowerment to African Americans. The organization began with the mysterious appearance of Master Wali Fard Muhammad in Detroit who, Nation of Islam members believe, came from the Holy City of Mecca with the express purpose of identifying and reclaiming the Lost Tribe of *Shabazz*. Master Wali Fard Muhammad started by going from house to house teaching African Americans "knowledge of self." He taught them that Islam is the natural religion of the Black man, that African Americans "were descendants of a great civilization and that the white man is a 'devil by nature'—absolutely incapable of living with anyone who is not white" (Lincoln, p. 161). He taught that the white man:

. . .is the natural enemy of all Black people, just as the hawk is the enemy of every bird that flies. The hawk will even attack the eagle, if he finds the eagle on his back. But when the eagle screams and spreads his wings, the hawk flees for his life. Similarly, there must be a day of reckoning between Black and White. It is the Battle of Armageddon promised in the Book of

Revelation, when the forces of evil will contend with the forces of good and be destroyed (Lincoln, p. 161).

Master Wali Fard also taught that in the meantime all Muslims should obey the law, submit to all "constituted authority," and live in peace with all who will live in peace with them (Lincoln, p. 162). In addition, he taught African Americans not to carry guns, as this is the white man's chief weakness, and it is this that will lead to his demise. Overall, as indicated above, he taught that the key to empowerment is "to know thyself."

Master Wali Fard Muhammad disappeared in 1934 as mysteriously as he came, and the Honorable Elijah Muhammad, assuming the title "Messenger of Islam," took the movement to new heights, infusing the Nation of Islam with his teachings of racial pride, self-protection, and economic self-help. The three underlying principles in Elijah's Islam were to "know yourself (and your kind), protect yourself (and your kind) and to do for yourself (and your kind)" (Lincoln, p. 166). Consistent with the teachings of Master Wali Fard Muhammad, who is deified by the Nation of Islam as the "Savior of Black Muslims," Elijah Muhammad also taught African Americans not to carry weapons as "the devils want you to carry weapons so that they can justify killing you" (Lincoln, p. 162). Overall, viewed as the "final Messenger" of Allah who received his teachings from Allah in person, the Honorable Elijah Muhammad's "influence in changing Black self-concepts and fostering Black pride among the masses has been unmatched by any individual since Marcus Garvey" (Lincoln, p. 156).

The Honorable Elijah Muhammad died on the eve of Savior's Day, in 1975. After this, his seventh son, Wallace Deen Muhammad, as head of the World Community of Al-Islam in the West (WCIW, later to become the American Muslim Mission) began to change the direction of the Nation of Islam and placed emphasis on traditional Islam and the teachings of the Prophet Muhammad as recorded in the *Qur'an*. He shifted emphasis from *asabiya*, the needs of local African American communities, to *ummah*, connection with the broader Muslim community, which McCloud (1995) contends has been a continual area of conflict for African American Muslim communities.

Because of his disenchantment with Wallace Muhammad's new directions, Minister Louis Farrakhan, on November 8, 1977, announced that he was leaving the WCIW to reestablish the old Nation of Islam based on the principles of the Honorable Elijah Muhammad. Others also left and began movements that are variants of the Nation of Islam. They include the five percenters — Nation of Gods and Earths, and those under the leadership of Silis Muhammad and John Muhammad (Elijah Muhammad's brother).

Although the Moorish Science Temple and the Nation of Islam are the two most known Muslim communities in the African American world, there were other earlier Muslim communities. They include the Ahmadiyyah Movement in Islam (1921), Universal Islamic Society (1926), First Muslim Mosque of Pittsburgh (1928), the Islamic Brotherhood (1929), Addeynu Allahe Universal Arabic Association (1930's)*, African American Mosque (1933), Islamic Mission Society (1939), State Street Mosque (1929) and the Fahamme Temple of Islam and Culture (1930's)*. Contemporary communities include the Nation of Islam, the American Muslim Mission, those listed under early communities (with asterisks), in addition to the Islamic Party, Islamic Brotherhood, United Submitters International, Shiite Communities, Ansarullah Nubian Islamic Hebrews, 'Isa al Haadi al Mahdi, Nasqshabandi Community, the Tijaniyyah Community, Darul Islam, and those who pledge allegiance to Jamil Al-Amin. Two of these communities — the American Muslim Mission under the leadership of Wallace Deen Muhammad and the Islamic community under the leadership of Jamil Al-Amin — are discussed further.

American Muslim Mission

As indicated above, Wallace Deen Muhammad's goal has been to change the direction of Islam. In the first year of his leadership, he began purging the myth of Master Wali Fard Muhammad as God, clarifying the concept of the devil, and redefining the role of the Honorable Elijah Muhammad (Abdullah, 1995). For example, with regard to Master Wali Fard Muhammad as God in person, he explained that Fard Muhammad had been called many names by Elijah Muhammad to emphasize the enormous task before him of changing the condition of African American people (McCloud, p. 73). He also contends that this was an expedient appeal to get the attention of African Americans (Abdullah, p. 14).

With regard to the white man being the devil, or a "grafted race," W. D. Muhammad revised this to mean that any human being with corrupted behavior and mentality could be characterized as such (p. 11).

W. D. Muhammad also explained that the role of Elijah Muhammad under Islam was to restore African America's humanity; their sense of self that had been stripped from them through the slave experience as was evidenced by their taking on the names of slaveholders. He explained that because restoring their humanity was a priority, Elijah Muhammad could not give them true Islam. As "it would not make sense to 'empty vessels' (African Americans) who were unable to understand themselves as actors in this world" (McCloud, p. 74). Before African Americans could be given the full teachings of Islam, they needed "to be fully human with a self- or group-determined identity — along with myths that entails — as well as [have] homes, goals, institutions, and so on" (McCloud, p. 75). After these objectives were met, "the community could now enter the world community on its own terms as a 'people' appropriating Islam just as other Islamic communities in the world had done before them" (McCloud, p. 75).

Through newspapers, speeches, and his own actions, W. D. Muhammad began to infuse the teachings with the five pillars of Islam. He also encouraged members to identify with their African heritage through Bilal Ibn Ribah who had been a former slave and who was instrumental in the development of Islam (See also Yosef Ben-Jochannan, *Africa, the Mother of Western Religion*), and to take on Islamic names (removing the X) as an indication of their identity with Bilal and the Islamic world community.

There was also a change in the title of the newspaper from *Muhammad Speaks* to the *Bilalian News* (Abdullah, 1995; McCloud, 1995). Other initiatives included a Muslim-Christian Dialogue Program, which was fueled by the Committee to Remove All Images that Attempt to Portray the Divine (CRAID), that was founded in 1977 and the *dawah* (essentially a proselytizing or propagation of Islam) program. The focus of CRAID was to eliminate pictures portraying Jesus as white. Meetings were held throughout Christian churches and synagogues to engage in discussions about this. Through the *dawah* program, members visited homes of non-Muslims, sold newspapers, and handed out flyers on lectures by W.D. Muhammad.

W.D. Muhammad also initiated changes in the organizational structure. In 1976, "the community's enterprises and properties included Chicago's Muhammad's Temple No. 2 and its school, the *Bilalian News*, Good Foods, Inc., Chicago Lamb Packers, Inc., Your Supermarket, Salaam Restaurant, Temple No. 2 Clothing, National Clothing Factory, Shabazz Bakery, Shabazz Grocery, Shabazz Restaurant, Capital Cleaners, Muslim Imports, an office building, farms and underdeveloped land" (p. 16). Despite such holdings, the Nation of Islam was debt ridden. Complicating the situation even more, after the death of the Honorable Elijah Muhammad, some of his heirs filed suit, which made the financial situation of the Nation even more tenuous. W.D. Muhammad, however, eventually decentralized operations and transferred all local business activities and administrative duties associated with *masjids* (mosques) to local Imams. He became resident Imam of Chicago's *masjid*.

Jamil Al-Amin

According to McCloud, "There are at least thirty communities in the United States and the Caribbean who have pledged their allegiance to Imam Jamil Al-Amin" (p. 85). Under Jamil Al-Amin's movement, there is an emphasis on *salat* (prayer) as an organizing principle, *zakat* (charity), which focuses on sacrifice and self-restraint, and *sawm* (fasting) as another form of discipline to "bind the community and to teach the Muslim how to 'guard against evil'" (p. 86). In his book, *Revolution by the Book*, Imam Jamil Al-Amin (1994) emphasizes "that it is [in] the historical acts of the Prophet and his companions that we see a clear blue print for changing a society, for bringing about revolution" (McCloud, p. 86). Through *zakat* one learns not only the values of giving, self-restraint and sacrifice, but also how crucial these are for economic development and perpetuation of Islam, which can ultimately change society. Fasting provides a means to gain "God-consciousness." In addition to this, Muslims learn not only to abstain from a diet of food that deteriorates their health but also to refrain from information, imagery, etc., which come into their households through the various media, resulting in spiritual deterioration.

Women in Islam

There is much misunderstanding about the status of women in Islam. Women are generally thought of as being oppressed or subjugated under male supremacy. There have been, however, major differences in the status of women in pre- and post-Islamic Arabia. In pre-Islamic societies, women, depending on the type of marriage, were generally under male rule in their father's house or in their husband's house and had little social or political status. Through Islam, women's socioeconomic status in the Arab world improved. This status, however, has waxed and waned according to broader socio-political developments. The following is an overview of the status of women in marriage in Arabia from pre-Islam to the present.

Pre-Islam

In *Women in Muslim Society and Islam,* al Faruqi (1991) divides the status of married women into four periods in the Arab world. These include seventh century pre-Islamic, early Islamic, 1250-1900, and 1900-1970. Marriage during the pre-Islamic period was an admixture of customs characterizing both sedentary and nomadic societies. There were essentially two dominant marriage forms. One was called the *sadiqah* marriage, where lineage was traced through the female, and the other was *ba'al*, where lineage was traced through the male.

Sadiqah was derived from *sidaq* which is "a gift given at marriage, in contrast to the *mahr* gift, which originally was given like a compensatory payment to the bride's parents or close relatives" (p. 3). There were two kinds of *sadiqah* marriages, one called *benna* and the other *mut'ah*. In *benna* marriages, there was generally a permanent arrangement between the man and woman; the woman, however, remained with her kin. Because she remained under the protection of her own tribe, "she retained a good deal of power in her marriage relationship" (p. 3). The *mut'ah* were generally "temporary unions, often between members of different, even hostile groups in which the husband visited the wife . . . at regular intervals" (p. 3). In both marriages, the agreement was made between the two parties, and they could be dissolved by either party. The children remained heirs and dependents of the tribe of the wife.

Ba'al marriages, those in which "dominance and kinship evolve around the male side of the union" included (1) those achieved by capture of a woman through war and (2) "those contracted by arrangement with the family of the woman, in which a *mahr*, or dowry price, was paid to the father or guardian of the bride as compensation for her being taken away from her parental home to live with the kin of the male and for the children to be under the complete control and dependence of their father's kindred group" (p. 3). These marriages were based on a contract between the prospective groom and the father or guardian of the bride. She did not have to consent; "the males alone made the agreement or contract" (p. 3). In these marriages the women were essentially the "captured or purchased possession of the man and little better than a slave" (p. 3).

With regard to civil-political affairs, in *sadiqah* marriages, women along with their offspring were protected and provided for by the members of her own tribe. In *ba'al* marriages, women became possessions of their husbands. In regard to divorce, in *sadiqah* marriages, in both the *beena* and *mut'ah*, women could instigate divorce. In *ba'al* marriages, only the man had unlimited power to do so. In addition, he was not obligated to provide any compensation to his wife and could prevent her from remarrying. Whichever form of marriage, a woman was completely dependent on male members of their family; she could not inherit, as inheritance was determined through the male side of the family, and she played little part in the political life of the tribe, which was always headed by a male.

With regard to social affairs, al Faruqi points out that what illuminates through various literary forms is generally "male domination of strong over weak... honor and prowess dominating the female world rather than one of sexual equality" (p. 5). Women are depicted as being dependent on men and submitting to either their fathers, relatives, husbands or captors. Moreover, she was "a daughter of her father, niece of her uncle, wife of her husband, and mother to her son" (p. 5). In some tribes, the custom of female infanticide existed. Although knowledge of the role of women in religious life is limited, occasionally there were priestesses and diviners among pre-Islamic Arabs. However, they were the exception under male supremacy.

Early Islam

It is often said that it was through the Prophet Muhammad that women in the Arab world were given status as independent persons. During early periods of Islamic history women were granted rights equivalent to that of men in all levels of life, especially in marriage. Even before the Islamic period "older maternal kinship ties had become weaker and less frequent," whereas "male dominance and kinship were becoming the rule" (p. 6). Thus, Islam brought about reform. Through the *Qur'an,* and *hadith* (the example of the Prophet Muhammad) and *shari'ah,* (Islamic law), married women were now "subject rather than object of the contract in marriage" (p. 6). The contract was now to be a legal written agreement between both the man and woman rather than the man and male relatives. Relatives could not coerce a woman into marriage. The wife could dictate the terms of the contract for marriage. The dowry was given to her rather than her family. Polygyny, where the number of wives had been unlimited in the past, was now censured and the number of wives restricted. Concubinage was prohibited with both free and slave women. Women could instigate divorce. She had rights to maintenance, and in the marriage contract, she could specify grounds on which she would divorce as well as specify compensation.

In civil-political affairs, a woman "became a legal entity who could own and manage property herself" (p. 8). "Her property remained her own even when she married" (p. 8). She could earn a living and enjoy the proceeds as an independent person. She could inherit and had power over her inheritance. Women also began to achieve power in state affairs, as was the case of one of Prophet Muhammad's wives, A'ishah, who is reported to have been active in political disturbances following the murder of the third caliph 'Utman and led the famous Battle of the Camel in 656'.

In social affairs, because of the insistence of the *Qur'an* on equality of the sexes, "[w]omen became poets, writers and leaders in various fields" (p. 9). "The Sufi orders admitted women who at times became leaders of those religious communities" (p. 9). Female infanticide was prohibited by Prophet Muhammad and the *Qur'an*.

Through the *Qur'an* women became equal to men in religious life. Both men and women were obligated to Islamic religious duties and could pray in the mosques. There was no concept of original sin blamed on women, both Adam and Eve were equally guilty (7:20-25; 20:121), and both had to repent and ask for forgiveness. In the Creation, God created both male and female out of one soul; thus, neither had importance over the other.

Islam, 1250-1900

During the period 1250-1900, the rights of women declined. al Faruqi proposes several explanations for this. One is the political and physical disasters stemming from Mongol and Turkish invasions. Following these invasions there was a period of conservatism as a result of Islamic communities trying to maintain their "equilibrium under the impact of the new influences from outside" (p. 13). Islamic communities then sank into feudalism, from which they have still not escaped today. al Faruqi points out that "because of the law of the jungle which feudalism encourages and because of the resultant need for protection, the women became gradually a drag on society because they could contribute little and were always in need of protection" (p.13).

Another explanation for the deterioration of women's rights is the movement to foreign or urban environments. When tribal people live in secure familiar surroundings with relatives and friends, there are "few dangers to the preservation of the tribe's exclusiveness, its normal kinship patterns and the control of its members" (p. 13). However, as they move to unfamiliar terrain in urban areas, control is endangered, and they begin instinctively to protect their women. It was during a period like this "that the Muslims took on the Persian and Byzantine customs of the face veil and the harem. Women were gradually forced into a more and more secluded and oppressed life" (p. 13). Another "explanation is that after the weakening of the initial strength of the Islamic movement the basic customs and practices of the areas where Islam brought its message began to reassert themselves in opposition to the beliefs and principles of the *Qur'anic* teachings" (p. 14). Whichever of these and/or other factors produced a reversal of the advances that women had made during the early Islamic period. By the late 19th century there was need for reform.

Islam, 1900-1970

During the period between 1900-1970, the rights of women under Islam were restored. Much of this can be attributed to influences from Europe and America during the Enlightenment period, the Industrial Revolution with its need for women in the work force, and an awakening from within the Muslim world. "Reformers in various countries began advocating a new look at women's rights" with those of the Islamic faith reaching back to their own legacy in the *Qur'an* as well as the *hadith* and the original sources of *shari'ah*, reinterpreting them without alien cultural influences (p. 14). These are the sources that guide marriage in the Islamic world today, no matter where one finds those of the faith.

Marriage in Islam

Marriage in Islam is seen as a sacred institution. However, it is important to note, that in Islam, there is no separation between that which is sacred and that which is secular. Every aspect of life is the creation of Allah and therefore has divine significance. Everything that humanity does works to fulfill the will of God on earth. Thus,

256

marriage is no more sacred than any other aspect of life and does not surpass any other institution in this regard. al Faruqi explains that it is not regarded as a religious sacrament, necessitating "the involvement of any clergy," or presupposing "a numinous or divine involvement" (p. 64). Nor is marriage regarded as indissoluble. However, it is recommended for everybody and is seen as much as the joining of two families as it is a joining of two individuals.

Marriage under Islam, according to al Faruqi, fulfills several purposes. "First, it provides a balance between individualistic needs and the welfare of the group to which the individual belongs. As such, it is regarded as a social and psychological necessity for every member of the community" (p. 65). Second, it provides a mechanism for control of sexual behavior and procreation. Since sex under Islam is viewed as a normal and healthy human drive, it is believed that it should not be denied to members of either sex. In fact, it is believed that lack of sexual satisfaction leads to "personality maladjustment" and can "endanger the mental health and efficiency of the society" (p. 65). Thus, Islam "commends sex as natural and good but restricts it to participants of a union which insures responsibility for its consequences" (p. 65). Third, marriage provides a stable environment for raising children. Fourth, marriage provides economic benefits for women during their childbearing years, a period of time for women that can be difficult. A fifth purpose of marriage is to provide companionship and ultimately emotional gratification for both men and women.

Islam prescribes specific requirements for pre-marriage, marriage, and divorce. Some of these are outlined below.

Limitations - There are several limitations under Islamic marriage. They essentially concern whom one can marry, and how one goes about doing so. With regard to whom one can marry, the *hadith* and *Qur'an* prohibit marriage between certain blood relatives, affinal relatives — those through marriage and lactational relatives — those nursed by the same woman. These boundaries were set to prevent the negative biological effects of inbreeding. There also limitations on interactions between members of the opposite sex.

Muslims believe that excessive familiarity between members of the opposite sex can cause sexual indifference in partners. Thus, to realize a sexually successful marriage, the possibility for familiarity must be limited and the "aura of mystery and excitement engendered" by members "of the opposite sex preserved" (p. 67). Thus, segregation between the sexes helps to achieve this. There are also religious affiliation boundaries to marriage. Muslim men are allowed to marry Muslim or non-Muslim women, but women are only permitted to marry Muslim men. This custom emerged because men traveled and lived in different parts of the world, in non-Muslim societies where there were no Muslim women available for marriage. Thus, they were permitted to marry non-Muslim women under certain conditions.

Polygyny - Prior to Islam, the number of wives a man could marry was unlimited. This often led to abuses, and concubinage was widespread, particularly when women were captured in war. Islam not only prohibited concubinage with those taken in war and abuse of orphans but also limited the number of wives a man could marry and the conditions under which he could marry more than one. It is stated:

Marry women of your choice, two, or three or four; but if ye fear that ye shall not be able to deal justly (with them), then only one or (a captive) that your right hand possess that will be more suitable, to prevent you from doing injustice. (4:3)

Thus, it is important for a man considering polygyny to understand that if feels he cannot be just, he should not take on more than one wife.

Written contract - The written contract is between the man and woman and specifies the dowry, signature of the parties, and two witnesses, one representing both the bride and groom (whenever possible, fathers of the couple) and other terms agreed upon by the parties. Important also is the *su'al* and *ijab*, question and consent. The contract is a legal document that is filed with the local Islamic registry and can be upheld in court.

<u>Dower</u> - This is the gift to the bride by the groom. It may consist of anything deemed suitable by the parties. It may be large or small, according to what is agreed upon, and may be given during the signing of the contract (*'add nikah),* or may be divided, a portion given at marriage, after, or in the event of death or divorce. A woman may also choose to forego her dower. Whatever is fitting for the couple may be arranged, and whatever the wife receives, in the case of money, may be used for what she desires.

<u>Divorce</u> - Marriage may be dissolved through divorce in one of four ways: (1) initiation by the husband, (2) initiation by the wife, (3) mutual agreement, or (4) judicial process. With regard to the husband, to divorce his wife he must announce on three different occasions in front of two witnesses, "I divorce you." Referred to as the *talaq,* ("letting go free") these three announcements must be spaced such that they are made after the woman's menstrual cycle (al Faruqi, p. 72). The first two times he makes the statement, the divorce is revocable. This time may be used for reconciliation, counseling, and/or arbitration by family and friends. The wife may still live in her home, and the husband still provides maintenance for her. After the third time the statement is made by the husband, the divorce is irrevocable, and the husband and wife cannot live together or remarry unless the woman marries again and is divorced. As for the woman, she cannot marry again until after three months to ensure that she is not pregnant. If she is pregnant, she cannot remarry until after she gives birth.

There are four circumstances in which a wife may initiate divorce. First, the right to divorce by way of the *talaq* may be stipulated in the marriage contract. A second way is that she stipulates in the contract that she is free to ask her husband for divorce if he fails to follow through on pre-marriage promises. A third way is a court divorce in which a woman may be free to leave the marriage if the husband stays away for a long period of time, deserts her, is impotent, abusive in anyway, or fails to provide adequate support. A fourth type is *khul,* where the woman can be released from the marriage if she agrees to compensate the husband (al Faruqi, pp. 73-74).

The *mubara'ah* is a mutual agreement between the husband and wife to dissolve the marriage. A marriage may also be dissolved through judicial process. The *Lian* or "double testimony" is the dissolution of a marriage when a husband accuses his wife of adultery (al Faruqi, p. 74). However, he must provide four eye-witnesses. If he does not have the witnesses, "he must swear by God four times that his statement is true" (p. 74). Likewise, the wife must admit her guilt or testify to the contrary in the same manner that it is not true. If either of them has been dishonest, they will "invoke divine curses for false swearing" (al Faruqi, p. 74). If there is no further proof for or against the accusation, "reconciliation between the two parties is deemed impossible, and the marriage is dissolved by judicial process" (p. 74).

Gender - Equality of the sexes is emphasized throughout the *Qur'an*. In the *Qur'an* Allah created both male and female from a single soul.

O mankind! Reverence Your Guardian-Lord who created you from a single person [self or soul] created of like nature, his mate and from them twain scattered (like seeds) countless men and women. Fear Allah, through whom ye demand your mutual (rights) and (reverence) the wombs (that bore you): Allah watches over you. (4:1)

Notice from this Scripture that men are implored to reverence the womb from whence they came. Although the sexes are equal in status and worth, this does not necessarily mean that they are "equivalent or have perfect identity." Males and females are different in their physiological and psychological emotional make-up and function. This is why in the *Qur'an* it is specifically stated:

[Husbands] are the protectors and maintainers of their [wives] because Allah has given the one more strength than the other, and because they support them from their means. (4:34)

al Faruqi observes that the trend towards a unisex society is one where the male role is more valued than the female's, and women, now imitating men, are forced "to live a life devoid of personality and individuality" (pp. 38-39). In the *Qur'an* there is emphasis on a dual sex society. She explained:

The *Qur'an*, recognizing the importance of this complementary sexual assignment of roles and responsibilities, alleviates the greater economic demands made on male members of the population by allotting them a larger share than women in inheritance. At the same time, it grants women the right to maintenance in exchange for her contribution to the physical and emotional well being of the family and to the care she provides in the rearing of children. The unisex ideology generates a competitive relationship between the sexes which we find in America and which is disastrous for all members of the society: the young, the old; the children; the parents; the single and the married; the male and the female. (p. 39)

Marriage in African American Islamic Communities

Two African American Imams and two Muslim scholars, one of Asian origin, were interviewed about marriage. I was interested in their understandings of Islamic marriage and nuances in African American Islamic communities. Areas discussed included pre-marriage, gender, economics, legalities, dress code, and polygyny. As with other Muslim communities, marriage in African American Islamic communities is guided by the *Qur'an* and the *hadith*. As understood by the interviewees, the underlying philosophy of marriage is that it is sacred, as is every aspect of life. Man and woman are thought to be half and become whole through marriage. Although regarded as a religious act, marriage is also very practical, which is reflected in the primacy of the contract (Na'im, 1998). Marriage is also a religious duty. In fact, the duty to marry assumes such importance that it is said to be half the religion, while belief in God is the other half (El-Amin).

Pre-marriage - Generally, marriages are arranged in African American communities. However, they are arranged not so much in the traditional sense by families, but by friends and acquaintances. An advantage of an arranged marriage is that it gives one the opportunity to ascertain information about a person of interest through other members of the community. When courting, the man and woman are to see each other only when accompanied by a third party or in the presence of other persons. This is to avoid the temptation of fornication or adultery if the man is already married.

A major factor in African American Islamic marriages is that they occur rather quickly. One Imam indicated that the longest pre-marriage period is approximately six months. This is to avoid the temptation to engage in sexual activities. A major aspect of pre-marriage is the involvement of the *wali* or guardian. The *wali*, usually a male relative of the woman, is the person who stands in for the woman to counsel her, negotiate the dower (to avoid placing herself at a disadvantage), and provide overall protection. In the event that no male relative is available, one may be appointed by the Imam.

Dress Code - A dress code applies to both men and women. Both are supposed to be modest in their dress. The dress code for women is that clothing be loose, cover them except for their hands and faces, and that their hair be covered. The same applies to men. One Imam (Na'im, 1998) explained that hair is covered because in some societies it is considered a symbol of sexuality. Also, every society has a notion of what modesty is; for example, there are only a small minority of Muslim societies throughout the world where women cover their faces. It was noted by Na'im (1998), that in the last ten years the number of women covering their hair in the Muslim world increased dramatically. For example, in urban communities in Egypt in 1970, approximately 10 percent of women covered their hair. Today 90 percent of women do so. This is done to demonstrate "a rejection of blind imitation of Western civilization that occurred in the 1930s, '40s and '50s" (Na'im, 1998). Although many do not cover their hair to avoid job discrimination or because of peer pressure, it is a violation of religious law to go out inappropriately dressed.

Gender - As indicated, women and men were created from a single soul and therefore are equal. Interviewees emphasized, however, that women and men are different. With the coming of Islam, women were encouraged to work and pursue their talents.

However, it was explained that whatever they do, women should not try to imitate a man but perform their work as a woman. Women should use what God has blessed them with naturally. It is thought that if a woman tries to proceed in the world in the manner of man, she is going to be inferior to the male, just as a male trying to live in the world in the manner of a female (El-Amin, 1998).

Economics - The general understanding among members of African American Islamic communities is that the legal obligation to provide for the family, rests on the man. The man is obligated to maintain the woman and to do so at a level to which she is accustomed. It is also understood that a woman is not obligated to contribute toward household expenses but may do so if she chooses. If she does, then it is considered charity. I was particularly interested in the idea of the man as the sole provider, considering the marginalization of African American males in the U.S. economy, and the larger number of African American females in the labor force, with incomes, in some instances, that exceed those of males. One interviewee asserted that "God put into the nature of man" to want to take care of his wife (El-Amin, 1998). When asked whether that is due to socialization, it was pointed out that as "faith" people, there is an understanding that there are "inner differences in the physical, emotional and spiritual make up of man and woman that manifests in various ways" (El-Amin, 1998). Thus, it is believed that generally no man would be comfortable being provided for by his wife, as it "can affect his dignity" (El-Amin, 1998). In addition, it was explained that Muslim men are trained in self-sufficiency and taught to abstain from "wasteful things," such as drinking, smoking, and playing the numbers, behaviors that are a drain on financial resources. Thus, many men in Islamic communities are capable of being the sole provider (El-Amin, 1998).

Legalities - The informants noted the importance of contracts. One Imam thinks it might be best that real property be put in the names of wives (El-Amin). This is especially the case for second and subsequent wives because if the husband's name is on the deeds of other wives, the first wife would have some claim to the properties. Although this is suggested, it was pointed out that husbands may be reluctant to put property solely in the name of wives because in the event of divorce they might lose legal claim to the property, which is problematic if they are making financial provisions for it. Other legal issues are related to how disputes are handled. When legal issues arise in Muslim communities, particularly when husbands and wives dispute issues regarding what is Islamic or unIslamic, including polygyny, judges ask ministers to handle such matters (Ibn-Stanford, 1998). Generally, such disputes are recognized as religious matters, particularly when a husband says it is his God-given right to have another wife. The courts generally do not want to get involved (El-Amin, 1998; Ibn-Stanford, 1998).

Arbitration courts are also being established to handle disputes between husbands and wives, and Imams are getting licensed as arbitrators (El-Amin, 1998; Ibn-Stanford, 1998). If a case is handled in an arbitration court, the arbitrator will usually get the parties to sign an agreement. Once the parties sign, they cannot go back to the general courts.

Polygyny - The informants explained that Allah permitted polygyny to remedy the excess number of women to men throughout the world. One Imam reported that the Prophet Muhammad said that there will be a time when one man will be responsible for seventy women (Al-Amin, 1998). The informants explained that polygyny has not been the norm in a traditional sense, and religious law does not treat it as such. There is, however, a whole body of law that establishes what is permissible (Ibn-Stanford, 1998; Na'im, 1998). Polygyny is treated as permissible under exceptional circumstances, for example, after a war when the male/female population is disproportionate or disrupted. Because sex is seen as natural, it is considered "cruel and unusual to expect women in a society where there are few men not to have the opportunity to have sexual relations" (Na'im, 1998). In circumstances where polygyny is not allowable, the woman goes unprotected. It is the woman who is left with the burden if she gets pregnant. Thus, polygyny is preferable to people having extramarital sex. Polygyny also provides protection for women.

Compared with other Muslim communities throughout the world, with the exception of Africa, polygyny is more widespread in African American communities. Na'im (1988) pointed out that African American women are more open to polygyny than women in other parts of the world. He also observed that in his experience he has yet to come across a polygynous marriage in the U.S. involving a non-African American person (Na'im, 1998).

Although some men think that they can marry additional wives without the consent of the first wife, the informants indicated that there is a school of law that states that polygyny is only allowed with the consent of the first wife (Na'im, 1998). If a woman is not interested in polygyny, she may stipulate that in the marriage contract. Marriage to a second wife is not supposed to break up the marriage to the first wife. Because the *Qur'an* emphasizes the fate of orphans, the fathering of children is a good reason to marry in polygyny. Marriage is also encouraged when a young woman has lost her parents.

After marriage, each person should have a separate residence, including the man, and the household economics of each residence should be kept separate. When I asked how realistic this is, considering the socioeconomic circumstances of African Americans, it was explained that polygyny is for those who can afford it, and that this standard functions as a "weeding out process." There are men in the communities, however, who abuse the right of polygyny because they are "twisted on the idea" (El-Amin, 1998). What occurs in some instances in African American communities according to informants, is that wives are not provided for equally. In some instances, money that should be given to one woman is given to another one, or money from one household may be directed to another one. Some men also marry several women who receive public assistance, and others may marry several working women for their own benefit. Although polygyny could be a solution for the many women who are taking care of themselves, but are without a husband, men are not supposed to use a woman's wealth to enrich themselves (El-Amin, 1998).

Despite some of the peculiarities that occur in African American communities, Muslim men are taught that they have to look at polygyny as a responsibility, not a right. The man is encouraged to ask himself, "Can I bear the responsibility of being another husband?" instead of seeing it from the perspective of getting himself another wife (El-Amin, 1998). Moreover, polygyny should be seen as a sacrifice to relieve the woman, and the woman should see it as a sacrifice of the privileges she would have in a monogamous marriage.

Structure - I was interested in whether Muslims in general and the two communities in which I conducted interviews had instituted a structure to guide men and women in marriage and acclimate them to the practice of polygyny. In one community, the Imam indicated that couples are encouraged to have three counseling sessions prior to marriage, but it is not a requirement. Workshops are offered every other month on marriage and approximately every six months on polygyny. In the other community, the Imam indicated that the *wali* counsels the woman.

The Women

I interviewed twelve women primarily from two Muslims communities in the Atlanta area. Of ten women who had been in polygynous marriages, five were no longer in them, and five still were. Two women who had never been in polygyny, provided their perspectives based on their longevity in the Muslim faith and their observations of other women in polygyny. Of all the women, eight were currently married; three were divorced; and one was widowed. The women's ages ranged from 39 to 55, with a mean of 47½ years. All but one had some college education. Two had completed high school; one had completed an associate degree; six had bachelor degrees; and three had master degrees. All were employed, three part-time, nine full-time, and five were self-employed. Some of their occupations include business owners, policy maker, administrator, media and marketing consultant, disability examiner, assistant manager, graphic designer, account executives, and teachers. The number of years as Muslim ranged from one to 30 with an average of approximately 20.

In Islam, all women who are married are held to be of equal status regardless of whether they are a first, second, or a subsequent wife. The women's experiences, however, were generally similar, depending on whether they were the first or already existing wife, or a second, or incoming wife. According to the interviewees, there are some things about being a first wife that makes polygyny difficult. Overwhelmingly, it is because they generally do not accept their husbands' marrying another woman and the way polygyny is entered into by their husbands. It also depends on how the first wife's sense of being central in the husband's life is displaced by a new wife. For second wives, polygyny is easier because those who enter into it, are generally more open to it. However, the negative experiences of second wives appear to stem from first wives' opposition to their marriages. The following describes the experiences of women who were or had been first or second wives. I did not meet or interview any woman who was or had been a third wife.

Displaced First Wives

> I think where the controversy has come in . . . in the cases that I know of and in the cases probably that other sisters have witnessed seems to have been situations where the present wife seems to have been displaced in a sense. And it also seems that the conditions that were laid out for how this takes place were not met.
>
> Muslim Woman, age 53, 20 years in a monogamous marriage

Back Door Marriages

There appears to be a great deal of conflict in marriage in African American Muslim communities due to the practice of polygyny. A major reason, it seems, is the manner in which polygyny is entered into by men. According to a majority of the interviewees, the first wife, for example, may have no awareness of her husband's interest in another woman until he announces his intentions to marry her. In other instances, an already existing wife may not find out about the new wife until after her husband has already married her. One woman did not find out that her husband had married another woman until a year after they had separated (They had apparently moved to different cities during the time of the separation). She found out when the woman called her and asked her when she was getting a divorce, so she could get one. What was interesting in this case is that the second wife and a third woman were pregnant by this woman's husband at the same time her own son was born.

This participant also had another bad experience in polygyny. In this particular instance, she and her husband were living separately until he got himself "established." They had agreed to this to avoid problems that would arise because of his unstable financial status. However, they agreed to stay married, continued to see each other, and decided to seek counseling. Then, according to her, "all of a sudden," he presented her with his interest in marrying another woman, saying, "'You know, I've been talking to another sister, and we're talking about getting married, and I would like for us all to be, you know, one big happy family.'" Her response was, "We're not one big happy family now. . . .How are you going to take on another wife when you're not even taking care of yourself? You're living in a boarding house, and you're not taking care of your situation with being married to me."

What sometimes occurs is that if an Imam will not marry a couple, they will get married by another one in a different community. In the case of the participant above, her husband was discouraged by the Imam from marrying another wife. Against the Imam's advice, however, he went to another community and got married. When she approached the Imam about it, he responded, "Oh my god! I had no idea. . . .The brother never told me." Interestingly, in this case, although her husband told her of his desire to marry the woman, he had already done so the night before.

In other instances, a husband may approach the first wife about his decision to marry another woman but fail to get her input. One woman explained that although she had already "begun to sense the presence of another person in his life," after her husband made *hajj*, . . . he started talking about this other person he had met. He felt that he needed the woman "to join [their] family," so he indicated that "if she [the incoming wife] agreed to accept Islam, he would marry her. There was no asking [her — the already existing wife] how [she] felt about it. It was just this is what I am going to do."

A husband may also tell his first wife of his intentions, but she may be opposed to it. Although it is common that a husband may marry a second wife without first informing the first wife, nearly all the interviewees reported that their own husbands' did tell them of their interest in marrying another woman. The women did not, however, approve of it. What happened in most of these cases is that their husbands married the second wives anyway, bringing them through what has been described as the "back door." By this it is meant that the new wife came in without the awareness and / or consent of the already existing wife.

However polygyny is entered into by men, the women indicated that they had felt "disrespected" by them and their new wives. One woman said it felt like somebody had "robbed you," like "theft in the night. . . . Like somebody had come into your house in the middle of the night and stolen something." It is for these reasons, according to interviewees, that women are opposed to the practice of polygyny. What makes matters worse is that some wives may find out from someone else in the community that her husband has married another woman, and, to add insult to injury, some husbands may marry another woman while the existing wife is pregnant. Not only do the women feel disrespected but some also "lose respect" for their husbands, as in the case of one woman who stated, ". . . he was a coward. I have respect for a man if he will stand-up and say, 'I'm going to take another wife.'"

Although the way polygyny is entered into by men may lead some women to abhor the practice, it is important to note that a majority of women in Islam, at least in the two communities where I conducted interviews, appear to be generally opposed to polygyny despite its permissibility in Islam. Thus, it appears that no matter how husbands may present the matter, some are so vehemently opposed to polygyny, it makes little difference. Thus, many men may be in a Catch-22 situation. If they communicate their interest in another woman to their wives, it may create conflict and subsequently strain the marriage. If they do not communicate with them or do so on a limited basis, their wives may feel they are carrying on with another woman in "secret," which also puts a strain on the marriage.

In fact, the belief that their husbands had carried on a relationship clandestinely is why first wives felt disrespected. Some also speculate that their husbands and incoming wives did not follow Islamic protocol while in courtship. As indicated previously, when a man and woman become interested in each in each other, they are not to be alone. The couple is expected to have a chaperon when they are together. Overall, what appears to contribute significantly to bad feelings experienced by first wives is the feeling of being displaced in the lives of their husbands by the second wife.

"She Got the Prize": Insecurity

Insecurity is the primary emotion a first wife may experience when her husband marries another woman. A significant factor contributing to this is the perception of why husbands marry other women. The interviewees pointed out that although Prophet Muhammad had 13 wives (8 and 11 have also been reported for the number of wives of the Prophet Muhammad) after the death of Kadijah, his first wife, "each relationship had a special meaning," and was an act of "charity" or "mercy." Thus, it is generally understood that if a man is going to marry more than wife that he does so for these reasons. The new wife is expected to "be widowed," "have children and need a father for her children and/or need financial assistance," or be "older," or "unattractive and have a good heart, but might be passed over by the average man." A woman should not be married because she is beautiful or for sexual reasons. The women were concerned about their husbands taking on another wife simply because she is "prettier" or "younger" or for their own reasons, such as "ego" or for variety. As one woman said, "It's like saying okay I got this ice cream here. I got vanilla, but I want some chocolate too. . . .I want this one, but I want that one too, and why can't I have it? Well, God said I can."

270

Another reason wives may feel insecure is that they are not prepared for polygyny. There appears to be a general lack of guidelines in Islamic communities to orient women to the practice of polygyny so that they know what to expect and how to conduct themselves in such marriages. Thus, they usually have no support mechanisms other than female friends, many of whom are themselves opposed to polygyny. Despite this general situation, some women are fortunate enough to find support. For one interviewee, although her husband's marrying another woman "was a painful thing," she was determined not to "walk out of her marriage" and sought help. She was "coached by two sisters," one a counselor and the other who was in a polygynous marriage.

It appears that some of the insecurity experienced by already existing wives might stem from not having a relationship with the new wife. Some said that they felt "estranged" from the second wife. These feelings, arising prior to the marriage, continue during the wedding ceremony and after the marriage. With regard to the wedding ceremony, some admitted feeling like an outsider, and others were invited to the ceremony but chose not to attend, which they believe sent a clear message of their disapproval of the marriage.

Feeling estranged from the new wife after the marriage has transpired may stem partly from how the first wife treated the new wife prior to the ceremony. Second wives seemed to be open to having a relationship with first wives in the beginning. But the first wife's opposition to the marriage and perhaps how she responded to and/or treated the second wife prior to the marriage, may contribute to why the second wife refuses to have a relationship with her after the marriage. Women who were interviewed who were first wives took responsibility for the role they played in the second wife's refusal to have a relationship with them and admitted that they did behave badly during the ordeal. One woman described herself as being "ugly" and confessed, "I was so horrible a person. I was just miserable with myself, with the notion, and how I found out." She admitted that the second wife wanted to talk to her, but she did not feel comfortable, particularly because of the way things were done prior to the marriage; they were "free-styling" (not following Islamic rules for courting). After the marriage, however, she "wanted to talk because [she] was thinking, if I am going to stay in this marriage, then maybe we need to try to have some type of civility." But "now she [the second wife] didn't want to talk, and I felt like now that she got the prize, now she doesn't want to talk; she's married now, so she don't even want to talk." Another first wife also said:

I really began to see the positive side of it. . . . When I started to make myself available that's when I saw him retreating, saying, "You are trying to interfere. You told me you wanted me to call her and invite her to mass, and I did, but she doesn't want to be bothered with you now." So that's when I began to see that this isn't really what I thought it was. I thought this was a come together thing.

Because she has minimal or no relationship with the second wife and her relationship with her husband may now be tenuous, the first wife may feel that she is being "left out" or like an "outsider." A factor contributing to estrangement from the husband may be how his feelings evolved in response to her behavior during the period prior to marriage to the second wife. Husbands may feel reluctant to discuss their relationships with their second wives, with their first wives, because they know that they were opposed to the marriage from the beginning, and may now feel uncomfortable about it or desire to avoid conflict. After all the bad feelings that transpired prior to the marriage, husbands and their first wives may have a difficult time communicating at all. In addition, many men may not know how to handle two wives. This is because there appears to be little or no guidelines to teach men how to handle having more than one wife.

"Like I Am an Old Shoe": Taken for Granted

Another issue for first wives is the feeling of being taken for granted by their husbands. When I asked one woman, "So you felt like he was taking you for granted?" she responded, "Yes, yes, like I am an old shoe." First wives also felt that they were in competition with second wives, as if their husbands desired them more. They also felt that their husbands showed favoritism to the second wife. Being able to please their husbands was also a major concern. One woman complained, "I also used to think that I was in competition with another women — is she good at pleasing better in any way, whether it's sexual, cooking, or just her." When asked why it's important to do something better, she replied, "Because I think then there would be favor. I would think that I want to be the special person in his life." She also indicated that she felt she had to "screw him real good" and that she "was not enjoying her sex life any more because [she] had these demons in [her] head." In fact, it is their husbands' having an intimate relationship with another woman and knowing about it that is most difficult for some women. One interviewee explained why some women have difficulty with the intimacy.

I think most of us think polygamy is based on sex. It isn't, and even I had to come, and I can't say that I've honestly come 100 percent to grips with it, but I do realize that that isn't what this is all about. And that's why I feel a lot of women, a lot of sisters, don't want to do it because they are thinking, "Oh, I don't satisfy him anymore so he needs somebody else," and sometimes this isn't what they are looking for. It isn't that they are oh so unhappy with their first wife sexually. . . they're not looking for a sexual partner. They're looking for someone they can talk to, someone they can laugh with, someone they can share things with.

The former interviewee admitted, "The hardest thing for me in polygamy in the first couple of months was knowing that he was sleeping with another women." She pointed out that she would probably be more comfortable not knowing that he is with someone else in that way; that it is "not open." When asked what bothers her in knowing that he's sleeping with another woman, her response was, "Well, now she knows your husband's secrets. She knows his little noises, sex, and things like that. If sex is a private thing between two people, then it's a selfish kind of thing, this is my thing, and somebody else has my thing." She discussed how her friends would say, "It's only a dick, don't even trip," but she pointed out that it is not just a matter of his penis, "It's the whole spiritual bonding."

A major difficulty for first wives is the change in living arrangements. Husbands change from being full-time residents to part-time visitors. First wives have to adjust from seeing their husbands seven days and nights to three or four. As one woman put it, "I've been with you for five years, and now you're asking me not to see you for three or four days and three or four nights." In the case of this woman, it was her desire to see her husband every day, and when it was her time, spend the night with him. This, according to her, is what the Prophet Muhammad did. "He saw his wives everyday and then he would spend the night with one and the next one with the other."

Holidays may not be spent entirely together as well. In these instances, the husband may spend part of the day with one wife and the other part of the day with the other one. In other instances, the woman whose day falls on the holiday will spend the day with the husband, and the other will not see him at all. This is difficult to deal with for first wives, particularly if they were accustomed to spending holidays with their husbands. Equally difficult is the adjustment of sharing one's husband after one has been married to him for a long period of time, such as 20 years or more. In one case, a woman, who had been married to her husband for 33 years, was looking forward to spending time with him alone, as the children had grown up and moved out. His taking another wife, however, made this an impossibility. In addition, for this woman as well as for others, is the difficulty of attending public events alone while her husband is with his new wife.

Reduced Protector and Provider Roles

A major difficulty for first wives is the reduction in the primary roles of their husbands as providers and protectors. With regard to his role as a protector, one wife asked, "How can he be my protector when he is not there?" Apparently, her profession causes her to be out late. One night, she called her house to leave a message on her answering machine that she would be coming in around 9 p.m. When she got home, her husband was not there. But she did not think he would be out with the woman he was considering to be a wife. When he returned home at 10 p.m., his seven-year old daughter who, innocently telling about her day, told her that "they were over to the lady's house." She explained, "That thing hurt me. Because I am like, this is my husband. He is supposed to be my protector. I'm coming into a dark house, and he's over at her house. So I confronted both of them. I called her and I said, 'You are dead wrong because he is my husband and he has no right [to be] over [at] your house.'"

Economics is a critical issue for women in polygyny. It appears to contribute significantly to why first wives are so staunchly opposed to their husbands' marrying second wives. Most felt that their husbands were not in the position financially to support another wife or family. In many cases, the financial situation is already unstable. Thus, a husband marrying a second wife reduces his ability to provide adequately for the first wife and family. The women also expressed their resentment that the second wife comes in "after all the work is done." They have spent years building with their husbands, and now another woman comes in and takes advantage of their hard work. One of the worst cases is that of a 53-year old woman who had spent her life as a homemaker and never worked. After her husband married a second wife, their reduced family finances forced her to seek employment for the first time in her fifties. Because of the general financial status of African American men, the women feel that most cannot be fair in providing equitably for each family.

"I Felt Like I was Dying Inside": The Pain

The women expressed a great deal of hurt and pain over their husbands' marrying second wives. A major factor contributing to the pain is their unpreparedness for polygyny. One woman confirmed this: "I probably felt more pain than I ever felt in my life, because I was not prepared." She added that the most "painful part of it" was the rejection she got from both her husband and his second wife: "I felt that Allah was being misused; it was being done in the name of Allah, but I thought it was really a mockery, a sham or something." Another woman recalled, "I was trying to be patient

275

with myself and with him to the point where I felt like I couldn't take it anymore. I felt like I was dying inside." She added, "I had never really accepted it. I didn't even like to say, his wife. I didn't like to call her name." The women reported "crying all the time." The pain was so overwhelming that some became physically ill. There were also reports of "emotional" and "nervous breakdowns." Women also leave the faith because of the way polygyny is practiced, "blaming it on the religion." However, for those who stay, keeping their faith in Allah and staying strong in the faith is how they continue.

"My Husband was My God": Moments of Truth

The women admitted that they were opposed to polygyny. So no matter how their husbands might have presented the matter of a new wife to them, they would not have accepted it. One wife, as did others, admitted, "I had not gone into the *Qur'an*; I had not gone into the heart of the matter. I was just opposed to it." The moment of truth for this woman came when she "began to accept the fact that obviously he cares for her more than he does me. So what!" She continued, "When I came to that crossroad and accepted it, I was free. So I was no longer crying at night wondering if he would call me sometimes, when he was with her." From that point on, she began to go out on her nights off with other "sisters who were in polygamy." She said, "We would have fun. It was fun. There were sisters who were in polygamy with mates who were in the position to be able to afford it in a manner that they could have more freedom to do things. So they would take us out and have some fun." Also, what helped is when her husband was no longer the focus of her life. This woman continued, "I was praying and crying sometimes at night and wondering why am I feeling this pain, and finally I got it. There is no God but Allah; and I knew it intellectually, and I knew it in other ways, but when it came to my husband, he was my God. When I released that I was free. So when I did get that freedom, I became a real person."

Another woman, who was also initially vehemently opposed to polygyny, and who went through a great deal, to the point of near nervous breakdown, eventually divorcing her husband, was invited by a woman to become a second wife to her husband. Originally, she did not think of the woman her husband had married as a charity case, as she was financially capable of taking care of herself, and her children had a father who was involved in their lives. The woman had, however, been single for over eleven years. Now that she herself is divorced, she realizes that "being a single woman, you need love." With regard to the woman who invited her to marry her husband, she noted that after hours and hours of conversation with her, "it changed my whole perspective about polygamy. She was willing to accept me." She recalled, "So here I was going to come in as the second wife and having to talk with the first wife and have her to have compassion for me; it was just a wonderful experience for me." She, however, did not marry into the family because she believed that he would eventually divorce his first wife, and she "did not want to be the sister that boosted him out of that relationship"; she did not "want companionship at the expense of another person's happiness." She now contends, "I will never again divorce because of polygamy."

It's "His-lam, Hers-lam, Theirs-lam," Not Islam: General Observations of First Wives

The women described some specifics about how polygyny is practiced in African American Islamic communities that are quite revealing. One is that rather than keeping marriages together, polygyny breaks them up. This is particularly true for already troubled marriages. In some cases, polygyny is used to end marriages to already existing wives. As one wife declared, "He had already intended to divorce me, and polygyny was the way out instead of to keep me." She pointed out that one is prohibited in the *Qur'an* from "exchanging one wife for another! It warns against doing that. So if you enter into it with the intent of running away [from] the first wife, then it is really for the purpose of divorce. . . Not for the sake of polygyny."

Because Muslim men can marry non-Muslim women, the first wives perceive the men as sometimes marrying other women who have no intention of sharing. One wife asserted that sometimes "the second wife, especially if she is not Muslim, has not found it in her heart to be sharing," and she felt that her husband's second wife "never intended to really accept it." She explained, "I think she was amazed that he could even get away with it." Another factor is that some men use Islam as a vehicle to "sleep with more than one woman." Several women indicated that some men become Muslim just so they can have multiple wives. When men who have brothers or friends that are Muslim find out they can have multiple wives, they become Muslim "just for that." Thus, because their spirits may not be in the right place and because some are motivated by "lust," "sex," "ego," or "to be able to brag to friends, 'yeah man, I got me a second wife,'" they do not "do right by the first or second wife," while those who might have good motives, are generally not prepared. As one interviewee explained, "The brothers come and say, 'I want to marry someone else,' but they don't always come prepared to take on the responsibilities." More often than not, what results, as another interviewee pointed out, is "the same old bump and grind" while they "wear Islamic clothes." Because men do not know how to handle polygyny, they go about practicing it as it is typically practiced in U.S. society. This interviewee continued: "They don't know how to separate the wife from a mistress. . . .All we know in this country is wife and girlfriend, and that's the way they deal with polygyny."

A major problem is that many men have the misconception that it is their right to have more than one wife. One woman pointed out:

If he feels that he wants to go over there and get him some, he feels like that's his right. I mean it is very unfair to women; I mean very, very unfair. I can't make polygamy unlawful because Allah has made it lawful, its practice here in the U.S. is not polygamy.

She explained that "it's a *privilege* to have more than one wife, not a right." By privilege it is meant that an individual has "to have so much going for [him] in order to be able to exercise that right." They "have to be blessed by Allah with that opportunity."

In some communities, a man will marry multiple wives with several children who are receiving public assistance. Some of the Muslim women find this a source of embarrassment for the

Muslim community, particularly in their places of employment because it feeds the negative stereotypes of Muslim women as "uneducated," "oppressed," "beat-up," "on welfare," and "poor and ignorant." Because most Muslim men are not financially, emotionally, or spiritually capable of entering into polygyny, it creates more problems than it is worth in some marriages, exacerbates already existing problems in others, and ultimately leads to divorce. This accounts for the high divorce rate in some African American Islamic communities.

With regard to Muslim women, participants explained that they tend to be very hostile when they hear the word polygamy; some even react to the point of becoming violent. Their reaction may stem from the way polygyny is practiced by some men in Muslim communities and may also stem from negative socialization toward the practice in U.S. society. A critical factor also plaguing communities of Muslim women, it appears, is the general lack of sisterhood. This reveals itself in how some women respond to unmarried women. One woman recalled, "When I became Muslim . . . [the] first thing they ask you is 'where's your husband?' I responded, 'What, I'm not married?' Oh then, everybody runs away from you like you got warts on your face." When I asked why, another woman replied, "That means that you're a threat." The former woman added, "Because they might think that you want their husband." The women pointed out that the way polygyny is practiced "puts a damper on sisterhood" because women "don't trust other women."

An interesting factor is how some women become Muslim. Interviewees indicated that many women become Muslim through men, not because they are motivated by the religion itself. One woman asserted, "They don't accept Islam because it's something that's in their hearts. They accept Islam in order to have a man." The dialogue continued as follows:

Interviewer: So they might meet a Muslim man and he converts them?
Interviewee 2: Or he was the boyfriend.
Interviewee 1: Or he was the boyfriend, or the "baby's daddy," or the husband. . . .We call it His-lam, that's not Islam. His-lam, Hers-lam, Theirs-lam, that's not Islam.

Interviewer: So, a lot of women come into it because men are in it?

Interviewee 1: Yes

Interviewee 2: We both found that a majority of women, if you ask them how they came into the Deen, it's because of some man.

The women also pointed out that some women, for various reasons, including that they may have a lot of children, become Muslim out of "desperation" to get a man. Thus, many women dress in Muslim attire but are not Muslim in their hearts. With regard to covering, one woman stated pointedly, "A majority of sisters . . . can't tell you why they are covered. . . . They follow the majority and what their husbands say." It was also asserted that "it is some of the worst ones" whose "faces are covered." Overall, as with men who come into the faith because they can have more than one wife, for some women, "it's not about God" or their "spirit" it is just to get a man. Such factors ultimately plague many marriages in African American Muslim communities, whether they are monogamous or polygynous.

Misunderstood Second Wives

Obstacles to Getting Married

A reason that Muslim women give for why first wives are opposed to their husbands' marrying second wives is the manner in which marriage is entered into. They explained that first wives generally believe that husbands and incoming wives carry on relationships clandestinely or that Islamic rules for courting are not followed. Although about half the women had been second wives, there were a few who still were. The women in the two cases that are emphasized here, maintained that Islamic pre-marriage protocol was followed and that they deferred to their husbands regarding their first wives because they felt they knew the situation better.

One interviewee, whom I will call Carma, indicated that although she worked with her husband, meetings were brief, and there was never any intimacy between the two of them. Her uncle or sister would accompany them. Her husband chose not to inform his first wife of his interest in her because of past experiences. On three different occasions, according to Carma, when he attempted to marry another wife, he elicited his first wife's input. In two of the cases, the wife's behavior presented obstacles to the marriage. In one instance, what the first wife said led the potential wife to leave. In the other instance, the first wife called his family "crying and rambling and raving," and his family took her side.

Carma explained that she was displeased at her husband not telling his first wife and encouraged him to tell her. However, because he knew his wife better, she did allow him to control the situation. When his first wife approached her about the "underhanded" way she married, where she kept saying, "You should have come to me, you should have a mind of your own," Carma contends that she "felt it was his responsibility to bring the two of [them] to some kind of plateau. . . ." She explained, "I didn't know her at all, and looking over it, the way it went was I just let him decide based on his knowledge of his own wife." Furthermore, his first wife "didn't take into account the respect [she] might of had for him to try and handle it . . . . She just thought that [she] was a fool for doing it like that." Carma further explained, "He thought that if she [his first wife] had the inside first that I might respond to her instead of him. After Carma met the first wife, she understood why her husband did it the way he did concluding, "Unfortunately, I don't think he could have done it any other way."

In the second case, the wife, whom I will refer to as Mya, also maintained that there was no intimacy between her and her husband, and that she encouraged her husband to make his first wife aware of his interest in her. She even attempted to establish a relationship with her. Although the first wife responded positively in the beginning, it was the opposition of women in the community that contributed to their having difficulty establishing one. The general disapproval of polygyny by Islamic women presents major obstacles. It makes it difficult for wives to establish relationships, even when they are willing to do so. Women, particularly first wives, are embarrassed in the face of other women that their husbands are marrying another woman. Mya explained: "We were getting along pretty well, but then other forces, the others sisters who are married in monogamy and didn't want that to come into their lives converged on her, and this is what happens in a polygamy union. It is not so much the existing wives' displeasure, but it is all the other forces that come on you."

"I Unveiled Her": Interactions With and Feelings About First Wives

A major obstacle to the wives establishing a positive relationship is the way first wives behave when they think their husbands have taken interest in another woman, express interest in marrying her, and after they have married. According to Mya, although the first wife was at first willing to "talk it through," she described her as becoming "very, very ugly." According to Carma, the first wife would call her and remind her that they are not supposed to be alone.

Weddings also take place in the midst of controversy. In the case of Mya, the first wife, tried to discredit her in front of the community and attempted to sabotage the wedding. Although it did not occur, it was feared women in the community were going to boycott the ceremony. After the marriage, the first wife gave the husband an ultimatum to denounce his marriage to Mya publicly. She explained, "After we got married, she would try all kinds of ploys to get him to divorce me. Like if you want to stay married to me, you're going to have to divorce her. She wanted a public display; she wanted him to divorce me so that it would make him look like a fool before the community." What this did was to make Mya side with the husband. She pointed out that "the more unsisterly and ugly she became, it was almost like my heart was inclined more towards him because I said this is really unfair."

In the case of Carma, the first wife would call her up and call her names. She explained, "She would curse me out and would tell me that I was a whore and that I was wrecking her family, and she was going to spread my name around the community." In this case, the first wife blamed her for the problems in her marriage. Carma pointed out that the first wife "made me feel like it was just me, she said that 'we were happy until you showed up. You are the cause of all of our problems.'" In addition, the first wife asked, "Why can't you go find a man of your own, why you got to find my man?" However, it appears that the marriage was already troubled. In fact, this became a source of conflict between the husband and

Carma because he did not tell her "how [bad] things were" between him and his first wife. There were times when the first wife tried to "sit down and talk" with Carma. Then days later, she would go into fits as though they had never talked. Ultimately, Carma believes that what she did by marrying him was to "unveil her (the first wife)."

Although all marriages should be known to the wider community, situations such as these, described by second wives as "ugliness," "torment," and "criticism," explain why relationships are entered into clandestinely, and marriages occur speedily and through the "back door." It seems that those who do it, want to avoid the negative reactions from the first wife and/or the community of women in general, to keep them from destroying the relationship. They therefore "rush the process."

Despite the reactions of the first wife and other women in the community, women go on and marry for various reasons. Mya saw herself as a charity case and her husband as "compassionate, responding to a single woman for 11 years with two children." She also saw the marriage union as being "pure" and "honorable" and decided that "rather than say, 'Well no, it's not for me,. . .'" she said, "'Allah knows best. . . .If Allah says it's permissible, we know our intentions are clean and good; we don't have to duck and hide.'" Mya also pointed out the hypocrisy that plagues marriage in American society.

I was clearer on the mercy and benefits and the purity of polygamy. . . .But the society we live in says that it doesn't matter how many relationships you have, what gets the attention is when you try to legitimize them. It is all right for your husband and boyfriend to have this one or that one and women usually go along with it as long as you don't "bring it in my face." So it's a double standard, and so Islam is a perfected way of life for the human being.

Furthermore, she believes that the difficulties she faced is a blessing from Allah for which she is "grateful," in that there was "growth" and her dealings with the first wife was a "thorn" that has made her "stronger."

How second wives feel about the husband is noteworthy. Second wives said that they feel extremely compatible with their husbands as compared with first wives. Carma, for example, thinks it "unfortunate" that her husband is married to his first wife, because they are "totally incompatible." When asked if she thinks his marriage to his first wife will last, she responded, "I don't know if you call that last or torture." She explained how her husband and his first wife use his marriage to her to placate their already existing problems: "The other part that kills me the most is they won't really look at themselves aside from me. I just gave them another reason to exist together." Some second wives sincerely believe that they have met their "soul mates." Carma described her husband as "a man who really touches [her] soul."

Time Arrangements

Women who had been or were in the position of a second wife indicated that they generally conceded to first wives. In an attempt to be fair, they are willing to allow already existing wives to work out time arrangements with their husbands. However, the women generally feel that husbands cater to their first wives, and "bend over backwards," at times even allowing themselves to be unfair. This is a general source of insecurity for second wives and sparks jealousy. The women explained that first wives (those who were opposed to the marriage) use their husbands' willingness to accommodate them to their advantage, and whenever a chance presents itself, take advantage of the situation. They may claim to be going through an emergency or find "little reasons" to need the husband on the second wife's time. Because their husbands might feel guilty for marrying the second wife, they accommodate them. One described it as the first wife's attempt to create situations whereby the second wife is neglected or abused. Second wives said they often do not challenge what is occurring in order to keep the peace, but, at times, they feel compelled to remind their husbands that they are not being fair.

In the cases in this research, the men made minimal financial contributions to the households of second wives because they were fairly established and financially capable of taking care of themselves. According to second wives, the marriage is not about taking from the first wife's household. They described themselves as independent, as Carma explained, "I've never been the kind of woman to expect a man to take care of me." She was just "happy he was Muslim so that she could be one of his wives." Similarly, Mya said "I was established. I had a home. . . .Let's just say the only thing I did not have was a husband." Although, under Islam, Mya knew she could require him to "take care of everything," she could put her house up for rent, and he would have to put her in one and take care of her kids, considering that he would have to start from "scratch," it was not realistic, nor did she did see the need to require him to "jump through a hoop." Furthermore, Islam gives a woman the right to waiver financial support, and "Allah gives you a heart," not to take advantage when you can.

Because husbands are required to provide equally for all their wives, the women pointed out that some already existing wives "structure in unfairness." They run-up expenses to ensure that their husbands will not be able to marry additional wives, and when there is already more than one wife, make it difficult to provide equally for both of them, thus causing conflict. According to Mya,"It is designed to drive a man crazy."

Considering that second marriages are not legitimate under civil law, women were asked if they feel like they are really married. The general response was that "Islamic law takes precedence over state law," that the "ultimate authority" over Muslims is Allah. It is believed that if a man is unjust, if he violates a woman's rights, "Allah will take care of him." As long as both men and women are obedient to him, try and do their best by him, and "engage his protection," then Allah will bless them.

One thing that stands out about second wives, at least in this study, is that they seem to be unconventional in their thinking about relationships and marriage. First, they generally do not see relationships or husbands in terms of ownership. Mya pointed out, polygyny "really puts you on another level because when you can engage in it for the pleasure of God, it puts you on a different level spiritually because you see this man that's not your possession." Carma declared that throughout her life she never "cared if [men] went out with any girl or had to always call to see where they were." While she was married she did not like the fact that her husband "was at the house all the time." She really needed him to have another life, and she sees herself as "just another kind of person, not just the monogamous type." The women do not seem to mind sharing a man and also seem to think it is natural for a man. Mya explained:

A lot of what we see in terms of infidelity is not just men being "dogs." I think God has given them the compassion to relate to more than one woman. Allah knew what the social circumstances would be that we would be in. So that he's a good clean decent man, and he's an enhancement to my life and he could also be an enhancement to your life, why does that have to be dirty? Why does that have to be ugly? Why can't we love each other?. . .But the society we live in is designed to make me feel, well, if you let him go with her that means that you are less of a person or you would be devalued; no, that may mean that I am bigger.

Carma described it as the man needing to continue to grow, wanting to expand his faith, and wanting to avoid adultery or divorcing his first wife. She also commented on the negative effect marriage can have on women, particularly if they marry young. She believes that it can stifle their own personal growth and development. The dialogue continued as follows:

Interviewee: I feel that in his case that was something in his heart [taking another wife] that he really wanted to do, and it was almost deceiving her all these years into believing that he would never do it if she would put up enough fight. [He had tried three times in the past.] I feel sorry for her in that sense but, on a personal level, I just feel that anybody who marries at a young age and stays married for a long time has an arrested development of character and I think that's the way she is.

Interviewer: What do you mean by "arrested development of character?"
Interviewee: I feel that in a sense that they got married, and she became Muslim because he did. And not deciding on her own to do it because of something that she felt. Then him marrying her so young, they almost like exchanged moms and dads for the husband and the wife at a young age. They didn't quite develop their character. He had more of an opportunity to . . . whereas [her character] was predicated on him and the kids that she has.

The women also think that when men do not practice polygyny openly, women use it as an excuse for their opposition to the practice. Carma continued, "Some of the ones who say, 'Well, I don't like it because the way it's done,' wouldn't be open to it if it was done right." She then asked, "What is the way that would please you? They couldn't come up with it because they really don't want it." In addition, first wives blame problems they are already experiencing in their marriage on second wives. Overall, with regards to sharing, Mya summed it up as follows:

You have a husband, someone to share your life and give your children and to be there with you, and I have the same thing. So we both may have to take a little less, but so what. Both of us can benefit. . . .When men see us fighting and this kind of thing over them, it reinforces something that is not healthy in them.

Finally, Mya asked, "These people existed before I came on the scene so what's the big deal? God existed before we all came on the scene, and our mates existed before we came into each other's lives, so what's the big control issue about?"

Two Case Summaries

As discussed above, most of the women who were interviewed, particularly those who were in the position of the first wife, were opposed to polygyny for various reasons already indicated. There were, however, a couple of first wives who were open to polygyny and therefore had more positive experiences with it. In case summary 1, the wife welcomed it and discussed why she did so. Case summary 2 is unique. The first wife, having witnessed the practice of polygyny in the African Hebrew Israelite community, became an advocate of it. She is also a strong advocate of sisterhood and has developed and directed an organization with this focus in Atlanta. Because she is for polygyny, she decided to become involved in it and asked a Muslim woman she had become friends with to marry her husband.

Case Summary 1

"Rather than leave him, my alternative was to extend my family."

The above statement describes how this woman, whom I will refer to as Amora, came to terms with her husband marrying another wife. In this case, Amora and her husband had discussed the possibility of his taking on another wife for several years. One reason that he was interested in doing so, according to her, was the pressure he was feeling from his colleagues. Highly paid professional men of high status are expected to engage in relations with multiple women, whether married or single. Much of Amora's husband's time in the job setting was spent with colleagues discussing their extramarital affairs and relationships with girlfriends. Her husband, however, although confessed to her that he "loves" women and had the economic means to engage them, having reached a certain level of consciousness, desired to protect his family and be responsible. Because he had the means to do so, he expressed interest in helping to improve the economic conditions of another woman and her children. Amora eventually agreed to her husband marrying another wife. When he and Amora's co-wife got married, she "was present at their ceremony," which signaled her "permission." She described the event as a "very wonderful day." After that, she went and did her thing, and they "left together for a day or two."

An adjustment for Amora initially was allowing her husband space to develop the relationship with his new wife. She said, "I felt myself starting to micro-manage. . . 'You need to do this

288

or that,'" but she had to balance "letting him be" while at the same time "letting him know the impact he was having on her and their children." The key was communication and having people who are willing to work through the issues. Another adjustment was how to deal with the public. Because Amora's family lives a "visible, active life in Atlanta," the questions that emerged were: "Who do you tell? Who don't you tell?" She and her husband decided to "selectively" tell family members and friends, "one at a time." They both understood that "irresponsible behavior is more acceptable than being accountable," and that his ⁄having a woman on the side is much more acceptable."

Amora and the second wife do not have a close personal relationship because they are "different people, very different people, but they have a cordial one. . . a healthy friendly relationship." When asked whether she ever wonders what he saw in the second wife, she said that her husband "saw an opportunity to help somebody who was in a really bad situation," that "he has that kind of compassion." This she believes stems from his own childhood experiences in poverty. With regard to jealousy, Amora believes that "it's good," "it's healthy," that one should "feel jealous as long as it's not uncontrollable rage, anger and destructive." She stated, "If it didn't bother me, I think I would need to re-evaluate; like I must [not] like him that much." Amora also believes that as a result of his marriage to her co-wife, her husband is "much more committed" to their relationship and has developed a "greater appreciation" for her. The advantages, in her own words, are that:

Another family is not in poverty; another woman is not exposed to the social ills of this environment. I became a better person, and my children are better people because they have extended themselves . . .beyond their own selfish needs. I have a society that respects my extended family in terms of not looking at them as being illegitimate children, as if she just had an affair. . . .I know, God willing, there's got to be a good deed in here somewhere for him, and for me, and the children, and for everyone involved. There's a great good in it more than not doing it.

Overall, Amora believes that accepting this has helped her to "evolve in the same way that having women friends and children have." She added, "I knew if I could do this, if I could rock and roll with this, then I was going to come out of this looking real good. Now and in the hereafter." Ultimately, Amora believes that it is dealing with feelings of loss that women have to overcome. Some "women are so fearful that they destroy themselves and their families." She contends that no matter how their husband's may have announced it, it has to be dealt with. Women must understand that in Islam there is no loss. She explained: It is a "function of fear of losing something that is nowhere by any standard of your imagination for a Muslim believing woman possible. . . .The lower self is just riding itself. . . . The only thing you are going to lose is your ugly self in the end. . . ." Finally, Amora concludes: "If you can elevate and get your heart to a point where it can hold to that belief, which is faith in Allah, there is really nothing that is diminished. If anything, I'm increased because of the giving, what is really called for me to do. Allah has increased me in everything."

Case Summary 2

Wife 1

Penis Possession

In this case, the first wife, whom I will refer to as Kanika, had been exposed to polygyny in the African Hebrew Israelite community about 15 years ago. Because she had the opportunity to see the positive side of it, it was a "profound moment" for her. She was "impressed" by how the women "took care of each other and each other's children and covered each other's backs and made sure that the brother was maintained." It is her perspective that "in America there is a covetous energy about my man." She stated, "Penis possession is what I call it. Where it is just one penis per woman." It is her opinion that there is a misconception that women are not sharing when in actuality they are and believes it to be a "rarity" to find a woman who is not. To her, the idea is "to bring everything on top of the table and really design something that is in the best interest of the whole; the family." A major reason Kanika thinks this is important is that "we have too many children who don't know who their father is, or who are not living in households with men." This along with a culture that is "arrested" or "retarded," so to speak, stunts the growth of the African American male, thus leaving a "very small pool" from whom to choose fathers and husbands. Thus, it is her belief that those men who are capable need to be shared.

Another motivation for Kanika for entering into polygyny was to expand her family. She explained, "The idea is that I not only have the two children that I birthed and the six children that he birthed, but I also have the five children that she birthed. And that is how villages are made. . . .It is the ideal of something larger."

In the Water

Kanika had frequently counseled women who were in polygyny but had never done it herself. One day she thought to herself, "It is easy for you, say, sitting back there in the comforts of your own home." She compared how she counseled on polygyny with how she used to instruct on swimming, saying, "I used to coach swimming standing on the side of the pool, and I would say, "No, stroke like this, stroke like that." But she realized that "it's not the same until you get in the water, dive in, and then you can really show first hand how to swim." Thus, she decided to experience polygyny from "in the water instead of on the side of the pool."

Another reason that Kanika decided to enter into polygyny was for her husband. She explained, "Love is not supposed to be based on conditions. The ideal is that I want whatever is in the best interest of that man. I genuinely want that. . . .Whether I'm in his life or not. I genuinely love him to that extent." Because he is Muslim and she is not, she wanted him to have a Muslim wife. She pointed out, "There is a nourishment that he gets from that faith, but I'm real clear that I'm not the one." So it was important that the new wife be a Muslim woman. Another factor in the choice of a wife for her husband was that she be health conscious, especially because Kanika is vegan. She explained, "It was very important to me whoever this person was that I'd be sharing body fluids with, that she also have a higher integrity with her diet." In addition, it was important that she'd be open and honest.

The woman who would soon become Kanika's co-wife was someone she had not known for a long time, but they talked and shared, and she trusted her. The woman's circumstances were such that her children were not living with her, and she was concerned about her getting them back. Because Kanika was looking for a co-wife, the woman suggested that she consider her, and she gladly accepted. Ultimately, a motivating factor for Kanika is her love for sisterhood. She pointed out the necessity of women applying some of the love they have for men to women.

You know we have all this love for the brotherhood. I mean we just can't live without them. . . . And I'm saying we need to be able to transfer that on a very high spiritual level to accompany sisters. . . . You'll see sisters cluster and support each other, just love each other unconditionally, . . . but they are usually aghhhh when it comes to sharing the penis. . . . So there is a higher idea and a higher imperative. Here that means you want for your sister that which you have for yourself.

Weeding My Garden

The transition to having a co-wife was relatively easy from a logistical standpoint. Although both Kanika and her husband claim the home of the other, they maintain their own residences. He has his own that he retreats to, and she has her own. Thus, for the incoming wife, it was easy because all she had to do was move into her husband's home. Although entering into polygyny was relatively easy for Kanika because she had 15-16 years to prepare herself for it, there were still a few adjustments. One is not having 24-hour accessibility to her husband. She also misses the spontaneity. She expressed, "I've just been used to having him at my whim." Even in the evening when he stays at his residence, "If I picked up the phone and said, 'Hon, I need you to come home tonight,'" there wouldn't be any issue. Although she can call him anytime she needs to and may even see him during the day, "there are respect zones" that now have to be maintained. She puts very little pressure on him during the week that he is with her co-wife.

292

From a financial standpoint, again, there were no radical changes that needed to be made. The household budgets are separate. Kanika did, however, point out that the van her co-wife received as a dowery from her husband, comes from surplus finances that would have been "earmarked" for her, especially since she is now having car troubles. She, however, understands that "there is a bigger picture," and there is sacrifice that comes with it. In addition, Kanika pointed out that there is an idea level that they would like to get to. They may be functioning at "B" level and sometimes at "C" level, but they are pushing to get to "A" level and to maintain it. In addition, as a result of both her and her co-wife being raised in America, there is some "deep seated" conditioning that they both have to work through. Once you "dive in the water," things like "rivalry, jealousy, [and] competitiveness," rear their ugly heads, and, according to her, you "weed [your] garden; pull them out one at a time when [you] see them." She exclaimed, "I have to pull them out. I have to pull them out."

A New Toy

When asked about jealousy, Kanika indicated that initially those were the biggest weeds, but it was not so much jealousy as it was insecurity with intimacy; the "sexuality." She explained, "Even children as much as they love this bear, if they get another one, this is the new toy. So there is this whole ideal of the old toy not being as exciting as the new toy." She, however, pointed out that she does not feel rivalry or jealousy for her co-wife. One thing that helps is that they live in separate residences. Although economically, it makes sense to share the same home, she thinks the "sensitivities" would be too "intense," and it would be too emotional for women. As much as she loves her co-wife and husband, "their holding hands going into the room" to "get down" would be too much to handle. Although when he's not with her for the week, she knows about it, it is different from having it "right on top" of her and "hearing the bed thumping." That would require that they'd "have to really expand."

With regard to how she handles her husband having another wife, Kanika pointed out that the "nitty gritty," or the "heart of the matter" is that she knows her husband loves her. Knowing your husband loves you gives you a certain security. It is your "starting place" because no matter "where your imagination takes you, you can always come back there." She reiterated, "I know without a shadow of a doubt that my husband loves me. That's my foundation."

With regard to benefits, she pointed out that there are no material ones for her. However, it has "made a bigger and expansive woman out of [her]." She explained, "To be able to love unconditionally, to be able to want for my sister, that which I have for myself, to be able to share and not expect anything in return, to be able to yield when I really don't want to yield; those kind of things [have] actually made a new woman out of me. A higher spiritual woman." With regard to disadvantages, it's Kanika's view that the greatest are to the second wife. This is because she, as the first wife, has a longer history with her husband, his children, and his extended family.

When asked if she has any regrets, Kanika indicated that only when her husband is stressed out about the other marriage. Sometimes when her car is down and she "sees somebody riding around town with a van," it sometimes crosses her mind, but she knew when she went in she would have to "weed her garden." The regrets are only temporary. Overall, unlike most of the others interviewed in the Muslim community, they are committed to family meetings, with her husband and co-wife, whereby there is open and honest communication.

Wife 2

What About Me?

The second wife, whom I am referring to as Tyra, had ended a marriage of 18 years and found herself without her children in a rooming house, with "nothing to nurture." Tyra had been approached by "many brothers who were married, but she would say, 'No. If you want to be married to me, then I have to meet your wife.'" Then one day the man she would marry came into a store in which she used to be employed. He asked Tyra whether she

294

knew a brother by the name of "Y", who incidently is her son and who looks like her. According to her, "It was just that spark, it was like this light was around him." She later asked her children if they knew him, and they said he is married to this sister that looks just like her. After finding out he was married, it just "went out of her head."

At another time Kanika came into the store, and she and Tyra exchanged telephone numbers. At the time, Tyra did not know that Kanika was the wife of the man she was attracted to. They began doing research, spending time together, sharing, and listening to each other, but Tyra still did not know Kanika was the wife to man she had already met until she called his name. During their discussions, Kanika shared with her that she was looking for a co-wife. According to Tyra, Kanika kept saying, "I'm looking for a co-wife, I'm looking for a co-wife." She discussed it on about three or four occasions. Because Tyra, herself "needed some support," and Kanika "was open to it," one day, when "she all of sudden" mentioned it, Tyra asked, "What about me?"

Kanika responded by saying, "Oh I would be delighted if you would be my co-wife." Tyra continued, "And she [Kanika] got out of her car and did a jig and dance and all of this stuff, because I think, because we had connected some, she felt secure as opposed to his going out and bringing a sister home." While Kanika was expressing her excitement, Tyra was thinking, "This is different," "Oooh, did I do that?" A week after that was Father's Day, so Kanika asked Tyra if, as a present to him, she could propose for him to marry her. Tyra agreed, and after they agreed to meet each other, they "hit if off pretty good," and then talked every night until they got married.

Like Kids in a Sandbox

There are two major issues in the marriage for Tyra. One has to do with boundaries and space. The other has do with the decision-making process. With regard to the first challenge, having been married monogamously for 18 years, with her life focused around her husband and children, Tyra views the "marriage space" as "sacred"; a place where "another person [does] not enter." Her home "has always been private." This is in contrast to Kanika who in her view "opens her home to the world."

Another factor is polygyny itself. Apparently because it is new to this family and particularly because Kanika is excited about it, polygyny is a point of focus in the marriage. Tyra pointed out that, just as in her other marriage she "wasn't always talking about being married all the time with her husband," she doesn't want to always have to talk about polygyny. She doesn't like the idea of bringing a third party into her marriage with her husband. She stated, "I think in my head it is better if there are two separate marriages." Tyra is "sensitive" about her "intimate" or "private zone." She also stressed that she is just really "needing time to build the relationship." This is particularly important because "you are already sharing half the time, so there is not as much bonding as it would be if it was just an all- the- time marriage, a monogamous marriage." It is especially difficult in that Tyra has come into an already bonded situation. Moreover, she seems plagued by the feeling that she is having to "fight [her] way in."

A factor that seems to contribute to the challenges regarding Tyra's private space has to do with her friendship with Kanika. First, there seems to be some differences in terms of their views of where they are with regard to evolution of the friendship. Tyra believes that in Kanika's "mind we are very tight (close)." However, in Tyra's "mind she is new." So different expectations emerge as a result of this. Tyra is having difficulty with how to have a friendship with Kanika and at the same time keep it separate from the marriage space with her husband. She stated:

I care about her. I feel like she is family, but it is a different kind of family. I think, for her she is wanting a lot of friendship with me, and I don't know how to be that way . . . in certain zones in marriage. I have many friends, but they are not in my marriage zone.

Another factor has to do with feeling like a wife. Tyra indicated that this has been a problem for her. She also needs to be assured that Kanika respects her as a wife with a marriage to her husband in spite of that fact she is also married to him. She wants Kanika to recognize that her marriage "is a real marriage. It is not something that you just allowed." She explained, "I don't know if it is easier for women to think that they have something on the side than to think wife. The word *wife* is stronger than just somebody on the side. In this case, it is supposed to be equal; equal everything." Tyra goes on to emphasize:

I won't be second here even though I'm second. I don't think second marriage. I'm coming in respectful. I'm coming in being patient and taking a back seat many times because I think it is necessary. I don't want to just take over. I'm not that type of person. But, at the same time, I don't want to always be second wheel or third wheel. And that is many times what I've felt.

Tyra indicated that when they got married, Kanika "wanted to have it where we were all getting married. She wanted me to be like a wife to her. That's not my concept. I can share because I'm coming in. I know I'm sharing. But to always be together and that whole thing, I don't think I had it in my head like that going in." In addition, she doesn't want to feel from Kanika that "I will give you permission to be with him when I want you to be with him," and for her to recognize that she needs "her household to be her household, and mine to be mine. Then, if we want to do something as a family together, that is fine." Also important to Tyra is to be respected as an independent person who makes her own choices and designs her own life. She indicated that her Kanika "is very much a leader, and she likes to take charge." She, however, has "always taken charge of [her] own life and kind of resents when people try to push [her] in another direction."

The second area that presents a major challenge for Tyra is when all three of them meet as a group and agree on something, and then she finds out later that what they agreed on has been changed without her input. This contributes to her having low morale about meeting because she wonders "what's the use?" What "they decide" seems more important than what all of them decide. It is at these times that she "starts not feeling like a wife." This is when she begins to question, "Well then, who am I? What am I?" She, however, does not think that it is malicious, or that her co-wife is trying to "hurt" her. "These are normal things." She explained, "We are learning. . . .We are learning as we go."

I just think we are kids in a sandbox. . . .We throw sand sometimes, but it is not vicious, it's not malicious. Throwing sand, . . . I don't think kids think they are going to hurt you. Yeah, I think they just want to see . . . or just think it is fun. And then you just cry, it startles them so. . . . Why are you crying?. . .They experience that sand in the eye, they cry, they rub eyes. . . .And then, other times, they make shakes together and they play. And so I'm saying I think that is what we are. We don't have examples, so we are just being human to each other.

Although Tyra understands, it still "hurts [her] feelings" when she feels left out of the decision making. When it happens, she'll "just be quiet and go away for awhile; like be in seclusion for a while."

When asked whether she thinks she will stay in the marriage for the long haul, she indicated, "There has been a lot of flight times," when she has "wanted to leave," but what keeps her there is her love for her husband. She also knows that this is not how he is approaching the marriage and knows that he goes to great lengths to make her feel assured. It is a matter of his being accustomed to his relationship with Kanika and now becoming accustomed to her. Because they were raised on the same street as children and did not know each other and, before getting married, lived on the same street "in a different house" as adults and also did not know each other, in addition to their fathers being born in the same hospital, she considers their meeting to be divine, while Kanika provided the link. With regard to Kanika, she thinks she's "a beautiful sister," and although they have differences, she "appreciates" that she "has a big heart," "opens up her life to people," and "opened up to her." She, however, still needs her to respect the boundaries and allow bonding time with her husband, which she thinks Kanika genuinely wants them to have.

"Try to Tell Yourself About the Rainbow, and Sunshine, and the Moon"

With regard to jealousy, Tyra experienced it a lot in the beginning because her husband spent a lot of time talking about Kanika. This made Tyra feel like he married her for his wife. So she "felt it was a burden for him and if it weren't for her he wouldn't be in it." He, however, would assure her by throwing a "tantrum" if she tried to "pull out," and is "always trying to prove to [her]" that he wants her to stay. She feels that the less she knows about his relationship with Kanika, the better. Some of this goes back to the friendship issue. Tyra thinks that not getting too close to Kanika helps to mitigate jealousy. She explained, "I don't want to feel jealousy, and I don't want her to feel it. . . I don't want to hear her talk about him," pointing out, "With my other girlfriends, they are not talking about your husband. With her, she is talking about my husband, and I'm talking about her husband. So if we are tight, it's going to happen because he's in our lives." Finally, when she was asked how she deals with jealousy, Tyra replied, "Breathe . . . pray. Try to tell yourself about the rainbow, and sunshine, and the moon."

With regard to economics, Tyra indicated that because her husband pays the household expenses, she is able to do more for herself and children. She is also able to save. She pointed out, "Whatever is supposed to be for me, nobody can take it. Whatever is not, I'm not going to get it. I'm looking to the Creator for that. I'm not hooked into the material like that."

Overall, the challenges in the marriage seem to result from incompatibility between the wives. Both women have early developmental differences that contribute to personality differences. Kanika has a sister to whom she is close and places high value and priority on sisterhood. Tyra has no sisters, and does not place a great deal of importance on sisterhood. Tyra seems extremely sensitive while Kanika seems tough-skinned. Kanika is outgoing, extroverted, gregarious, and extended-family and community oriented. Tyra is introverted, private, and nuclear-family oriented. Tyra is more conventional with regard to her perspective on marriage and family. Kanika is unconventional and more innovative. Tyra has had little exposure to the subject of polygyny, and all this is new to her vs. Kanika who has had 15 years to play with the idea and the time to make certain adjustments in her mind. Tyra is Muslim, and Kanika seems to pull from various spiritual-development systems. Ultimately, these differences result in different expectations.

In spite of their differences, the one thing that both Tyra and Kanika have in common is their undying love for their husband. They both hold him in the highest regard and have a great deal of love, admiration, and respect for him. He was described as "sweet," "empathic," "understanding," and one who "will not leave a problem unresolved." They expressed their concern about him being burdened or stressed out over the marriages and their desire to make sure he is relieved of it. The women also seem to genuinely care about each other and each is concerned about the feelings of the other. With what each brings to the marriage, including the husband, in terms of intellect, talent, business savy , and, most importantly, spirituality, as well as being physically attractive people, it was the first time in my experience with the subject of polygyny that I got a full understanding of the African philosophy of expanding the family not only quantitatively but qualitatively. It is my opinion that they really have something.

What is Necessary for Polygyny to Work

"There Must Be Value in it if Allah Would Allow it"

Finally, I asked first and second wives what they think is needed for polygyny to work in African American Islamic communities. They indicated requirements on the part of both men and women. For men, it was stressed that they should not take another wife through the "back door." When it is done in this manner, "the trust factor is damaged in the very beginning," and the "first sister could never take the second sister in" because she "feels violated." Not only does it "undermine the trust between the women," but it "breaches the confidence with the brother" as well. When this occurs, "there is nothing"; "the children don't benefit; the women don't benefit. Nobody really benefits." The women also emphasized that men must understand the seriousness of the undertaking. In fact, the women believe that it "requires a superhuman kind of person." Men must look past whether the woman has some physical characteristic that they find appealing, or their motivations for sex. They must understand that when they marry another wife, they are marrying a family. One woman explained:

When you're marrying into a family just as in a monogamous relationship you're marrying more than just that person. . . .You're marrying two families, you're marrying co-workers, you're marrying friends, you're marrying all kinds of people together and when you divorce you're divorcing all these people too.

If they are going to take another wife, it is also important for men to understand that women have different needs; they have different emotional, intellectual, sexual, material, financial, and spiritual needs. It is also important to ensure that the woman's rights are "protected" and "preserved." This is crucial. Most importantly, if a man should take another wife, he should be able to "handle it" and should treat them "justly." It was indicated that he should first "be able to handle what is required in a monogamous marriage." Then, if he desires to take a second wife, he should be able to "handle it doubly." Overall, it is critical that the man be prepared financially, emotionally, and spiritually to maintain all households in a "fair and just manner."

With regard to women, it is believed that some are not equipped to handle polygyny. Some believe that women have to "be almost born with something inside" them; that there are those who have the capacity for it and those who just do not. One woman for example explained:

Some women are made to have a lot of kids, some are made to be married for twenty years and live through their husbands, [and] some are made for polygamy. You just have to find what really fits your person. You better search yourself out and find out what you really dig and what's important to you.

In any event, this interviewee warned, women need to be prepared for polygyny when they marry a Muslim man, saying, "You just better not decide that you want to be Muslim and married to a man and hope that he never takes another wife. You better not do it."

Overall, the interviewees believe that polygyny could solve some serious problems in American society. As one woman pointed out, as she has "grown in her understanding," she has come to realize that "there must be value in it if Allah would allow it." If Allah permitted it for men, "then we have to look at it." But "it requires emotional growth, it requires us to be intellectually aware of the situation, and also, it requires empathy." Women also have to overcome their fear of loss. As stated by another woman, "You have to really work on your own heart; you have to feel free enough and loved enough by Allah that nothing is going to be taken from you as long as you're coming to do the right thing." You have to be "selfless" and "consider other people." In addition, women must understand "that this person wants to get married too." One woman explained:

Maybe she has three children or four children. Maybe her husband has been killed or left or whatever. What opportunities might she have? She's in competition with a lot of younger women who are single. That might give her some protection too and allow her to raise her children and educate them so that they have a more secure future. It takes an openness and willingness to really look at it . . . to look into it and not just make quick judgments.

Finally, it was indicated that a woman has to "develop the heart and spirit to be willing to allow her husband to take another family as his responsibility." One participant summed it up: "One of the main *hadiths*, from the Prophet Muhammad, is that none of you are truly a believer until he wants for his brother what he wants for himself. So for the Muslim sister who wants to object to it, she knows that she is not truly a believer, unless she wants for her sister what she wants for herself."

302

Chapter 12

STEPPING UP: MEN WITH MULTIPLE WIVES

The Husbands

As with women, I interviewed men from the African Hebrew Israelite, Ausar Auset and a Muslim community. Because they have multiple wives, there were substantially fewer men than women. Thus, I combined their interviews into this chapter. Of the men I interviewed formally, five were from the African Hebrew Israelites, five were from Ausar Auset society, and four were from a Muslim community. A total of 14 men were interviewed, all of whom were in polygynous marriages.

The men in the African Hebrew Israelite community resided primarily in Israel. Two had two wives, two had three wives, and one had four. Their ages ranged from 43 to 60 years, with an approximate mean of 47. Their functions in the community included, prince, African envoy, priest, minister of information, and overseer of transportation. I also interviewed others among them informally.

Of the five men I interviewed in the Ausar Auset society, two had two wives, two had three wives, and one had four. Their ages ranged from 34-47 years, with an approximate mean of 42 years. The number of years married to their first wife ranged from 5 to 25 years, with a mean of 16. The number of years married to the second wife ranged from 5 to 17 years, with a mean of 12. The number of years married to third wives ranged from 6 months to 16 years, with a mean of 8 years. Only one had a fourth wife, and he was married to her for 1 ½ years. The number of years of education ranged from 16-20, with a mean of 18. Two have bachelor degrees, three have master degrees, and one was enrolled in a doctoral program. Their occupations include: A college administrator, adjunct professor and on-line communicator, a salesman, and two federal government employees—a management analyst and a commodities supplementary food program specialist.

The number of years as members of Ausar Auset society ranged from 6 to 25 years, with a mean of 15 ½ years.

All the men in the Muslim community had two wives. Their ages ranged from 43 to 56, with a mean of 45 ½ years. The number of years married to first wives ranged from 9 to 25 years, with a mean of 17 years. The number of years married to second wives ranged from 2 to 9 years, with an approximate mean of 6 years. All had some college level education. One had a bachelor degree, and one had a masters. All of the men were self-employed. One of them was also an Imam. The number of years as a Muslim ranged from 19 to 30 years, with an approximate mean of 23 years. Men who were not in polygynous marriages were interviewed formally and informally in other communities.

The following provides an overview of the experiences and perspectives of these men on polygyny. I describe how the men pursue wives, their motivations for doing so, the challenges and difficulties of having multiple wives, the strategies they use to maintain fairness and balance, how they divide their time, and general perspectives. The interviews with men in the African Hebrew Israelite community are limited because, when I visited the community in Israel, I originally sought to interview the women only. I was, however, provided men to interview. Because the men provided interesting insights, I developed a questionnaire for men in the other two communities. The information provided by Ausar Auset and Muslim men is therefore more extensive than that of the African Hebrew Israelite men.

Pursuit of Wives

One aspect of polygyny I thought was important to explore is how men go about pursuing additional wives. I thought it was important to know whether existing wives have any input, since their lives can be greatly affected with the addition of a new wife. Though similar in some regards, the way men pursue additional wives varies slightly according to the community.

African Hebrew Israelites

The men in the African Hebrew Israelite community explained that the way to pursue another wife is to let one's already existing wife know of one's interest as soon as possible. The way to do it is to ask her, "'How do feel about this sister?'; or by telling her, 'These are some things I like about her, and I'd like for you to get to know her. Let me know what you think.'" It was indicated that "the sooner the better," so that the wife cannot later say, "'Well I didn't know. You only told me....'" It was also indicated that, although this is the "proper way" to pursue another wife, some men still "have 'Negro' tendencies in them and are dishonest." Pursuing wives properly in the beginning, according to this interviewee, helps to neutralize "the 'Negroisms' in the Black woman that begin to come out."

Ausar Auset Society

Among Ausar Auset society men, when a husband is interested in pursuing another wife, a decision is usually made by the family — the already existing wives and himself. According to one interviewee:

I don't bring in a new wife, we bring in a new wife. We sit down, we get counseling, because I can't force them to live with somebody and have somebody sharing their children; all kinds of intimate things that'll come up and their not prepared or willing to do that. So it's something we have to decide on together. Just like if we would buy a house, or we make any major moves as a family, we have to do that; everybody has to be in support.

Consulting the oracles also helps families figure out "what's right or what's wrong." In some instances, it is not the man who makes the suggestion, it is the women: "Sometimes a person will just be talking casual and say, 'Yeah, we should marry that sister....We should get her on our team.'"

305

Muslim

As already indicated, there is a great deal of conflict in some Muslim marriages, due to the practice of polygyny. This is because some Muslim men do not tell already existing wives of their interest in another woman until they announce their intentions to marry her or after they have already married. I was therefore interested in why men approach marriage to new wives in this manner. Generally, the men explained that they bring in second wives in this fashion because they believe that their wives will not accept the new wife. As one man explained, "They really give you an air about that . . . like they are not going to tolerate it." He continued:

It is already set up by their demeanor and everything. Because I guarantee you, most brothers say, "Well, if I take another wife, [already existing wives will say,] 'Well, hey, you won't be coming here. I ain't going for it.'" They even said it years ago. And they think the brother forgot that, that they said that or even mentioned it one or two times. Instead of already existing wives being open to it, in the first two years she ain't saying, "Well, if you ever think about taking another wife, make sure you let me know baby and bring her around and so and so and so." No, you know you are going to have some problems once you take another wife. So you say, "Well, I'll do it my way."

The interviewees also explained that husbands put off telling their wives about their interest in another wife to shorten the period of conflict they will undergo. As one man put it, "I knew I was going to have a lot of static anyway, and I just said if I tell her it is going to be a battle. It'll just start the process that much earlier."

Another husband also said, "Well I didn't think it was necessary because I felt at the time that it was a relationship between me and her. It had nothing to do with her." He further explained:

You see, there are relationships between people and they are based on things. I'm saying, if we've got a friendship based on sharing this mango, . . . we share the mango. But then I get another mango, and I'll tell you about it. Well, that's okay because we are still sharing that mango. But you found out about this other mango, and you are like, "Why didn't you tell me about the other mango?". . . So, I'm saying as long as I've got this other mango and you don't know nothing about it, it is no hassle. We just continue to share that mango.

Although this may have been the case, as with others, it appeared that he was just delaying inevitable conflict. He continued, "I didn't want the flack. . . .I didn't want to deal with the hassle prior to doing it. So I said, "'Well, I'll do it, and then I'll tell her.'" Ultimately, although the interviewees married a second wife before telling the first one, they now contend that this is not the way to do it and vow that they will not do it this way again. One reason for this is: "That will be their first excuse, when you get married. They will holler at you and say, 'Well you did it the wrong way. [You] went around the back door,' and this, that, and the other." However, the men explained that although women behave this way, "they were never open and fair in their understanding towards it in the very beginning," the new marriage is used as an "escape clause for [first wives] to always have something on you."

One man claimed, "I will tell them to go ahead and let them know because they'll hit you in the head with the way you did it . . . the rest of your life, or it may just destroy the whole marriage." He added that it is important for everyone to meet so that "everybody will be on the same page, and if they are not, have the opportunity to say, 'I don't want this,' and step out of it if they so choose."

The men also provided perspectives on the approach they think wives should take with their husbands marrying another wife. One husband explained:

When you love someone, do you love them because of their physical self or are you really telling them that I don't love your soul, and I rather condemn your soul to hell? So you go and do what you need to do but just come back to me. So when a woman loves you then she says, "Well, my husband has a need for another wife, I see him to be extra friendly with sister such and such. . . . Do I love his soul to say that I feel that my husband may be getting ready to do something wrong? Am I going to tell my husband, 'Baby, it is all right you like; I see you kind of inclined to such and such. . . .why don't you marry her? Save your soul. Don't go the wrong way.'"

The men suspect, however, that the "women prefer if they never knew" about it or "if you cheated." They are more comfortable with it this way, and because of the numerical disparity between African American males and females, it is "easy to have a girlfriend," particularly if "you travel a lot. . . .People see you with money, see you trying . . . know you ain't a slouch . . . you are clean and decent." Especially since "some [women] don't have even temporary help." The men also pointed out that although they could probably "get away with some things" if this approach were taken, they know that "Allah sees you; you ain't getting away from the angels recording of it, or Allah's understanding and knowing that [you] had a girl and chick on the side." Some of the men "begin to feel this struggle," and ask themselves, 'Do I worship Allah and what Allah says is correct, or do I worship this woman? Do I fear her and how she feels about what Allah said I can do, or do I fear this woman?'" Rather than engaging a woman of interest the wrong way in the eyes of Allah, they decide to marry her.

There also appears to be little or no guidelines to teach men how to pursue potential wives, at least among the men I interviewed. Many therefore adopt a trial and error approach.

Motivating Factors

The men were asked what motivated them to enter into polygyny. The most common response was the desire to care for women. Other reasons, some of which still stem from the desire to make sure women and their children are taken care of, include the desire to expand their already existing family, to pool resources, to make a potential relationship lawful (in Islam), and to make a difference.

African Hebrew Israelites

When I asked one man what motivated him to want a third wife, he pointed out in no uncertain terms that it was not a matter of "wanting," a wife. "God brings two people together." He then explained that because of the excess number of men to women in the kingdom (community in Israel), it is the responsibility of the men to ensure that the women are taken care of. He asserted:

For me to lay cozy, say, "Well, I got it made, I ain't got no troubles," . . . and there's a hundred or so sisters—good, clean, sweet, talented, kingdom-rooted sisters, committed, dedicated—where are they supposed to get husbands, on the streets? No it's us, the warriors and soldiers, who say we believe in this and *step up* and say, "*Abba* [how the leader is referred to, which means *father*] I'll take that responsibility on gladly."

Ausar Auset Society

The desire to care for women is a motivating factor for men in Ausar Auset society as well. One man expressed a need to take care of women because of what he saw his mother, whom he described as "independent and educated," go through as a single parent. He even expressed his wish to marry all African American women without husbands because of how much it hurts him to see them struggling alone. With regard to his second wife, who is thirteen years his senior, he said, "I just couldn't see her going [about] without being married."

When asked why he needed another wife, one husband indicated that there is never "a need to bring in other wives." There, however, "may be circumstances." Although he also felt an attraction to his second wife, a motivating factor for him was to pool economic resources with a woman who was already a part of his family. He explained, "We were functioning like a family anyway, but we weren't having sex. What I mean is we did laundry together, we bought food together, we did shopping together, we had a bank account together. We did everything a family would do." A major impetus for him was that the rent was going to increase. "So we were going to pay collectively about $800 rent together. I said, 'The hell with that man, let's buy a house.' When we bought the house, we were only paying $500." Furthermore, he "felt she could fit in"; they had "rapport with [their] families and [he] thought [they] could make it work."

The idea to marry another woman also comes to men or their wives "through spiritual suggestions," for example, meditations and dreams. Some are also encouraged by already existing wives. One husband's wife, whom he described as a "very sharing person, a loving person," proposed the idea to him.

My first wife had experience with a polygamous family, not personally, but she had a friend that was polygamous and they happened to have a very harmonious relationship. She commented on how she could never tell whose children were whose, and she thought that was such a beautiful thing to have an environment where children had more than one mother and there was such sharing that you couldn't tell whose children each were. So that had a powerful impact on her, and it was something she suggested. . . . It was something that she wanted to do.

Muslim

A woman's children may also be a motivating factor. This was the case for one Muslim man. When asked why he married another wife, he explained, "Well I thought . . . that men Allah had blessed should handle the responsibility of the community, and there was a sister who had two children, and they were not being fathered. The father was not there, and the sister needed some help." When asked whether it was really because he was attracted to her, he replied, "No, it was more of a help situation. I mean I meet women everyday that are attractive." He went on to explain how attraction works for him, and the role he plays in providing for both of his families:

The attraction is that you have a woman that you feel like you want to work hard to maintain, protect, and provide for. . . . So I have two families, eight children, [who] each . . . receive private education, which means that [what] is not paid for by the mother is paid by me. And their house notes, their car notes, their insurance, their electric bills, their gas bills, all are paid by me.

Another husband indicated that a man is motivated "because of his desire to serve." He further pointed out that polygyny "is a crucible that can increase exponentially the amount

310

of love and concern and care that individuals get," and "it can be a source of another role model for children."

Wanting to make a potential relationship "lawful in terms of Islam" is a factor for Muslim men. One participant explained, "In Islam there are no relationships, there is no cohabitation, there is only marriage, or there is adultery and fornication. So rather than being in the adultery or fornication category, I wanted to be in the married category."

The desire to expand their family was also a motivating factor. One man, for example, expressed the opinion that "you need more people; you need to expose your kids to more family." He discussed how his children grew up without a grandmother, and, if he had another wife, maybe his children might have one in Atlanta. He continued, "I'm about expanding family and having the kids exposed to . . . three sides of the family. . . .You need counselors in all different areas. A counselor ain't just a psychologist, but it could be an aunt, it could be an uncle, it could be a co-wife. Maybe my second wife has a good friend. . . .that could be a friend to one of my sons or somebody. . . .You have different people. There is a much broader sense of unity in the community and strength in family."

Men are also motivated to marry another wife because it energizes them and challenges them to reach their highest potential, as one explained:

Ain't no way there is nobody that could tell me that I would come in here at 9 o'clock in the morning and leave at 4 [a.m.] in the morning if I didn't have their motivations at hand. It is the energy that I give them, and there is some energy that they give me. And that energy helps me, motivates me to be the best person that I can be.

He described how his business has increased as a result of the energy he gets from his wives.

I was in business at one level, and then I married another woman. And my business, just the energy to succeed, it was like it just increased. Because I was making money, but I wasn't as successful as I would say I am right now. And eventually I may become more successful because when their demands and energies increase, then my energy increases.

311

Furthermore, he contends that his expanded family helps to move the entire family to another level:

It's like you've got one person working, and they can only develop a certain level of materials and products. But when you have six or eight people who are really praying for you, who make and do for you, you ask Allah to give you strength, "energy to provide for my *abi* so he can provide for us." What kind of energy do they give you? What kind of energy does that give a man when he walks in and sees all his people full in their bellies, their tummies from that which his sweat has provided by Allah?

Overall, some men are motivated by the need to make a difference. The interviewee above explained, it as an "humanitarian" act. "A man sometimes has the need to do more. . . .[H]e can't truly call himself a success unless other people have benefitted from him living."

Challenges and Difficulties

The men cited several challenges or difficulties with polygyny. Probably the most difficult challenge has to do with economics. Others include adjusting to different personalities, the demands of the women and children, and maintaining health, including potency.

African Hebrew Israelites

~"It brings out all the man that you ever
dreamed you could possibly be."~

One man thought that "the degree of difficulty really depends on the level of sincerity of the man. If you're not fully committed to it and sincere to the highest level, there's a number of things that become difficult for you." For him, however, "because I'm trying to carry everybody at that thousand percent level, the only difficulty I experience is if I don't achieve it. I continue to press." He also discussed the time he spends trying to do things to make his wives happy:

When I'm out traveling throughout Africa and places, I buy them garments. I hang 'em up in the room where I'm at and look at 'em, and I say, "Now, is that really gonna make E happy? Is that gonna make S happy?" Clothes spread out all over the room, fabric, and I go to stores and so that's the only difficulty I experience. But with them their growth has been phenomenal, but they are two, in my estimation, unusual, highly educated, spiritual women. So I'm blessed.

Another participant also pointed out that he has never had any difficulties. It is because God is kept at the center. He said, "I have to keep saying this, and I can't stress it enough. If you keep the holy one of Israel in your life, the problems are minute. I haven't had any arguments or fall outs or an inability to take care of the family. I just enjoy it, and I constantly thank Yah for blessing me with two wives." Overall, he reiterated: "It's a great challenge. It's a rewarding challenge. It brings out all the man that you ever dreamed you could possibly be."

Ausar Auset Society

~"You could lose yourself in polygyny."~

One challenge for men in polygyny is dealing with different personalities. It was noted that wives have very different personalities, and this can be "very troublesome," "very challenging," and "emotionally taxing." Other challenges include meeting the demands of their wives and having time for themselves. A man with three wives commented as follows:

Just keeping your energies to deal with the needs, and I'm not just talking about sexual needs, I'm talking about all the needs and to really do the best for everybody. Because wife B does not know what you just went through with wife A, and she does not necessarily care. I'm not saying that in a negative sense, I'm just saying she respects that this is my problem. This is what I've got to deal with: "My child needs this; I need you to handle this for me; I have this demand; my father just went through this situation. I need you to help me".... She doesn't know you're getting that pull from three different directions. She does know, but she doesn't know specifically. She doesn't know how it feels to you. . . .That's the side of polygamy people miss. They look at the man and say, "You got more than

313

one wife," but they don't know what it really is like to be demanded of by three or two people.

What contributes to the challenges is when women initially enter into polygyny saying what they are willing to deal with, that they are willing to "put up with this" or "put up with that," but when it comes down to reality, they really are not. In addition, are the challenges in dealing with them when things change and their expectations are not being met. With all the demands of wives, children, earning a living, and, if one is intensely involved in the community, trying to maintain a sense of self can be particularly difficult. Therefore, according to this interviewee, it is important not to become over-involved in the women's affairs. He explained:

Another difficult piece in polygyny is to realize that I've got a life too. I ain't got to be up under these women all the time. I ain't got to be trying to resolve issues. Resolve it yourself. We've got the same tools (the oracles). I don't mind playing that role, but resolve issues yourself. I've got a life. I'm going bike riding. I'm taking my trips. I've joined a new club. I'm saying I think you could lose yourself in polygyny by staying involved and getting up all into the women. . . and forget about your own life and your own goals.

Another challenge is children. Difficulties with children emerge when individuals have different parenting styles. One husband pointed out, "If you believe in spanking and I believe in talking, we gotta sit down and talk and come up with what the procedure is going to be because we can't have some children in the family being dealt with in a different way." The family has to "come up with a consistent approach as to how the children should be dealt with on all levels: diet, discipline, education, what they can watch, what they can't watch." This can be challenging with different wives who may already have children when they come into the family. This is especially important, because, as one interviewee noted, "everybody comes into marriage with their own values and their own scripts." He pointed out that "step-kids" are the "worst problem" for him because "they ain't your kids when they are pissed off at you. . . .If they get sick, and you've got to go to school and pick them up, if you ain't their father or their mother, they ain't your kids either." Children's fathers can also present challenges, especially if husbands don't get along with them. Children may also be torn between them and their biological fathers. One participant noted that fathering his step-son might become a serious challenge when he has to do "some fatherly things with him, especially on the discipline side." Overall, it was noted that issues with children can be "astronomical" in polygamy.

~"*If you don't have no money, stay the hell out of polygyny.*"~

The greatest challenge of being in polygyny is economics. One man stated, "You know what women put men through when you've lost your job and all that kind of stuff. That economic piece, that is a big piece." He further declared, "If a brother ain't got no money, stay the hell out of polygamy . . . because it is rough. You need money after the honey. The honey lasts about a month. After the newness, it [boils] down to money." He went on to point out that although he is not expected to take care of everybody, he is expected to "maintain financial continuity." There are many needs, especially if one has a big family; wives "are going to get pregnant"; and family members "are going to come out of the work force." He therefore emphasized over and over again, "You need money in polygamy." This interviewee stated, "I don't think no man should really get into polygamy unless he's got money, or he's got a plan . . . where he thinks he can make some money. If you ain't got that, don't do it." Although he noted that you "do not have to wait until you get money before you do it"; he also stressed that " if you ain't got no plan of action . . . stay your butt out of this polygamous piece. . . .That's real. . . .It is really real."

~"*You ain't superman.*"~

Men who have multiple wives also deal with insecurities. As one explained:

There is a lot of pressure that we go through as men that we don't say. . . . A lot of men, especially in polygamy, are insecure. We've got insecurities. Maybe we are overweight. The women ain't dead; they are looking at them [other men] with them washboards [abdomens]. . . .And then we don't talk to nobody, thinking that what we're going through is new, and it is my business. That is a challenge in polygamy.

Fortunately, for those in Ausar Auset, there are persons one can turn to. Insecurity may emerge specifically in regards to potency. As this interviewee further explained:

We've got some serious frailties. . . .[They] don't understand that in them forties my brother it don't work. You get your hint in your thirties. . . .It's a problem in polygyny. You've got to maintain your potency. You have to do whatever you've got to do to maintain your potency. . . .Even the women, if they don't want it often, they are going to want it when they want it.

Health in general is a factor. Not only with regard to potency but in marriage. When I asked the above interviewee what was most difficult with having two or more wives, he replied, "As you get older, health. . . .You ain't superman. I ain't thirty no more. I'm not twenty no more." He pointed out that men have to check out their prostate. They worry about cancer and their heart. Overall, he pointed out, "A lot of problems that people have in relationships are health related," and declared, "I believe I could have saved one of our marriages if I just knew enough about. . . PMS." The importance of a good diet was stressed. This interviewee stated, "I've seen marriages saved over changing the diet."

Muslim

Economics is also a major challenge for Muslim men, especially because, as part of the Islamic creed, men are expected to provide for their wives. This can be particularly difficult because households are kept separate. When one man was asked the most difficult thing about having two wives he pointed out, "Economics is crucial, and when you talk about maintaining two families, the economics is really crucial." When I asked if maintaining separate households is a limitation of polygyny in the Islamic community, because it inhibits the ability of families to pool resources, the men pointed out that "there are levels of pooling," it depends on whether the women want to be "interwoven." One interviewee explained, "It is one thing to share a husband, but it is another thing to share hopes, dreams, and aspirations." Although that might be ideal, it may not materialize because of differences in outlook.

Another difficult challenge in polygyny, according to one Muslim man, is the role husbands sometimes have to play in "representing the absent party," or "defending someone who is not there." He explained what he means by this:

If you and I were in polygamy . . . and my other wife wasn't here . . . you might tell me, "Well, so and so did so and so and so, and she said so and so, and I don't like da, da, da, da, da." And I have to take the position, "Oh yeah? Really? Okay, I'll look into it, or do you want to talk to her?"

This is compounded by "listening to their emotional expressions," and the "double talk." One husband complained that what is most difficult, is "there is a lot of talking, and sometimes I don't feel like talking. . . .It is more talking than I ever imagined."

Balance and Fairness

The men cited several ways they balance and attempt to be fair with regard to treatment of wives. The methods include keeping wives' issues or problems separate, having a sense of fairness, prayer, and keeping God at the center.

African Hebrew Israelites

~"It's God that she sees in him that
keeps her balanced."~

One male was asked how he is able to divide his time and attention without showing favoritism. He explained, "Love transcends that. Coming into the kingdom, you even look at sex in a whole [different] way. . . .You can get the same gratification just from being hugged. Time, sharing, and intimacy [go] on throughout the whole day, not just in the bedroom." One thing that was pointed

317

out is how divine marriage alleviates the deceit and guilt that one can experience when engaging in relations with more than one woman simultaneously. This man continued:

I mean I ain't restricted because this is the week *E* is spending in my bedroom. I ain't restricted from making love to *S*. She has a room. She's there. I might go over there, and me and her start playing some cards and stuff, and I stay. I don't have to walk in the room the next morning like I stayed out all night and lie about the lipstick on my shirt and say the boys locked me in the poolroom while I played poker. I don't have to live with all that guilt like Black men in America. You don't have to deal with none of that. That's why I'm grateful to the Father (the leader) for freeing me.

When another interviewee was asked if he ever feels more attracted to one wife and is subsequently pulled in that direction, he responded:

You can love two women, but you can't love them the same. If you were trying to do that in just a physical way, you couldn't. It's spiritual too. Every woman doesn't need the same thing. . . .If a man has two wives, one of them may be okay with taking a walk once a week, or one may love flowers. It is again up to the man to keep spiritual harmony and love between him and his wives. . . .One wife may ask, "Can we go for a walk?" and that may be all it takes is a 20 minute walk for her to express herself, whereas another wife may not require you to say or do anything but listen. It has nothing to do with whether you love one or the other. If you keep God at the forefront it balances out.

In addition it was noted, "Without God at the forefront, it is impossible because it is He who sets the rules for divine marriage. It's God that she sees in him that keeps her balanced."

Ausar Auset Society

~ *"They've (the wives) got to help you."*~

Several of the men indicated that no man can "honestly" say he is not more attracted to one wife over another for various reasons. They compared it with having several friends and having certain things in common with some and other things in common with

318

others. Just as no friendship or relationship is the same, so it is with wives. One man said, "There is something that I share with one wife that just happens naturally. There's something I share with another wife that happens naturally with her that doesn't happen with the other wife. So it's kind of balanced in an unbalanced way."

Although a man may be more attracted to a wife, it was pointed out that no matter what a man's "personality," "likes or dislikes," or how he "clicks with one person over another," it is his "job to be mindful of that and not follow [his] instincts." In addition, although one might not want to be with one but wants to be with another, it is important not to always follow what they feel at the time. A man having a "sense of fair play" is also important. Women can also play a significant role, as one man explained:

I think it is not me trying to balance it out by myself. You can't. They've got to help you. . . .I think any man who says I can balance this out by myself is lying. You never balance it out by yourself. They contribute to that balance because you are going to make some mistakes in judgment, and they are going to throw some red flags up in your face, like, "What's your problem?"

Following the oracles and counsel also helps, but again the role of the women was stressed, "Then your regular old pressure of the women. Because if you ain't fair, you'll see it. You'll see it. None of them are 'yes' women. . . .They ain't no 'yes' women. And that helps you [to] be fair."

Whatever the case, scheduling helps to keep the men fair. No matter whom a man might gravitate toward more naturally, the "objective schedule" is important, and "it is up to the brother to bring the quality to that interaction." That indeed, is the "challenge." In addition, spiritual focus is paramount.

Muslim

When one man was asked how he deals with being more attracted to one wife over another, he said:

The law in the *Qur'an* is that the things, matters of the heart, [are] something that you really don't control. You see, one wife may cook better

319

than the other wife. So naturally, you would be happy when you have to go over there to eat. That is just natural. . . . One wife may iron your clothes a certain way, so you will be happy when you see your clothes ironed.

Keeping the problems and issues of wives separate requires strategy. One husband pointed out that "it is all about [the] management of the man. It is like you don't go home to one situation talking about what happened over there, and don't go over there talking about what happened over there. . . . So it's how you manage yourself." He also stressed the separate relationship with each wife:

When a man is separate with a woman, just him and that woman, then he shows his love for that woman. And then when he goes to be with that other woman, then he shares his love for that woman. That's why I don't mix. Because I'm so passionate with that one, that if the other one sees that then it may be a conflict. When I'm with her, I'm with her. And when I'm with the other sister, I'm with her. This husband discussed some of the misconceptions people have about what is fair:

It's like if your refrigerator went out, and we were married, and then I bought you a refrigerator, would I have to buy her a refrigerator? Her refrigerator didn't go out, and so that wouldn't make sense. But people look at it . . . as not being fair. Fair is basically that you try to handle them in terms of their needs and provide for them what they need. You try to be fair. . . . You may be in a marriage with a situation or a wife where you all have been married a long time, and you have already acquired certain things. So that [doesn't] mean that you have to rush to acquire those things for the second wife. In due time, you hope to see these things progress in her life as well.

One man observed, "Allah says that between the women you will never be fair." From the wives point of view, no matter how hard you try to be fair to them . . . between themselves they will say he ain't fair." It was also noted that fairness is "subjective"; it is "in the minds of the women," and ultimately it "comes from the women, not from the men." For example, one participant explained that "if you saw one of those women only one day a week and four days with the other one, to them that could be fair if they said you do that brother. I only need to see you one day a week."

320

The necessity of women showing "understanding" and "charity" towards each other and the man was also stressed. It was noted that it "really begins with how they view each other and how they show their *ikram*, which means, wanting for your brother (in the case of women, your sister) what you want for yourself. However, men often think that many women do not have that *ikram* and therefore to them they "are never going to be fair." Rather than being open hearted when someone is sick and saying, "Why don't you stay over there," or when someone has kids and might need more help, by showing charity with regard to time, "they will hold you to the letter." One man indicated, "They dictate the fairness. When they do it, everything will be beautiful, and Allah will be praising and the angels will be writing it down. But they don't want to do it; they think, 'I'm going to hold you to this. No, uh, huh.'" This is because for some "women there is really no respect or love between them"; "women in general don't love each other. . . .They have that envy." And this makes it difficult for men, no matter how hard they try. Whatever the circumstances or situation a man might be handling, the men indicated that following the example set by the Prophet Muhammad in his treatment of his wives is a guideline they can use to achieve balance and be fair. Ultimately, prayer is the key.

Time Arrangements

A variety of schedules are used by the men. For African Hebrew Israelite men, time is divided equally between wives in blocks of time. If there are two wives, each usually spends time in his bedroom for a period of two weeks. If there are three wives, each spends ten days. For the Ausar Auset, the same time arrangement applies. In both communities, because the men and women share the same house, time is also shared during the day with all the wives. The only difference is who shares the same bed with the husband at night. There may be some flexibility depending upon the relationship between the wives and the specific family culture. A husband, for example, may sleep alone at times or even fall asleep on the couch.

The Muslim men experimented with a variety of schedules before settling on one. The most common is that they alternate between the two wives every other night, every two or three nights, or every other week. One interviewee pointed out how he started with every other night but found that it involved too much adjusting. He therefore settled on every other week.

The difference between Muslim men and men in the other communities is that some may not see one wife during the entire time they spend with the other one. This is because the households and interaction between wives are kept separate. Because of hostility between wives, the wives may hold their husband to the letter. There are occasions, however, when a wife may give up time for the other one because she may be sick or have relatives in town. However, the men are generally expected to make up the time, and it becomes stressful. As one man pointed out, "In real life that becomes impractical at times. You can't make up all these days. You really can't. You really can't do it. The women know the situation, and they have to have that *ikram*. They have to be willing to show their love, or they have to be able to show up sometimes when your other people are in town and be hospitable to them. But they don't even want to learn that."

Perspectives

Men Marry Wives for Sex and Ego

I asked the men other questions, for example, how they would respond to assertions that men desire to have multiple wives for sex, ego, or to look good in the eyes of other men. Other questions included what they would tell other men who might be considering multiple wives, and their perspectives on the idea of women with multiple husbands. The men also discussed other issues without my asking questions, for example, their belief that polygyny is needed. With regard to reasons that men marry multiple wives the following were their responses.

African Hebrew Israelites

The question was asked: "Now coming from the American male perspective, having several women is often looked at as a macho thing, like the individual is 'the man,' because he's got all these women. How would you respond to something like that?" One interviewee responded, "I wouldn't. 'Cause that is not the level of where my thinking is. The only way I can control them is to be correct. The only way I can get maximum cooperation from this is to be as right as I possibly can and that's what I try to do."

Ausar Auset Society

One participant in Ausar Auset society had this to say. "If the man is motivated to have another wife because he looks [about] and says, 'Well she looks good and we can have a sexual thang'. . . .That wouldn't happen, just like in monogamy, if that's what's motivating it. Because that's gonna get worn out. I mean that's not going to sustain you. It's going to be fun for a minute or fun for a while, but it's going to calm down, and then you're going to realize it's a person here. This person has a destiny and they have things that they gotta do."

Muslim

When asked if he thought sex was a major motivator for some men, one man responded, "Yeah, I think initially. But see again, you can start a lot of things but to be able to maintain them is a different thing. You know you can start a lot of things, but the effective people look to how they want something to end before they start it." Another one had this to say:

I would definitely say that . . . there is a misconception because sexual orgasm lasts just such a small time and that if a man is just into that after two or three weeks of being with the woman, he won't want it no more. . . . But to sustain a family and to groom a family is really something that is very different, and he gives up so much of himself, for instance, if a man is taking care of two families, paying two rents, two light bills.

When asked whether a man pursues another wife after a lot of years with one wife for something different or variety, one said, "Sex is a small part of it," and another declared,

[You] can't even get it sometimes. It ain't worth it. All this drama? All this drama? You think all this drama is worth the sex part? Ain't no way in the world. All the headache, all the struggle, all the stuff you have to do to maintain and try to make things work and keep your family together and provide. . . .No!

He also pointed out that he "had a spurt in [his] life where Allah blessed [him] to go and buy both of [his] wives brand new cars in the same day." He said, "When the women talk about you did it for sex, I'm looking like I could have taken my money and done what I wanted to do. . . .You can get sex for virtually free, $5.00, $10.00, and you can get it anywhere."

With regard to ego, one man commented: "A man could go and buy himself a Mercedes Benz and get more play, more everything than having a woman and saying that I'm going to take care of her kids." He also stated, "you get more benefit in the eyes of Allah to take care of the young kids" than putting your energy into "cars," "diamonds," a "rolex watch," and other things to massage your ego. In fact, the men indicated that they could probably get more women if they possessed these things. However, to "watch over children, take them to football practice and to educate them for 18 years," puts a whole different perspective on it.

What Would You Tell Men Considering Polygyny?

I asked the men what they would tell men who might be considering entering into polygyny. The following were there responses.

Ausar Auset Society

~*"You've got to have women skills."*~

One interviewee declared: "You've got to have women skills. . . . You've got to have not people skills [but] woman skills in polygamy. If you . . . haven't been in relationships with women before, stay . . . out of polygamy until you learn. If you don't have no women skills you are going to mess it all up. You are going to show favoritism, not because you want to, . . . but because of your lack of skill set. You are going to have this woman pull you over here, that one pull you over there; you are not going to know when to take a stand."

~*"He has to pray."*~

Another interviewee said, "He has to pray. One thing I notice is that people give you a lot of respect. Oh, you got more than one wife, but I don't think they understand that it not like a macho [thing]. That's not what it's about. Cuz if that's what it is about, then you're just doing what everybody else is doing. You're just messing around with more than one woman. . . .That's not what it's about; it's not the bedroom. In addition, they must focus on "their own spirituality, their own strength, centeredness, [and] their health. It is very key."

Muslim

~*"It is more than a notion."*~

Another interviewee offered this view: "I think men that have not been in polygamy, and I was one of them, fantasize about polygamy. Fantasize. It is fantasy. Because you are talking about dealing with the psychological, emotional, social, economic needs of another human being. That is what marriage is. . . .And now, you're talking about dealing with not *one* other being, but with *two* other human beings. . . .They think about the sexual aspects of it. But even that requires emotional, psychological [strength]. I'm

325

saying all of that is involved even in the intimacy aspect of it. So it is more than a notion. Yeah, it is more than a notion."

~*Pray to Allah Much*~

Another interviewee advised: "I would tell them to make sure they know their religion. Make sure they are financially and economically stable. Make sure they are mentally stable to be able to manage people. Because it is managing the people. And pray to Allah much. Much. Because nothing happens without the mercy of Allah, his grace."

Polygyny is Needed

The men also shared the perspective that polygyny is needed for African Americans; not for men but for women and children.

Muslim

One Muslim man thinks polygyny is in the interest of women:

I think that for some of us it is already obvious that the right of every woman to feel secure, protected, respected in the community should be the primary purpose of polygamy. . . .I'm sure polygamy is for women. I'm sure of that. In the United States, there are too many ways that men can satisfy the need for multiple women without polygamy. In Islam those ways are unlawful. They are unlawful. They are called *haram*, which means unlawful. . . .There is the need for women to be honored or cared for and taken care of, and therefore being able to pass that on to children.

One man believes polygyny to be necessary, but he observed, "Sometimes you may have to shatter one of your families just to know you can create a better situation because of the mind set of some people." He also pointed out the importance of being careful with whom one chooses as a mate because most African Americans don't take seriously the "pedigree of people, their family members, where they come from and what you desire and project where you want to see your family down the line." He feels that it is important to be "better in the selecting process, when you pick and choose your mate."

Ausar Auset Society

Although most of the men believe that polygyny is needed, there are those who don't think it is for a majority of people. One man had reservations: "I don't think it is a viable alternative. I think it is a viable alternative for a few people. Because most people don't have their emotions together. Most people have no accountability."

What About Women with Multiple Husbands?

I asked men how they would respond to the idea of multiple husbands for women. I did not think of this question, however, until I began interviewing Muslim men. Therefore, the responses are those from Muslim men only. One pointed out the potential problems with in-breeding. If a woman had four husbands, it would be difficult to tell which man is the father of the child. If these men subsequently fathered children by other women, the children of a common father, not knowing who their father is, may marry and subsequently have children, and thereby risk the hazards of in-breeding.

They also questioned whether women could meet the needs of several husbands. They indicated that many women are not able to handle the needs of one husband, particularly when they are pregnant and afterwards. Although they conceded that a woman may be able to handle two boyfriends on a sexual level, they asked whether she could she handle two husbands and children and all the obligations that come along with them. It was also asked: "Women are saying that they can't find one man, so where are [they] going to get two?"

Lastly, it was stressed that in Islam it is unlawful for a woman to have more than one husband. When I asked why they think this is so, one interviewee's response was "Because Allah said it wasn't lawful," and, "Maybe Allah knows something about the nature of human beings that maybe we don't know."

As already indicated, there is a great deal of conflict in African American Muslim communities due to the practice of polygyny. One reason for this is general opposition to the practice among African American Muslim women. In response to this, Muslim men shared their perspectives.

One factor, according to the men, that seems to contribute to the general dislike of polygyny may be that, like everybody else, women "want their own." The men pointed out, however, that "it is a matter of submission (to Allah); it is a matter of faith, and realization that you are going to own nothing. There ain't no your own. And what happens when Allah takes the individual away? You don't own nothing."

Another factor that Muslim men believe inhibits women from seeing the value of polygyny is the need to feel special. One interviewee explained: "A lot of women, and men too, they want to be so special. They want to feel special in your eyes, like they are the only one in the world. They want the knight in shining armor to love only them and care for only them." It was expressed, that this is "really a fantasy," and the problem with this kind of thinking is that they want it "at any cost." However, "the cost for that is too high when you've got lives and children." The men also responded to the claim by Muslim women that their husbands and their new wives had disrespected them, or that they did not feel respected. One interviewee's perspective on the issues of respect and the need to feel special was:

If you don't feel special to yourself, you are not going to feel special. . . . And it is just like respect. Some people want respect without giving respect. "They should respect me because I was with you this amount of time and you aren't respecting me." But when you come around, you're nasty, you've got a funny look on your face, you've got terrible vibes, but you want to be respected because of a past, because I was married to you for a hundred years before that. . . . No, you earn respect of other women, and other people, and other children. . . . And I think that respect begins on the inside, on how you do yourself and how you treat people, and the same with feeling special. . . . You've got to give in order to receive. And when you give a certain amount of things, then you will be special to other people too. But you earn all of it. It's a constant earning process.

It was also pointed out that what women need to understand is that "the goal is not to be the only one. The goal is to get to paradise. To know that Allah is pleased with what you are doing and know that you are being pleasing to him. And know that your man is making a sacrifice to try to please Allah too, and don't put him in situations where you make him make bad decisions where he is not pleasing to Allah." In addition, they should "want all the souls to be correct in their relationships," particularly in the eyes of Allah.

The general negative attitude towards polygyny in some Muslim communities prohibits some women who might be open to it from entering into it. The men pointed out that there are "some sisters who have been single for 10, 12, 15 years and they have a need to be married, but they don't want to go on record and say, 'I'll marry brother A, I'll marry brother such and such. . . .They don't want to go on record, but in their heart they are ready to accept polygamy." One husband added, "A lot of communities say that they don't want to accept polygamy, but when I get with individual members, they are whispering to me, 'How do you do this? Brother, show me how to do this.'"

The men also criticize how women sometimes pass their hostility toward other wives to their own children. One explained, "She don't really like her kids to like her (his second wife) either. So that is what she will teach them: 'I don't want you to go around her because I don't like the way they got married.'. . . So they spread that understanding to the children."

In spite of negative attitudes of women to the practice of polygyny, the men still see it as valuable and necessary. They point out that although polygyny may be difficult, women must evolve to see the value in it. They also see polygyny for women as comparable to holy war for men. An interviewee asserted:

Allah says that one of the greatest tests for women is polygamy. It is like *Jihad*. *Jihad* is like the holy war for men. *Jihad* is the holy war for us when we go out to battle, and *Jihad* for the woman is polygamy. And a lot of people, you know, don't want to go to war. Because war is going to teach you some things about yourself and about your manhood, about everything. It is going to test every fiber of your [being], how you believe and define what life is all about, everything. . . .Polygamy will, I think, it will shake those women and see what [they] are going to be about. . . . They are going to have to answer those real questions within themselves.

Finally, he pointed out that, essentially,

it becomes a test of their faith, their *ikram* (wanting for your sister what you want for yourself). Like anything else, it becomes a test of their *ikram*. This is how you get closer to Allah, by doing what Allah said. Whether they like it or not, whether they understand it or not. . . .I may not like getting up in the morning and coming to prayer every morning, but it is not an issue. It is not a question. To get closer to Allah, to approach Allah as he said he is to be approached, I've got to do this. And that goes along with it.

Chapter 13

COMPARATIVE SUMMARY OF THE THREE COMMUNITIES

A common factor in all three communities is their commitment to a higher power. There is focus on the presence of an omnipotent being or third entity. It is this which provides moral sanction for polygyny. The ideal of "wanting for your sister what you want for yourself" guides the women even though the way polygyny is practiced varies in each community and among members. Focus on spiritual development helps individuals rise above the challenges presented by polygyny.

The African Hebrew Israelites consider themselves to be self-governing, and even though they have communities in cities throughout the U.S., West Africa, and the Caribbean, the seat of government resides in Israel. There is a deep commitment to building a Kingdom of God, as demonstrated by the exodus its members made out of the U.S. in the late 1960s and their willingness to live in the wilderness in Liberia until they eventually ended the journey in Israel. A major component in reaching their spiritual goal is the development of economic and social institutions to provide for the physical, emotional, and spiritual needs of its members. Such helps to circumvent social ills that can emerge when basic human needs are not met. Ultimately, the aim of the institutions among the African Hebrew Israelites is to provide mechanisms whereby each individual can reach his or her fullest potential.

Divine marriage, whereby a husband may marry more than one wife simultaneously, is socially structured to ensure that in circumstances of an imbalanced sex ratio, all women can have the social, economic, and emotional support that comes with a primary relationship through marriage. A major goal of polygyny in divine marriage is to eliminate the potential exploitation of women and other negatives that can occur under a monogamy only policy with a preponderance of women. The women in the community in Israel are emphatically committed to the goals of the kingdom. This includes a commitment to sisterhood, even if it means sharing their own husbands.

Ausar Auset society is committed to a way of life based on traditional African culture. As was the case throughout traditional Africa, the goal was to construct social structures that maximize human potential. Social structures, in Ausar Auset society, including marriage, are therefore designed to meet this goal. Polygyny is incorporated into the socio-political-spiritual structure to ensure that all women can have the potential to marry. The oracles, through which one communicates with the supreme being, help members to fulfill their incarnate objective, including how it might be met in marriage. The oracles are also used to guide individuals in their daily lives.

The *Qur'an* as revealed to the Prophet Muhammad provides a guide to living for practicing Muslims. The *hadith* can also be used as a guide to follow the practice and teachings of the Prophet Muhammad. The *Al Nisa* (Surah 4, or the fourth chapter) of the *Qur'an*, outlines the rights of both men and women in marriage, including polygyny. The *shari'ah*, or Islamic law, also covers matrimonial law. The Imam is the spiritual link between humans and Allah, to whom all submit and defer to live a righteous life.

Marriage

All three communities have guidelines for marriage. However, it appears that the African Hebrew Israelites have the most rigid *prerequisites* for marriage, and the Muslim communities (at least those in which I interviewed individuals) have the least. Living through one's higher spiritual self is supposed to underlie all relationships (intimate or otherwise) in all three communities.

In Ausar Auset society, members are encouraged to get an oracle reading prior to marriage to determine whether they should get married. Although members are strongly urged to seek premarital counseling, it is left to the discretion of the individuals.

In the African Hebrew Israelite community, individuals in *michodeshet* (engagement) are required to have ten sessions with a priest before getting married. If the prospective marriage is polygynous, the already existing wife may also participate in some of the ten sessions. Premarital counseling under divine marriage teaches men and women what to expect in marriage, helps the parties determine if they are ready for it, provides them guidance on how to relate to one another, introduces them to the difficulties they may encounter, gives them a chance to gauge whether or not they are compatible, and teaches all the parties what commitment is and the importance of remaining true to it. Within the community, men have other men to whom they can turn for advice on parenting and husbanding, and women have other women to whom they can turn to for the same things. Divine marriage also has a mechanism that permits one to go to someone outside the family, mainly priests, if problems arise that the spouses are unable to settle among themselves, or if a spouse's behavior is out of order.

The same exists within Ausar Auset society. One may seek counseling from a shekhem, or priest, who will generally use the oracles to help resolve conflicts. As with the African Hebrew Israelites, there are also other men and women to whom individuals can turn to for advice.

For Muslims, although individuals are encouraged to seek an Imam for advice to become married, there are few or no premarital counseling requirements in the communities in which individuals were interviewed. The Imam in one community indicated that individuals are encouraged to go through at least three premarital counseling sessions, but attendance is not a requirement. There are classes once every other month on marriage in general and one about every six months on polygyny. In the other community, it was indicated that the *wali* is expected to counsel the woman.

With regard to the practice of polygyny, there are both similarities and differences among the three communities. A major factor distinguishing the communities is that two of them, the African Hebrew Israelites and Ausar Auset, have separated themselves from the social and cultural values of U.S. society. Although both groups still share the same land and are subjected to the same laws governing the land, they have made a shift from the cultural values of the U.S. and have instituted a spiritually focused social and economic-political system (even though the

African Hebrew Israelites have physically moved the seat of government to Israel, they are still subjected to the laws governing Israel and where they have extensions in the U.S., the same applies).

This is in contrast to Muslims under the American Muslim Mission. Unlike the Nation of Islam (of the past), there is no organized nationalistic effort. This is a major reason that there was a separation between the Nation of Islam led by Minister Louis Farrakhan and the American Muslim Mission led by W. D. Muhammad. In the communities that have made a cultural shift, there is a general commitment of members to the goals of the community. In the Muslim community under W. D. Muhammad, the teachings come primarily from the *Qur'an*. Thus, the members become Muslim as they would any other religion in a society that supports religious diversity. Even though Islamic communities allow polygyny because it is permitted in the *Qur'an*, and the Prophet Muhammad had several wives, there may be few if any institutions that provide education on African or Western history or a critical analysis of European cultural hegemony. There also appears to be no mechanism to re-orient or help individuals make the paradigmatic shift from socialization to monogamy only. The result is that although many profess to be Islamic, they have little or no understanding of it or the political milieu out of which it emerged. They therefore remain captive to the social orientation of the Western world, which includes exclusive monogamy.

In both the African Hebrew Israelite community and Ausar Auset society, women are open to polygyny because they are committed to the goals of the communities, one of which is an ethic of care for all its members. Among the African Hebrew Israelites, it did take some years for the women to accept polygyny. The women eventually made the adjustment and now assist their husbands in choosing sister-wives and even seek them out. They express a great deal of love and concern for their sister-wives, as well as women in the broader community. The sisterhood is, in fact, remarkable. The women also hold the men in the community in the highest regard and express undying love for their husbands even though they have multiple wives. The benefits they see in polygyny include being a part of a family and having help with childcare and domestic responsibilities. There is also emotional, sexual, and domestic assistance for husbands. The women provide companionship for each other, and there is more autonomy to pursue individual interests. Jealousy is a major challenge for some women, particularly when a husband is in the room with a sister-wife. However, spiritual focus and concern for each other enable the women to rise above this.

Commitment to sisterhood among women in Ausar Auset society is mitigated by the daily realities of living in the social milieu of the U.S. Relationships between the women range from close friendships to estrangement. Some issues between the women stem from how husbands deal with them. If a husband is unfair or does not show balance in his treatment of one wife, it may spark jealousy or resentment in another wife. Other issues seem to stem from a general incompatibility of wives, which may range from personality differences to differences in household maintenance. There may also be cliques between wives, particularly if there is differential compatibility between and among them. This stems from individuals being naturally drawn to whomever they feel more comfortable with.

A major challenge for wives in Ausar Auset society who do not have a marriage license is dealing with feelings of insecurity about whether they are really a wife. Another challenge is how to present themselves to the public, for example, in the work place and on documents. Incoming wives may also feel like outsiders with husbands and wives who are already emotionally, socially and economically bonded. They may also feel left out of the decision-making process, or, in some cases, input from the several parties in decision-making slows it down and can be frustrating for newcomers.

Different styles of household maintenance is also a challenge. Economics and differences in parenting styles are also challenges. Overall, many of the challenges seem to stem from the women living in the same household. The women are, however, committed to the goals of the community and see major advantages to being in polygyny. These include help with childcare for women who were single parents prior to marriage, not having to run a household completely alone, sisterhood, help with providing husbands' sexual needs, being a part of a family with children, and spiritual growth. There is continual focus on living through the higher self, and the oracles are consulted to resolve conflicts.

The Muslim community differs from the other two communities in three ways: There is little or no support for polygyny, there is general unacceptance of it by women, and the women live in separate residences. In some Muslim communities, at least those in which members were interviewed, there are few guidelines other than the *hadith* and *sunnah* (which most know about but probably have never read) to guide men and women on how to be in polygyny. Many Muslim women speak of the moral philosophy of "wanting for your sister what you want for yourself," but few seem willing to practice it. This may stem partly from the less than optimal way polygyny is entered into and practiced by Muslim men. Because of the lack of guidance, women's general unacceptance of it, and the dishonest and deceptive manner in which some men enter into it, many Muslim marriages are plagued with instability and discontentment.

As far as some of the dynamics of polygynous Muslim marriages, already existing wives may feel displaced by an incoming wife. First wives often suspect that the husband and incoming wife failed to follow protocol during courtship. The feeling of being displaced coupled with insecurity stemming from such suspicion in turn generates feelings of estrangement from the husband and his new wife. Already existing wives also feel like outsiders to the marital triad, and feel that they are taken for granted. Such feelings are compounded by knowing their husband is being intimate with another women.

Women's perceptions of why some men become Muslim also contribute to problems in polygynous marriages. Many suspect that men convert to Islam to get legitimate support to be with other women, and that some marry other women for reasons other than those indicated in the *Qur'an*, for example, because she is prettier or younger, or for sex, lust, ego, variety, or to brag.

The challenges for incoming wives stem primarily from the opposition to polygyny by Muslim women in general and first wives in particular. There are fewer problems and more stability in marriages when both wives consent. The challenges for such marriages are generally the same as they are for those in the other communities: Incompatibility between wives, feeling like an outsider to an existing husband-wife bond and the decision-making process. Also challenging is keeping jealously at bay and taking into consideration the other person.

Under Islam, women in polygyny live in separate residences. An advantage of this is that it helps to alleviate the strain that can occur when women live together in close quarters. Each woman has her own space and does not have to endure conflicts or feelings of jealousy stemming from the other wife's interaction with their husband. By contrast, women in the African Hebrew Israelite community and those in Ausar Auset society are constantly challenged to rise above conflicts and feelings of jealousy; though they expressed how this helps them to grow spiritually. Although separate residences offer some advantages, the disadvantage is that most men are incapable of contributing to two or more households. At times, resources that should be used in one household may be used for another one. In some instances, a husband may not even contribute to a household. Also, it seems the Islamic creed that men are responsible for providing for women can encourage them to become economic dependents. If a women is providing most of the childcare and domestic support, it would seem logical that men would make the economic provisions. However, it does not seem logical that educated, skilled, and talented women should be encouraged to become dependents, especially given the socioeconomic circumstances of African Americans as a whole. With this as the operative, polygyny could do little in broad terms, because of the small number of African American men who are able to support more than one household. Most are not in the financial position to be the sole provider for one household, let alone two. It does, however, help to weed out those who might not be prepared to enter into polygyny.

Muslim women are told that polygyny is permissible, and Scriptures are used to support it, but there appear to be no mechanisms to prepare them for it emotionally. Men are taught to take on more than one wife only if they are able to be fair. Otherwise, they are discouraged from doing so. There are Scriptures to support this. However, the *Qur'anic* Scriptures as the only support mechanism for men and women in polygyny in this social milieu do not seem adequate. The guidelines in the *Qur'an* focus on the dower, the contract, inheritance, etc., matters related primarily to rights, but they do not provide a mechanism for African American men and women to make a paradigmatic shift from monogamy to polygyny. Islamic law provides legal guidelines, but what prepares men and women for marriage in general? Men are referred to the *hadith* for guidelines on how to be with their wives. But what prepares women on how to be with their husbands? How are women to make the shift psychologically and emotionally? The *wali* is expected to stand-in for the woman, to protect her in the negotiations for the dower. However, from my understanding from interviewees, women can and do choose any man to stand in for them. This man may have little or no training or qualifications to negotiate a contract, let alone, education, or skills, to assist a woman in making the paradigmatic shift to polygyny, or how to be with her husband and his new wife.

An important factor to note is that Imams are charismatic leaders. Therefore, no one governs them or requires that they have education, training, or skills. Some become Imams by the mere fact that they have good oratorical skills. There is also no oversight to ensure that the Imam is equipped to help individuals work through emotional and psychological problems. If the Imam lacks education and skills, members may not benefit from his advice whether in monogamous, or polygynous marriages. Overall, as in the broader culture, there seems to be little or no preparation for marriage in Islam in general, let alone for those entering into polygyny. It would help the Islamic community if there were a governing body to set the standards for the entire Muslim community. In addition, if there were some organized way for local Imams to meet, it could preclude problems at the local level, such as a man using an Imam in another community to marry a second wife when the Imam in his own community will not do so.

A major challenge to being in polygyny for Muslim men is the general opposition to it by women. The men proclaimed that this is the reason that marriages are entered into without making already existing wives aware or obtaining their consent. It is conflict between wives which leads to distress for Muslim men.

A challenge for men in all the communities is maintaining a sense of independence and autonomy, that is, refraining from becoming too involved in the affairs of the women. Another challenge is establishing consistency with regard to rules and goals for children. Another challenge has to do with health, including potency. Representing an absent partner when a complaint is being made is another challenge, along with having the patience to deal with the "all the talking" that is required with multiple wives. The men must also maintain good judgment, fairness, and balance. It is scheduling, however, which helps with this. The greatest challenge for men in Ausar Auset society and the Muslim communities is economics. This is generally not a problem for African Hebrew Israelite men because the communal economic structure assists them in providing their family needs.

Finally, for the most part, the men would not admit that they may be drawn to women for reasons that men generally are, sex, variety, ego, etc. Regardless of what motivates them, however, there are structures in Ausar Auset society and the African Hebrew Israelite community that ensure that men pursue women in a way that is constructive. These structures also help to keep them on track if they should fall short of expectations. Overall, the men hold steadfast to their belief that polygyny is needed for women and children, and that it is they, who are men of God, who are charged with the responsibility of setting the example.

Gender

Among the African Hebrew Israelites, the man is the head of his family and household. The hierarchical structure comprises God, man, woman, and child. As far as the decision- making process, the man functions as a figurehead, and his wife(s) as counsels. If a man should operate in a manner that discounts his wives, there are places women can go to appeal. There are also rigid gender roles for men and women. The sole responsibility for domestic tasks and childcare is placed on women. They are also expected to provide domestic support to their husbands whether or not they work outside the home. Although some families may approach an egalitarian arrangement, within the social structure the ultimate responsibility for domestic tasks falls on women. Thus, those who work outside the home and have to assume childcare and household responsibilities may experience role overload.

Although there are rigid gender roles, in the African Hebrew Israelite community, women are still encouraged to pursue their interests. Most of the women with whom I spoke were well read (some were even brilliant), independent, strong-willed, creative, and by profession were international entertainers, business owners, midwives, nurses, public relations spokespersons, culinary artists, nutritionists, fashion designers, teachers, and authors. Through the Crowned sisters, the women also participate in decisions regarding the direction of the kingdom. Although women may experience role overload from rigid gender roles, it is important to note that men may also experience the same thing. The men work just as hard as the women. This is because the community, just over 30 years old, is in its early stages of development. This means that everyone has to go above and beyond the call of duty for the community to sustain itself. It is the responsibility of men to be the major providers for the family, which allows women to focus in the domestic arena if they so desire. Thus, the care and support African Hebrew Israelite women provide their husbands appear to be mutual.

Important to note is that studies indicate that when societies are in their early stages of development, women generally focus in the domestic sphere, particularly when the domestic and public spheres are almost indistinguishable. With regard to the political hierarchy, the highest level to which women participate is in the Crowned sisters. They do not participate at higher levels of government, such as the council of ministers, and it is only recently that efforts have been made to allow them into the priesthood.

Under Islam, the man assumes the ultimate leadership and decision-making role in the family. This does not mean that women are subjugated by men. The man is compared to a political leader with his councilwomen. Even though there are laws under Islam to protect women, male supremacy still seems to be a part of the Islamic creed, and women are still socialized to be dependent. There are also rigid gender roles that may derive from Arabia when women were not allowed to work in the public arena. Although

Islam helped to liberate women, social and political hierarchies under Islam still seem to be male-dominated. There are also few, if any women who are Imams.

It is only in the Ausar Auset society that women participate on all levels of the spiritual-political hierarchy. They are queen-mothers, shekhems, and priests. Even though there are gender-roles, e.g. women as primary nurturers and responsible for domestic care, they are also encouraged to fulfill their incarnate objective.

With regard to gender roles, it is important to note that rigid gender roles early in human development were necessary for survival. There was a need for women to be responsible primarily for childcare and to assume less physically demanding tasks (although labor intensive) while men assumed more physically demanding and stressful tasks such as building, hunting, fishing, security, etc. Women were focused on maternity, but they also contributed to overall economic production. In fact, in hunting and gathering and horticulture (a simple form of agriculture) societies, women produced a large proportion of the food. As such, they had high status. They were also able to self actualize in other arenas, including becoming priestesses. Because of the nature of the tasks they performed, they were able to nurture their children in the fields and in the market place.

Industrialization, however, changed the material reality for some parts of the world. One factor in the development of industrialization was the shift in economies from the homestead where women made substantial contributions and held a great deal of status, to the public arena. The result, particularly in U.S. society, was that labor around the home front came to be less valued and unpaid, by contrast to paid labor in the public arena (Collins, 1991; 2000). Through the "cult of domesticity," women of the 19th century were relegated to the private domestic sphere and men the public sphere. From this emerged the white-middle class ideology of the "housewife" (Davis, 1983). However, while these socioeconomic dynamics were occurring among white Americans, African American women were enslaved, and working in the fields and in the houses of slaveholders. Interestingly, under slavery, the labor of both African American males and females outside the domestic arena was also unpaid, while white males and females were the benefactors of the wealth their labor helped to produce. Angela Davis, in *Women Race and Class*, (1983) has argued that because of the social and economic conditions during slavery and after, the African American family, may very well be the first in America to approach an egalitarian arrangement. Thus, relegating women to the role of "housewife" leaders may unknowingly be subscribing to white American middle-class ideology (and one that is outdated).

Whatever the economic and social circumstances, it seems individuals should be skilled in both areas. Both women and men need basic survival skills, which includes being able to cook a meal and maintain a clean environment, and they need skills that they can take to the market place. A strategy might be for both women and men to engage in tasks necessary to sustain the family, including household maintenance and childcare, with each taking responsibility for tasks based on need and each leading in the areas in which they possess the greatest strength, especially in situations where women work outside the home. This would allow both men and women the time and energy needed to do what is necessary to maintain the family and self-actualize.

The traditions of both the African Hebrew Israelites and Muslims, although out of the Abrahamic tradition have African origins, also evolved through Indo-European cultural peculiarities which include extreme forms of patriarchy. In the 3,000 or more years that it took Eurasians to overthrow female deities (see Merlon Stone's *When God was a Woman*, 1976) and, ultimately, the feminine aspects of God, not only did they strip women of a most crucial source of power but also men, and nations that do not recognize the importance of the feminine for balance at all levels of society, including the highest level of government.

Thus, there is a need for the African Hebrew Israelite and Muslim community leadership to rid their political-spiritual structures of rigid gender roles. Some profess equality for women, but the absence of women in higher levels of government, or in the sanctuary, as priests or Imams, reflects a different reality. Making women responsible for childcare and domestic tasks, while men are free to self actualize does not seem like equality. It is important to recognize that God is both masculine and feminine. Being so, s/he speaks to woman in a way that s/he does not speak to man. Thus, there is a need not only for the masculine voice of God, which God speaks through man, but also the feminine voice of God, which God speaks through woman. It is necessary that both aspects of God exist at all levels of society, including in government, so that there is balance. This it seems, is necessary for any nation to reach its highest potential.

Finally, according to members of the communities, the most crucial element for polygyny to be a reality is that women have an open heart. It is also crucial that there is a community structure to provide moral sanction and pre-and post-marital support and guidance. Individuals must be encouraged to live through their higher spiritual selves. Ultimately, it is necessary that God be at the center.

PART IV: CO-PARTNERING: A VIABLE ALTERNATIVE?

Chapter 14

TOWARDS CO-PARTNERING

Co-partnering is defined as two or more women openly consenting to being married to, or in a relationship with a man at the same time. I believe that instead of women and men expending time and energy on the negative consequences of dishonest, closed polygynous formations, they could potentially work together. This could be advantageous for not only women, but families, communities, and the African American world.

What would be the benefits of co-partnering for women? As with our African, African Hebrew Israelite, Ausar Auset, and Muslim sisters, the benefits include: participating in the selection of one's co-wife, the opportunity to participate in deciding how time and resources will be shared, assistance with childcare, the opportunity for more children to have fathers, a mechanism to build wealth, and, most of all, the potential for all women to have the love and support of a mate. Co-partnering would invariably benefit one, depending on one's existing marital and socio-economic status, whether or not one has children, and one's area of focus: career, or children and domestic life. How one would benefit also depends on the type of relationship the women choose to have with one another, and whether they agree to merge their resources.

For women who are already married, co-partnering can provide the opportunity to participate in selecting whom one's husband becomes involved with. This may help to prevent a woman from becoming an appendage to one's family without one's awareness, and whose personality and spirit may not be in accord with it. It can also prevent a woman from becoming a drain on a family's resources without making contributions in some way or other to the existing wife and children.

For single women, especially those who have moved away from their families of origin, co-partnering can offer an alternative to loneliness and isolation. Considering the shortage of marriageable men, co-partnering can potentially increase the number and quality of men in the selection pool. In cities, such as Washington, D.C. and Atlanta, the sex ratio imbalance puts men in the position to pick and choose from among the most eligible women without having to make a commitment or be accountable to any of them. Co-partnering would shift the advantage from men to women. It would put women in the position to choose from among the most eligible men because, whether a man is single or married, he could potentially be available. Ultimately, single women would not be limited to men who are unwilling to be responsible human beings.

For women of all marital statuses, co-partnering can provide a mechanism for assistance with children. For married-couple families with two working spouses, a third party could potentially provide relief for both mothers and fathers. If the parties all work cooperatively, it could provide women who desire to focus in the domestic arena, the opportunity to do so, while others can focus on their work. For single mothers, trying to juggle work, children, household, transportation, and personal responsibilities can be overwhelming. This does not even consider the economic burden they may carry. In fact, approximately 40 percent of African American female householders are below the poverty level, and approximately 33 percent of African American children under age 18 live below the poverty level (U.S. Bureau of the Census, 2000). Co-partnering might not only provide women assistance with their many responsibilities, but also potential economic help.

Women without children might also benefit from co-partnering. Some women may have missed the opportunity to have children because of focus on their careers. Others may have missed the opportunity because of their inability to find a suitable mate. For those who are reluctant to take on the burdens of single motherhood by birth, adoption, or foster care, co-partnering with a woman who already has children might provide the opportunity to participate in the nurturing and development of children.

Depending on the level of cooperation, the women could also provide emotional support and companionship to one another. Overall, co-partnering can provide a mechanism for women to expand their families, to exchange time, skills, talents, and expertise, and to improve the overall quality of their lives.

A major advantage of co-partnering is that it may be a way for African Americans to build wealth. In *Black Wealth/White Wealth*, Melvin L. Oliver and Thomas M. Shapiro (1997) defining net financial worth as assets minus debts, and net financial assets as available resources minus equity accrued in a home or vehicle, indicate that the African American middle-class has very little by way of liquid assets. The middle-class status of African Americans derives largely from income, not wealth. Using data from the 1987 Survey of Income and Program Participation (SIPP), Oliver and Shapiro found that the net worth of middle-class African Americans range from $8,000 to $17,000 for white collar workers, and this largely represents home equity. Whites possess nearly twelve times as much median net worth as African Americans, and the financial assets of African Americans are minuscule, ranging from zero dollars for white-collar workers to $175 for those with college degrees. When one compares the wealth of African Americans and whites, African Americans have between $8 to $19 of wealth for every $100 that whites possess. For the latest year for which they had data (1984), it was found that African Americans "owned only 3 percent of all accumulated wealth in the U. S, even though they received 7.6 percent of the total money earned and made up 11 percent of all households" (p. 97). Because African Americans may have virtually no liquid assets, many may be one or two pay-checks from poverty.

Factors contributing to this were racialized U.S. government policies that supported slavery, apartheid, and economic exclusion, whereby legislation prohibited African Americans from obtaining certain licenses, operating certain kinds of businesses, and working outside certain employment arenas — domestic service and farming (See Charshee McIntyre's, *Criminalizing A Race*). Because the African American middle-class has little in net assets and maintains its status primarily through earned income, it continues to be extremely vulnerable, particularly

346

to shifts in the labor market. In an article, "Upward Mobility Across Generations in African American Families," Harriet Pipes McAdoo (1997) asserts, "Middle-class Black families are where they are because of their own efforts, not because the financial surplus of earlier generations has been passed on, as is frequently the case in non-Black middle class populations" (p.158).

The general understanding is that in societies in which polygyny is practiced, men marry as many wives as they can provide for financially. This is a misconception, at least as it pertains to traditional African societies. As indicated in chapter 2, women in traditional African societies contribute substantially to economic production, and this is a primary incentive for men and their wives to seek additional wives.

In U.S. society, most African American women work. In fact, there are more African American women in the labor force than African American men. This means that most women contribute substantially to overall family income and well being. With the disparity of income between African and European Americans, African Americans need more wage earners to approach the standard of living of whites, and a majority of African American families that reach middle-income status do so because of a working wife. Thus, co-partnering can provide African American families the flexibility to own and operate businesses, and have multiple incomes when all parties are employed. This would give them the leverage needed to build *real* wealth.

There may also be substantial benefits for children. Co-partnering can potentially provide children with full-time fathers and multiple-mothers. Nearly 77 percent of female householders with no spouse present have related children (Bureau of the Census, 1997). Growing up in fatherless homes may be related to mounting social problems among youth, including delinquency, school dropout, drug and alcohol abuse, and homicide, especially among African American males. Those who have no consistent positive male role models in their lives, particularly if they live in communities plagued with crime and violence, may be especially vulnerable. The need to bond with other males may lead them to seek out males in their communities who may be involved in activities that lead them to be incarcerated or killed or

347

marginalized in the economic sector, thereby continuing the cycle of fatherless homes.

Growing up in families without fathers may also lead adolescent girls to seek acceptance from males, making them vulnerable to participating in premature sexual activity. There also is no threat of a male to intervene on their behalf. These factors have implications for the continuing cycle of teenage motherhood, poverty, and its associated problems.

Overall, it is important to note that all the benefits outlined here are possible in community building with or without co-partnering relationships. However, the single most important aspect of co-partnering is that it eliminates the element of deceit. With this, relationships can be based on openness and honesty, which is critical for community building. In addition, it provides a mechanism to call men to accountability. Ultimately, it is holding men accountable, I believe, that is necessary to ensure that all women can potentially have the social, emotional, physical, and spiritual support they need.

I feel compelled to emphasize that polygyny has been a socially accepted and morally sanctioned marriage practice throughout most of the world. A reason for its wide acceptance, particularly among African women was that it provided a structure to ensure all women and their children would be socially, economically and emotionally supported and protected. With such a social structure, it was unheard of for women to remain unmarried or to be exploited in the manner they are in the U.S. with monogamy as the only morally and legally sanctioned marriage practice. In fact, in some societies when a woman's husband died, her deceased spouse's brother would assume responsibility for supporting her and her children. Polygyny was also necessary because, given the material conditions, it would have been virtually impossible for anyone to survive alone. Everyone had to be tied to a family or larger kinship group. This was necessary not only for material but also for emotional survival. It is important to note that because women were tied to larger kinship groups in African societies, their spousal relationship was not the only one that provided emotional and social support. Sudarkasa (1980) explains:

The extended family provided social security in the form of companionship, counseling, and emotional reinforcement for the society's youth, adults, and aged. Africans did not subscribe to the view that "true" emotional gratification, and support come primarily through relationships based on sexuality. In fact, husbands and wives looked to their wider extended family relations as well as to each other (sometimes more than to each other) for companionate, gratifying, and satisfying relationships. (p. 49)

Because the husband-wife relationship was not the only significant relationship, it may have made polygyny easier for women to accept. In the U.S., African American women, particularly those of middle-income status, may not need to be attached to a man, family, or kinship group for material survival. However, there are many whose emotional survival is at stake. And this is because they do not have a mate or other significant social attachments. This may especially be true for those who have moved away from their families of origin to pursue education and/or careers.

Some family theorists have raised questions about the all-consuming monogamous relationship. Ramey (1974), for example, points out that in marriages throughout the world in the past, psychological and interpersonal needs were satisfied in a variety of ways through kin, neighbors, and friendship. Using a statement from Bott (1957) he indicates:

Couples in close-knit relational networks maintained a rigid division of labor, were deeply involved in external bonds, and placed little emphasis on shared interests, joint recreation, or a satisfying sexual relationship. Couples in loose-knit networks, on the other hand, show little division of labor, emphasize marital togetherness, and are highly self-conscious about child-rearing techniques. The transition from working class to middle-class status and from urban villager to suburban environment tends to bring about a loosening of relational networks and is therefore usually associated with an increase in the intensity and intimacy of the marital bond and a decrease in marital role differentiation. (p. 106)

He also quotes Komarovsky (1962) to depict the nature of the current marriage relationship:

Spouses are now asked to be lovers, friends, mutual therapists, in a society which is forcing the marriage bond to become the closest, deepest, most important, and putatively most enduring relationship of one's life. Paradoxically, then it is increasingly likely to fall short of emotional demands placed upon it and be dissolved. (p. 108)

African American kinship systems in rural communities in the U.S. were similar to African extended networks described by Sudarkasa. Neither men nor women relied on the other to provide all their needs but relied instead on same sex peers and extended family and kin networks in closely knit communities. As African Americans migrated to urban areas in the South and North to escape extreme racial oppression and to seek employment opportunities, they became increasingly isolated from kinship and family networks. Many, however, still remained closely knit in segregated communities. Now, as social and economic apartheid becomes dismantled and as African Americans become increasingly middle-class, suburban, and assimilated to white middle-class values of the monogamous, nuclear family, they rely less on family and kinship networks for emotional and material support. As others in suburbia middle-class America, they expect an enmeshed marital relationship to meet most if not all of their needs. African American women, in particular, as Komarovsky points out, expect a man to be their lover, friend, and therapist.

Such expectations, however, can present problems for single African American women because of the few available men. Many women suffer deeply from feelings of loneliness because the dearth in males makes it impossible to have an exclusive mate, let alone one who can perform all these roles. This may be especially true of women at higher education and income levels. Many may find it difficult to meet men of the same or higher status, especially in light of the fact that the number of African American women with professional degrees is more than double that of African American men. When some do meet such men, they find that they are in high demand, simply refuse to become committed to a primary relationship, and engage in multiple secondary ones; or they may already have a primary relationship and are only willing to engage them secondarily or casually. As discussed previously, what often occurs under such arrangements is that the woman's sexual needs may be met, but her emotional and social needs may not. This is because, in many instances, she is little more than an extra-curricular sexual activity for the male. There is clearly a need to explore other options.

The crux of the matter, I think, is that the majority of women would be content if things remained as they are. But then we wonder why there is so much strife in our relationships and marriages, and our families and communities are falling apart. Besides little or no understanding of the purpose of marriage and what is necessary to maintain one, most of which stem from Western ideas of love and romance, a people cannot continue to live with lies and deceit, especially under oppression, and expect not to experience tremendous hurt and pain, and utter chaos, and devastation. We do, however, have the power to change things. As agents in our own empowerment, we can choose to structure our relationships in ways that work for the benefit of all women, our families, and our communities. Co-partnering can provide a way.

Chapter 15

MORAL, LEGAL, CULTURAL, AND PERSONAL CONSIDERATIONS

In considering whether co-partnering is a viable option for African American women, there are moral, cultural, legal, and personal factors that must be taken into consideration. Because there are strong proscriptions against such a practice in all these areas, and structural constraints to support them, overcoming these may indeed be a great challenge.

Moral

One cannot make an argument for co-partnering without considering it from a moral standpoint. In doing so, I think it is important to first examine the foundation upon which morality is constructed in the Western world. The question of what is moral or what is good has been pondered throughout human experience. How we understand it in the Western world is based largely on Judeo-Christian and Greek ideas.

In an essay in the analytic-positivist tradition, "What is the Meaning of 'Moral'?" Morizt Schlick (1966) identifies two expressions of morality in the West. According to him, morality in the Judeo-Christian tradition expresses itself as renunciation, that is, it is based on the curbing of self, considerateness, the rejection of egoism or self-interestedness, in favor of the other person or, in other words, selflessness. By contrast, the Greek expression of morality is based on self-desire, self-realization, and self-affirmation (p. 469). Schlick further explains that for the Greeks, the 'good' originally meant what is desired and was based for the most part on the idea of hedonism or pleasure. The Greeks could not see the good as nothing other than "what is desired,"or "what is imagined with pleasure" (Schlick, p. 470). The underlying question from the Greek tradition, according to Schlick, then, is: "How must I live to be happy?" (p. 470).

Thus, in the Judeo-Christian tradition, what is considered to be moral is what is good for others. In the classical Greek tradition, what is considered to be moral is what is good for self. The two prevailing ideologies of morality are contradictory and, it seems, create a dilemma in the structure of morality. There is no other place in which this contradiction is more apparent than in the economic and social goals of U.S. society.

In examining morality from an economic standpoint, one must look at capitalism. Although it is defined as an economic system characterized by open competition in a free market, in U.S. society it is driven by three prevailing ideologies as defined here from the America Collegiate dictionary. The first and primary one is *materialism*, which is the doctrine that well being and worldly possessions constitute the greatest good and highest value in life.

The second is *individualism.* From an economic standpoint, individualism is the idea that one should be free to pursue one's interests and succeed through one's own initiative. From a social standpoint, individualism is the doctrine that the interests of the individual should take precedence over the interest of the state or social group.

Competition, the third ideology is the striving or vying with others for profit, prize, position, or the necessities of life. An associated aphorism of competition is survival of the fittest. Survival of the fittest, derived from Charles Darwin's theory on natural selection, is the idea that only those organisms best adapted to existing environmental conditions survive. Herbert Spencer applied Darwin's theory to social phenomena and asserted that those who have the edge in the competition for survival are favored.

From an economic standpoint, one finds the Greek equivalent of what is moral or good in that the "individual" "competes" to attain what is desired or pleasurable for self, which by the doctrine of "materialism" are worldly possessions which constitute the greatest good and highest value in life. Thus, it is the acquisition of worldly possessions that fulfills how "I" the individual must live to be "happy."

From a social standpoint, morality is concerned with the goodness or badness of human conduct or action. From a utilitarian standpoint, it is concerned with the "greatest common good," or what is good for society. In such an expression of morality one finds renunciation and selflessness for the good of others. It is this expression that defines what is moral as a social goal in U.S. society. The contradiction occurs in that as it regards material, or the economic means to attain material possessions, the individual or self becomes the center of focus. The individual should compete by whatever means to his/her disposal to make him/her self happy, even if it is to the disadvantage of the other. On the social level, human action that is considered moral is what is good for the other and society.

Thus, on the one hand, there is the prevailing ideology to seek what is pleasurable or desirable for self, which often manifests in the material, since this is the greatest good. On the other hand, the good is renunciation of self for others. Only if "how I must live to be happy" is through the happiness of others are the two reconcilable. Ultimately, the crux of the moral dilemma in American society is that economic goals and principles are inconsistent with its social goals. This conflict is internalized at the individual level and permeates all areas of social life, including marriage.

The question of morality in marriage is fundamentally a question of what is good or right in the relationship between man and woman. A monogamy only principle proposes that marriage between one man and one woman is what is good or right. A cultural normative that coexists with this, however, is that it is also acceptable among men, to engage in sexual relations with other women so long as their doing so does not interfere with the primary relationship (whether they are married or single, although fidelity which is also considered moral, is promised by those who are married). It is to these "other" women that the man has no moral, legal, social, emotional, or economic accountability.

As previously noted, this is a cultural retention from the Greco-Roman world. Although monogamy was the only legitimate marriage form for Roman citizens (besides the acceptance of polygyny among the Jews until A. D. 285, Hillman, 1976), a complex system of prostitution coexisted along with it. Supported by the state, prostitution, emerged because of the low value placed on women in the Greco-Roman world. Women were restricted to two primary roles: the wife, whose sole purpose was to reproduce heirs to inherit the property of their fathers, and the prostitute, whose role was to provide sex for men. *Hetaerae* (higher level prostitutes) and others even lower on the hierarchy were there for no other reason than to provide men with an escape from the doldrums of married life and to provide them a sexual outlet. There were also concubines who provided both sexual and domestic services. Under this social arrangement, some women, unprotected by marriage laws, were essentially reduced to their sexuality and labor.

By contrast, in other societies, particularly African, where polygyny is an acceptable and desirable form of marriage, all women can potentially marry. This means that they and their children can be legally, and potentially socially, emotionally, and economically supported. Social scientists contend that before European colonialism in Africa, prostitution did not even exist. In contemporary U.S., with monogamy as the only legitimate marriage form, as in the Greco-Roman world, there are some women, especially when there is a surplus, who will not be married and, as mistresses, lovers, prostitutes, and pornographic sex objects, reduced to their sexuality. In the African American world, where the surplus is disproportionately high, women and their children are at the greatest disadvantage.

Important to understand is the role that Western systems of domination play in women being reduced to such a status. Afrocentric theorist, Marimba Ani, in her work *Yurugu* (1994), notes that an overarching component of systems of domination is "despiritualization." Under this, all phenomena are reduced to a material dimension. This makes it easy to control, dominate, or otherwise destroy. Afrocentric feminist Patricia Hill-Collins (1991; 2000), in *Black Feminist Thought*, examines three major components of systems of domination and the impact they have on women. These include dichotomous thinking, oppositional pairs, and objectification.

In dichotomous thinking, people, things, and ideas are categorized in terms of their difference from one another.

Oppositional pairs means that the designated difference is defined in oppositional terms. One part is not simply different from its counterpart; it is inherently opposed to it. For example, Marimba Ani, (1990, formely Donna Richards) in "African Culture: The Rhythms of Unity," observes that "some opposing pairs in the European world view include knowledge/opinion, objective/subjective, science/religion, mind/body, male/female, man/boy, white/Black, and so forth" (p. 210). However, not only are pairs opposed to each other but "one...becomes valued, while its converse is understood as lacking value. One is good, and the other is bad" (p. 210).

Dichotomous, opposite pairs, are central to objectification. Collins (1991) states, "oppositional dichotomies rarely represent different but equal relationships, they are inherently unstable. Tension is resolved by subordinating one half of the dichotomy to the other. Thus whites rule Blacks, men dominate women, reason is thought superior to emotion in ascertaining truth; facts supersede opinion in evaluating knowledge, and subjects rule objects" (p. 70). As these three components become operative in human relationships, one is "subject" and superior, and the "other" is "object" and inferior. These components are evident in the male approach to relations with females in the Western world. In either/or dichotomous thinking, women are classified as "virgin" or "whore." There are those who are "good" and worthy of the status of wife vs. those who are "bad," and unworthy. The wife becomes a valued "subject," and women who are used for their sexuality become the "objectified" "other." Ultimately, it is women as "other" who become despirited objects, and denied value and worth as human beings.

A fundamental element of marriage in Western culture is an emphasis on structure rather than the male-female relationship itself. Men in sexual relationships with multiple women have existed throughout human experience in most of the world, even in Western cultures. Given this reality, it would seem that the moral question should be not whether it is good or right for a man to have relations with more than one woman simultaneously (because it occurs and under certain social circumstances is needed) but rather the moral question should be on what principles are these relations based.

There are two fundamental principles that appear to be universally valued and form the basis of relationships not only between man and woman but all human relationships. These principles are trust (which stems from honesty) and respect.

With regard to trust, societies that promote men having relations with more than one woman simultaneously and have moral, social, and legal structures to support them, provide the basis for these relations to be based on honesty (which promotes trust). Societies that promote such relations but have no moral, social, or legal structures to support them encourage relations based on dishonesty (which promotes distrust). Those societies that have structures to support such relations can teach what is good and right conduct for both men and women. Those societies that do not, set the stage for relationships to be based on lies and deceit, and further exploitation of one sex by the other. As such, it is impossible to teach what is good and right conduct for either men or women.

Respect, the other principle, simply means to hold another in esteem and to honor the person. With monogamy as the only legitimate marriage form, at the most fundamental level, by becoming a wife, a woman as "subject" is at least honored. If her husband should enter into a relationship with another woman without her knowledge of it (or her consent), she is violated and dishonored by both her husband and the woman. The woman with whom her husband enters into relations as "other" or in some cases, "object," is not honored. In both instances, the women are dishonored and disrespected.

Thus, with regard to the question of what is moral, several questions arise. Is it moral that some women are given honor and respect as a wife, and other women, although engaging in the same type of sexual and sometimes emotional exchange with men, are not? Is it moral that under such circumstances some women are given moral and legal and potentially emotional and social support while others are not? Is it moral that some women are allowed to live with truth in the light, while others are compelled to live with lies in the dark? And should a woman choose not to dishonor or

357

disrespect herself or another woman by taking up with her husband, is it good that she may be expected to live her life without the love and support of a mate? And what about the children? Is it moral that children who come into the world through such associations are bastardized and, like their mothers, are forced to live in the dark? Finally, is it moral that any marriage practice is so rigid that it fails to give every man, woman, and child the moral, legal, and social support that validates their inherent worth as human beings?

Cultural

There are several cultural considerations, one of which is the ideal of romantic love. Romantic love in contemporary U.S. society is a considerable prerequisite for marriage. However, this has not always been the case throughout most of the world, including Europe. Knox & Schacht (2000) indicate:

Love in the 1100s was influenced by economic, political and family structure. In medieval Europe, land and wealth were owned by kings controlling geographic regions—kingdoms. When so much wealth and power were at stake, love was not to be trusted as the mechanism for choosing spouses for royal offspring. Rather, marriages of the sons and daughters of the aristocracy were arranged with the heirs of other states with whom alliance was sought. Love was not tied to marriage but was conceptualized, even between people not married or of the same sex as an adoration of physical beauty (often between a knight and his beloved) and as spiritual and romantic. (p. 36)

However, as European societies evolved after the English and French revolutions, power was transferred from the aristocracy to representative national bodies, such as Parliaments and Congresses. Thus "marriage became less of a political and business arrangement and more of a mutually desired emotional union among spouses" (p. 36). Rather than individuals being bought and held together by business and political arrangements, "love would now provide the emotional and social bonding" (p. 36).

Even outside Europe, marriage throughout most of the world was arranged by families. Feelings of love were expected to develop after marriage. This was particularly the case for Africans. Radcliffe-Browne & Forde (1967) observe:

The African does not think of marriage as a union based on romantic love, although beauty as well as character and health are sought in the choice of a wife. The strong affection that normally exists after some years of a successful marriage is the product of the marriage itself conceived as a process, resulting from living together and co-operating in many activities and particularly in the rearing of children. (p. 46)

Romantic love became popularized in the U.S. through novels and various media and thereby became the primary basis for mate selection.

Another consideration is how women are socialized. In societies in which polygyny is practiced, particularly in traditional Africa societies, women are socialized to share their husbands. The survival of the group assumes importance over survival of the individual. This social value is carried over to and naturally informs the conjugal union. There are also moral, legal, social, and economic structures to support polygyny. Women in the U.S., on the other hand, are socialized to monogamy only and to expect to have an exclusive mate. Survival of the individual and, by extension, the conjugal union assumes importance over survival of the group. Thus, it is socially acceptable to be concerned only with oneself and one's own marriage relationship. In addition, there are no social or legal structures to support any marital union other than monogamy.

Another cultural consideration is that the monogamic, nuclear family is propagated as ideal. Under this model one's spouse is expected to provide all of one's emotional and social needs. Thus, if a woman is completely dependent on her husband in this way, it would make it difficult to see sharing him with another woman. As previously indicated, because of the division of labor between males and females in the past, each played a different role in what they provided to the overall economic well being of the family. Women, working in female occupations, primarily around the homestead, and often in female networks, provided one another emotional support. Their mutual efforts were

359

translated into the social arena as well. However, as the division of labor becomes less segregated and Africans throughout the world are becoming more suburban, individualistic, nuclear family oriented, and therefore more assimilated, it is becoming increasingly difficult for men and women to rely on same sex networks and family and kinships for emotional and social support. A consequence of this, is that husbands and wives are expected to become completely enmeshed, socially and emotionally bonded, and dependent on each other.

Another factor is that the only role the state plays in marriage in American society is in setting licensing requirements and when it enters into court—typically through divorce. Because most states do not require pre-marriage education, most people have no skills on how to co-exist with someone else, especially in light of contemporary challenges to patriarchy and gender roles. This may contribute to why the divorce rate is close to 50 percent. Through the work of some organizations such as the Coalition for Marriage, Family and Couples Education—Smart Marriages, churches, and a few states, efforts are just now being made to require pre-marriage education. Interestingly, what these groups are doing is something that African peoples have been doing for thousands of years through rites of passage institutions—preparing young people for life and the challenges of marriage and children. American society essentially takes a reactive approach to marriage, where individuals seek help after the marriage is in trouble, rather than a proactive approach, where individuals are prepared for the challenges of marriage. Thus, most people are not prepared for a monogamous marriage, let alone a polygynous one.

For co-partnering to become a viable option, it would require changes in all these areas. First, it would require that criteria for mate selection be shifted from romance to practical standards. For example, an individual's values, whether they are compatible with one, and whether they can help one in one's spiritual growth and development would be the major criteria for mate selection. Second, it would require a shift from seeing one's mate as someone to provide all one's emotional and social needs. Other relationships with friends and extended family and fictive kin would be just as important. Third, and most important, is it would require a paradigmatic shift in how we think about relationships and marriage and a shift in values underlying our approach to them. The "WEUSI" concept discussed previously might provide the basis for this. Finally, it would require that the approach to relationships and marriage is proactive, rather than reactive. Africanist scholars and family and relationship practitioners might develop a nationwide spiritually based marriage and family educational and support institution. Using the guidelines and principles of the communities which were the focus of this work, this organization might provide pre- and post-marital education and support for individuals in both single and plural marriages.

Legal

With regard to legal aspects of co-partnering, there are two primary considerations. One has to do with marriage itself, and the other has to do with property. The following is a brief historical overview of marriage and legal considerations for one entering into co-partnering.

Marriage

Many of the characteristics of modern marriage have their roots in Greco-Roman culture. If one recalls from chapter one, under Roman law there were two ways in which a person could be married. One was through consensual marriage, and the other was ceremonial. Consensual marriage was based on two adults consenting to, and living together for more than a year. Ceremonial marriage involved a ceremony with witnesses and consent by the parties. However, with the spread of Christianity in Europe, marriage began to be regulated by canon law. Consequently, although consensual marriage was still recognized, "the law directed that parties *ought* to marry only in religious ceremonies after the publication of public notice of the intended marriage between the parties, known as *banns*. In 1563, at the Council of Trent, the Catholic Church ordained that marriages were not valid unless contracted in the presence of a priest and two witnesses, and

<u>divorce was no longer permitted</u>" (Jasper, p. 3). Although Christianity began to influence marriage throughout Europe, England, under the Anglican Church, retained jurisdiction over marriage, recognizing both consensual and ceremonial marriages. It was not until 1753 under the Lorde Hardwicke Act that consensual marriage was abolished "due to abuses such as fraudulent claims of marriage and property rights" (Jasper, p. 8). With the passage of the Lorde Hardwicke Act, "marriage performed without the required formalities were deemed invalid for all purposes and were considered felonies punishable by death" (Jasper, p. 8). The American colonies, still under British rule during the time, however, did not adopt the act and held two types of marriage to be valid: common law, which is essentially consensual marriage, and ceremonial marriage.

In the U.S., regulation of marriage falls under state jurisdiction. For a ceremonial marriage, in all states the parties must acquire a license. Most states also require that the "marriage is solemnized by a minister, priest, and rabbi, or other public official, such as a justice of the peace" (Jasper, p. 5). In only eleven jurisdictions is common-law marriage still recognized (Knox and Schacht, 2000).

There are two primary considerations for those entering into a co-partnering arrangement. The first has do with the marriage not being legally recognized, and the other is the social and psychological implications of this. Because the latter concerns were discussed in previous chapters, only the legal aspects are discussed here. The Uniform Marriage and Divorce Act of 1974 defines marriage as occurring between *two* persons, one man and one woman. Thus, if a man is already married through license and marries another woman by license, this is considered bigamy and is punishable by law. If he marries another woman (that is, a ceremony is performed), but does not obtain a marriage license one would presume he has not committed a crime. However, this can be more complex depending on the state. The Mormon, Tom Green, was convicted of bigamy in a state that recognizes common law marriage. Because he held out to the public as the husband to the five women, and they held out as his wives, this was used to convict him. Even though he married each of the women and

362

annulled the marriages, he was still convicted based on common law marriage. Also, it is considered bigamy in Utah if one is married and cohabitates with someone else simultaneously. Thus, it seems that if one claims two or more wives in states in which common law marriages are recognized, it could put one at risk. Also important to note is that cohabitation is a illegal in some states.

In addition to the risk of the man being convicted of a crime, it is the woman who is not married by license who is most vulnerable, particularly in the event the husband seeks to dissolve the marriage. Even if she lives with the man and his legal wife, she has no legal rights. This is also the case if a man and his already existing wife do not have a license but have cohabitated for a period and have presented themselves to the public as husband and wife in common-law states.

The husband may also be vulnerable if the legal wife seeks to dissolve the marriage. "The primary grounds for divorce based on fault include adultery, cruelty, abandonment, and constructive abandonment — when one spouse is ready and willing to engage in sexual relations, but the other spouse refuses without cause to do so" (Jasper, p. 17). "Although there is a growing trend to eliminate fault as a consideration in granting a divorce, most states have retained fault grounds for divorce while incorporating some form of no-fault provision in their divorce law" (Jasper, p. 16). Because adultery is defined as voluntary sexual intercourse of a married person with someone other than their lawful husband or wife, on these grounds alone, the first wife may be able to sue for divorce. In the event that divorce does occur, it may have implications for how property is distributed, the second major area of consideration.

Property

Property that is owned by either of the spouses in a legal marriage is considered marital or separate. Marital property, although not uniformly defined among the states, refers to any that is acquired from the date of marriage. Separate property refers to that owned by either spouse before marriage as well as any acquired by gift or inheritance after marriage. In the event of divorce, there are two ways in which property is distributed. One is through equitable distribution law, and the other is through community property distribution. In equitable distribution states, property is distributed equitably whether it is jointly or individually held. In community property states, all property owned by either spouse is considered community property unless it can be proven to be separate. In what is considered community property, each spouse has an undivided one-half interest. The Uniform Marital Property Act (UMPA) approved by the National Conference of Commissioners on Uniform State Laws in 1983 is a model for states to follow in forming their laws.

Although property is regarded as marital or separate, there are other legal instruments that can be used to handle property. These include those that fall under concurrent estates. Concurrent estates exist "whenever two or more persons have a concurrent and equal right to the possession and use of the same parcel of land" (Cunningham et al., 1993). The forms of concurrent estates derived from common law include joint tenancy, tenancy in common, tenancy in the entirety, tenancy in coparcenary, and tenancy in partnership. "Tenancies in coparcenary have been absorbed into the tenancy in common," and tenancy in partnership has been eliminated in all states by the adoption of the Uniform Partnership Act (p.187). Tenancy in common, joint tenancy, and tenancy by the entirety still survive in the U.S. and may be created in personal and real property. For the purposes of this discussion, only two, joint tenancy and tenancy in common, are discussed. Tenants by entirety applies only to a husband and legal wife.

Tenancy in common - means that all tenants in common have equal rights of possession and use of the property, which is referred to as "unity" of possession. Every owner can have equal fractional interest; however, they do not have to. The forms of ownership may vary; for example, some may have a fee simple (unqualified ownership and power of disposition), while others may have an estate for life (for the duration of their life only). One's interest may be left to heirs, and in the event that there is no will, pass by intestate succession to their heirs.

Joint tenancy - for joint tenancy to exist there must be four "unities" of time, title, interest, and possession. This means that "all tenants must acquire their interests at the same time and by the same instrument (deed or will) and that the interests of the co-tenants must be identical as to individual fractional shares, quantum of estate and quality of estate (legal or equitable) and carry with them equal rights of possession and enjoyments" (Cunningham, p. 194). The distinguishing feature of joint tenancy is the right of survivorship, which means survivors become the sole owners of the property in the event of the death of the others. Some states have abolished joint tenancy by statute, whereas others have made significant modifications to the law. However, it is still recognized if it is specified in the agreement in some form or another, for example, a transfer "to A and B" (Cunningham et al., p. 195).

Under both tenancy in common and joint tenancy, an individual may be able to transfer his undivided interest by conveyance. If an individual under joint tenancy conveys his interest, he "severs" it from the joint tenancy and destroys the right of survivorship as to that interest. Both tenants in common and in joint are subject to the laws of transfer, possession and use, rights based on carrying charges of common property, partition, and sale and division of proceeds.

A tenancy in common might be considered in cases where all wives reside in the same residence. This means that each spouse, whether they are legally married or not, can have equal rights and use of the property and pass these rights to their heirs. A joint tenancy might be considered in cases where a wife lives in a separate residence, particularly a non-legal wife, especially if it is desired that she owns property separate from the legal wife. In cases in which there is no joint tenancy, if the husband and non-legal wife purchase property together, in the event of his death, his legal wife may have claims to his portion unless he specifies in a will his desire for the non-legal wife to have it. Even if he does specify in a will that the non-legal wife inherits the property that she and he have purchased together, his legal wife may still be able to claim his portion, depending on whether he followed state laws with regard to spousal inheritance. The benefit of joint tenancy is that in cases in which property is acquired, in the event of the husband's death, the non-legal wife will have sole survivorship rights.

Overall, If the wives and husband choose tenancy in common, it means that each spouse may have an equal interest in the property. If a husband and non-legal wife have a joint tenancy, this means that she may be entitled to the property in the event of his death.

Another option to consider is corporations. If a family chooses to set up a corporation, shares would be closely held by its members. Under corporations, wives and husband would become members of the board of directors, officers, and shareholders. For all shareholders, in the event of their death, their shares would pass to their heirs. For those considering corporations, it is important to take into consideration several factors. First, is that there are costs associated with maintaining corporations. Depending on the state in which they are registered, there are state fees. If the corporation uses an accountant and/or lawyer, the costs can range from a couple of hundred to thousands of dollars per year. Second, because corporate records and minutes must be maintained, they can be time consuming. There are also forms that must be filed annually.

If spouses do not consider any of these options, it is probably best that the property of the non-legal wife be kept separate from that of the husband and his legal wife. If a non-legal wife resides in the same residence as the legal wife and her husband and is making payments toward the mortgage, her name might be added to the deed. In any event, it is important that all parties, especially non-legal wives, keep records of property. I would also suggest contractual arrangements between all parties where needed and wills to protect parties in the event of death. In addition, all the parties should consult legal counsel to ensure that everyone is covered.

Personal

The experiences of the women and men in the three communities in which I conducted interviews provide some indication of the personal considerations for a co-partnering arrangement. These considerations can be divided into three primary dimensions: Economic, emotional, and spiritual. The economic dimension comprises basic material requirements of food, clothing, shelter, transportation, and other comforts. The emotional dimension concerns issues and problems that may arise from the interaction between the parties. It essentially has to do with each party's feelings of security. There are at a minimum three dyads and one triad relationship with an incoming wife. These include: the husband and already existing wife, husband and incoming wife, the already existing and incoming wife, and the husband-wife-wife triad. If there are more than two wives, the emotional dimension can become even more complex, and with children even more so. The spiritual dimension has to do with how much each has to expand to maintain emotional balance.

Already Existing Wife

For an already existing wife, an incoming wife may pose an economic, emotional, and spiritual threat. Critical considerations are how the incoming wife will add to or detract from the marriage and overall family well being. The impact can be determined by the extent to which the new wife becomes integrated into the corporate family structure. This is further determined by whether the wives keep separate residences and maintain private lives or live in the same residence.

From an economic standpoint, the most important consideration for the already existing wife is how much the incoming wife will need from the husband and family by way of financial support. Will she be a drain? If she will require financial support, then one might consider what she can contribute to basic family maintenance functions, such as child and household care, her special skills or talents, and/or personality attributes.

From an emotional standpoint, the already existing wife will have to consider how she will feel about her husband's relationship with his new wife. Her concerns might include: Will she still feel loved by her husband? Will she be able to handle knowing that her husband is being intimate with another woman?

Will she be able to make the adjustment from having a full-time to part-time husband if there are separate residences? And if she and the incoming wife live in the same residence, will she be able to handle seeing her husband and his new wife together. There are also considerations with regard to the incoming wife. Since the relationship with her can range from an enmeshed friendship to a cordial interaction, or to no interaction at all, the already existing wife has to consider the type of relationship she expects to have with the new wife. In any case, it seems that it would be better for the entire family if the women at least like each other and there is some compatibility between them.

Other important considerations are the incoming wife's social circumstances and emotional state and history — what kind of emotional and family problems might she be bringing, and what she will expect with regard to time and attention from the husband. Other considerations concerning the new wife include: What are her interests? Is she interested in being a team player, or is she just interested in the husband? What are her expectations with regard to friendship? Finally, a consideration for the already existing wife might be whether she has anything in common with the incoming wife and how important this is.

How much the already existing wife has to stretch spiritually would be based on fairness of the husband and incoming wife, and the degree and amount of problems that emerge because of inconsistency between expectations and agreements, and what actually occurs. Spiritual centeredness would be required to mitigate feelings of jealousy and to be fair in her treatment of the incoming wife with regard to time, attention, and resources.

If the wives maintain separate residences, the dynamics, it seems, would be less complicated. However, it seems that if an incoming wife does not become incorporated into the family life in some respect, she could become a detractor rather than an asset to the family, especially since she will require time and attention and may be in need of material resources.

Two major questions an incoming wife might consider are what marital problem she is being brought into the marriage to help resolve, if any, and how the already existing wife will receive and treat her. Many of the considerations pertaining to her economic, emotional, and spiritual well being are the same as those for the already existing wife. From an emotional standpoint, what the incoming wife has to think about is how complicated her life might become by becoming involved with a man who already has a wife and children. This could be further complicated if she is being brought into the family to resolve a problem between the man and his wife, either economic, emotional, or sexual. If it is for sexual or emotional reasons, it may lead the already existing wife to feel insecure which may evoke feelings of jealousy.

The incoming wife may more than likely be entering into a situation in which the husband and wife are already economically, emotionally, and spiritually bonded. This may lead her to feel insecure. Because she is not recognized by the state as being married, she may feel insecure about whether she is actually a wife. She may also not be recognized as being married in the eyes of her family and circle of friends, which could compound her feelings of insecurity. In addition, there may be uncertainty as to how to present herself to the public, particularly in her place of employment and on legal documents. The incoming wife must also consider the kind of relationship she would like to have with the existing wife, and whether this is compatible with the existing wife's expectations.

From an economic standpoint, a major consideration for an incoming wife is whether she is being brought into the marriage for economic support. If a family is having financial difficulties, it could detract from what she has already built on her own and from her material quality of her life. With regard to property, the incoming wife must be careful about being legally protected in the event the marriage is dissolved or of death. Thus, she may have to keep separate property. She must also have her own health insurance in place and prepare for old age since she will not be entitled to social security benefits from her husband.

From a spiritual standpoint, the incoming wife has to consider whether the husband and his first wife will be fair. She has to also work on being fair herself. Spiritual focus is necessary to resist the urge to become competitive, and to deal with feelings of jealousy.

Husband

The major question for the husband is whether he is physically, financially, emotionally, and spiritually capable of handling more than one wife. Although economics should not be the only determining factor, if he is not financially stable, it can lead to problems of astronomical levels. It may be difficult for either marriage to have emotional and spiritual well being if finances are unstable. From an emotional standpoint, the question is whether he is emotionally stable himself and whether he is capable of handling the emotional needs of more than one wife and children. From a physical standpoint, health, including potency, is an important factor. Trying to meet the sexual needs of more than one wife on a consistent basis may be more than most men can handle, especially in middle- and old age. Spiritual steadfastness is absolutely a must to maintain emotional balance and fairness. Overall, the man must ask himself and answer honestly whether he thinks he will be able to provide the different, emotional, intellectual, material, sexual and spiritual needs of the women.

Children

All parties must consider the potential impact of co-partnering on children. Although there may be many benefits for children — multiple mothers and a father (if they did not have a relationship with one before the marriage), the extent to which they may be able to gain would depend upon the emotional stability and interactions between the spouses. The disadvantages could be just as many as the advantages, and in some instances outweigh them if the relationships between the spouses are unstable and plagued with conflict.

There are also other considerations. If living in the same household, children are expected to merge with other children and share resources, space, and time. They must also adjust to different expectations from the adults, and parenting styles, the same considerations for blended families. Differential treatment by parents and extended family members can breed jealousy between the children. Already existing problems may be exacerbated by the addition of new spouses and children. Adults must also consider the pressures children may undergo from their peers, since polygyny is an unacceptable marriage practice. If a marriage is dissolved, children undergo the same emotional turmoil as the adults. It may, however, be more difficult because of having more people to detach from.

Finally, good conflict resolution skills are a must. Living through the higher spiritual self—is critical. As indicated by members of the communities who were interviewed, this is necessary to rise above the many challenges that polygyny may present. Ultimately, for African American women to see co-partnering as an option requires a conversion to an ethic of care for sisters. Black womanist ethics might provide the way.

Chapter 16

REMOVING THE "VEIL" SEPARATING THE "WIFE" AND "OTHER" USING A WOMANIST ETHIC OF CARE FOR SISTERS

Removing the Veil

In the third chapter, I referred to Gerda Lerner's historical investigation into the wearing of the veil. In *The Creation of Patriarchy*, Lerner (1986) explains that in Indo-European history, wearing of a veil, based primarily on the sexual position of women to men, was used to separate classes of women. Married women and some concubines were required to wear it. Those women who were not under the sexual control of men were not allowed to wear the veil. Some women were therefore granted status and respectability, while others were not. The effect of this was that some women were regarded as superior, and others were regarded as inferior.

It is my belief that women in general, and African American women in particular, are still separated by the veil, albeit, an invisible one. It is this veil which prevents women from becoming a unified force. As long as women are divided by dichotomies that abet gender oppression, e.g. standards of physical attractiveness — Caucasoid vs. Africoid, "virgin" vs. "whore," "respectable," vs. "unrespectable," and, ultimately, "wife" vs. "other," all of which pit women against one another in the competition for men, they will not be able to effectively challenge the structures that exploit some, while holding others up. African American women can, however, remove the veil.

A critical reading for African American women is Patricia Hill Collins' *Black Feminist Thought*. In this work, Collins (1991; 2000) provides an poignant analysis of the manifold oppressive forces that shape the lives of women of African descendant. This work also illustrates ways in which African American women have resisted. It is this critical work which guides what I think is necessary for African American women to remove the veil that separates us and move towards copartnering.

First, African American women must become active in the pursuit of information. Information is power and it is empowering. Active pursuit of information can lead to consciousness. Consciousness can lead to a shift in how one understands the reality of African peoples in general, and women in particular. And it is consciousness, that can lead one to understand the necessity of taking action, the second step towards co-partnering.

Women of African descent, according to Collins, have an activist tradition that has challenged domination and is characterized by two dimensions. One is group survival, and the other is institutional transformation. Women in Africa and throughout the diaspora have fostered group survival through their various social institutions — families, community organizations, churches, etc. They have also participated in various organized efforts such as maroon societies, the abolitionist movement, the civil rights and Black power movements, and in government, to transform Western policies and institutions. It is necessary that African American women continue this tradition.

Third, we must deconstruct ideologies and values undergirding systems of domination and construct new ones. Afrocentric theorists/feminists continue to work vigorously to do this. Ideologies and values such as survival of the group, collective responsibility, and cooperativeness stemming from the African social philosophy, "I am because we are" provide "old" but new values upon which to construct human relationships.

Finally, we must construct social structures with these values as the foundation. The women in the communities that are the focus of this work have done this; they provide practical models for the African world. That two of these communities have sustained for over 30 years is a testament that such models can work, even under domination.

Forging A Womanist Ethic of Care for Sisters

There is one dimension of this new value system that is critical for African American women; an ethic of care for sisters. Quoting from June Jordan's *Civil Wars*, Collins (1991; 2000) asserts that in any relationship, especially under multiple systems of oppression, the decisive question for African American women should always be: *"Where is the love?"* Collins also proposes that African American women use the principles espoused by Katie Cannon as the basis for their relationships. In *Black Womanist Ethics*, Cannon (1988) emphasizes the necessity of using the Black theological tradition for the development of an ethic for Black women. To this end, she adopts the Christian ethics of Howard Thurman and Martin Luther King, Jr. The recurring themes she identifies from Thurman and King include the divine in human personality, love grounded in justice and as a means to bring about social change, and interrelatedness in community.

Maulana Karenga (1999) using Kemetic (Egyptian) ethics, an African ethics older than Christianity and the basis upon which much of Christianity is founded, also provides a way to break the crippling effect of individualism on our minds, bodies, and spirits, by using an expanded way to look at the "self" or what it means to be human. Karenga (1999) breaks down the Kemetic conceptions of self into five dimensions. These include: the spirituality of self — *worthiness;* naturality of self — *at oneness;* the sociality of self — *human relatedness;* the corporeality of self — *bodiliness* or physicality; and the personality of self — *uniqueness* [his emphasis]. Both Black womanist ethics and the expanded self, I think, are necessary to forge a womanist ethic of care for sisters. A womanist ethic of care for sisters, I believe, is necessary to move towards co-partnering (p. 41).

Self as Divine and "Worthy"

Seeing the divine in self and in others is the first step in forging a womanist ethic of care for sisters. Karenga, using the Kemetic ethic of the expanded self, and Cannon, using the ethics of King and Thurman, stress the importance of recognizing:

(1) We are created in the divine image of God. Therefore, in each and every one, is the "presence and power" of the divine (Cannon, p. 160).
(2) Being "offspring of the divine, issues of the divinity himself" obligates one to be like God, which means one should seek good and rightness—*Maat*, so that one may reach the ultimate goal which is to
(3) *Stand worthy* before God, family, community and friends (Karenga, pp. 44-45).
(4) Being in the image of God, all "possess an inviolable and inalienable dignity" (Karenga p. 45) are "sacred," and have "inherent" and "equal" worth and value (Cannon, p. 163).

The critical challenge, here, is for African American women to understand that we all are of God, and being so, we all are, or should be, seeking *Maat* or good and rightness in our relationships. Seeking *Maat* helps us to achieve *worthiness* before ourselves, before our families, before our communities, and before God. For some women to be right and good in their relationships, while others are compelled to less, denies their divine selves to themselves, their families, their friends, their communities, and to God. If we say we love God, and are of God, then it is the divine moving in us, that ought to move us, to want to ensure that we all are accorded dignity and value, so that we are all able to stand worthy.

Self as Related and in Community

The second step in forging a womanist ethic of care for sisters is to understand the need we all have to feel love and security in relationships, in family, and in community. Karenga points out that "in Kemetic and other African [traditions] to be human is to be a person-in-community" (p. 41). "In other words it is to be a person-in-relationships (i.e., in family, community, nation and indeed the world. . .)"(p. 41). Also, an aspect of self as related and in community is being "one who hears." Karenga points to emphasis in Kemetic ethics of knowing how to listen; to hear especially those who are in need, and to act.

Both Thurman and King, according to Cannon, also stressed the importance of relationships in community. It is community, they believe, that is necessary to help all persons reach their potentiality and to maintain life and further it to its highest level. With this understanding, then, if a woman recognizes her own need to be loved and supported in a manner that only a relationship with her natural, God-given mate can provide, she recognizes this need in her sister. If she recognizes her own yearnings to have relationships in family and community, she recognizes these yearnings in her sister. This means opening her *God ear* to listen to sisters in need, to hear them, and to act. It is also crucial to understand the necessity of a mate, family, and community for all to reach their potentiality.

In order to bring about community Cannon, also calls for African American women to unify, and to confront and defy any affronts to unity, even laws. She expounds on what King had to say about this: "King believed... when the government and its laws do not uplift 'the solidarity of the human family,' but instead unjustly degrade members of society, then [there is] no alternative but to engage in direct action in order to defy [them]" (p. 170). With this as a guide, African American women, as moral agents, then, must confront and defy any laws which by their oppressive nature, disavow the diversity of the human family, experience and condition or because of their inflexibility lead to social interactions that diminish "human beingness" (p. 173). Ultimately, it is an ethic based on love and care for sisters that is necessary to confront any "barriers to common unity" (p. 164).

Self As-One and as Restorator

The *naturality of self* according to Karenga, means that we share a "common origin" or "essence with all modalities of being" that makes us all one with all (p. 51). We therefore have a "moral obligation to preserve and restore the world" (p. 53). In the manner of the ancient ones, Karenga states that we are morally obligated to "raise up and rebuild that which is in ruins; to repair that which is damaged; to rejoin that which is severed; to replenish that which is lacking; to strengthen that which is weakened; to set right that which is wrong; and to make flourish that which is insecure and underdeveloped" (p. 53). The third step, then, in forging a womanist ethic of care for sisters is recognizing the role that we must play in repairing the damage in our relationships with men, and with each other, due to adherence to practices that diminish human capacity, and the obligation we have to strengthen each other, so that our families and communities can flourish.

In order to act as restorators, however, it is first important to see our interrelatedness. Cannon indicates that King and Thurman believed that "interrelatedness" is needed to make right that which is wrong, and love can help us to see our interrelatedness. Cannon outlines three ways that Thurman believed interrelatedness can become manifest. These include: (a) reconciliation, (b) reclaiming those who help perpetuate oppressive structures, and (c) "'common sharing of mutual worth and value' in the wider community" (pp. 164-165).

With regard to reconciliation, Cannon states that Thurman believed:

Love restores unity within the infrastructures of Black life. Parents and children as well as all those who are not related by blood or marriage who make up the aggregate of the Black community, must take the initiative to break down barriers that divide them. By dealing with the root causes of hostility among family members and neighbors, . . .Black people would recognize new forms of mutual responsibility to each other. (p. 164)

With regard to reclaiming those who help to perpetuate oppressive structures, Cannon notes the necessity of calling upon "those persons from within the. . . community who function as cohorts with the malevolent social structures" (p. 164). She quotes Thurman: 'There are always those who seem to be willing to put their special knowledge at the disposal of the dominant group to facilitate the tightening of the chains. They are given position, often prominence, and above all a guarantee of economic security and status' (p. 164). The challenge for African American women is to call upon these individuals to step forward in support of our goals to restore our relationships, families and communities, to set the example, and to use their affluence to make co-partnering an alternative that is recognized by the state.

For "'common sharing of mutual worth and value' in the wider community," Cannon explains what Thurman had to say on this:

377

Each must be seen in the context of common humanity. For instance, the "white necessity" to maintain privileges of supremacy must be eradicated. The 'male necessity' to protect privileges of superiority also must be broken down. When the heavy weight of status is sloughed off, 'each person meets the other where he is and there treats him as if he were where he ought to be.' (p. 165)

Applying this to marriage, white supremacy holds monogamy to be superior and other marriage forms as inferior. Male supremacy allows men to engage women in a manner that holds some up while others are inferiorized. Through both of these practices women that are held up are given status of wife, while those who are inferiorized become "other."

The third step in forging a womanist ethic of care for sisters, then, is first to be clear on how these practices damage our relationships with men, and each other, and ultimately community and nation building. We must also see that it is our interrelatedness through God's love that is necessary to restore and rebuild our relationships and communities, and to make co-partnering a reality. It is necessary that the "heavy weight of status" of "wife" be "sloughed off" so that we all meet each other and move as a unified force to build relationship, family, and community structures so that we each may be treated as we ought to be — with love, honor, dignity, and respect. Ultimately, it is through every woman extending herself to every other woman that African American women, and African American people as a collective, will be able to repair, rebuild, replenish, restore and strengthen our relationships, families, communities and nation.

Self as Person and Unique

The *personality of self,* according to Karenga, is concerned with the unique way in which one asserts oneself in the world, whereby one is worthy. Worthiness of remembrance and justification for eternal life are the focal points of the self as unique. In traditional African ethics, it is one's specific purpose or destiny that also gives one uniqueness as a person.

These principles are also useful in forging an ethic of care for sisters. We should all be moving to actualize our purpose. It is, however, relationships in family and community that strengthens us to do this. Each, then, must do what is necessary so that all are able to realize self and thus our uniqueness as individuals. What is also important, is to do good by one's sisters, so that one may be worthy of remembrance and justified in one's quest for eternal life.

Self as Body

The body, in ancient Kemetic thought, "is an expression of self as a concrete living reality that is not separated from the other constituents parts of the self" (Karenga, p. 48). As an "articulation of self" in this world, it is perceived as a locus of beauty, sacredness, and of heart, mind [and will]" (p. 48). It is also "the center of rationality and sensitivity" (p. 48). Karenga explains that beauty is recognized in the expression of an ancient Kemetic women, 'I am beautiful by what comes from my mouth' and by "what I do" (p. 48). Sacredness of the body is in its image of divineness. Because "the body as the concrete expression is subject to needs and desires and is thus vulnerable to thought, emotion, speech, and conduct" which serves to "undermine its capacity for maximum self realization," the goal is to discipline "the body to realize self by cultivating the heart mind and will" (p. 49). Cultivating the heart, mind, and will is necessary to develop one's "capacity for rationality and moral sensitivity" (p. 50).

An ethic of care for sisters helps African American women to recognize that we all desire to be beautiful to ourselves and to others. To be beautiful, one must feel beautiful. To feel beautiful, one must not engage in any relationship that diminishes one's capacity to do so. Our bodies, as part of self, should not be detached from emotionality of self or spirituality of self in our interactions with men. Any practice that seeks to reduce us to our bodies only; any practice that denies us from being beautiful to ourselves and to others; any practice that diminishes our sacredness in the image of the divine must be eradicated. For all of us to be beautiful to ourselves, our families, and communities, it is necessary to discipline our hearts, minds, and wills to rise above "thought, emotion, speech or conduct" that gives force to envy and jealousy. Rising above these helps us to cultivate our hearts, minds, and wills to an ethic of care for sisters. We must discipline our hearts, minds, and wills to rise to the capacity for "rationality" and the "moral sensitivity" necessary to extend ourselves to our sisters.

Morality of Sacrifice and Truth

There are two additional principles that African American women must also incorporate into our way of being in order to forge a womanist ethic of care for sisters. One is a "morality of sacrifice" and the other is to uphold truth. Karenga (1999b) notes in the *Odu Ifa* the importance of a "morality of sacrifice" in traditional African Ethics. In an interpretation of one of the *Odu*, (sacred texts) from the Nigerian Ifa tradition, he explains the meaning of morality of sacrifice as: "to give more of self in the struggle, [that is] more dedication, more discipline, more effort" (p. vii). He explains that sacrifice means "an expanded dedication, discipline and effort – an *expanded giving of self*" (p. vii). It is through the expanded self "that one prospers and make her way clear. . . .Indeed. . .the *clear way* and *the good life* require a *morality of sacrifice*. . ." (p. vii-viii).

The example set by Harriet Tubman provides a way for African American women to incorporate a morality of sacrifice into our way of being. As stated in the beginning of this work, it took tremendous sacrifice and deep love and care for African people for Tubman to return nineteen times, with one of the largest bounties in the history of America on her head, by foot, in the woods, at night, to free her brothers and sisters — blood and extended from the monstrous grips of slavery. It took tremendous sacrifice to give her life to the cause of freedom for African American people in the form of fund raising for the abolitionist movement, service to the military during the Civil War without pay, use of her own money to establish a resting place for elderly, ex-slaves, not having children of her own, and not marrying again after she escaped from slavery until late in her life. It took tremendous sacrifice for women of African descent to participate in warfare and in the staging of revolts and mutinies with millions dying; to participate in maroon societies, the abolitionist movement, the nineteenth century club

380

women's movement, the civil rights and Black power movements and various other efforts for the freedom of people of African descent. It is was this kind of sacrifice which freed us from physical bondage. It is this kind of sacrifice which is now necessary to free us from psychological and emotional bondage to ways of thinking and being that leave too many of us detached from family and community, subsequently leaving us without the love and support we need for emotional, psychological, and spiritual survival.

Also important is upholding truth in all aspects of our lives, including in our relationships. As indicated previously, we cannot build strong, healthy, and loving relationships, families, and communities when lies are an integral part of them. The notion that one would rather not know that one's mate engages in intimate relationships with "other" women, is not a heathy foundation upon which to build relationships, families or communities. What is built on lies will eventually crumble. Furthermore, we cannot stand worthy before God without truth. Love, faith, and trust in God can help us to reach deep inside ourselves to face truth in our lives and in our relationships. As Cannon puts it, "Love provides the Black woman with confidence to be bold and defiant, to risk all and stand by truth no matter what the cost" (p. 165). For it to be acceptable to say that one is too "selfish" to extend oneself to one's sisters is to ignore the pain, suffering, hard work, and sacrifice our ancestors went through to get us to where we are now. Love can help us to move to a morality of sacrifice for our sisters.

Finally, to forge a womanist ethic of care for sisters African American women must evolve to see the moral obligation we have to one another. We must tune into our expanded self, the God-self that is also others. This will help us to understand our relatedness to others, our at oneness with others which sensitizes us to hear those in need. Through our expanded self we must align with others so that we see the necessity of extending ourselves, so that we stand worthy, others stand worthy, we all stand worthy before ourselves, before our families, before our communities, and before God. We are one in the same; the same in one. Henceforth, when one sister is out there stranded, we all are. Every woman is somebody's daughter, and all women are everybody's sister. As daughters of God, we all deserve love, honor, respect, and support.

African American men, as sons of God, must purge themselves of any thought or action that prohibits them from recognizing the divine in themselves and in their sisters. African American women, too, must rise to their divine selves; the self that seeks to stand worthy and to help others to also stand worthy; the self that understands the need we all have to be loved and cared for; the self that moves to replenish and strengthen those in need; the self that sees self and others as sacred and as beautiful; the self whose uniqueness in doing good by her sisters is worthy of remembrance and justified in her quest for eternal life. It is these selves, that can empower us to remove the veil that separates us. It is our expanded self that is necessary to incorporate a womanist ethic based on genuine love and care for sisters. It is a womanist ethic of care for sisters that will help us to move toward co-partnering for ourselves, our families, and our communities. As with our African Hebrew Israelite, Ausar Auset, and Muslim sisters, the move in this direction can begin with one simple question: Can you want for your sister what you want for yourself?

REFERENCES

Abdullah, M., & Bilal, W., & Muhammad, F. N., & Waheed, A.H., & Zambezi, S.Q. (1995). *Evolution of a community.* Calumet City, IL: WDM Publications.

Ajanaku, K. (1998). *Interview.*

al Faruqi, L. (1991). *Women in Muslim society and Islam.* Indianapolis, IN: American Trust Publications.

Al-Amin, J. (1998). *Interview.*

Al-Amin, J. (1994). *Revolution by the book.* Beltsville, MD: Writers' Inc. International.

Ali, Abdullah, Y. (1997). *The Holy Qur'an.* Beltsville, MD: Amana Publications.

Altman, I., & Ginat, J. (1996). *Polygamous families in contemporary society.* New York: Cambridge University Press.

Amen, R.U.N. (1992). *An Afrocentric guide to a spiritual union.* Bronx, NY: Khamit Corp.

American Civil Liberties Group. (1999). *ACLU of Utah to Join Polygamists in Bigamy Fight* [Web page]. URL http://www.aclu.org/news/1999/w071699b.thml.

Ammi, B. I. (1999). *Written Interview.*

Ani, M. (1994). *Yurugu.* Trenton, NJ: Africa World Press.

Asante, M.K. (1980). *Afrocentricity: The Theory of Social Change.* Buffalo: Amulefi Publishing Co.

Asante, M.K. (1989). *Afrocentricity.* Trenton, NJ: Africa World Press.

Ba, M. (1981). *So long a letter.* London: Heineman.

Bachofen, J.J. (1967). *Myth, religion, and mother right.* Princeton. New Jersey: Princeton University.

Barrett, R. E. (1994). *Using the 1990 U.S. Census for Research.* Thousand Oaks, CA: Sage Publications, Inc.

Black, D. P. (1997). *Dismantling Black manhood.* New York: Garland Publishing, Inc.

Bondojia, T. J. (2000). An Analysis of Polygyny Within the Infrastructure of Racism (White World Supremacy). *National Council for Black Studies, 24th Annual International Conference.*

Boserup, E. (1970). *Woman's role in economic development.* London: St. Martin's Press.

Bott, E. (1957). *Family and social network.* London: Tavistock.

Brannon, R. (1976). The male sex role: Our culture's blueprint of manhood, and what its done for us lately. In D. David, & R. Brannon (Eds.), *The forty-nine percent majority.* Massachusetts: Addison Wesley.

Briffault, R. (1993). *The mothers: A study of the origins of sentiments and institutions.* New York: The MacMillian Company.

Campbell, B. M. (1989). To be Black, gifted and alone. In N. Hare, & J. Hare (Eds.), *Crisis in Black sexual politics* (pp. 127-140). San Francisco, CA: Black Think Tank.

Cannon, K. G. (1988). *Black womanist ethics.* Atlanta, GA: Scholars Press.

Cazenave, N. A. (1981). Black Men in America: The quest for "manhood." In H. P. McAdoo (Ed.), *Black families* (pp.176-185). Newbury Park, CA: Sage.

Chapman, A. (1995). *Getting good loving.* New York: Ballantine Books.

Chapman, A. (1986). *Mansharing: dilemma or choice.* New York: Kayode Publications.

Clatterbaugh, K. (1990). *Contemporary perspectives on masculinity.* Boulder, CO: Westview press.

Collins, P.H. (1991). *Black feminist thought.* New York: Routledge).

Collins, P.H. (2000). *Black feminist thought (Rev. 2ⁿᵈ ed.).* New York: Routledge.

Cunningham, R.A. & Stoebuck, William B. & Whitman, Dale, A. (1993). *The Law of Property.* St. Paul, MINN: West Publishing Co.

Darwin, C. (1936). *The origin of the species and the descent of man.* New York: The Modern Library.

Davis, A. Y. (1983). *Women, race & class.* New York: Vintage Books.

Deen, N. F. (1998). *Interview.*

Diop, C. A. (1990). *The cultural unity of Black Africa.* Chicago, Illinois: Third World Press.

Diop, C.A. (1974). *The African Origin of Civilization: Myth or reality.* Chicago, IL: Lawrence Hill Books.

Dorman, D. Unpublished. Developing an Afrocentric family formation model: An Exploratory Study into Polygyny within the African American Community.

Doyle, A. J. (1983). *The male experience.* Dubuque, Iowa: Wm. C. Brown Company Publishers.

El-Amin, P. (1998). *Interview.*

Ellwood, R.S. (1982). *Many peoples, many faiths.* (2ⁿᵈ ed.). Englewood Cliffs, NJ: Prentice -Hall, Inc.

Embers, M. (1974). Welfare, sex ratio and polygyny. *Ethnology,* 13(April), 197-206.

Emecheta, B. (1979). *The joys of motherhood.* New York: George Braziller, Inc.

Engels, F. (1942). *The origin of the family, private property and the state*. New York: International Publishers.

Fattah, G. (2000). *Loose lips doom Tom Green* [Web Page]. URL http:\\www.polygamy.org/articles/010620/1846243.shml.

Frazier, E. F. (1939). *The Negro family in the United States*. Chicago: The University of Chicago Press.

Frazier, E.F.,& Lincoln, E.C. (1974). *The Negro church in America & The black church since Frazier*. New York: Schocken.

Friedman, J. R., Martinelli, N., & Hyman, P. (Composers). (1995). *i refuse to be lonely*. New York: Philadelphia International.

Garcia, G. (1997). *Phyllis Hyman: Phyllis Hyman's friend/manager Glenda Garcia talks about the suicide* [Web Page].URL http://geocites.com/ Sunset Strips/Palms/4299/glenda. html.

Glasgow, D. G. (1981). *The Back underclass*. New York: Vintage Books.

Goody, J. (1973). Polygyny, economy, and the role of women. In J. Goody (Ed.), *The character of kinship* (pp. 175-191). New York: Cambridge University Press.

Grier, W. H., & Cobbs, P. (1968). *Black Rage*. New York: Basic Books Inc.

Grossbard, A. (1980). The economics of polygamy. In J. DaVanzo, &. D. J. Simon (Eds.), *Research in population economics* (pp.321-350). Greenwich, CT: Jai Press, Inc.

Hallwas, J. E., & Launius, R. D. (1995). *Cultures in conflict*. Logan, Utah: Utah State University Press.

Hannerez, U. (1969). *Soulside*. New York: Columbia University Press.

Heath, D. (1958). Sexual division of labor and cross-cultural research. *Social forces*, 37(1-4), 77-79.

Henriques, F. (1962). *Prostitution and society: A survey*. New York: The Citadel Press.

Hillman, E. (1975). *Polygamy reconsidered*. Maryknoll, NY: Orbis Books.

hooks, b. (1993). *Sisters of the yam: Black women and self-recovery*. Boston, MA: South End Press.

Howard Hogan, & Gregg Robinson. (Unpublished). *What the Census Bureau's coverage evaluation programs tell us about differential undercount*.

Ibn-Stanford, A. (1998). *Interview*.

Jasper, M. C. (1994). *Marriage and divorce*. New York: Oceana Publications Inc.

Jordan, W. D. (1974). *The White man's burden*. Oxford: Oxford University Press.

Joyce, G. H. (1948). *Christian marriage: An historical and doctrinal study*. London: Sheed & Ward.

Kambon, K. (1992). *The African personality in America*. Tallahassee, FL: Nubian Nations Publications.

Karanja, W. W. (1994). The phenomenon of 'outside wives': Some reflections on its possible influences on fertility. In C. Bledsoe, & G. Pison, (Eds.), *Nuptiality in sub-saharan Africa: Contemporary anthropological and demographic perspectives* (pp. 117-129). Oxford: Clarendon Press.

Karenga, M. (1993). *Introduction to Black studies*. Los Angeles, CA: University of Sankore Press.

Karenga, M. (1999b). *Odu Ifa: The ethical teachings*. Los Angeles, CA: University of Sankore Press.

Karenga, M. (1999). Sources of Self in Ancient Egyptian Autobiographies. In J.L. Jr. Conyers (Ed.), *Black American intellectualism and culture: A study of American social and political thought* (pp. 37-57). Stamford, CT: JAI Press.

Karenga, M. (1989). The Black/Male Female Connection. In N. Hare, & J. Hare (Eds.), *Crisis in Black sexual politics* (pp. 45-48d). San Francisco, CA: Black Think Tank.

Kilbride, P. (1994). *Plural marriages for our times: A reinvented option?* Westport, CT: Bergin & Garvey.

Kimmel, M. S., & Kaufman, M. (1995). Weekend warriors: The new men's movement. In M. S. Kimmel (Ed.), *The politics of manhood* (pp.15-43). Philadelphia, PA: Temple University Press.

Kimmel, M.S. (1995). Introduction. In M. S. Kimmel (Ed.), *The politics of manhood* (pp. 1-11). Philadelphia, PA: Temple University Press.

Komarovsky, M. (1962). *Blue-collar marriage* . New York, NY: Random House.

Lee, G. (1982). *Family structure and interaction: A comparative analysis*. Minneapolis: University of Minnesota Press.

Lee, G. (1979). Marital structure and economic systems. *Journal of marriage and the family*, 41, 701-713.

Lee, G., & Whitbeck, L. B. (1990). Economic systems and rates of polygyny. *Journal of comparative family studies*, XXI(1), 13-24.

Lerner, G. (1986). *The creation of patriarchy*. New York: Oxford University Press.

Lerner, G. (1972). *Black women in white America*. New York: Vintage Books.

LeSueur, S. (1987). *The 1838 Mormon war in Missouri*. Columbia, MO: University of Missouri Press.

Lincoln, E.C. (1961). *The Black Muslims in America*. Boston: Beacon Press.

Macionis, J. J. (1993). *Sociology.* Englewood Cliffs: Prentice Hall.

Madhubuti, H. R. (1990). *Black men: Obsolete, single, dangerous?* Chicago, IL: Third World Press.

Maillu, D. (1988). *Our kind of polygamy.* Nairobi, Kenya: Heinemann.

Majors, R., & Billson, J. M. (1992). *Cool pose: The dilemmas of Black manhood in America.* New York: Lexington Books.

Mbiti, J. S. (1969). *African religions and philosophy.* Oxford: Heinemann.

McAdoo, H.P. (1997). Upward mobility across generations in African American families. In H.P. McAdoo (Ed.), *Black families* (3rd ed., pp. 139-162). Thousands Oaks, CA: Sage Publications Inc.

McCloud, A. B. (1995). *African American Islam.* New York: Routledge.

Morgan, L. (1963). *Ancient society.* Cleveland, OH: The World Publishing Company.

Murdock. (1949). *Social structure.* New York: The Free Press.

Murdock, G. P. (1967). *Ethnographic Atlas.* Pittsburgh, PA: University of Pittsburgh.

Murstein, B. I. (1974). *Love, sex, and marriage through the ages.* New York: Springer Publishing Company.

Na'im, R. (1998). *Interview.*

Nobles W. W. (1978). Toward an empirical and theoretical framework for defining Black families. *Journal of marriage and family,* 679-688.

Oliver, W. (1989). Sexual conquests and patterns of Black-on Black violence: A structural-cultural Analysisl. *Violence and victims,* 4(4), 257-272.

Osmond, M. (1965). Toward monogamy: A cross-cultural study of correlates of type of marriage. *Social forces,* 44(1), 8-16.

Pitshandenge, I. N. A. (1994). Marriage law in sub-saharan Africa. In C. Bledsoe, & G. Pison, (Eds.), *Nuptiality in sub-saharan Africa: Contemporary anthropological and demographic perspectives* (pp. 117-129). Oxford: Clarendon Press.

Pleck, E. H., & Pleck, J. H. (1980). *The American man.* Englewood Cliffs, NJ: Prentice Hall, Inc.

Partoun, T.M. (2001). *He Makes a Village* [Web Page]. URL http://www.time.com/magazine/article/0,9171,110101054-108 793,00.html.

Radcliffe-Brown, A. R., & Forde, D. E. *African systems of kinship and marriage.* London: Routledge & Kegan Paul.

Ramey, J. W. (1974). Emerging patterns of innovative marriage behavior. In J. R. Smith, &. L. S. G. Smith (Eds.), *Beyond monogamy* (pp.103-137). Baltimore, MD: The Johns Hopkins University Press.

Richards, D. (1990). *African American spirituality.* Trenton, New Jersey: Africa World Press.

Schacht, D. & Schacht C. (2000). *Choices in Relationships.* (6th ed.) Belmont, CA.: Wadsworth/Thomson Learning.

Schillebeecky, E. (1965). *Marriage: Human reality and saving mystery.* London: Sheed & Ward.

Schlick, M. (1966). What is the meaning of "moral"?. In J. A. Mann, & G. F. Kreyche (Eds.), *Approaches to morality* (pp.468-478). New York: Harcourt, Brace & World Inc.

Scott, J. (1976). Polygamy: A futuristic family arrangement for African-Americans. *Black books bulletin.* 4, 13-25.

Solway, J. (1990). Affines and spouses, friends and lovers: The passing of polygyny in Botswana. *Journal of anthropological research,* 46, 41-66.

Staples, R. (1982). *Black masculinity.* San Francisco, CA: The Black Scholar Press.

Sterling, D. (1984). *We are your sisters.* New York: W.W. Norton & Company.

Stone, M. (1976). *When God was a woman.* New York: Harcourt Brace and Company.

Sudarkasa. (1989). African and Afro-American family structure: A comparison. *The Black scholar,* 37-60.

Taylor, L. (1971). *Deviance and society.* London: Michael Joseph.

Thompson, E.H., & Pleck, J.H. (1987). The Structure of Male Role Norms. In M.S. Kimmel, (Ed.), *Changing men: New directions in research on men and masculinity* (pp. 25-36). Newbury Park, CA: Sage Publications.

Tiger, L. (1978). Omnigamy: The new kinship system. *Psychology today,* 12(2), 14-17.

Toropov, B., & Buckles, L. (1997). *The complete idiot's guide to the world's religions.* New York, NY: Alpha Books.

Tucker, S. (1990). A complex bond: Southern Black domestic workers and their white employers. In D. Clark Hine (Ed.), *Black women's history: Theory and practice* (pp. 1-18). Brooklyn, NY: Carlson Publishing Inc.

U.S. Bureau of the Census. (2000). *Poverty 1999.* [Web Page]. URL http://wwwcensus.gov/hhes/poverty/poverty99/pv99est 1. html.

U.S. Bureau of the Census, C. P. R. (1999). *Marital status and living arrangements: March 1998(Update)* [Web Page]. URL http://www.census.gov/prod/99pubs/p20-514v.pdf.

U.S. Bureau of the Census. (1992). (Report No. 1990 CPH-R-1A). Washington, DC: U.S. Department of Commerce.

Van der Vliet, V. (1992). Traditional husbands, modern wives? Constructing marriages in a South African township. In Speigel A. & McAllister P. (Eds.), *Tradition and transition in Southern Africa* (pp. 219-241). New Brunswick, NJ: Transaction Books.

Villarosa, L. (1994). *Body & Soul: The Black women's guide to physical health and emotional well-being.* New York: Harper Perennial.

Ware, H. (1979). Polygyny: Women's views in a transitional society, Nigeria 1975. *Journal of marriage and the family,* 41, 185-195.

Welsing, F.C. (1991). *The Isis papers.* Chicago, IL: Third World Press.

Westermarck, E. (1922). *The history of human marriage* (Vol. III). New York: The Allerton Book Company.

White, D.G. (1985). *Ar'n't I a woman?* New York, NY: W.W. Norton & Company, Inc.

Whiting, J. (1964). Effects of climate on certain cultural practices. In W. Goddenough (Ed.), *Explorations in cultural anthropology* (pp. 511-544). New York: McGraw-Hill Book Company.

Williams, R. (1981). *The collective Black mind: An Afro-centric theory of black personality.* St. Louis, MO: Williams & Associates.

Willis, W. B. (1998). *The Adinkra dictionary.* Washington, DC: The Pyramid Complex.

Wolfe, N. (1991). *The beauty myth.* New York: Anchor Books.